Telerobotics, Automation, and Human Supervisory Control

Telerobotics, Automation, and Human Supervisory Control

Thomas B. Sheridan

The MIT Press
Cambridge, Massachusetts
London, England

Set in Times Roman from disks provided by the author.
Printed and bound in the United States of America.

Library of Congress Cataloging-in-Publication Data

Sheridan, Thomas B.
  Telerobotics, automation, and human supervisory control / Thomas B. Sheridan.
    p.   cm.
  Includes bibliographical references and index.
  ISBN 0-262-19316-7
  1. Remote control. 2. Robotics. 3. Man-machine systems. I. Title.
TJ213.S45522   1992
620'.46—dc20   92-2666
                                                                            CIP

Contents

TJ
213
S45522
1992

for Paul and Kate, Rich and Nancy, Dave and Cynthia,
Margie and Keith

Preface

Why this book

This book is about a growing technological phenomenon: remote control of physical systems by humans through the mediation of computers. This new form of technology, which is taking over the way people work in government, industry, and many other sectors of the economy, includes but is more than automation. People are still very much involved. This is because many of the jobs to be done are nonrepetitive and unpredictable, and therefore cannot be done by special-purpose machines that can be set up, preprogrammed, and then left to work by themselves. Or the jobs are one-of-a-kind, such that dedicated automatic devices to do them are too costly. So human perception, planning, and control are still required.

Unfortunately, many worksites are hazardous to human health or survival. This includes outer space, deep water, nuclear or biologically or chemically toxic environments, mines, construction sites, fires, and police or military operations. Therefore, remote control by human operators using video inspection and master-slave mechanical manipulation (called *teleoperation*) is considered. However, such direct human teleoperation often poses serious problems of getting sufficient sensory information and controlling the remote devices with sufficient dexterity. The alternative is to use artificial sensing, along with computer intelligence and control, to augment human sensing, intelligence, and control—but at the same time to keep the human very much involved.

Many operations, even though they may not be hazardous to nearby humans, are being automated to achieve greater performance and reliability. Aviation and process plants are examples. But even in highly automated systems the human is still considered a necessity for monitoring, detection of abnormalities, and intervention when necessary. Thus, interaction between human and computer is a problem here as well.

We have hardly begun to understand how best to integrate human and artificial brands of sensing, cognition,and actuation. One thing is clear, however: to cast the problem in terms of humans versus robots or automatons is simplistic, unproductive, and self-defeating. We should be concerned with how humans and automatic machines can cooperate. This cooperative relation between human and machine has been called *telerobotics* or *supervisory control*, with small distinctions between the meanings of these two terms. Here the term *telerobot* is generic to any system that has its own sensors, actuators, and computer decision/control capability, yet receives supervision from a human.

This book was written to fulfill a perceived need to bring together in one place the diverse ideas of telerobotics, automation, and human supervisory control that are rapidly emerging in a number of application fields. There was a need to show the common themes, and to interrelate the theories and experiments that have been published in a great many different meeting proceedings and journals by people who often don't know that the others exist.

What the book is and is not

The book emphasizes human-machine interaction in telerobotics, automation, and supervisory control. It brings in a variety of relevant theories and technologies, using experiments and hardware embodiments as examples. It is neither the first word nor the last word on this restricted topic, and it makes no claim to be a comprehensive or even-handed review of human-machine interaction experiments. It surely is biased by including a much higher fraction of the work of the author and his students than of others in the field.

There are by now many books on the hardware and software of tele-manipulators (for example, Vertut and Coiffet 1986a,b) and on robots in general (Nof 1985; Asada and Slotine 1986). No attempt is made to supersede these. There are a few works on the human in relation to automation in transportation and process control (e.g., Billings 1991). There is an even greater literature on human-computer interaction (Helander 1988), sensory psychology (Stevens 1951), conventional human factors or ergonomics (Salvendy 1987), expert systems (Harmon and King 1985), and other topics referred to but not covered in any depth in this book.

For whom the book is intended

The book is intended as a reference for human-machine researchers and system developers, and as a text for graduate students in engineering and psychology who may be interested in this emerging field. A modicum of mathematics is used in a few sections where the ideas cannot otherwise be explained. Mostly, ideas are described in words and diagrams, with examples from the experimental literature.

How the book came to be written

The author and his colleagues in the MIT Man-Machine Systems Laboratory have been doing experimental research in the area of teleoperators, telerobotics, vehicle and process automation, and supervisory control for 30 years. Over this period a great many master's and doctoral theses on these topics have been completed in the Lab; these have been published in widely scattered places.

In 1974 the author, together with William R. Ferrell, published *Man-Machine Systems: Information, Control, and Decision Models of Human Performance*. That book was designed to present the experiments and the aspects of theory that were well codified at the time. The decision was made to exclude teleoperation, telerobotics, automation, and supervisory control. Though these were topics the authors were then actively researching, they were too new and were not sufficiently codified. Now, they still are not what could be called well codified, but they are maturing. With their increasing emphasis on computer-interaction and cognition, telerobotics and supervisory control have turned out to be more complex, more encompassing, and less amenable to concise definition and mathematical modeling than, for example, manual control, which was once at the center of "man-machine systems." Therefore, though much has happened, the field has continued to lack a book to tie together the experiments and fragments of theory that are there. It seemed due time to provide such a book.

Organization of the book

The book consists of an introduction and four chapters.

The introduction defines important terms used throughout the book and offers a brief history of the idea of supervisory control.

Chapter 1 (Theory and Models of Supervisory Control: Frameworks and Fragments) includes a diversity of relevant theoretical ideas, both qualitative and quantitative. It discusses reasons why a single integrated model of supervisory control is not currently seen as an achievable goal.

Chapter 2 (Supervisory Control of Anthropomorphic Teleoperators for Space, Undersea, and Other Applications) deals with various aspects of conventional (anthropomorphic) teleoperator and telerobot technology: application needs; forms that devices and interfaces take; command language; visual, force, and tactile feedback; telepresence; deleterious effects of time delay; state estimation and decision aids; and performance measurement.

Chapter 3 (Supervisory Control in Transportation, Process, and Other Automated Systems) concerns computer-mediated control of vehicles (aircraft and automobiles), process control (using the nuclear power plant as the primary example), flexible manufacturing systems, and other systems that may be called non-anthropomorphic teleoperators (i.e., that do not have arms and hands and do not look like humans). It fills in a number of ideas about the supervisory control and the human interface not covered in chapter 2, such as goal setting and "satisficing," monitoring displays, failure detection, mental workload, intervention by the human into the otherwise automatic control, and human error. A main point is to show the parallels between chapters 2 and 3 with regard to supervisory control.

Chapter 4 (Social Implications of Telerobotics, Automation, and Supervisory Control) comments on the advantages to be gained from the new technology and form of human interaction, then raises a number of worries as regards the future.

Acknowledgements

I owe special thanks to many close colleagues for contributions to this book in the form of ideas, financial support, and moral support. Among them are William (Russ) Ferrell, Daniel Whitney, William Verplank, William Rouse, Dana Yoerger, Jens Rasmussen, Neville Moray, Gunnar Johannsen, Henk Stassen, Jean Vertut, Antal Bejczy, Melvin Montemerlo, Gerald Malecki, Norman Doelling, Demitrius Jelatis, Robert Cannon, Larry Leifer, and, of course, Rachel Sheridan. Particularly important are the contributions of many of my former graduate students, for they have also been my teachers.

Introduction

Some Necessary Definitions

Human supervisory control, supervisory control

Since *human supervisory control* is the pervasive theme of the book, it will be defined first and in the most detail. *Supervisory control* means the same thing; the human is implied (and we will drop the adjective *human* from now on). The term is derived from the close analogy between the supervisor's interaction with subordinate human staff members in a human organization and a person's interaction with "intelligent" automated subsystems. A supervisor of humans gives directives that are understood and translated into detailed actions by staff subordinates. In turn, subordinates collect detailed information about results and present it in summary form to the supervisor, who must then infer the state of the system and make decisions for further action. The intelligence of the subordinates determines how involved their supervisor becomes in the process. Automation and semi-intelligent subsystems permit the same sort of interaction to occur between a human supervisor and the computer-mediated process (Ferrell and Sheridan 1967; Sheridan and Hennessy 1984).

In the strictest sense, *supervisory control* means that one or more human operators are intermittently programming and continually receiving information from a computer that itself closes an autonomous control loop through artificial effectors and sensors to the controlled process or task environment.

In a less strict sense, *supervisory control* means that one or more human operators are continually programming and receiving information from a computer that interconnects through artificial effectors and sensors to the controlled process or task environment.

In both definitions the computer tranforms information from human to controlled process and from controlled process to human, but only under the strict definition does the computer necessarily close a control loop that excludes the human, thus making the computer an autonomous controller for some variables at least some of the time.

The accompanying figure characterizes supervisory control in relation to the extremes of manual control and full automatic control. Common to the five man-machine system diagrams are displays and controls interfaced with the human operator, and sensors and actuators interacting with a controlled process or environmental task. System 1 represents conven-

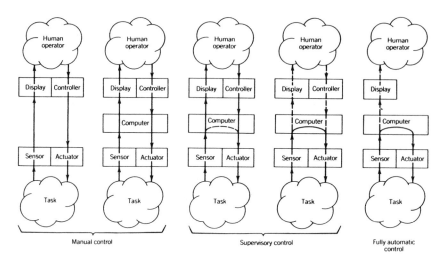

Manual control   Supervisory control   Fully automatic
                                                                            control

The spectrum of control modes. Broken line indicates minor loops are closed through
computer, major loops through human. Solid line indicates major loops are closed through
computer, minor loops through human.

tional (i.e., not computer-aided) manual control. In system 2 significant
computer transforming or aiding is done in either or both of the sensing
and acting (effector) loops. This corresponds to the less strict definition of
supervisory control. Note, however, that in both system 1 and system 2 all
control decisions depend upon the human operator. If the human stops,
control stops.

When either a minor (system 3) or a major (system 4) fraction of control
is accomplished by control loops closed directly through the computer and
exclusive of the human, this is supervisory control in the strict sense. If,
once the control system is set up, essentially all the control is automatic
(system 5)—that is, if the human operator can observe but cannot influence the process (other than by pulling the plug)—it is no longer supervisory control. The five diagrams are ordered with respect to degree of
automation. The progression is not meant to imply either degree of sophistication or degree of desirability.

The strict (systems 3, 4) and not-strict (system 2) forms of supervisory
control may appear the same to the supervisor, since he or she always sees
and acts through the computer (analogous to a staff) and therefore may
not know whether the computer is acting in an open-loop or a closed-loop
manner in its fine behavior. In either case the computer may function

principally on the efferent or motor side to implement the supervisor's commands (e.g., do some part of the task entirely and leave other parts to the human, or provide some control compensation to ease all of the task for the human). Alternatively, the computer may function principally on the display side (e.g., to integrate and interpret incoming information from below, or to serve as an "expert system" advising the supervisor as to what to do next. Usually it does some of each.

In the strict forms of supervisory control (systems 3, 4), the human operator (supervisor) programs by specifying to the computer goals, objective tradeoffs, physical constraints, models, plans, and "if-then-else" procedures. This specification is usually and most conveniently put in high-level "natural" language—in terms of desired relative changes in the controlled process, rather than in terms of control signals. Once the supervisor turns control over to the computer, the computer executes its stored program and acts on new information from its sensors independently of the human, at least for short periods of time. The human may remain as a supervisor, or may from time to time assume direct control (this is called *traded control*), or may act as supervisor with respect to control of some variables and direct controller with respect to other variables (*shared control*).

Automation

Automation is the automatically controlled operation of an apparatus, a process, or a system by mechanical or electronic devices that take the place of human organs of observation, decision, and effort. (This definition is adapted from Webster's Third International Dictionary.)

Robot

A *robot* is an automatic apparatus or device that performs functions ordinarily ascribed to human beings, or operates with what appears to be almost human intelligence (adapted from Webster's Third International Dictionary). *Robotics* is the science and art of designing and using robots.

The Robot Institute of America has defined a robot as a reprogrammable multi-functional manipulator designed to move material, parts, tools, or specialized devices through variable programmed motions for the performance of a variety of tasks. The average person thinks of robots as having human form, as in science-fiction movies. Actually, so long as a robot fits the above definition—which means it must have sensors, effectors, memory, and some real-time computational apparatus—its form is best determined by its function.

Thus, perhaps for short periods of time, many modern chemical or oil plants can be called robots, since they can be programmed to carry and process fluids or other materials automatically in a great variety of ways. Similarly, modern aircraft might be called robots, because they can be programmed to take off, navigate, and land automatically. As we shall see below, they are better designated *telerobots*. However, in this context it is more common to speak of *human-centered automation*.

Teleoperator

A *teleoperator* is a machine that extends a person's sensing and/or manipulating capability to a location remote from that person. A teleoperator necessarily includes artificial sensors of the environment, a vehicle for moving these in the remote environment, and communication channels to and from the human operator. In addition, a teleoperator may include artificial arms and hands or other devices to apply forces and perform mechanical work on the environment. The term *teleoperation* refers most commonly to direct and continuous human control of the teleoperator, but can also be used generically (and literally—i.e., "operating at a distance") to encompass *telerobotics* (see below) as well. In this book *teleoperation* will be used both in the generic sense and in reference to control by a person using a joystick or a master-slave positioning device. *Telemanipulation* is sometimes used as a synonym for *teleoperation*, unless one means remote control of a vehicle for inspection only. *Telechirics*, the Greek etymological roots of which means "remote hand," has also been used.

Telerobot

A *telerobot* is an advanced form of teleoperator the behavior of which a human operator supervises through a computer intermediary. That is, the operator intermittently communicates to a computer information about goals, constraints, plans, contingencies, assumptions, suggestions, and orders relative to a remote task, getting back integrated information about accomplishments, difficulties, and concerns and (as requested) raw sensory data. The subordinate telerobot executes the task on the basis of information received from the human operator plus its own artificial sensing and intelligence.

Whereas the term *supervisory control* is commonly used to refer to human supervision of any semi-autonomous system (an aircraft, a chemical or power plant, etc.) regardless of the distance separating it from its human operator(s), the term *telerobotics* commonly refers to supervisory control of a teleoperator (a machine that is remote from the operator).

As the telerobot's sensors, effectors, and computers become more powerful, and as the capability and correspondingly the authority assigned to any one telerobot by its human supervisor becomes greater, each of the supervisor's acts of committing the machine to execute the program becomes more critical. Thus, a major problem is to help the supervisor and the telerobot communicate sufficiently well and fast that the supervisor understands the implications of what he or she has programmed and the robot does what is intended.

Anthropomorphic teleoperator or telerobot

An *anthropomorphic* teleoperator or telerobot has a human-like form, in that it senses its environment with what resemble eyes, manipulates mechanical objects with what resemble arms and hands, and/or moves in many directions with what resemble human body motions. Its human operator is usually located remote from it and, in controlling it, must conceptually map its form and motions onto his or her own body. That is, the anthropomorphic teleoperator or telerobot must provide the operator with a remote body image or *physical alter ego*.

Non-anthropomorphic teleoperator or telerobot

A *non-anthropomorphic* teleoperator or telerobot does not have a human-like form, does not have appendages resembling arms or hands, and/or does not move in a human-like way. It may move around in its environment to do its mechanical work, or it may remain at a fixed location. Its human operator is likely to be in it or around it; perhaps for that reason, or perhaps because the operator's task itself does not demand it, the transference of body image is not so important.

Modern automated airplanes and computer-based process-control systems, which for short periods of time may function (respectively) as moving and fixed-base *robots* in the general sense described above in the third paragraph of the *robot* definition, strictly are intermittently reprogrammed by human supervisors. Thus they can be called *non-anthropomorphic telerobots*. There can, of course, be anthropomorphic telerobots performing jobs inside process-control (e.g., nuclear power) plants. There can also be non-anthropomorphic telerobots operating in space or under the sea. It is the form of the teleoperator or telerobot and its relation to the human operator that makes the distinction, not the application.

Teleproprioception and telekinesthesis

Teleproprioception refers to the human operator's sensing and keeping track of the location and orientation of the teleoperator and its arms and hands relative to its base, to each other, to external objects, and to the location of the operator's body, arms, and hands. The closely associated term *telekinesthesis* refers to the operator's ability to identify the dynamic movements of the teleoperator and its arms and hands relative to its base, to each other, to external objects, and to the velocity or forces imposed by the operator's body, arms, and hands.

Telepresence

Telepresence means that the operator receives sufficient information about the teleoperator and the task environment, displayed in a sufficiently natural way, that the operator feels physically present at the remote site. This can be a matter of degree. Naturally, an operator, upon reflection, knows where he or she really is. Nevertheless, the illusion of telepresence can be compelling if the proper technology is used.

A more restrictive definition of *telepresence* requires further that the teleoperator's dexterity match that of the bare-handed human operator.

Telepresence is sometimes used to mean *virtual presence* (see below).

In spite of the considerable current popularity of the term, the usefulness of imparting telepresence is obscure at the present time. The topic will be addressed in chapter 2.

Virtual presence, virtual environment, virtual reality

Virtual presence, or synonymously a *virtual environment* or *virtual reality* or *artificial reality* (the latter two are more fashionable but linguistically more troubling terms), is experienced by a person when sensory information generated only by and within a computer compels a feeling of being present in an environment other than the one the person is actually in.

With sufficiently good technology a person would not be able to discriminate among actual presence, telepresence, and virtual presence.

Human-computer interaction

Literally this means any interaction between human and computer, and in that sense it includes telerobotics. However, the term is most often applied to human use of computers in the office, or to other situations where the computer and its database are the end objects, and are not mediators in the control of a physical dynamic system on the other side of the computer from the human. This use of *human-computer interaction* is distinct from our use of *telerobot* or *supervisory control*.

Human operator

This is the person doing the observing (monitoring) and the acting (controlling), whether in direct or supervisory control. Throughout this book the pronoun forms *she* and *her* are used generically to refer to the human operator.

History of the Idea of Supervisory Control

Supervisory control is emerging rapidly in many industrial, military, medical, and other contexts, although this form of human interaction with technology is not well recognized or understood in a formal way.

From the pyramid-building pharaohs of Egypt through all of the history of technology there has been concern about how best to extend the capabilities of human workers. Early in the twentieth century, against the backdrop of the newly mechanized production line, F. W. Taylor's *scientific management* (see Taylor 1947) catalyzed a formal intellectual consciousness about the human factors involved. Taylor intended a new interest in the sensorimotor aspects of human performance; he did not intend that his essentially mechanistic approach be criticized as dehumanizing, as it was.

The 1940s and the 1950s saw the emergence of *human factors* (*ergonomics* in Europe), first in an empirical "knobs and dials" form concentrating on the human-machine interface. This was supported over the next decade by the theoretical underpinnings of "man-machine systems" (Sheridan and Ferrell 1974). Such theories included control, information, signal-detection, and decision theories originally developed for application to physical systems but now explicitly applied to the human operator. In contrast with human-factors engineering, with its emphasis on the interface, man-machine systems analysis considers characteristics of the entire causal "loop" of decision, communication, control, and feedback through the human operator's physical environment and back to the operator.

From the late 1950s on, the computer began to intervene in the causal loop (via electronic compensation and stability augmentation for control of aircraft and similar systems, electronic filtering of signal patterns in noise, electronic generation of simple displays, and so on). It was obvious that once vehicular or industrial systems were equipped with sensors that could be read by computers, and with motors that could be driven by computers, then (even though the overall system was still very much human-controlled) control loops between those sensors and motors could be closed automatically. Thus the operator of a chemical plant was relieved of keeping the tank at a given level or the temperature at a reference—she needed only to set that desired level or temperature signal from time to time. So too, after the autopilot was developed, the human pilot needed only to set the desired altitude or heading; an automatic system would strive to achieve this reference, with the pilot monitoring to ensure that the aircraft did in fact go where desired.

The automatic building elevator, of course, has been in place for many years, and is certainly one of the first implementations of supervisory control. The supervisor in this case programs by indicating the desired floor. Monitoring is essential, for the human supervisor in this case must take action to get off at the correct floor. So too the "automatic" washing machine and dryer require the human operator to set a simple timer or other controls in addition to pushing the "on" switch, but do not require monitoring. They verge on being robots.

Recently developers of new systems for word processing and for the handling of business information have begun thinking along similar lines (Card et al. 1986).

Beginning in the early 1960s a small community of researchers interested in manual control (mostly of aircraft, but also of cars and other systems) met annually on a relatively informal basis, in a meeting that came to be known as the Annual Manual. It was becoming evident that control of many systems was becoming automated, and that some theory was needed to characterize people functioning in high-level discontinuous control loops, where the operator's function was to specify the parameters of an automated action as contrasted to the conventional continuous manual control skill. This higher-level control was initially called *meta-control* (Sheridan 1960).

The full generality of the idea of supervisory control later became apparent (Ferrell and Sheridan 1967) as part of research on how people on earth might teleoperate vehicles on the moon through three-second round-trip time delays (imposed by the speed of light). Under such a constraint, teleoperation of lunar roving vehicles or manipulators was shown to be possible only by performing in "move-and-wait" fashion. This meant that the operator could commit only to a small incremental movement "open loop," i.e., without feedback (which actually is as large a movement as is reasonable without risking collision or other error), then stopping and waiting one delay period for feedback to "catch up," then repeating the process in steps until the task was complete. This was unacceptably tedious except for simple tasks where long waits were acceptable.

It became evident that if the human operator, instead of remaining within the control loop, communicates a goal state and some instructions for getting there (including if-then-else information for responding to artificially measured information along the way), and if the remote teleoperator incorporates sufficient capability to measure variables both internal to the machine and in the external environment, then the achievement of this goal state can be turned over to a remote subordinate control system for implementation. In this case, where the computer executing the operator's commands is colocated with the teleoperator, there is no delay in the control loop that implements the task and thus there is no instability. One might assert that this is just programming the computer. What makes it supervisory control is that the operator continually monitors and iteratively updates or modifies the program. Automation (loop closure through the computer, its sensors, and its actuators) is usually much faster than if the operator had to do the sensing, deciding, and controlling. Yet the human is still there observing and revising the instructions, or taking over control if necessary.

There necessarily remains, of course, a delay within the supervisory loop. This delay in the supervisor's confirmation of desired results is acceptable so long as (1) the subgoal is a conveniently large "bite" of the task, (2) the unpredictable aspects of the remote environment are not changing too rapidly (i.e., the disturbance bandwidth is low), and (3) the subordinate automatic system is trustworthy. More will be said of these points below.

As computers gradually become more capable both in hardware and in software, it is evident that telemetry transmission delay is in no way a prerequisite to the usefulness of supervisory control. The incremental goal specified by the human operator need not be simply a new steady-state reference for a servomechanism (as in resetting a thermostat) in one or even several dimensions. (An example of the latter is resetting both temperature and humidity, or commanding a manipulator end point to move to a new position including three translations and three rotations relative to its initial position.) Each new goal statement can be the specification of a whole trajectory of movements (as the performance of a dance or a symphony) together with programmed if-then-else branching conditions (what to do in case of a fall or a broken violin string, or how to respond contingent upon audience applause). It can be a specification in terms of the environmental objects to be moved and the goals to be met, rather than in terms of the teleoperator control signals or motions.

In other words, the incremental goal statement is a program of instructions in the full sense of a computer program, which makes the human supervisor an intermittent real-time computer programmer, acting relative to the subordinate computer much as a teacher, a parent, or a boss behaves relative to a student, a child, or a subordinate. The size and the complexity of each new program are necessarily functions of how much the computer can (be trusted to) cope with at once, which in turn depends on the computer's own sophistication (knowledge base) and on the complexity (uncertainty) of the task.

Supervisory control is now emerging in various forms in various industries—usually without being called that. (More likely, each developer or vendor has its own cute acronym emphasizing how "smart" and easy it is to use the new product.) Aircraft autopilots are now "layered," meaning that the pilot (the "flight manager") can select among various forms and levels. At the lowest level she can set a new heading or rate of climb. Or she can program a sequence of heading changes at various way-points, or a sequence of climb rates initiated at various altitudes. Or she can program her inertial guidance system to take the aircraft to (within a fraction of a mile of) a distant city. Given the existence of certain ground-based equipment, she can program an automatic landing on a given runway, and so on. Wiener and Curry (1980) provide a good review of how such automation crept into the aircraft flight deck. Modern chemical plants can similarly be programmed to perform heating, mixing, and various other processes according to a time line, but including various sensor-based conditions for shutting down or otherwise aborting the operation.

The examples cited above characterize the first or stricter definition of supervisory control given above, where the computer, once programmed, makes use of its own artificial sensors to ensure completion of the assigned task. Many familiar systems, such as automatic washing machines, dryers, dishwashers, microwaves, and stoves, once programmed, perform their operations in "open-loop" fashion—i.e. there is no measurement or knowledge of results. If the task can be performed in such open-loop fashion, and if the human supervisor can anticipate the task conditions and is good at selecting the right open-loop program, there is no reason not to employ this approach. To the human supervisor it is often unknown or unimportant whether the lower-level implementation is open-loop or closed-loop; her only concern is whether the goal is achieved satisfactorily. For example, a programmable microwave oven without the temperature sensor in place operates open-loop, while the same oven using the temperature sensor operates closed-loop. To the human supervisor/programmer, they may both look the same.

A very important aspect of supervisory control is the ability of the computer to "package" information for visual display to the human operator. Data may be included from many sources, from the past, the present, or even the predicted future, presented in words, graphs, symbols, pictures, or some combination. The ubiquitous examples of such integrated displays in aircraft and air traffic control, chemical and power plants, and various other industrial or military settings are too numerous to review here. Some examples will be considered below.

General interest in supervisory control became evident in the mid-1970s (Edwards and Lees 1974; Sheridan and Johannsen 1976; Baron et al. 1980, 1982), and continues to grow. A report by the National Research Council (Sheridan and Hennessy 1984) outlines current problems of supervisory control, especially with regard to experimental research (which is particularly difficult because of the inherent complexity and capital cost of real supervisory control systems, inhibiting both simulation and experimental control) and system design. For general reviews, see Moray 1986, Sheridan 1987, and Stassen 1991.

The current motivations to develop supervisory control are

(1)   to achieve the accuracy and reliability of the machine without sacrificing the cognitive capability and adaptability of the human,

(2)   to make control faster and unconstrained by the limited pace of the continuous human sensorimotor capability,

(3)   to make control easier by letting the operator give instructions in terms of objects to be moved and goals to be met, rather than instruments to be used and control signals to be sent,

(4)   to eliminate the demand for continuous human attention and reduce the operator's workload,

(5)   to make control possible even where there are time delays in communication between human and teleoperator,

(6)   to provide a "fail-soft" capability when failure in the operator's direct control would prove catastrophic, and

(7)   to save lives and reduce cost by eliminating the need for the operator to be present in hazardous environments, and for life support required to send the operator there.

1 Theory and Models of Supervisory Control: Frameworks and Fragments

This chapter provides a variety of qualitative characterizations of supervisory control in the form of diagrams, lists, and words. In addition there are a number of qualitative models which at best can be said to describe and predict experimental data for some limited aspect of supervisory control. The very diversity of the modeling ideas that have been put forth in the name of supervisory control conveys its complexity and inclusivity. No comprehensive mathematical model or representation is in sight at this time. One might say that the current status of supervisory control theory is "fragments in search of unification."

First, some qualitative paradigms and taxonomies which cover the generality of supervisory control, including several ways of representing its multi-loop, multi-level nature, are presented. Then the modeling efforts that stem from application of conventional control theory to human operators are reviewed. Next, models of human attention allocation are reviewed, including multi-person and multi-task considerations. The relevance of cognitive science and mental models are then discussed, along with that of artificial intelligence.

An elaborated taxonomy of the functions of the human supervisor is then presented, together with suggestions for how computers might aid human decisions at each for these functions. Finally there is a discussion of the factors that limit our ability to model supervisory control.

The references to salient literature in this chapter are far from comprehensive. Many of the issues will be revisited in subsequent chapters.

1.1 The Basic Supervisory Control Paradigm

Figure 1.1 illustrates the concept of supervisory control. The human operator provides largely *symbolic* commands (concatenations of typed symbols or specialized key presses) to the computer. However, some fraction of her commands may be *analogic* (hand-control movements isomorphic to the space-time-force continuum of the physical task) in order to point to objects or otherwise demonstrate to the computer relationships that are difficult for the operator to put into symbols. The *local* or *human-interactive computer* (HIC) thus should be human-friendly, able to indicate that it understands the message, and able to point out that a specification is incomplete. In this way it should help the operator to edit the message correctly. It also needs to interpret signals from the distant telerobot,

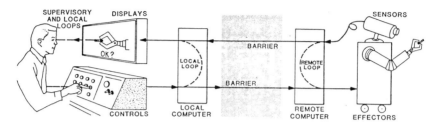

Figure 1.1
Basic concept of telerobot supervisory control, showing separate computers for loop local
to human and loop remote from human, separated by a barrier of distance, time, or
inconvenience. [From Ferrell and Sheridan 1967; © IEEE.]

storing and processing them to generate meaningful integrated graphic
displays. Finally, this local human-interactive computer should contain a
knowledge base and a model of the controlled process and task environment and be able to answer queries put to it by the operator.

Meanwhile, the subordinate "remote" or *task-interactive computer* (TIC)
that accompanies the controlled process must receive commands, translate
them into executable strings of code, and perform the execution, closing
each control loop though the appropriate actuators and sensors.

1.2   Five Generic Supervisory Functions

The human supervisor's functions are

(1)   planning what task to do and how to do it,

(2)   teaching (or programming) the computer what was planned,

(3)   monitoring the automatic action to make sure all is going as planned
and to detect failures,

(4)   intervening (which means that the supervisor supplements ongoing
automatic control activities, takes over control entirely after the desired
goal state has been reached satisfactorily, or interrupts the automatic
control in emergencies to specify a new goal state and reprogram a new
procedure), and

(5)   learning from experience so as to do better in the future.

These are usually time-sequential steps.

Planning

This is the hardest function to model. Formally it means

(1) gaining experience and understanding of the physical process to be controlled, including the constraints set by nature and circumstances surrounding the job,

(2) setting goals that are attainable, or objectives along with tradeoffs, that the computer can "understand" sufficiently well to give proper advice or make control decisions, and

(3) formulating a strategy for going from the initial state to the goal state.

Teaching the computer

The supervisor must translate goals and strategy into detailed instructions to the computer such that it can perform at least some part of the task automatically, at least until the instructions are updated or changed or the human takes over by manual control. This includes knowing the requisite command language sufficiently well that goals and instructions can be communicated to the computer in correct and timely fashion.

Monitoring automatic control

Once the goals and instructions are properly communicated to the computer for automatic execution of that part of the task, the supervisor must observe this performance to ensure that it is done properly, using direct viewing or whatever remote sensing instruments are available. The prompt detection of the presence and location of failures, or of conflicts between actions and goals, and the anticipation that either of these is about to occur, are essential parts of the supervisor's job.

Intervening to update instructions or assume direct control

If the computer signals that it has accomplished its assigned part-task, or if it has apparently run into trouble along the way, the human supervisor must step in to update instructions to the computer or to take over control in direct manual fashion, or some combination of the two. Since the controlled process is an ongoing dynamic system, not a machine that can be arbitrarily stopped and started again like a computer, the takeover itself must be smooth so as not to cause instability. Similarly, reverting to the automation must be smooth.

Learning from experience

The supervisor must ensure that appropriate data are recorded and computer-based models are updated so as to characterize current conditions with the most accurate information. Historical data must continuously be analyzed for trends or contingencies leading to abnormalities. All such information must be in a form usable in the future in the four preceding steps.

1.3 Multiplicity of Loops and Levels in SC

Supervisory functions as nested control loops

We may view these functions as operating within three nested control loops, as shown in figure 1.2. The innermost loop, monitoring, closes on itself. That is, based on what evidence is interesting, the supervisor redirects her attention and formulates hypotheses or makes minor system adjustments in the automatic control system that require no significant intervention. The middle loop closes from intervening back to teaching;

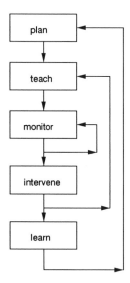

Figure 1.2
Five supervisor functions as nested loops.

i.e., human intervention usually leads to programming of a new goal state to the process. The outer loop closes from learning back to planning; intelligent planning for the next subtask is usually not possible without learning from the last one. The three supervisory loops operate at different time scales relative to one another. Revisions in monitoring behavior take place at brief intervals. Interventions and/or reprogramming occur at somewhat longer intervals. Learning and revision in task planning occur only at still longer intervals.

This nesting of functional control loops is not novel in systems involving human operators. Hess and McNally (in press) have shown how conventional manual control models can be extended to such multiloop situations, each inner loop having a set point determined by the next outer loop. In aerospace vehicles (figure 1.3) the innermost of three nested loops is typically called "control." For aircraft this is primarily pitch and yaw control relative to offsetting air turbulence and crosswinds; for spacecraft it is thrust directional control. The intermediate loop is "guidance," having to do with airspeed and altitude in the aircraft and with total thrust and fine trajectory adherence in the spacecraft. The outer loop, "navigation," has to do with planning and execution of route way-points in aviation or with gross trajectory shape in spacecraft. Similar levels of control occur in automobile driving: fine-level steering is an inner loop, speed and lane changing constitute an intermediate loop, and trip planning and route selection constitute the outer loop.

Supervisory control is the way spacecraft are controlled, so that the five-step functional taxonomy fits that situation rather well. In modern aircraft the supervisory control functions apply when the autopilot is used,

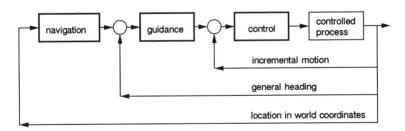

Figure 1.3
Navigation, guidance, and control as nested loops, as applied to an aircraft or another vehicle under multi-level control.

but at the pilot's option all three loops can be and often are under manual control. In car driving, automatic gear shifting and cruise control are primitive forms of supervisory control; more sophisticated forms are being considered for obstacle avoidance and other functions.

Rasmussen's "skills, rules, knowledge" paradigm: The levels of behavior

Rasmussen (1976) introduced a paradigm for describing three levels of human behavior: *skill-based behavior* (continuous, typically well-learned, sensorimotor behavior analogous to what can be expected from a servo-mechanism), *rule-based behavior* (what an "artificially intelligent" computer can do in recognizing a pattern of stimuli, then triggering an "if-then" algorithm to execute an appropriate response), and finally *knowledge-based behavior* ("high-level" situation assessment and evaluation, consideration of alternative actions in light of various goals, decision and scheduling of implementation—a form of behavior machines are not now good at). Figure 1.4 is an abbreviated version of Rasmussen's qualitative model showing in particular the nesting of skill-based, rule-based, and knowledge-based behavioral loops.

Referring back to the three supervisory loops discussed above, we see that system monitoring is a semicontinuous, well-learned, and largely perceptual-motor skill. It fits the Rasmussen "skill" level rather well. Teaching and intervening, and the loop within which they fit, involve computer

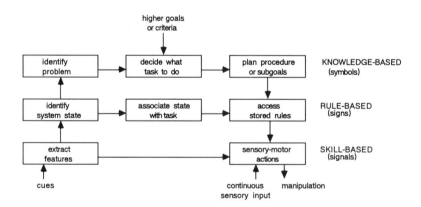

Figure 1.4
Rasmussen model for levels of human behavior: skill-based, rule-based, and knowledge-based, from lower to higher levels. Stimulus cues (patterns) are processed up, across, and down at the corresponding level of behavior.

instructions and task protocols initiated by established criteria, and therefore tend to be rule-based. Planning and learning, and the outer loop within which these functions fit, clearly involve much greater attention to goals and problem formulation, and thus tend to be knowledge-based. Although teaching and learning are often said in the same breath, in the supervisory control context learning is an inductive activity, generalizing from experience, and therefore at a higher level than teaching the computer, which amounts to reducing general ideas to specific instructions.

The classical S-C-R paradigm: Loci of biological activity

We will also make use of a traditional classification of behavioral activity (figure 1.5) according to apparent physiological locus: (S) sensory (in this case referring usually to exteroceptors—vision, hearing, taste, touch, smell, vestibular senses), (C) cognitive activity without apparent sensory or motor components (remembering, making decisions), and (R) response or motor functions (referring usually to skeletal muscle activity). Clearly the body's major sensors have muscles to control them, and muscles have internal or interoceptive sensors to close their control loops. Nevertheless, a coarse differentiation of S, C, and R is often useful.

Supervising many tasks simultaneously

More and more supervisory control systems use many computers to control many tasks simultaneously (figure 1.6). In this case the supervisor must provide sufficient instruction to each low-level task-interactive system to

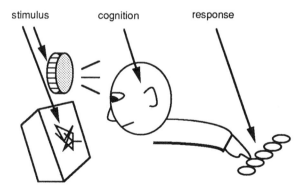

Figure 1.5
Traditional stimulus-cognition-response loci of behavior.

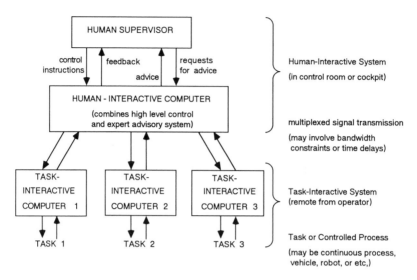

Figure 1.6
Supervision of multiple computers and tasks.

keep it occupied for sufficient time until she can return her attention to monitor and/or reprogram it. She must also multiplex her own time and attention. Typically a large human-interactive computer is in the control room to generate displays and interpret commands. It, in turn, forwards those commands to various microprocessors (task-interactive computers), which close individual low-level control loops through their own associated sensors and effectors. In some process plants there are over 1000 TICs, some serving simply as conventional feedback control stations and some performing higher-level decision functions.

Combining supervisory functions, behavior levels, and S-C-R loci into a single paradigm for control of multiple tasks

Considering the above three meta-characteristics of the supervisor described in the preceding sections (function, loci, and level) as three independent dimensions of such behavior, we may then represent any behavioral element to be within one cell of a three-dimensional array, as shown at the top of figure 1.7.

Immediately below this array of supervision behaviors in figure 1.7 lies the human-interactive computer (HIC). This is conceived to be a large

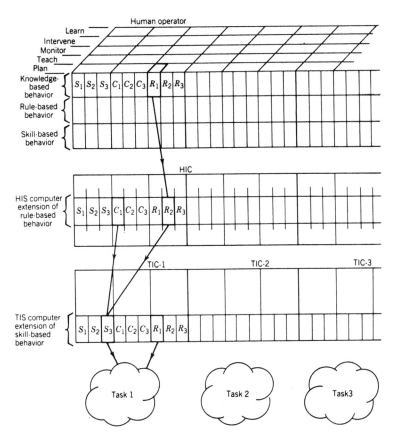

Figure 1.7
Combining supervisory functions, levels of behavior (skill, rule, knowledge), and loci (stimulus, cognition, response). Upper three-dimensional matrix represents human operator. Middle matrix represents human-interactive system (HIS). Lower matrix represents multiple task-interactive systems (TIS).

enough computer physically to communicate in a human-friendly way, using near-natural language, good graphics, and so on. The HIC should be able to recognize patterns in data sent up to it from below and decide on appropriate algorithms for response, which it sends down as instructions. Eventually the HIC should be able to run "what would happen if …" simulations and be able to give useful advice from a knowledge base, i.e., include an "expert system."

The HIC, located near the supervisor in a control room or cockpit, may communicate across a "barrier" of time or space with a multiplicity of task-interactive computers (TICs)—which probably are microprocessors—distributed throughout the telerobot, plant, or vehicle. The latter are usually coupled intimately with artificial sensors and actuators, in order to deal in low-level language and to close relatively tight control loops with objects and events in the physical world.

The human supervisor can be expected to communicate with the HIC intermittently in information "chunks" (alphanumeric sentences, video pages, etc.) while the task communicates with the TIC continuously in computer words at the highest possible bit rates. The availability of these computer aids means that the human supervisor, while retaining the knowledge-based behavior for herself, is likely to "download" some of the rule-based and almost all of the skill-based programs to the HIC. The HIC, in turn, should download a few of the rule-based programs, and most of the skill-based programs, to the appropriate TICs.

In terms of this paradigm, researchers and designers of supervisory control systems must cope with questions such as these: How much autonomy is appropriate for the TIC? How much detail should the TIC tell the HIC and the HIC tell the human supervisor? How should responsibilities be allocated among the TIC, the HIC, and the supervisor?

Johannsen's interface management system

Johannsen (1990, 1991) proposed a formal system structure or architecture for process control decision support systems similar in many ways to the generic structure of figures 1.6 and 1.7. At what here is called the HIC level, and in addition to the human interface itself, Johannsen places what he calls the "user model." By this he means the knowledge base for the human functions of procedure support, plan evaluation, and error recognition (which he also relates to Rasmussen's knowledge-based, rule-based, and skill-based behaviors). This model, as well as the operator interface components, communicates through a versatile "dialog system" capable of handling not only analog signals but also symbolic messages. On the distal side (the other side from the human) of the dialog system, within what is here called the TIC, is the "application model," the knowledge base for support of lower-level control, including process models and failure criteria.

NASREM task/computer hierarchical architecture

Albus, McCain, and Lumia (1987) proposed a reference model telerobot control system architecture consisting of a hierarchy of six levels of sensory processing, world modeling, and task decomposition. Their proposal, originally conceived for computer-aided manufacturing and more recently applied to spacecraft, is really a qualitative taxonomy of hierarchical levels, based in part on the Albus (1975) model of the animal cerebellum and how it mediates control. Figure 1.8 is a diagram of the NASREM architecture. A global data store is accessible by the sensory processing module at any level, and each sensory processor also receives new data from the next-lower-level sensor system. The task-decomposition modules at each level

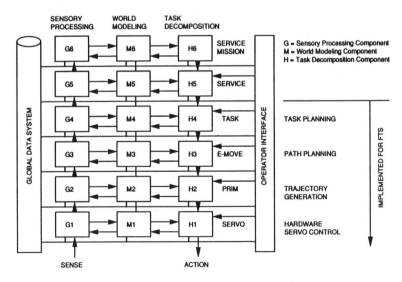

Figure 1.8
NASREM task/computer architecture being built into the NASA Flight Telerobotic Servicer. [From Albus et al. 1987.]

receive commands as appropriate from the human supervisor and from the next-higher-level task-decomposition module. There is other intermodule communication as shown. The level breakdown is as follows.

Level 1, the bottom-most or *servo level*, is assigned the most primitive closed-loop servo-hardware control; i.e., observed sensor data is compared against commands and signals given to actuators to null the differences. Kinematic coordinate transforms are also handled at this level, as are interpolations of actual trajectory points between servo command updates.

Level 2, the *primitive level*, generates smooth, dynamically efficient trajectories in a convenient coordinate frame. The criteria for dynamic efficiency can vary, but would most likely be some function of the time, the maximum force, and the energy used. This is the level at which a single arm-hand or vehicle or sensor mechanism would be commanded to make a limited continuous movement.

Level 3 is called the *elemental move (E-move) level*. At this level, symbolic commands for movement are transformed into intermediate poses of one or a combination of arm-hands or mobility devices or sensors in such a way that these poses define pathways free of collisions with obstacles and kinematic singularities. World models at this level would be specific to manipulation in general, or to mobility generally (vehicle control), or to a single category of exteroceptive sensing (including the actuators that position and focus the sensors) such as vision or touch.

Level 4 is called the *task level*. At this level, goals specified from above are transformed into control-system actions designed to achieve these goals. This is the level at which a single complete telerobot would be commanded to perform a relatively straightforward and constrained task. The world model at this level would include manipulative control as well as control of the vehicle.

Level 5, called the *service level*, deals with a larger set of tasks to be performed at one location.

Level 6, called the *mission level*, deals with an entire mission and all telerobotic and computational elements that participate.

NASA is implementing NASREM in the Flight Telerobotic Servicer, but for now is including only the first four levels.

Resolving conflicts among tasks

Note that the "tasks" in figure 1.6 are at the same level and appear to be controlled independently. One problem is that otherwise independently

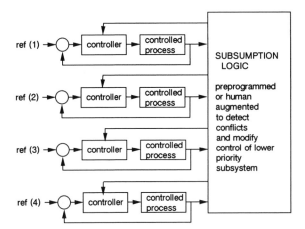

Figure 1.9
R. Brooks' subsumption architecture, with potential human supervisory conflict resolution in place of computer logic (right-hand box).

controlled processes can conflict with one another, as, for example, if they are vehicles which move about in the same space, or if one loop controls temperature and the other controls flow of the same physical system. R. Brooks (1986), using robot-like "insect" devices consisting of multiple semi-autonomous loops programmed to strive for different goals simultaneously, has shown how, in the case of conflicts, higher-level logic can prioritize or inhibit (or otherwise *subsume*) the actions of one element relative to another (figure 1.9). Brooks' robots do indeed exhibit robust behavior and appear intelligent. This so-called *layered control* or *subsumption architecture* is not unlike the situation faced by the human supervisor of multiple automated subsystems or "tasks." In fact we assume that the human supervisor can provide greater robustness in resolving conflicts than can Brooks' computer logic. Bellingham and Humphrey (1990) proposed doing this with undersea telerobot vehicles. There are strong parallels to layered control in fully human organizations.

Multiple information loops through the physical system

The above discussion identifies different functions, behavioral levels, and physiological loci inherent in supervising a single computer-controlled machine or task. Figure 1.10 indicates yet another breakdown of ways in which information is processed in supervisory control, in this case by

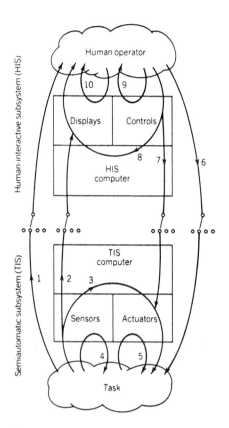

Figure 1.10
Supervisory control as multiple and mirrored loops through the physical system.
(1) Task is observed directly by human operator's own senses.
(2) Task is observed indirectly through artificial sensors, computers, and displays. This task-interactive-system (TIS) feedback interacts with that from within human-interactive-system (HIS) and is filtered or modified.
(3) Task is controlled within TIS automatic mode.
(4) Task is affected by the process of being sensed.
(5) Task affects actuators, and in turn is affected.
(6) Human operator directly affects task by manipulation.
(7) Human operator affects task indirectly through controls interface, HIS/TIS computers and actuators. This control interacts with that from within TIS and is filtered or modified.
(8) Human operator gets feedback from within HIS in editing a program, running a planning model, or etc.
(9) Human operator orients herself relative to control or adjusts control parameters.
(10) Human operator orients herself relative to display or adjusts display parameters.

information channels or loops which differ from one another with respect to their paths through the physical system external to the human. In this figure the human-interactive subsystem (HIS) and the computer-interactive subsystem (CIS) form mirror images of one another. In each case the computer closes a loop through mechanical displacement (hand control, actuator) and electro-optical or sonic (display, sensor) transducers to interact with an external dynamic process (human operator, task). The external process is quite variable in time and space and somewhat unpredictable. The numbered arrows identify individual cause-effect relations, with explanations of the loops in the caption.

There are three types of inputs into the human operator: (1) those that come by loop 1 directly from the task (direct seeing, hearing, or touching), (2) those that come by loops 3, 2, and 8 through the artificial display and are mediated by the computer, and (3) those that come by loops 10 and 9 from the display or manual controls without going through the computer. (The last is information about the display itself such as brightness or format, or present position of manual controls, which is not information which the computer has to provide.) Similarly, there are three types of human outputs: (1) those that go by loop 6 directly to the task (the human operator bypasses the manual controls and the computer and directly manipulates the task, makes repairs, etc.), (2) those that communicate instructions via loops 8, 7, and 3 to the task, and (3) those that modify the display or manual control parameters via loops 10 and 9 without affecting the computer (i.e., change the location, forces, labels, or other properties of the display or manual control devices).

Correspondingly, there are three types of force and displacement input into the task: (1) direct manipulations by the operator via loop 6, (2) manipulations mediated by the computer via loops 8, 7, and 3, and (3) those forces that occur by interaction, over loops 4 and 5, with the sensors and actuators, and are not computer-mediated. Finally, there are three types of outputs from the task: (1) information fed back directly to the operator over loop 1, (2) information fed to the operator via loops 3, 2, and 8, and (3) information (in the form of forces and displacements) that modifies the sensors or actuators via loops 4 and 5 without being explicitly sensed by the computer.

When the task is physically near to the operator, the HIS and TIS computers can be one and the same. When the TIS is remote, the HIS and TIS computers are usually separated to avoid problems caused by bandwidth or reliability constraints in telecommunication (loops 2 and 7). Multiplexing switches are shown in loops 1, 2, 7, and 6 to suggest that one HIS may be time-shared among many TISs as described above.

Figure 1.10 should make it clear that the human supervisor may intervene at various levels—to perform continuous direct control herself, to make parameter adjustments in any of the multiple control loops, to switch control from one preprogrammed mode to another, or to enter more complex statements about goals, contingencies, or conditions. In other words, teleoperation may be controlled along a continuum from direct manual control to quite high-level supervisory command and control. Further, any of a variety of control modes may be in operation for different subordinate teleoperator systems.

In considering supervisory control, we are interested in which functions can be done by either a human or a computer, and which are best done by a human and which by a computer. We may design a system with some duties assigned to the human and some to the computer; but then in evaluating the performance of the resulting system it is likely to be very difficult to establish whether an error was caused by the human or the computer, or which is to be credited with good performance. We will know only which human-machine combinations resulted in what system performance. It may be easier to model the performance of the human and the computer in combination. There is a precedent for this in the modeling of simple manual control systems, which will be discussed next.

1.4   Extensions of Manual Control Theory toward SC

The idea of human plus controlled process as invariant

Since roughly 1950 there has been much effort devoted to using conventional linear control theory to model simple manual control systems (figure 1.11), where the human operator is the sole in-the-loop control element and the controlled process can be represented by linear differential equations. A primary motivation for this work was the need to establish predictive models for control of aircraft, where having good differential equation models for the controlled process (airframe plus control electromechanics in this case) was of no use unless models of the pilot were factored in as well. Initially it was believed that an independent model of the pilot was appropriate, so that the pilot model could then be combined with whatever controlled process was of interest. This was soon found to be impractical,

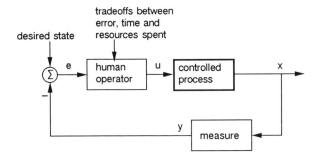

Figure 1.11
Simple compensatory manual control paradigm. Action **u** causes simple nulling of error **e** between current measured state **x** and desired state (goal).

since the characteristics of the human operator proved to be very much *dependent* upon the controlled process, varying to compensate for the controlled process so as to stabilize the closed-loop system and provide satisfactory transient response.

It was then proposed to model the human operator and the controlled process as a single forward loop element, to combine the two upper blocks of figure 1.11 as shown in figure 1.12. The idea was that there would be only minor variation of the combined human and process from application to application. This approach proved very successful. The result is the *simple crossover model* of McRuer et al. (1965), which has the form

$$\mathbf{x}/\mathbf{e} = Ke^{-j\omega T}/j\omega.$$

This is essentially a combined pure time delay and integrator, ω being frequency. The (small) variations of parameters K and T are well established in the literature. Direct man-in-the-loop control is well covered elsewhere (McRuer and Jex 1967; Sheridan and Ferrell 1974).

What is important here, other than to mention this bit of classic human operator modeling background, is the idea of a model in which *human operator plus controlled process is what is invariant,* not the human operator *per se.* This idea surely applies to supervisory control in some form, but it has not found explicit application there as yet.

Kalman filter and optimal control

A second widely accepted class of models of direct manual control is based on so-called optimal or modern control theory. Inherent in such models is

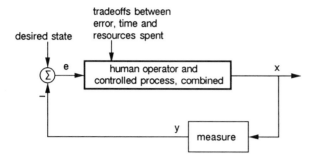

Figure 1.12
McRuer's simple crossover model assumes human action-decision element and
controlled-process act as an invariant (forward loop) combination.

the use of a model-based controller, which in turn contains a model-based
state-estimator (*observer*, or *Kalman filter*) to provide an optimal estimate
of controlled process state variables. Once true state variables are known,
there are well-established control laws for forcing the controlled process in
order to minimize some criterion—for example, some function of state
variable deviation from the desired state (control error) and resources
expended (control action). In most real-world cases, true state variables are
not available or not known precisely and must be estimated on the basis
of current (noisy) measurements and on the basis of the effect of past
control inputs on the process (to the extent that the process dynamics are
known).

If state variables can be accurately measured, then control is relatively
straightforward by traditional means. If, by contrast, one has a perfect
model of the controlled process and there is negligible disturbance, one
need not bother to measure state. Knowing the past and present inputs to
the process allows precise determination of the state; control can be "open-
loop." Seldom is either condition true. One must use both noisy state
measures and the best available model. The Kalman filter (Kalman 1960)
is a way to combine information from both.

The configurations of the model-based controller, and the estimator or
Kalman filter itself, though well known to control engineers, are shown in
figure 1.13 for the benefit of those not familiar with these ideas. **A**, **B**, and
C represent the gain matrices that shape the actual vector variables for
state feedback in the controlled process, for control, and for measurement
as shown in the figure. **A′**, **B′**, and **C′** are the best available *models* of these,

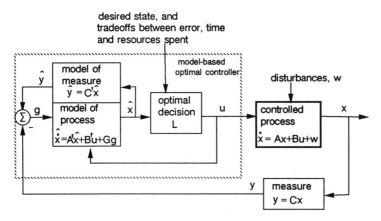

Figure 1.13
Modern (optimal) control paradigm, using the model-based estimator of state **x** (Kalman filter). Action **u** is based on model's estimation of current state **x**. The process model is continuously updated by nulling discrepancy **g** between modeled and measured states.

and, together with knowledge of the disturbance statistics, the observation noise statistics, and the known deterministic inputs, constitute an *internal model* of the external reality that is the heart of the Kalman filter. The modeled output measurement vector $\hat{y}$ is compared against the actual measurement **y**, and the discrepancy or residual **g** is used for a continual Bayesian correction from prior to posterior estimate $\hat{x}$ of state **x**.

Roughly speaking, this correction (the *Kalman filter gain*) is made proportional to **g**, proportional to confidence in the previous measurement (more confident the smaller the observation noise covariance), and inversely proportional to confidence in the *a priori* state estimate (more confident the smaller the state-variable error covariance). We shall see in chapter 3 that the Kalman residual is useful not only as a correction factor but also as an indication of a process actively deviating from what was supposed to be—in other words, for failure detection.

This approach produces a minimum variance state estimate with white noise residuals if one assumes that the controlled process is linear, that its internal model matches the actual process perfectly, and that noise terms are Gaussian and random. With such a "best" estimate of state, the control law **L** can perform its criterion-minimizing function independently of the estimation. Again, it is not the purpose of this book to provide a tutorial on modern estimation and control, but to provide some idea of the basis for some important models of supervisory control. The general and powerful idea of an internal model will be referred to again below.

Baron (1984) comments that a model based on the Kalman filter estimator can become so confident of its prior state estimates (based on the model) that it virtually operates in open-loop fashion and ignores exteroceptive feedback for short periods. He suggests, and the present author agrees, that such behavior is often observed in human operators.

Kleinman-Baron-Levison optimal control model (OCM)

Kleinman, Baron, and Levison (1970) made use of the idea of optimal control in developing a model of the human operator in a simple control loop. This model, pictured in figure 1.14, while considerably more complex and requiring more assumptions than McRuer's simple crossover model, has nevertheless proved quite robust in fitting experimental data.

Baron and his colleagues subsequently added to the OCM "event detectors" triggered by state variable (estimates) being abnormal or having reached some critical point in a mission. They also added logic by which monitoring procedures and activities are changed. Pattipati, Ephrath, and Kleinman (1979) extended this model to make selections among N independent targets (tasks) and utilized N Kalman filters to make estimates

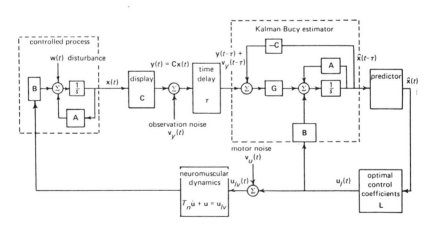

Figure 1.14
The Kleinman-Baron-Levison optimal control model (OCM) of human operator. In effect, a predictor (to compensate for the operator's time delay) and neuromuscular dynamics are added to the modern control paradigm. [From Kleinman et al. 1970.]

which in turn were used as a basis for selecting the most important task to do. They used a multi-task experimental paradigm of Tulga and Sheridan (1980) involving multiple bars appearing at random locations from a "deadline" and moving at constant speed across a computer display. Subjects had to select, one at a time, such a task to "work on" to earn points. Pattipati et al. report good predictions of probability of task completion and probability of decision errors (such as beginning a task that is bound to hit the deadline before it can be completed).

Critiquing his own and others' previous work, Baron (1984) comments on the above OCM work: "... none of these models considers any of the following: multiple tasks having different objectives; the detection of events not explicitly related to the system state variables; or multi-operator situations and the effects of communications among such variables. Perhaps the chief shortcoming of the models with respect to realistic supervisory control tasks is that they do not include the procedural activities of the operators or the discrete tasks that are often part of such procedures."

PROCRU

To satisfy the above kinds of concerns, Baron et al. (1980) developed PROCRU (procedure-oriented crew model) for analyzing commercial aviation flight crew procedures for ILS (instrument) approach-to-landing. PROCRU incorporates both "by the book" procedures and more unconstrained monitoring and control activities. It models both continuous control and discrete procedural tasks which are triggered by controlled process state variables. The particular task chosen at any moment by the procedure selector is the one having the greatest expected payoff, based on both mission priorities and perceived state as determined from both visual displays and auditory inputs from other crew members or from air traffic controllers (ATC). PROCRU models multiple crew members simultaneously. The model for any one crew member is as shown in figure 1.15.

Because of essential nonlinearities the basic Kalman estimation could not be used. The authors had to linearize the vehicle trajectory about nominal segments and estimate purturbations from the nominals, where the total state is then the sum of estimates of purturbation and nominal states. Auditory messages are treated as priority interrupts, but they also may be missed if workload is high. Procedure decision is a commitment to be locked in (and unable to do anything else) for a time specified by the procedure itself.

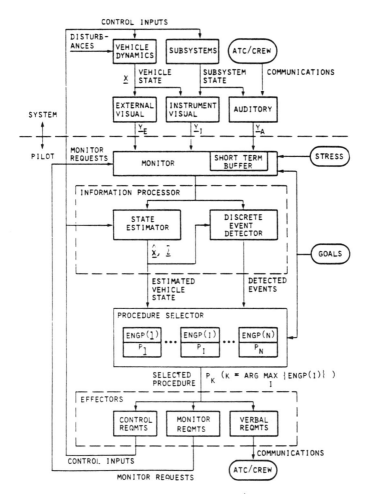

Figure 1.15
Baron's PROCRU. The extended optimal control model is further elaborated to
accommodate a variety of inputs, procedures and outputs. [From Baron 1984.]

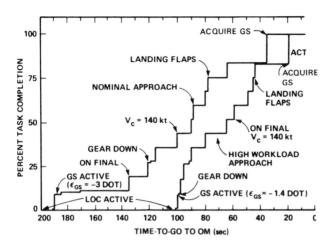

Figure 1.16
Procedure attention allocation histories in aircraft approach. [From Baron 1984.]

Outputs of PROCRU are vehicle trajectory, state estimation errors, and attention allocation of each crew member. Figure 1.16 shows portions of procedure attention allocation histories for two non-flying crew members. The two histories are identical in parameters except for an ATC request for an early turn toward the glideslope in the rightmost one, resulting in a higher workload and a shortened final glideslope segment.

Baron (1984) has discussed various possibilities for extending this type of modeling for supervisory control, including more sophisticated event detectors and situation assessors—for example, making use of *templates* on sets of system parameters or variables (what Rasmussen calls *symptoms*; see discussion in chapter 3 on failure detection) as a basis for triggering attention or action. He states that the model structure "provides an opportunity to go beyond completely myopic strategies and to incorporate at least some aspects of planning."

Kok-Van Wijk and Papenhuijzen-Stassen models of ship control

Kok and Van Wijk (1978) also extended the Kleinman-Baron-Levison (1970) model of the human operator as an optimal controller. They considered human control of processes which are slowly responding, in particular the supertanker, which has time constants of a number of minutes to respond to the helmsman's steering commands. As in the Kleinman et al.

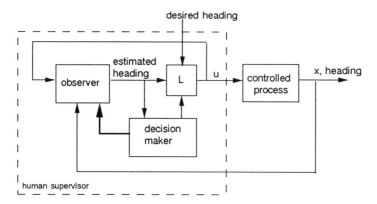

Figure 1.17
Kok-Van Wijk supervisory control model of helmsman. Heavy line indicates signal from
decision-maker element to make new estimate and update model inside observer. [After
Kok and Van Wijk 1978].

OCM described above, their model of the supervisor (figure 1.17) includes
a Kalman filter to provide a best estimate of system state and estimation
error covariance and an optimal linear control law to fit an objective
function appropriate to the given conditions. Their novel feature is the
addition of a decision-making element to decide, on the basis of estimated
state and estimation error covariance, when to observe (i.e., when to operate the Kalman filter and get a new estimate of state), and when to make
Kalman gain adjustments. These authors fitted their model to available
data on supertanker helmsman behavior. White (1981) fitted the same
model to the control of a petrochemical plant.

Papenhuijzen and Stassen (1987) extended this model to cope with the
two-person team of navigator and helmsman characteristic of large super-
tankers. In these the navigator is responsible for considering present position and course in relation to travel plans and the available map, setting
main engine speed, and giving course commands to the helmsman. The
navigator's decision-making includes an internal representation of the
ship's dynamics, its disturbances, and the environment. The authors experimented with both crisp and fuzzy rules as part of their model. The helmsman, in turn, compares the actual course against the commanded one, then
gives commands to the ship's steering machine. The navigator model is
diagrammed in figure 1.18.

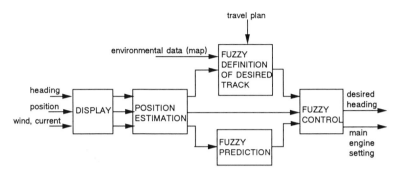

Figure 1.18
Papenhuijzen-Stassen model of supertanker navigator. [After Papenhuijzen and Stassen 1987.]

Self pacing and preview

Unlike physical tracking systems that respond as best they can to continuously imposed reference inputs which specify an ideal state "right now," human controllers can usually look ahead to what the desired position or other reference input value will be before it is necessary to start responding. The automobile driver can see "what's coming" on the road ahead; she does not base her control on seeing only the present lateral position of the car relative to the highway lane. The aircraft pilot can look ahead to the runway before landing or can fix her position on the map before increasing altitude to avoid a mountain. The power plant operator can look ahead to the procedural steps that must be taken up next. Although in systems that do not provide preview there is always a time lag, preview permits a response to be anticipated, prepared for, and initiated with no time lag and with some closer-to-optimal allocation of resources. Just as preview control is appropriate to direct manual control, it is also useful for the supervisor who must look ahead in vehicle control or other tasks and decide what goal to give to an automatic controller at each time step.

Given some assignment of the choices at each of a series of decision stages, and given the costs or rewards of taking any particular incremental decision at a particular stage, and assuming that costs or rewards are linearly independent, an optimal solution can be obtained either by dynamic programming (Sheridan 1966) or by modern control theory (Tomizuka 1975). Figure 1.19 illustrates an example of how dynamic programming might be applied in such a staged decision problem where the operator

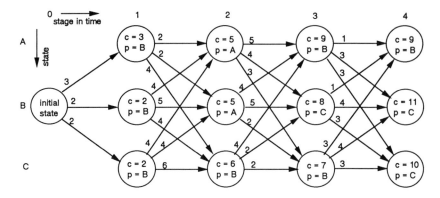

Figure 1.19
Example of dynamic programming.

Assume, at each of four stages in time after an initial stage, that there are three possible states of a system, represented by the circles in the figure. From each state at a given stage the incremental cost to get to each state at the next stage is some function of the two states, represented in the example by a number along the line connecting the states. Starting at stage 1, the cumulative cost (c) indicated within each circle (state) is given by the number along the line from the initial state. The least-cost path (p), a letter representing the least-cost state to have come from, is B in every case, since this is the only previous state.

At stage 2, the cost to get to state A (the circle at the top) is the least of path A (cost = 3 + 2 = 5), path B (cost = 2 + 4 = 6) and path C (cost = 2 + 4 = 6). The stage 2, state A circle is thus marked with the least cost (5) and corresponding path (A). Similarly, the cost to get to state B is the least of path A (3 + 2 = 5), path B (2 + 5 = 7) and path C (2 + 4 = 6), which is 5, along path A. Similar calculations are made for state C. Having completed the calculations for least cost and corresponding best path to get as far as stage 2, we can throw away all cost information about stage 1, since in determining costs for stage 3 we need know only the costs to the states at the previous stage. But best (least-cost) path information must be be retained. At stage 3 we similarly obtain least cost and corresponding path information for each of the states, and so too with stage 4.

At stage 4 one could require that one state, for example B, be the terminal state. In this case, tracing backwards, we observe that we should have come there via state C at stage 3, to there via state state B at stage 2, to there via state A at stage 1, and thence back to state B at stage 0. This, then, is the optimal, or least-cost, trajectory.

On the other hand we could have looked for the least-cost state at stage 4, found state A to be so, and traced back a different optimal trajectory: state B at stage 3, state C at stage 2, state B at stage 1.

The reader should note that in determining the least-cost paths from any stage to the next, the number of trial comparisons was 9, the square of the number of states, and only the three best previous values were stored. Both the total number of comparisons and the total number of stored paths were linear with the number of stages traversed. In general, for T stages and N states per stage, the dynamic programming algorithm requires at most TN comparisons, and TN stored "best path" values to determine the optimal trajectory. Compare this to trying all possible N paths, which gets quite large as the number of states and stages increases!

could preview, and hence anticipate what obstacles or other costs lay in store at each future point in time. Human behavior can then be compared to this optimal behavior.

Reality dictates that the human operator cannot see infinitely far ahead, only a relatively short distance, and that the farther ahead one looks, the poorer is the quality of the information at that instant. The operator knows this and surely discounts information as a function of distance (time) ahead. Thus, preview models must include some preview-discounting function.

Seeing ahead and anticipating helps not only in lateral control of a vehicle but also in longitudinal control—speeding up on the straightaways and slowing down on the curves. In discrete-task telerobotics this is equivalent to moving more quickly through the assigned tasks when they are easy and less quickly when they are hard. The term *self-pacing* may be applied in both continuous and discrete control situations.

State trajectories and state-space search

Any end-point control task, i.e., going from an initial state to a final state, can be defined as the problem of finding a satisfactory trajectory through the hyperspace of all salient states from the initial state to the final state. Here the term "state" can refer to position, velocity, pressure, or any other variable with respect to which there are absolute bounds or good-bad weighting. Figure 1.20 illustrates the idea in the very simple case of grasping a block with manipulator jaws, moving it from 2 to 3, releasing it and moving the jaws back to 2, closing the jaws, and pushing the block into the slot at 4. In this case the jaws have two state variables: one for movement along the axis shown, and one for open-close. The block has one state variable for movement along the axis. Clearly this is a three-dimensional state space and can be drawn (a higher-dimensional one cannot). There are obvious constraints, such as the fact that the jaws when grasping the block cannot both occupy position 4, which translates to a forbidden zone in the state space (the point is missing). Arrows indicate possible pushes. Searches in such state spaces can be based on criteria of least cost according to some criterion of distance, time, etc. Whitney (1969a) showed how manipulations could be modeled in this fashion. Recent obstacle-avoidance research in AI has referred to this as *configuration space*.

Hardin (1970) demonstrated that when a human supervisor can break a task into subtasks (thereby reducing the number of variables and/or the

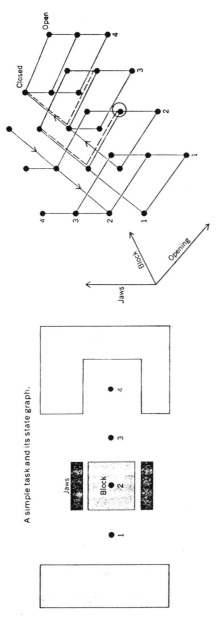

Figure 1.20
Representing manipulation operation by state-space trajectory. From a starting state (open jaws and block at position 2, the circled point in the state space diagram), to move the block to position 4, the jaws close and both move to 3 (dashed line). Then the jaws open and move back to 2. Then they close, and push the block to 4 (dashed line). [From Ferrell and Sheridan 1967; © IEEE.]

number of alternative combinations of states those variables can take within each subtask) the requirements on the computer in searching for "optimal" solutions (the size of the state space) within each subtask can be reduced by several orders of magnitude. Hardin's computer simulations suggest that the key is careful selection (by a human) of starting and stopping conditions for each of a number of subtasks, leaving the computer to do the detailed trajectory optimization.

1.5 Human-Attention-Allocation Models as Supervisory-Control Components

Given the roles that humans and computers may play in supervisory control systems, what are the strategies and tactics by which the computer and the human supervisor should share their attention among these different functions? A safe assumption, considering the bright future of computer capability and speed, is that the computer functions can be performed in parallel by essentially different computers, or that there is plenty of time available for a single computer to time-share functions. But the same cannot be said about the human operator. The human, by contrast, is very slow. Whether the human can attend to more than one thing at a time is a matter of continuing debate, but most researchers adopt the one-task-at-a-time assumption.

To properly allocate limited human resources to meet demands, it is useful first to break the task down into elements (this is called *task analysis*). Then, for each of the task elements, one should ask: (1) What human resources (particular senses, motor capabilities, memory, etc.) need be assigned to perform each task element in a supervisory control mode? (2) How much time and effort will it take to do the element? (3) How much time or energy is available to do the element? (4) What is the reward for successfully completing that task element, or what is the cost of not doing it?

Clearly this simple characterization treats task elements as though they are independent of one another (which they almost never are), that they are apparent and obvious (yet often one has to be very knowledgeable about the task), and that the operator attends to each task element in order and in some completely deterministic way. It is only natural that models of attention allocation start with simplifying assumptions, though, as with control models, we will find that these assumptions get us into some trouble.

Time-allocation comparison of supervisory and direct control

Any task performed under supervisory control requires time for the human to program (teach) the operation, and then time to monitor while the operation is being executed by the computer. Each of these components takes more time as the complexity of the task increases. There are many indices of task complexity. One might be the information content of movement selection plus the information content of move execution (see next section). Presumably, once the computer is programmed it can perform the task more quickly than the human could by doing it directly (or by teleoperation).

The human programming time and the machine (computer) execution times add to make up the supervisory control completion time (see figure 1.21, heavy line). This can be compared with the time for direct manual (teleoperated) control (broken line). For very simple tasks one might expect direct control to be quicker because instruction of a machine, as with that of another person, requires some minimum time. Common experience is that it is quicker to do some tasks yourself than to explain them to a helper.

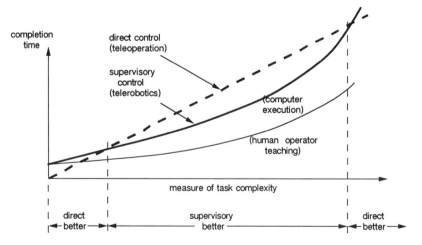

Figure 1.21
Time-allocation comparison of supervisory to direct control.

That means direct beats supervisory for the very simple tasks. As more complex tasks are encountered, there presumably will be savings in going to supervisory control because the computer is faster at execution than the human—the broken line will cross the heavy solid line. However, when very complex tasks are encountered it is likely that the sheer difficulty of programming them and/or the complexity of computer execution will consume time at a greater rate than direct control, and the lines will cross back. This diagram, of course, is hypothetical, and curves surely would depend on many factors.

Information measures for simple movements

Hick (1952) proposed a model, based on Shannon's (1949) information theory, for the time it takes to choose which of several alternative movements, i, to make when the choice is based on an immediately displayed signal calling for that move (figure 1.22), and the move time itself is brief and constant:

$$H_{choice} = \sum_i p_i \log_2(1/p_i), \quad T_{choice} = \alpha + \beta H_{choice},$$

where H_{choice} is information in bits, p_i is the probability of signal i, T_{choice} is the time required to choose, and α and β are scaling constants dependent on task conditions. α includes at minimum the base reaction time for making the slightest hand movement in response to a visual stimulus.

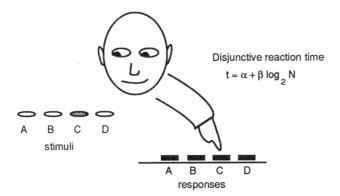

Figure 1.22
Hick's experiment for choice reaction time.

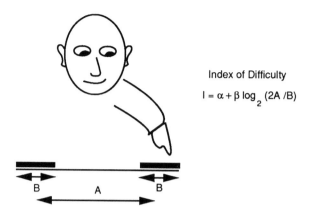

Figure 1.23
Fitts' experiment for moving a given distance to within a given tolerance.

Fitts (1954) also used the information measure for his model of the time required for making a discrete arm movement:

$$H_{move} = \log_2(2A/B), \quad T_{move} = \alpha + \beta H_{move},$$

where (see figure 1.23) H_{move} is information in bits (sometimes also called *index of difficulty*), A is the distance moved, B is the tolerance to within which the move must be made (for Fitts' experiment a tap between two lines), T is task completion time, and α and β are again scaling constants, different for different conditions. Fitts probably did not realize what wide application the model would find. When applied to simple one-dimensional movements to within tolerances, the model has withstood the test of time and been robust over a wide range of A's, B's, and other task conditions such as bare-handed vs. master-slave manipulator. It was successfully fitted to experimental data in a number of the studies described above. However, like so many elegant models for human behavior, Fitts' model breaks down for more complex manipulations.

If a person must first make a choice and then move, a first-order model for time required will then be

$$T_{total} = T_{choice} + T_{move}.$$

Caution is suggested about expecting such simple assumptions of independence to be borne out by experimental data.

Sturgis and Wright (1989) provide a thoughtful discussion of the problem of quantifying manual dexterity. They suggest, in relation to Fitts' model, the following:

(1) $H = \log_2(\text{greatest force/least force})$ for each DOF.

(2) Dexterity = (number of DOF)(frequency)/(resolution)
     = (number of DOF)(characteristic limb length to the
     $-3/2$ power).

(Sturgis and Wright argue this transformation on grounds of mechanics and biomechanics.)

(3) H = minimum, considering each DOF_i, of $(H_{\text{effector}} - H_{\text{task}})_i$.

(4) When linear transient response of repositioning by x is characterized by

$x = \exp(-t/T)$,

by then inverting and taking logs one gets

$\log_2(1/x) = (t/T)\log_2 e$,

and so the information H of $1/x$ taken as an A/B ratio is proportional to t.

Cannon (1992) suggests that the parameters of Fitts' law can be calculated using principles of control. Using the natural logarithm rather than the base-2 logarithm originally adopted from information theory, he predicts the values of the parameters α and β (see figure 1.24): β, he suggests, is the inverse of the dominant root (approximated if there is no clear dominant root); and α is the projected abscissa intercept of the dominant (or adjusted) root exponential superimposed on a control theory step response curve for the total system. Predicting these parameters leads to the possibility of evaluating a potential human-machine system before it is built, since step response curves can be made from control theory models. The terms of the human transfer function used in the model must, of course, be consistent with the type of controlled element proposed (see McRuer et al. 1965).

Cannon's rationale for why the form of Fitts' law applies to human-machine systems is straightforward. Most automatic control systems are designed to reduce error to a certain percent accuracy and therefore take

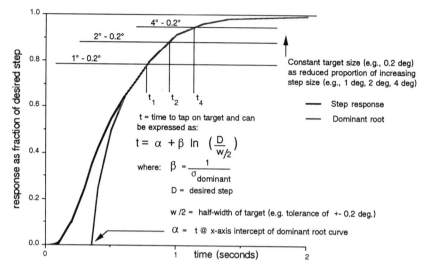

Figure 1.24
Cannon's theoretical basis for Fitts' law. [Courtesy of D. Cannon.]

the same step time for all step sizes. Humans, however, are intrinsically aware that a specific target size is a greater proportion of a small step than of a large step. Humans are, therefore, able to conclude a step action earlier for progressively smaller step sizes than can a system designed to achieve a certain fixed percent accuracy. Cannon believes that even autonomous systems, if imbued with sensors that seek to acquire constant target size rather than percent accuracy, will be seen to exhibit behavior consistent with this form of Fitts' law.

Thompson (1977), in his studies of manipulation, showed that the time required to mate one part to another was a function of the degrees of constraint (the number of positions and orientations that simultaneously have to correspond before the final mating could take place). Figure 1.25 illustrates the idea of degrees of constraint. Data based on both the Fitts and the Thompson measures will be shown later when time-delayed manipulation is discussed.

Nyquist interval model for sampling: The experiment of Senders et al.

Some kinds of attentional demands are simple to observe. When the resource constraint is the effort of switching attention (including focusing and reading) from one relatively simple display to another, it may be as-

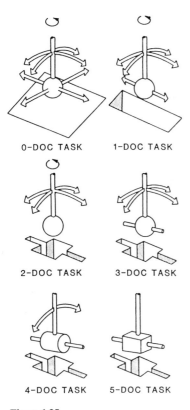

Figure 1.25
Thompson's degrees of constraint. [From Thompson 1977.]

sumed that observation time is constant across displays and that the time to transition from one display to another is negligible. In this special case the strategy for attending becomes one of relative sampling frequency. That means checking each of many displays often enough to ensure that no new demand is missed, and/or sampling a continuously changing signal often enough to be able to reproduce the highest-frequency component present, the bandwidth.

Where the bandwidth of any display input signal i is ω_i, the required sampling frequency, called the Nyquist frequency, is $2\omega_i$. That can easily be shown by considering that a Fourier series to represent any function of time duration T has two coefficients for every frequency multiple of the fundamental, $1/T$, up to the bandwidth ω_i. This is $2\omega_i T$ coefficients per T, or a time-average $2\omega_i$.

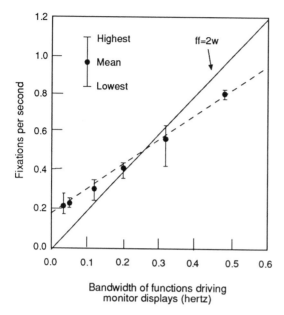

Figure 1.26
Senders' experimental results. Figure shows relation between fixation frequency and the bandwidth of the observed signal. Five practiced observers monitored four zero-centered meters at the corners of a square (separated by 60° visual angle). The meters were driven by sums of sinusoids, which appeared random. The task was to report excursions of the pointer to extreme values. The data show undersampling, but an otherwise strong linear correlation with the Nyquist model. [After Senders et al. 1964.]

A classical experiment by Senders et al. (1964) showed that experienced visual observers do tend to fixate on each of multiple displays in direct proportion to each display's bandwidth. Figure 1.26 shows some of the results. Each of five highly practiced subjects monitored four zero-centered instruments, each having signals of different bandwidth ω_i. Signals were actually sums of non-coherent sinusoids, a technique that makes them appear random. The instruments were located at the corners of a square, and were separated by approximately 60° of visual angle. The total Nyquist number of fixations, $\sum (2\omega_i)$, was selected so as not to overload the subject. The task was to report when any signal reached extreme values.

The model predicts that the data should lie on the solid diagonal line (i.e., $2\omega_i$) if a sample is instantaneous. Note that subjects tended to over-sample the lowest-frequency displays and undersample the highest-frequency displays—a "hedging toward the mean" that is found in other forms of decision behavior. The undersampling at higher frequencies could have been because samples were not instantaneous (actually they were relatively constant at about 0.4 sec, independent of frequency) and therefore the subjects were getting some velocity information too. If on each sample they got perfect velocity information, they needed to sample only at ω_i. Clearly they compromised between the ω_i and $2\omega_i$ rates; the slope for Senders' data is 1.34. Moray (1981), who believes that the oversampling at low frequencies (long time delays between samples) might result from forgetting, points to other evidence that very-low-frequency signals can be sampled at rates much in excess of $2\omega_i$.

Predicting sampling on the basis of the Nyquist interval assumes that averages are over a long time period, that all displays are of equal importance, and that there are no costs for sampling.

Balancing the costs of inattention with those of attending—another way to decide how often to intervene

The analysis above is based on displayed information content only. It ignores the relative costs of attending to the different information sources. However, most attention-allocation decisions involve the relative costs and benefits of attending to information sources (about inputs or controlled process outputs).

Normally the value of information is a function of how recently a particular display or source of information has been observed. At the instant an operator observes a display she has the most current information, but as time passes after one observation (action) and before a new one the information becomes "stale," eventually converging to some statistical expectation. How often should she sample to gain information and readjust controls, given that there is some finite cost for sampling as well as the gradually increasing cost of inattention?

Sheridan (1970a) sought a way of considering information content together with costs. His general representation of this is depicted in figure 1.27, where the supervisory operator observes a system "state" vector $\mathbf{x}$ and tries to take action $\mathbf{u}$ to maximize some given objective function $V(\mathbf{x}, \mathbf{u})$. Specifically, the question is how often to sample $\mathbf{x}$ and/or update $\mathbf{u}$. We assume that the state $\mathbf{x}$ in this case includes any directly observable inputs and/or outputs relative to the system that will help the operator decide what further sample or action to take (a more inclusive definition

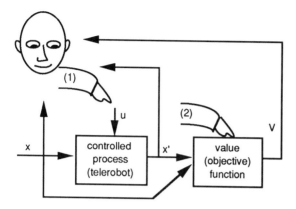

Figure 1.27
Supervisor's task: given observables **x**, maximize objective function **V** by controlling **u** or modify objective function.

than is usually assumed in control problems). The operator also is assumed to have statistical expectations about such signals.

The analysis is easier when x and u are scalars. Given assumptions about the probability of x and how rapidly it is likely to change, given a value (objective) function for consequences resulting from a particular x and a particular u in combination, and given a discrete cost of sampling, one can derive an optimal sampling strategy as follows to maximize expected gain.

Assume that x has a known prior probability density $p(x)$, that x_0 is its particular value at the time of sampling, and that $p(x_t|x_0, t)$ is a best available model of expectation of x at time t following a sample having value x_0. (Necessarily when $t = 0$, $p(x_t|x_0, t) = 1$ for $x_t = x_0$ and 0 elsewhere. Thereafter the density $p(x_t|x_0, t)$ spreads out, approaching $p(x)$ as t becomes large.) Assume also that $V(x, u)$ is the reward for taking action u when the state is x. The goal is to maximize EV, the expected value of V.

Clearly, without any sampling the best one can do is adjust u once and for all to maximize EV, i.e.,

$$EV \text{ for no sampling} = \max_{u} \left[\sum_{x} (V|x, u) \cdot p(x) \right].$$

If one could afford to sample continuously, the best strategy would be to continuously adjust u to maximize over u for each $(V|x, u)$ for the particular x encountered, so that

$$EV \text{ for continuous sampling} = \sum_{x_0} \left[\max_u (V|x_0, u) \cdot p(x_0) \right],$$

where $p(x_0) = p(x)$. For the intermediate case of intermittent sampling,

$$E(V|x_0, t) \text{ at } t \text{ after sample } x_0 = \max_u \left[\sum_{x_t} (V|x_t, u) \cdot p(x_t|x_0, t) \right].$$

Then

$$E(V|t) = \sum_{x_0} E(V|x_0, t) \cdot p(x_0),$$

remembering again that $p(x_0) = p(x)$. In this case, for any sampling interval T and sampling cost C, the net EV is

$$EV^* = 1/T \sum_{t=0}^{T} [E(V|t) - C/T].$$

So the best one can do is to maximize EV^* with respect to T. The components of these tradeoffs are represented in figure 1.28 as a function of time.

Sheridan and Rouse (1971) found in an experiment that, even after the $V(x, u)$ functions were made quite evident to subjects, their choices of T were suboptimal relative to this model. Moray (1986), however, points out that subjects with even moderate training are quite likely to demonstrate suboptimal behavior, and only after they "live the experience of the costs" for a long time (as Senders' subjects did) are they likely to converge on optimality.

The above theory can be applied not only for a fixed decay of knowledge of x and a corresponding decay of expected V following an observation or control intervention, but also where both $V(x_0)$ and $V(x_t)$ vary as a function of the planning/programming time put in by the supervisor, the "intervention time." This is shown in the upper plots of figure 1.29. For example, intervention T_{iA} might result in curve A, and intervention T_{iB} might net curve B. For either curve the best stopping time T can be decided by the above analysis. Then the running V curves can be plotted, showing the times of control inactivity during teaching intervention intervals (assume constant V during these intervals, or other assumptions can be made) and positive but decaying V starting when automatic control begins and lasting for period $T_{operate}$. An integration under either running V curve yields the total worth of the operation in that case.

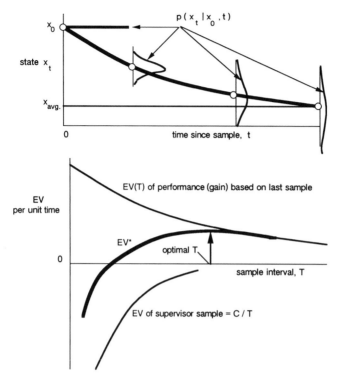

Figure 1.28
Tradeoffs in deciding how often to sample (intervene). Heavy line above is expected value of
x_t, given sample x_0. Probability density changes from a single value at $t = 0$ to $p(x_0)$ at
$t = \infty$. Heavy line below is difference between value gained by intervention and cost of
intervention.

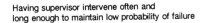

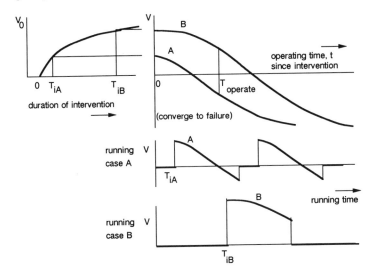

Figure 1.29
Optimizing the strategy, considering both the frequency and the duration of the planning/
programming intervention between periods of automatic control. The quality of
control V_0 is better the longer this intervention (upper left curve). Once on automatic,
quality of control deteriorates with time until the next intervention (upper right). The result
is a scalloped curve of quality of control with time (assumed here to be zero during
interventions).

Generalizing the expected-value optimization for states inferred from inputs

The above analysis treats the case of optimal sampling rate where salient
variables may be observed directly. This can be generalized (Sheridan
1976a) to the case of states x_i which must be inferred from observables y_j,
and where the supervisor must decide both what display n to attend to and
what motor action u_k to take. Again we seek to maximize expected value,
given in this case V_{ik}, and prior distributions $p_0(x_i)$ and $p_0(y_j)$. We also
assume to know the calibration of each of our sensors n, that is, $p_n(y_j|x_i)$,
what observable any sensor will indicate, given the true x_i.

Corresponding to the "imperfect information" case in the previous sam-
pling analysis which yielded $E(V|x_0, t)$, in this case, for a given sensor n and
observation y_j,

$$E(V|n, y_j) = \max_k \left\{ \sum_i [(V_{ik}) \cdot p_n(x_i|y_j)] \right\}$$

and

$$E(V|n) = \sum_j p(y_j) \left\{ \max_k \left\{ \sum_i [(V_{ik}) \cdot p_n(x_i|y_j)] \right\} \right\}.$$

From Bayes' theorem,

$$p_n(x_i|y_j) = [p_n(y_j|x_i)p_0(x_i)]/p(y_j),$$

$$E(V|n) = \sum_j \left[\max_k \left(\sum_i [(V_{ik}) \cdot p_n(y_j|x_i)p_0(x_i)] \right) \right],$$

and

$$EV = \max_n E(V|n).$$

The result is a "best" combination of where (what sensor) to look at (maximum n) and what to do (maximum k). From this one can fashion a kind of supervisory control model (figure 1.30).

Such a strategy might be fine if expected-value decision making were itself acceptable and if the necessary probability distributions were available. However, one is often "risk averse" and avoids altogether very high-cost events, or very low-probability events which have a moderate expected

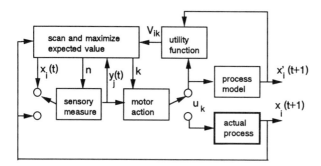

Figure 1.30
Supervisor model based on trial sampling and expectation. The sensory input and motor output boxes cycle between the test-and-optimize (upper) mode, and the operate (lower) mode.

cost. More will be said of this in chapter 3. Further, the probability distributions may simply not be available.

How far to commit to open-loop action: A probabilistic decision approach with some analogies to signal-detection theory

If the computer could be told how to respond to all possible contingencies, that would be "full intelligent automation" and there would be no need for a human supervisor except to monitor for failure. At the opposite extreme, if the supervisor did not trust the computer to assume control for any finite time, the only alternative would be continuous manual control and there would be no supervisory control. In supervisory control, the supervisor instructs the telerobot or other semi-automated controlled process to execute the subtask for some finite time period; i.e., control is open-loop with respect to the supervisor for that period (unless she seizes back the control). In setting up this finite open-loop program, the supervisor always has some uncertainty about "how far to tell the automatic controller to go" (in distance, time, force, or some other variable) to accomplish the given task but yet avoid known hazards. In business management this is the equivalent of what has sometimes been called the span of delegation or the span of authority, though in that context, to the writer's knowledge, no quantitative theories are available.

For example, consider the problem of how much force to instruct the telerobot to employ while inserting a circuit board. The force must be enough to ensure that the circuit board seats properly so that all electrical contacts are made. However, if too much force is imposed the board will be destroyed. Alternatively, it may happen that, with a given application of force, neither are contacts made nor is the board destroyed. Which outcome occurs first will be unknown until after it occurs. How hard to tell the robot to push?

Consider a planetary roving vehicle which is instructed to search for an object and return to base before it runs out of its limited stored energy. It may return to base having completed its job, may run out of energy, or may return to base having neither found the object nor run out of energy. How far to instruct the vehicle to go?

In each of the above cases the supervisor faces a tradeoff between (1) being too timid and risk-averse and not instructing the telerobot to move far enough to accomplish a given task, possibly accomplishing nothing, and (2) taking too much risk in her eagerness to be sure to accomplish the task by instructing the telerobot to go too far, with the high probability of experiencing serious penalty.

The problem will be formulated and then the correspondence to signal-detection theory discussed:

(1)   Let the extent of the open-loop commitment to action (along a continuum of distance, time, force, or some other *decision variable*) be x, as in figure 1.31(a).

(2)   Let the conditions of the task be such that each time the open-loop control is executed a *gain opportunity* (GO) occurs randomly with probability $p(\text{GO})$ and a loss opportunity (LO) occurs randomly with probability $p(\text{LO})$. One or both or none may occur during a trial.

(3)   For each of GO and LO, if they occur, let there be thresholds x_G and x_L respectively as shown in figure 1.31(a) which, when met by x, i.e., $x \geq x_G$ or $x \geq x_L$, cause a significant gain V_{yG} and/or loss V_{yL} outcome, respectively (where subscript y signifies "yes, the threshold is met"). In each case of occurrence of GO or LO when the corresponding threshold is not met by x the outcome is either zero or a smaller positive or negative value, V_{nG} or V_{nL} respectively (where subscript n signifies "no, the threshold is not met"). This amounts to a 2×2 matrix of outcomes V as shown in figure 1.31(b).

(4)   Let the conditional probability density of threshold x_G in the case of GO, $p(x_G|\text{GO})$, and the conditional probability density of threshold x_L in the case of LO, $p(x_L|\text{LO})$, have the approximate shape shown in figure 1.31(c). We assume that these density functions are offset relative to one another, so that with increasing x the indefinite integral of $p(x_G|\text{GO})$, which we shall call *cumulative probability* $P(x_G|\text{GO})$, rises sooner (at lower values of x) than the indefinite integral of $p(x_L|\text{LO})$, which we shall call $P(x_L|\text{LO})$.

(5)   The decision maker would like to select x so as to maximize the expected-value outcome, EV.

Any incremental increase in x may cross a threshold x_G or x_L. The problem is that one cannot know until after the fact whether it is an x_G or an x_L. Just crossing a threshold is advantageous when the expected value for doing so exceeds the expected value for not doing so. For any incremental x at which there is a threshold the incremental EV is

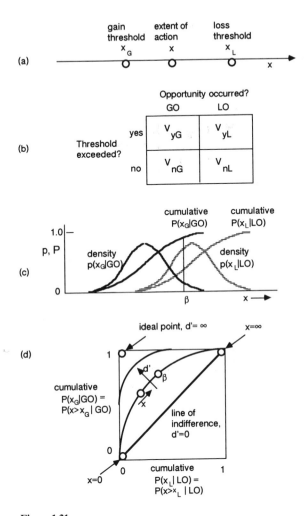

Figure 1.31
Applying signal-detection theory to optimizing open-loop commitment.
(a) Extent of move x, and relative locations of gain threshold x_G and loss threshold x_L.
(b) Outcome matrix.
(c) Densities $p(x_G|GO)$ and $p(x_L|LO)$ and cumulative distributions $P(x_G|GO)$ and $P(x_L|LO)$.
(d) Relative operating characteristic (ROC) curves.

$$\frac{dEV}{dx} = \frac{dP(GO)}{dx} V_{yG} + \frac{dP(LO)}{dx} V_{yL} = p(GO|x)V_{yG} + p(LO|x)V_{yL},$$

and when the incremental step is not taken

$$\frac{dEV}{\text{not } dx} = \frac{dP(GO)}{dx} V_{nG} + \frac{dP(LO)}{dx} V_{nL} = p(GO|x)V_{nG} + p(LO|x)V_{nL}.$$

One therefore takes the incremental step when there is expected advantage in doing so, or when

$$p(GO|x)V_{yG} + p(LO|x)V_{yL} \geq p(GO|x)V_{nG} + p(LO|x)V_{nL},$$

or when

$$\frac{p(GO|x)}{p(LO|x)} \geq \frac{V_{nL} - V_{yL}}{V_{yG} - V_{nG}}.$$

By Bayes' theorem

$$p(GO|x) = \frac{p(x|GO)p(GO)}{p(x)}$$

and

$$p(LO|x) = \frac{p(X|LO)p(LO)}{p(x)}.$$

Substituting, the left side of the previous equation is transformed, and the condition becomes

$$\frac{p(x|GO)p(GO)}{p(x|LO)p(LO)} \geq \frac{V_{nL} - V_{yL}}{V_{yG} - V_{nG}},$$

or

$$\frac{p(x|GO)}{p(x|LO)} \geq \frac{p(LO)(V_{nL} - V_{yL})}{p(GO)(V_{yG} - V_{nG})}.$$

The left side of the last equation above is called a *likelihood ratio L(x)*, and is a ratio of two terms we assume we know. The right side is a constant, which we call β, determined entirely by the prior probabilities $p(GO)$ and $p(LO)$ and the outcome gains and losses, all known *a priori*.

We now cross-plot the cumulative probabilities $P(x|GO)$ and $P(x|LO)$, that is, the indefinite integrals $p(x|GO) = p(x_G|GO)$ and $p(x|LO) =$

$p(x_L|LO)$ up to x, as shown in figure 1.31(d). This produces what may be called a *relative operating characteristic* (ROC). In this case

$$P(x|GO) = P(x \geq x_G)|GO), \quad \text{and} \quad P(x|LO) = P(x \geq x_L)|LO).$$

These are, respectively, the probability of exceeding the threshold (whatever it is) by an open-loop action x in the case of opportunity for gain, and the same in the case of opportunity for loss. The ROC curve shows the net risk of incurring significant gains or losses should the opportunity occur for various x selections. The slope of this curve at different values of x is $L(x)$, and the point having a slope β is the optimal x for the given V values. One would like to operate at the upper left corner of figure 1.31(d), but cannot because of the overlap of the two densities $p(x|GO)$ and $p(x|LO)$.

In applying this theory it is of interest to see if human decision makers are optimal and select $x = \beta$, or if they consistently are biased toward the lower left (risk-averse behavior) or the upper right (risk-prone behavior).

The less the two density functions $p(x|GO)$ and $p(x|LO)$ overlap, the closer the ROC comes to this ideal point, and the easier it is to decide how far to go to incur significant gain but not loss. In signal-detection theory (SDT) the amount of separation is characterized by a parameter called d'. The ROC for $d' = 0$ is a diagonal line (along which there can only be indifference to x). The upper left corner is where $d' = \infty$. The ROC for very large d' approaches the ideal point, as shown.

The reader familiar with SDT will note that the above modeling approach, which may be called *open-loop action theory* (OLAT), parallels SDT in many ways. (See Green and Swets 1966 and Sheridan and Ferrell 1974 for more detailed expositions of SDT. See Cohen and Ferrell 1969 for an application to discrete decision making in manual control.) However, there are important differences. In both cases the decision maker is assumed to know three things *a priori*:

(1) the prior probabilities of two independent conditions (in SDT the conditions are *signal-plus-noise* and *noise-alone*; in OLAT the conditions are gain opportunity (GO) and loss opportunity (LO), independent of the location of the threshold);

(2) the probability densities on a decision variable x for the thresholds under the two underlying conditions GO and LO; and

(3) a 2×2 matrix of outcomes corresponding to whether GO or LO occurs and how the variable x relates to some threshold criterion.

Two factors distinguish SDT from OLAT:

(1) In SDT the decision maker is assumed to *receive a stimulus* corresponding to some value of the continuous decision variable x, then *make an explicit binary decision*, either signal-plus-noise or noise-alone. In OLAT the decision maker makes an overt response x along a continuum, which turns out to be greater or less than the threshold set by GO or LO, so the greater-lesser factor is determined but not explicitly decided by the decision maker.

(2) In SDT it is usually assumed that on a given trial either signal-plus-noise occurs or noise-alone occurs, but never both and never neither. In OLAT any combination can occur. In fact, since the criterion is expected value and the equations are linear, on a single open-loop excursion OG and OL can occur multiple times. Only the ratio of OG to OL frequencies is important.

In an experiment (in either SDT or OLAT) we can motivate a decision maker to select various x values (and thereby determine this curve) by manipulating outcome penalties and rewards. Without such influence she will tend to operate at a particular "comfortable" x, which may differ from β. (There may be some other criteria in her head which can be inferred.) The variables d' and β are independent, and that is one beauty of this theory.

The problem of how long (or far) to make an open-loop commitment will be a critical one in supervisory control for years to come. This bit of theory is yet to be developed and used experimentally.

Allocation of personal presence: A dynamic programming model

One problem the supervisor faces is allocating her own attention to various tasks, where each time she switches tasks there is a time penalty in transfer—typically different for different tasks, and possibly involving uses of different software procedures, different equipment, and even bodily transportation of herself to different locations. Given relative worths of time spent attending to various tasks, dynamic programming makes it possible to establish the optimal allocation strategy (Sheridan 1970b). Moray et al. (1982) applied this model to deciding whether a human or a computer should control various variables at each succeeding moment. For simpler experimental conditions the model fitted the experimental data (subjects acted like utility maximizers), but as task conditions became complex the model apparently broke down.

In a similar study by Wood and Sheridan (1982), supervisors could select among alternative machines (differing in both rental cost and productivity) to do assigned tasks or do the tasks themselves. Results showed the supervisors to be suboptimal, paying too much attention to costs and too little to productivity and in some cases using machines when they could have done the tasks more efficiently by themselves.

Multi-task selection and pacing: The Tulga paradigm

Tulga and Sheridan (1980) developed a model of attention allocation among multiple randomly appearing task demands, based on an abstract graphic presentation. Tasks were displayed to the subject on a computer screen as is represented in figure 1.32. New tasks appeared at random times and locations on the screen as blocks of differing heights and widths, then moved at constant horizontal velocity toward a vertical "deadline" at the right. Upon reaching the deadline, a block disappeared and there was no

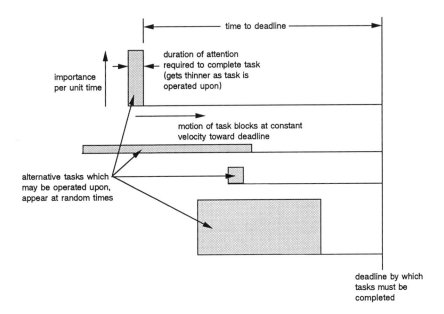

Figure 1.32
Tulga multi-task selection paradigm. Displayed blocks are "tasks" to be done, which convey importance, duration required for completion, and time to deadline.

further opportunity to "work" it. Working any particular block meant holding a cursor at the right margin in line with that block, which reduced the width of that block at a constant rate. There was but one cursor, while usually there were many tasks (blocks) on the screen, so the decision maker had to decide among them continually. Points were earned by completing a task block, i.e., reducing its width to zero. The total reward for a task was indicated by the area of that block, the reward earned per unit time by the height of the block. The human decision maker in this task did not have to allocate her attention in the temporal order in which the task demands appeared or in the order in which their deadlines were anticipated. Instead she could attend first to the task that had the highest payoff or took the least time, and/or she could try to plan ahead a few moves so as to maximize her gains. She could quit working on a task and go back to it later, but there was a finite transition time required to move from one block to another. The paradigm was rich with experimental variables and dynamic decision hypotheses, and variants of it have been used by other experimenters. Tulga and Sheridan also derived an NP-complete dynamic programming algorithm to find optimal solutions for the multi-task problem.

The experimental results of Tulga and Sheridan suggest that subjects approached optimal behavior (as defined by their normative algorithm) both when they had plenty of time to plan and when their workloads were reasonably heavy. The latter case, in which there were more opportunities than the subject could possibly cope with, amounted to selecting the task with the highest payoff regardless of the time to deadline. This was evident because the optimization algorithm required discounting of the future as the task interarrival rate increased, and models that fitted the human subjects' data required this also. The subjects' corresponding subjective reports were that their sense of mental workload was greatest when by arduous planning they could barely keep up with all the tasks presented. But as the screen filled with more task opportunities and/or there was less time available before the deadline (as the "objective mental workload" grew) there came a point where the strategy switched from "plan ahead" to "put out fires and shed all other tasks." The latter meant doing whatever had to be done in a hurry while there was still time—and never mind that some very important long-term task could be worked on "ahead of time," because there might not be time to complete it. Interestingly, the investigators found that as "objective mental workload" continued to increase beyond this point where "plan ahead" had to be abandoned in favor of "do what has an immediate deadline," the "subjective mental workload" (as measured on a rating scale) stopped increasing and decreased. A first-order quantitative hypothesis was that the mental workload is the disjunction (minimum) of utilized capacity (which kept rising up to saturation) and relative performance (which was constant until capacity saturation, then diminished). Mental workload is discussed further in chapter 3.

Levis' use of Petri nets to represent interacting decision makers

Levis and his colleagues (Boettcher and Levis 1982; Levis and Boettcher 1983 ; Levis 1990) developed a series of models to characterize various forms of interaction of decision makers in distributed decision making (i.e., various organizational structures). They used Petri-net representations of the hierarchical and distributed structure of communication and interactions, because Petri nets can be "run" like computer programs and also are particularly amenable to mathematical analysis.

A Petri net (Peterson 1977) is made up of two types of nodes—*places* (circles) and *transitions* (solid bars)—all interconnected by directed (one-way) *arcs*. Figure 1.33 shows a Petri net. *Tokens* (dots) represent the presence or absence at any node of some salient property (a signal, a physical object). A *marking* M of a Petri net at any time is a vector whose elements are the (non-negative, integer) number of tokens at each place.

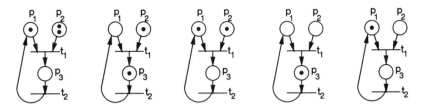

Figure 1.33
Example of how a Petri net works. *Tokens* (dots) t_i at different *places* (circles) p_j signify status of different variables in a system. For example, let tokens at p_1 and p_2 in the first diagram (1, left) signify the availability of a robot and parts to be handled, respectively, and p_3 signify that the robot is in operation. *Transitions* (bars with arrows) are events. For example let t_1 start the robot moving a part, and t_2 end that operation. When every input place to a transition is *marked* (has at least one dot), that transition is *enabled* to fire on a clock cycle, at which time one token is removed from each input place and one token is added to each (possibly many) output place. On the first cycle (1) only t_1 is enabled. At (2) transition t_2 is enabled. At (3) t_1 is again enabled. At (4) t_2 is enabled, and the transition to (5) ends the activity. [After diCesare and Desrochers 1991.]

Thus, the marking represents the *state* of the Petri net. Many alternative states are possible: if, for example, a place is allowed to hold at most one token, and there are n places, there are 2n possible states.

A transition is *enabled* to *fire* by a given marking M if there is at least one token at each of its input places. When a transition fires, a token is removed from each of its input places and a token is placed at each of its output places, thus generating a new marking. A *switch* is a special kind of transition (due to Levis) with multiple output places and a decision rule which, upon firing, places a token in only one output place. The decision rules can be deterministic or stochastic. The complexity of the decision rules and the size of the net determine the analytical complexity of a Petri net.

The marking vector determines the distribution of tokens over the structure of the network. A sequence of markings describes the information flow. From this one can define and derive entropy terms at various locations in the network and at various times by using Shannon information theory. (See Sheridan and Ferrell 1974 for a brief tutorial on application of the theory.) Levis et al. applied information theory to analyze experimental data for a simple command and control task performance of both parallel and hierarchical decision-making structures, the configurations of which were representable by Petri nets. On this basis they measured information throughput (transmission), information blockage (equivocation), internally generated information (noise), and information coordination (interaction). According to the partitioning theorem of information theory (the equivalent of partitioning of variance in analysis of variance; see Conant 1976), total information activity is the sum of these components. Levis et al. used this sum as a surrogate for workload, assumed that such workload must always be less than a fixed capacity if severe degradation of performance is to be avoided, and measured it experimentally. They also measured accuracy (in informational terms), response time, and required number of communications, each as a function of organizational structure, the pace of new task arrivals, and other factors.

Their experimental results showed, as they expected, that response accuracy decreases as task arrival pace increases. The variation in performance and the degradation of accuracy were generally less between different team structures than between individual decisionmakers within a team, a result which was consistent with predictions of the Petri-net/information-theory model. Levis et al. claim that their model is a reasonable guide for experimentation and is useful for predictive purposes.

Sharing and trading of control

The roles of the computer in supervisory control can be classified according to how much task-load is carried compared to what the human operator alone can carry. The computer can *extend* the human's capabilities beyond what she can achieve alone, it can partially *relieve* the human, making her job easier; it can *back up* the operator in cases he falters; and it can *replace* her completely. Figure 1.34 conveys the idea. Extending and relieving are examples of sharing control. More specifically, *sharing* control means that the human and the computer control different aspects of the system at the same time. Backing up or replacing can also be called *trading* control. Trading control means that either the human or the computer turns over control to the other (or the latter seizes it). In sharing control the main issue is: Which tasks should be assigned to the human and which to the computer? In trading control the main issue is: When (e.g., conditions with respect to time, completion of assigned task, error or deviation from nominal plan, expectations of the other's readiness) should control be handed over willfully and when should it be seized back? There are also forms of cooperative control where control is initiated by one agent (human or computer) and the other trims or refines it. None of these

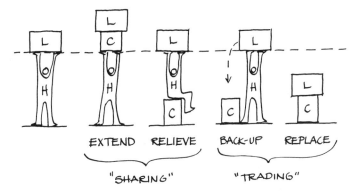

Figure 1.34
The notions of trading and sharing control between human and computer. *L* is the load or task, *H* the human, and *C* the computer. [Courtesy of W. Verplank.]

is purely hierarchical, with one agent always superior and the other always subservient (i.e., supervisory control as defined above).

Rouse (1977) utilized a queuing-theory approach to model whether from moment to moment a task should be assigned to a computer or the operator should do it herself. The allocation criterion was to minimize service time under cost constraints. Results suggested that human-computer "misunderstandings" of one another degraded efficiency more than limited computer speed. In a related flight-simulation study, Chu and Rouse (1979) had a computer perform those tasks that had waited in the queue beyond a certain time. Chu, Steeb, and Freedy (1980) extended this idea to have the computer learn the pilot's priorities and later make suggestions when the pilot is under stress.

Moray et al. (1982) experimented with an arrangement wherein the operator, faced with four independent control loops, could either monitor the systems and control them manually or leave them to automatic control. The aim was to keep all systems within fixed limits. They found that the initial attention of relatively unpracticed operators was almost equally divided between systems, in spite of markedly different time constants to reach critical limits.

1.6   Fuzzy Logic as a Model of Human Knowledge

Crisp and fuzzy discriminations

In everyday experience a human operator's knowledge about variables or relationships between variables can be called *fuzzy*. That is, the observations and thoughts of most people most of the time may be said to be mentally modeled and/or communicated to other persons in terms of sets of natural language words (such as "short," "medium," "long," and "very long" as applied, for example, to a train, or "urgent," "little," "normal," and "plenty" as applied to the time available for a train to meet its schedule). Expert operators of trains or other systems will describe their jobs and the criteria for their own decision making in such terms or by rules made up of such terms: "If the train is long or very long, and there is little time, or if time is urgent, then take action U."

Fuzzy mathematics was introduced by Zadeh (1965). It has been extensively developed in Japan and other nations—perhaps more than in the United States, where it is controversial. For some people the term "fuzzy" seems a contradiction to rationality (which it is not, though there remain some empirical problems, as noted below).

Precise quantification and Boolean logic imply "crisp" sets, wherein a number or symbol is identified with a well defined set of objects or events, and explicitly not identified with other objects or events. Any one object or event either is in the set corresponding to a given symbol or it is not; we can say its membership M in the set is either 0 or 1. Fuzzy sets are different. The membership M of objects or events of a fuzzy set can be 0 or 1 or anything in between. The meanings of words (the symbols of natural language) are fuzzy, in the sense that a word can apply very well (clearly, obviously) to some objects or events, can clearly exclude other objects or events, and can apply somewhat (more or less, partially) to still other objects and events.

Figure 1.35 gives a simple example of plausible meanings, in terms of membership functions M (relative truth, applicability, etc.), of the four terms mentioned above for each of two physical variables relating to train scheduling. Each of the four curves then defines a fuzzy set for the corresponding term relative to the associated quantitative and objectively measurable variable. Then any one quantitative value maps to a fuzzy vector M of different memberships corresponding to each of several different fuzzy terms; e.g., the train length indicated by the mark on the abscissa of figure 1.35 has membership $M = 0.8$ for "long," 0.4 for "medium," and 0.2 for "very long."

Thus, any physical state vector maps to a corresponding membership M for every fuzzy term or symbol. It follows that any logical "if—, then—" statement made up of fuzzy symbols (such as "If the train is long or very long and there is little time, or, if time is urgent, then take action U") yields a net membership or relative applicability for that particular physical situation. For the given particular value of the train length, the M of "long" is 0.8 and the M of "very long" is 0.2 ; for the given time, the M of "little" is 0.9 and the M of "urgent" is 0.6. Making the customary assumption that the conjunction "or" (logical union) means the *maximum* of the two associated terms and the conjunction "and" (logical intersection) means the *minimum* of the two terms, we have

$$\{ [(\text{long}) \ or \ (\text{very long})] \text{ and } [(\text{little})] \} \quad or \quad \{ (\text{urgent}) \} \rightarrow \text{Action U}.$$

This statement, for the current values of the length and time, has relative membership

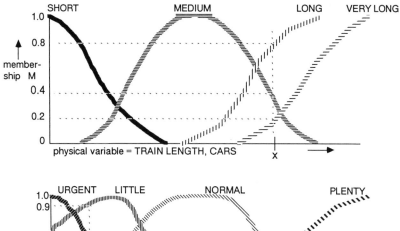

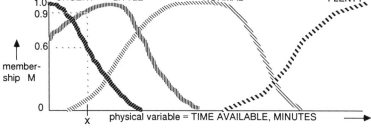

Available Rules:

(1) "If train is long or very long, and there is little time, or if time is urgent, then go."
(2) "However, if train is medium or short, and time is little or normal, stay."

Parse:

For first rule: If { [(long or (very long)] and [little] } or {urgent} then go.   Similar for second rule.

Evaluate membership for given case, (using or=max, and=min)

(1)   max [(long), (very long) train] = max [0.8, 0.2] = 0.8,
        min [(long or very long train) , (little time)] = min [0.8, 0.9] = 0.8
        max [(long or very long train, and little time), (urgent time) = max [0.8, 0.6] = 0.8 for go

(2)   max [(medium), (short) train] = max [0.4, 0] = 0.4
            max [(little), (normal) time] = max [0.9, 0.2] = 0.9
        min [(medium or short train), (little or normal time)] = min [0.4, 0.9] = 0.4 for stay

Take action with greatest membership (go), given that all available rules were evaluated
for case at hand.   Or, if evaluation of available rules for this case results in no membership
greater than some criterion, invoke other procedure.

Figure 1.35
Example of fuzzy membership functions, fuzzy rules, and decision based on fuzzy logic.

$$M = max\{min[max(0.8), (0.2)], [(0.9)]\}, \{(0.6)\} = 0.8.$$

Independent rules, all of which must apply, require an "and" between them.

There may be other rules that recommend different actions; for example, "If A is the case, then do U_1; if B is the case, then do U_2." The usual assumption for fuzzy models is that, in a given situation, the rule or combination of rules that has relatively greatest applicability (membership) should dominate. In other words, the action U with the greatest membership M should be taken. A second rule is given in the figure 1.35 to illustrate the point.

Applying fuzzy logic to modeling human behavior

Fuzzy rules and logic have been applied in many and varied kinds of human-machine systems. For example, Buharali and Sheridan (1982) demonstrated that a computer could be taught to "drive a car" by a person specifying rules, as they came to mind, relating when to accelerate and by how much, when to brake and by how much, and when to steer. At any point in the teaching process, the computer "knew what it didn't know" with regard to various combinations of conditions of rules, and then could ask the supervisor-teacher for additional rules to cover its "domains of ignorance."

Fuzzy rules and logic can be combined with crisp rules and logic. Papenhuizen and Stassen (1987) applied fuzzy rules to their model of a navigator's decision making in supertanker control.

When first exposed to fuzzy logic, humans associate membership functions with probability density functions. This is unfortunate, since probability density is an abstraction from empirical frequency, and thus is an aggregate property, indicating how often events occur in different ways—ways that are quite crisp and mutually exclusive after the occurrence. Fuzzy relations, by contrast, are properties of single events that are always there, and not different from occurrence to occurrence.

The attraction of fuzzy logic is that it captures an inherent and obvious property of most human communication, namely that it is not crisp. People communicate orally and in writing by means of words, and the meanings of many (even most) words with respect to the associated physical variables are fuzzy. This is not to say that one cannot use numbers in written or oral discourse, or add enough qualifiers that the meaning of a set of alphanumeric symbols becomes quite crisp. It is rather to say that the great majority of ordinary communication by ordinary people is through fuzzy terms. Nor is it to recommend that action be based on fuzzy terms and rules when there are trustworthy "crisp" measures and rules available. Rather, fuzziness is a reality to be coped with.

Fuzzy set theory is still far from rigorous with respect to certain basic operations. For example, what does it mean to have a membership of 0.5? Or, stated another way, when pressure is "0.5 high" and flow is "0.5 weak," in what sense are these equivalent? Are there experimental scaling operations to verify that the 0.5 membership has the same meaning in both uses?

Ren's method for capturing human knowledge in a fuzzy model

Ren (1990) demonstrated a use of fuzzy logic for directly capturing the knowledge or behavior of a person in terms of a *fuzzy relational matrix*. This is equivalent to an input-output mapping or transfer relation. The gist of the idea is as follows:

Suppose when a particular input display (say a bar graph representing level in a tank) is x^* a human subject outputs y^* (say she adjusts a valve). We seek to discover what is the mapping from input to output.

Suppose that each of the continuous physical variables x and y is coded into three fuzzy elements (e.g., level x = Lo, Med, Hi and valve setting y = Closed, Part, Open)—see figure 1.36. This is a coarse mapping. It could be finer, but the coarse mapping will make explanation easier. From the above,

$\mathbf{M}(x^*) = 0.2$ (Lo), 0.8 (Med), 0 (Hi),   and

$\mathbf{M}(y^*) = 0$ (Closed), 0.3 (Part), 0.7 (Open).

Where $\mathbf{M}(X)\mathbf{R} = \mathbf{M}(Y)$, the fuzzy relational matrix $\mathbf{R}(x^*, y^*)$ is the Cartesian product or minimum for each (ij) element pairing of $\mathbf{M}(x^*)$ and $\mathbf{M}(y^*)$, respectively.

$$\mathbf{R}(x^*, y^*) = \begin{bmatrix} 0 \text{ (Lo, Closed)} & 0.2 \text{ (Lo, Part)} & 0.2 \text{ (Lo, Open)} \\ 0 \text{ (Med, Closed)} & 0.3 \text{ (Med, Part)} & 0.7 \text{ (Med, Open)} \\ 0 \text{ (Hi, Closed)} & 0 \text{ (Hi, Part)} & 0 \text{ (Hi, Open)} \end{bmatrix}.$$

Now, given some $\mathbf{R}$, for any X, we can determine Y within fuzzy limitations as follows: Each jth element of $\mathbf{M}(y) = max$ over all $i\{min[\mathbf{M}(xi), \mathbf{R}(ij)]\}$.

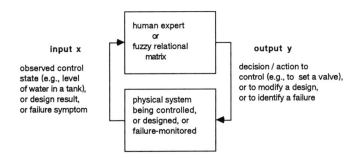

Suppose when a particular state of the system is x* the human expert decides y*, and suppose the continuous physical variables x and y are each coded into three fuzzy elements (e.g., level x = Lo, Med, Hi, and valve setting y = Closed, Part, Open).

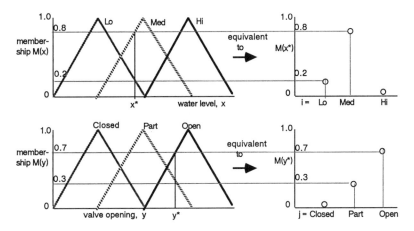

From the above M(x*) = 0.2 (Lo), 0.8 (Med), 0 (Hi), and M(y*) = 0 (Closed), 0.3 (Part), 0.7 (Open)

Where M(X) R ● M(Y), the fuzzy relational matrix R(x*,y*) is the Cartesian product or minimum for each (ij) element pairing of M(x*) and M(y*) respectively,

$$R(x^*,y^*) = \begin{vmatrix} 0 \ (Lo, Closed) & 0.2 \ (Lo, Part) & 0.2 \ (Lo, Open) \\ 0 \ (Med, Closed) & 0.3 \ (Med, Part) & 0.7 \ (Med, Open) \\ 0 \ (Hi, Closed) & 0 \ (Hi, Part) & 0 \ (Hi, Open) \end{vmatrix}$$

Now, given some R, for any X, then Y can be determined within fuzzy limitations as follows.

Each jth element of M(y) = max over all i { min [M(xi), R(ij)] }. In the above example
    M(y*) for Closed is Max of { Min [0.2, 0], Min [0.8, 0], Min [0, 0] } = 0
    M(y*) for Part is Max of { Min [0.2, 0.2], Min [0.8, 0.3], Min [0, 0] } = 0.3
    M(y*) for Open is Max of { Min [0.2, 0.2], Min [0.8, 0.7], Min [0, 0] } = 0.7
That is, M(y*) is fully recovered.

Figure 1.36
Example of building a fuzzy relation matrix.

In the above example

$\mathbf{M}(y^*)$ for Closed is max of $\{\min[0.2,0], \min[0.8,0], \min[0,0]\} = 0$

$\mathbf{M}(y^*)$ for Part is max of $\{\min[0.2,0.2], \min[0.8,0.3], \min[0,0]\} = 0.3$

$\mathbf{M}(y^*)$ for Open is max of $\{\min[0.2,0.2], \min[0.8,0.7], \min[0,0]\} = 0.7$.

That is, $\mathbf{M}(y^*)$ is fully recovered.

To demonstrate the method, Ren used a two-input, one-output process consisting of a tank with a very nonlinear shape (non-uniform cross section). The human subject observed the input flow rate and the level in the tank (the "inputs" to the human). The subject adjusted the output flow rate in an effort to keep the level constant. Each of the input variables was coded into triangular membership functions where $M = 1$ at the midpoint and $M = 0.5$ at the intersections with adjacent membership functions, and the output was similarly coded. After relatively little training Ren had the subjects perform the task for about 2 minutes, collecting roughly 200 samples. Then he showed that control could be turned over to the fuzzy relational matrix, which performed the task remarkably well.

1.7 Relation of Artificial Intelligence to Supervisory Control

What AI is

While roundly criticized for promising too much too soon, in the several decades of its existence *artificial intelligence* (AI) has clearly made major contributions to speech and picture recognition, expert systems, and other problems that have culminated in useful products. It is not my intention to review all of these contributions here, but only to discuss the relation of AI to supervisory control.

AI is not easy to define. Workers who associate themselves with the term develop computer programs that seem intended to perform in ways that are traditionally regarded as intelligent. Some AI workers are said to seek better understanding of the human mind by computer simulation of mental functions. Others are said to seek improved computational capability—without reference to the mind. Perhaps in between are those who seek improved cooperation between mind and machine.

AI, like other engineering science, is driven both by codified formal reasoning and by empirical trial and error. The formal theory is somewhat different from most of the rest of engineering science in that it is based less in continuous (cardinal) mathematics and more in discrete mathematics. Discrete mathematics is characterized by classical logic and "qualitative" kinds of reasoning that seem to bear a closer resemblance to the way humans think. The latter are often embodied in list-processing computer languages such as LISP. A good example is frame theory (Minsky 1975), which represents one very influential approach to modeling human intelligence. Minsky (pp. 212–213) states the essence of a "frame" as follows:

Here is the essence of the theory: When one encounters a new situation (or makes a substantial change in one's view of the present problem) one selects from memory a substantial structure called a frame. This is a remembered framework to be adapted to fit reality by changing details as necessary.... Once a frame is proposed to represent a situation, a matching process tries to assign values to the terminals (the detailed features) of each frame, consistent with the markers at each place.... Most of the phenomenological power of the theory hinges on the inclusion of expectations and other kinds of presumptions. A frame's terminals are normally filled with default assignments. Thus a frame may contain a great many details whose suppositions are not specifically warranted by the situation. These have many uses in representing general information, most-likely cases, techniques for by-passing logic and ways to make useful generalizations.

A common example of a frame is a room in a building. After one has seen a doorway, one's expectations about the room are determined by seeing windows or furniture. In addition to frames, other such terms are now common parlance in AI. For example *scripts* (Schank and Abelson 1977) have to do, as in the common example, with what people assume and what they say when ordering food in a restaurant, and how a computer might make sense of it.

From early in the development of AI there has been an interest in robots. Initially robots were seen as a way of demonstrating AI concepts rather than as a useful end in themselves. Video eyes could send pictures of environmental objects to computers. These could be processed on LISP machines to identify the objects and their geometric relations to one another. With this information the robot arms could then be controlled by the computer to pick up and manipulate the objects according to stated goals. Clearly this is essentially the same as what has been described above as functions of the task-interactive computer in the supervisory control paradigm. But from the AI point of view there is no supervisory control; there is no human being in the system of interest. Fully autonomous hand-eye operation is what AI has been about.

As AI has matured, the relatively hard line on consideration of the human operator as a salient element in the system of interest has softened somewhat. But the principle activity of AI in relation to robots has remained exclusive of human operators, and thus also of teleoperators. Robot vision, arm control, path planning, obstacle avoidance, grasping, and touch sensing have been worked on very actively in AI laboratories in recent years. Some of these contributions will be touched on in chapter 2. For now we are interested in the more general questions of theoretical contribution to human-computer cooperation in supervisory control.

AI and HCI

Hollnagel (1989) offers a thoughtful critique of the relation of AI to what has come to be called *human-computer interaction (HCI)*. Hollnagel accepts that much current HCI is restricted to the narrower domain of application as defined in the introductory chapter above, but emphasizes the importance of extending HCI to the role of mediation with the external dynamic system (that is, a telerobot or supervisory control system as we have been discussing it). He makes the distinction between (1) interacting *with* a computer, in such a way that the computer is in effect a prosthesis and the human experience is *of* the computer, and (2) working *through* a computer, where the computer becomes a *tool* (metaphorically in the operator's hand) to work on a *task*. In the former case the operator *experiences the computer*, while in the latter case she *experiences the task*. The latter case means *tranparency* between the human and the task, and that is what is sought.

Hollnagel goes on to describe how some early computer programs posed as intelligent—for example, Joseph Weizenbaum's ELIZA, one version of which could pose as a psychiatrist. ELIZA was understood by its users in two ways. The naive users saw it as a psychiatrist—they experienced the computer program itself. The more sophisticated users saw it as an interesting demonstration of the way context could be used by a computer to seem intelligent (for up to a few minutes, when the program began to behave in rather foolish ways). I am in full accord with Hollnagel's sentiments, and with the relevance of the *tool* and *working through* metaphors as goals for telerobotic and supervisory control.

Hollnagel asserts that the primary role of AI in HCI is not in understanding the human but in helping her by increasing her functional capability. AI techniques can augment the human in functionality by visual pattern recognition and discrimination, by monitoring for a particular variety of signals or patterns, by checking for insufficiency or redundancy or consistency, by offering "expert" advice, and by providing defaults when necessary, doing all of these things in parallel. HCI is already full of gimmicks—colors, fancy fonts, windows, icons, and other graphical tricks which may add little or no increased user capability. There is the danger, suggests Hollnagel, that AI may contribute its additional share of clever but profoundly useless gimmicks.

1.8 Cognition and Mental Models in Supervisory Control

It should be clear from all the foregoing that supervisory control puts new emphasis on the cognitive (perceiving, planning, evaluating, deciding, learning) aspects of the human operator's behavior in contrast with the sensorimotor aspects. *Cognitive science* was brought into being by AI and the computer model (or metaphor) of mind. *Cognitive systems engineering* (Hollnagel and Woods 1983; Norman 1986) was a result of systems engineers and psychologists acknowledging that they needed to team up in order to build computer-based systems of all kinds, including supervisory control systems. Distinctions between AI, HCI, cognitive science, and cognitive system engineering are becoming more and more blurred.

Mental models

The purpose of a mental model (sometimes called a user model) is to represent what a person thinks about some set of objects or events. The motivations for mental modeling derive from both practical and research considerations. The system designer wants to know how the user of a computer or some other system thinks about that system so that software or hardware can be designed to correspond to that model. For example, the icons on a computer screen should correspond to how someone thinks about and remembers certain functions which those icons call up. The same may be said about the terms of a command language. The trainer wants to know how a person learns so that training can be more efficient. Of course, the mental model itself is part of what is to be trained, so that the state of the model can also be used as an index of progress in training. The researcher wants a way to represent research findings and predict phenomena which might then be tested experimentally. The researcher needs to have control over the objects and events to be observed and experienced by the experimental subject. Mental-model research is reviewed in Gentner and Stevens 1983 from the viewpoint of cognitive science, and in Goodstein et al. 1988 from the viewpoint of systems applications.

A mental model can take two forms. A first form is qualitative, and usually this means it is essentially descriptive of the interrelationships for a particular set of objects or events experienced. For example, it may represent by a diagram how a particular device works—in a cause-and-effect sense. DeKleer (1979) and deKleer and Brown (1983) describe their approach to qualitative modeling of how an experimental subject thinks a doorbell system works. Having the model in hand, one could say what effects some imposed change (for example, operating a particular switch) might have.

A second type of model is a quantitative cause-effect relation. For example, it might be a model of how water in a tapered vase rises as it is being filled from a constant-rate faucet. The mental model of a nontechnical subject may or may not resemble the differential-equation model of the hydraulic engineer, but with a little experience it would have at least elementary quantification of water height and time. This might involve ordinal instead of cardinal relations, with coarse scaling on the physical variables. Or there might be some fuzzy rules: "If the water flow from the faucet is fast, then...; if it is slow, then...." Such a model is capable of being generalized and "run" willfully in one's head with differently shaped vases or different faucet flow rates. Presumably, from this mental model a quantitative "what would happen if" experiment can be posed, and an answer obtained.

From the user's perspective the best mental model is one that is simple, easy to learn, and easy to apply in the sense of providing a way of storing and retrieving all the relationships required (i.e., knowledge). From the computer's (that is, the computer designer's) perspective, again the best user model that contains all the required knowledge is the one that is easiest to interpret. To represent all of what the user knows and how she knows it appears to be a considerable undertaking. An alternative (one which Hollnagel (1989) recommends) is to represent what the person does not know—the gaps in knowledge.

In recent years there has been great interest in "mental models." This may be driven by the explosive growth of "expert systems" (Harmon and King 1985) and the urge to capture what is in the human expert's head and put it into a computer.

Research on mental models and expert systems naturally begs the question of exactly how the mental model is observed, measured, and validated. The difficulty is that mental events are not directly observable. More is said below on this problem. For us now there is also the question of the relevance to supervisory control, and whether mental modeling need be restricted to how teleoperator-task objects and events (the controlled process) "works," or whether the ideas can be extended to a supervisor's thinking about plans and goals, or other relevant aspects of doing the task. It seems only natural to imagine that humans carry around in their heads models of relations which can be useful in all the functions of planning, teaching, monitoring, intervening, and learning. In section 1.9, the role of mental models in performing these functions will be discussed in greater detail and will be tied to the possibility of computer decision aids in addition to mental models for all such functions.

Calibration

One of the most straightforward problems of extracting judgment information from a person is the degree to which the judgments people render about the values of variables in the physical world are biased. This problem has a solution, for those judgments can be made more accurate and therefore useful by the process of reverse bias, or *calibration.*

Calibration makes several assumptions: (1) Mental models and processes are relatively stable statistically, so that individual judgment biases about the same or very similar variables in the same or similar situations can be treated in the same way, i.e., as a probability density. (2) The human judge not only can render her "best guess" (mean of the judgment density function for that event) but can also provide fractiles (say 90% confidence limits) on the judgment, as a way of specifying "how sure she is." (Machines, by the way, are generally not capable of this.) (3) Eventually the judgments can be verified against events in the physical world (eventually the truth is known).

Assume that a number of judgments are made that relate to the same "situation." They can be judgments of the same variable at different times or places, or judgments of different variables, but all involve the same mental model. In this case, except for scaling factors, the biases and precisions of judgments on the different variables are likely to be the same. In each case the judge is asked to provide not only the best estimate (mean) but also the 90% confidence limits. The first three such judgments are represented by the ticks on the top three lines in figure 1.37. Eventually the truth about each judgment is determined, and that is recorded for each case (as the circle in each case). After a number of such comparisons, the results are aggregated on a common normalized scale, where the 90% confidence ticks are the same, and the units of each variable lose their meaning. Now the true values form a frequency distribution, and statistical estimates can be made of the mean and the standard deviation.

If the judge had no biases, either in her "best estimate" or in her 90% confidence estimates, the mean of the true values would lie at the 50% judgment fractile tick. The offset of the 50% judgment fractile relative to the mean of the true values is the expected bias. If the 90% fractiles of the true-value histogram lie outside the 90% subjective judgment ticks, that implies that the judge has more confidence than is warranted. If the 90% fractiles of the true value histogram lie inside the 90% subjective judgment ticks, that implies that the judge has less confidence than she should have in her own judgments. A chi-square statistic adapts easily to testing wheth-

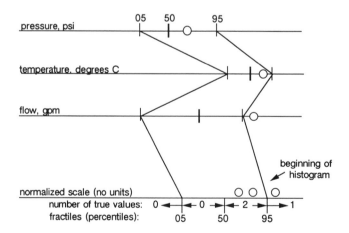

Figure 1.37
Example of calibration. For each of three tests, 05, 50, and 95 are fractiles of the judge's subjective probability function. Small circles the actual values. Both are aggregated on a normalized scale below for comparison.

er the expected number of true values appears in each of the interfractile intervals.

Mendel and Sheridan (1989) extend these ideas for getting calibrated "best measures" from multiple human experts or other information sources.

Rasmussen's hierarchy of abstraction

Rasmussen (1983, 1986) has made important and useful description of the functional properties of a system according to what he calls "goals-means" or "means-ends-relationships" in a functional abstraction hierarchy. Figure 1.38 is Rasmussen's schematic way of of representing these relationships.

"Such a hierarchy," says Rasmussen, "describes bottom-up what components and functions can be used for, how they may serve higher level purposes, and, top-down, how purposes can be implemented by functions and components.... During system design and supervisory control, the description of a physical system will typically be varied in at least two ways. The description can be varied independently along the abstract-concrete dimension, representing means-end relationships, and the dimension representing whole-parts relationships. The first dimension relates to

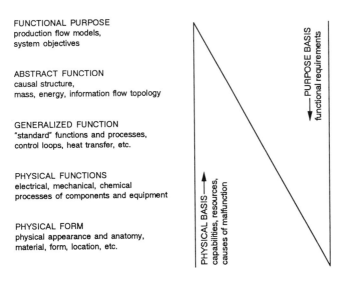

Figure 1.38
Rasmussen hierarchy of abstraction. [After Rasmussen 1986.]

Table 1.1
Examples of Rasmussen's hierarchy in three different contexts. [From Rasmussen 1986.]

Washing machine	Manufacturing plant	Computer system
Purpose		
Washing specifications;	Market relations;	Decision flow graphs in problem terms
Energy waste requirements	Supply sources;	
	Energy and waste constraints;	
	Safety requirements	
Abstract function		
Energy, water, and detergent flow topology	Flow of energy and mass;	Information flow;
	products, monetary values;	Operations in Boolean logic terms, truth tables;
	Mass, energy balances;	
	Information flow structure in system and organization	Symbolic algebraic functions and operations
Generic function		
Washing, draining, drying;	Production, assembly, maintenance;	Memories and registers;
Heating, temperature control;	Heat removal, combustion, power supply;	Amplification, analog integration and summation
	Feedback loops	Feedback loops, power supply
Physical function		
Mechanical drum drive;	Physical functioning of equipment and machinery;	Electrical function of circuitry;
Pump and valve function;	Equipment specifications and characteristics;	Mechanical function of input-output equipment
Electrical/gas heating circuit	Office and workshop activities	
Physical form		
Configuration, weight, and size;	Form, weight, color parts and components;	Physical anatomy;
Style and color	Their location and anatomical relation;	Form and location of components
	Building layout and appearance	

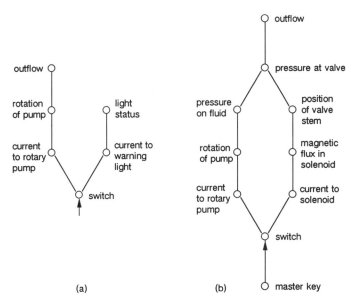

Figure 1.39
Moray's lattice model of a mental model. (a) Causality goes from bottom to top. (b) Lattice differs from tree in that for some events (e.g., pressure at valve) more than one causal factor must exist. [After Moray 1990.]

the concepts used for description; the second relates to the level of detail chosen for description.... Changes along the two dimensions are often made simultaneously, but can in fact be done separately. In the organization of abstraction hierarchies for design, there has traditionally been no major effort to distinguish between aggregation and abstraction.'

Table 1.1 gives examples of descriptions of the means-end hierarchy for three different contexts.

Moray's use of lattice theory to represent mental models

Moray (1990) proposes the use of lattice theory (Birkhoff 1948) to represent mental models. He asserts that this particular way of mapping isomorphisms efficiently captures the most important features of mental models, and is particularly amenable to interrelating concepts which assume different levels in a hierarchy of abstractions as discussed by Rasmussen (1983).

A lattice (figure 1.39 shows two examples) is a partially ordered set of elements (which become nodes on the lattice graph). Any two nodes are ordered by a diadic relation "$\leq$" or "$\geq$" (corresponding to "lower than" or "higher than" in the lattice), which can be assigned any kind of meaning, such as "causes." In figure 1.39 the switch causes the flow of current to both the pump and the solenoid, and these in turn have other causal effects upward in the lattice. Nodes on the left branch are not causally related to those on the right branch until the co-occurrence of both pressure on fluid and position of valve stem cause pressure at the valve.

The diadic relations in figure 1.39 can also be considered to mean "purpose"; i.e., the purpose of the switch is to turn on current to the two nodes above it. However, purpose can also be thought of as levels of aggregation and abstraction. Thus, in figure 1.39 the switch is considered part of each of eight pump systems, four of which are part of a normal pump system and four of which are part of an emergency pump system, both pump systems being part of the cooling system, the highest level of abstraction represented here.

Moray suggests that there are four criteria by which human operators map elements of the actual world into the same element or different elements at the same level of the abstract representation (formal lattice): (1) *physical resemblance* between elements, (2) *correlation* of the *behaviors* of elements, (3) *causal relation* between elements, and (4) *common purpose* among elements. The mental lattice is likely to be different for different criteria which the operator deems appropriate, even though the physical elements to be cognitively mapped may be the same.

Moray makes the point that the choice of the relation to be represented in the mental lattice and the degree of simplification or abstraction relative to the observed or accessible physical reality is a tactical decision imposing a cost-benefit tradeoff. To preserve detail may impose workload and perhaps inefficiency. To simplify means throwing away detail that may not be available when needed, since returning from the abstraction to the detail can result in returning to the *wrong* detail (since one-to-many mapping is indeterminate). In this sense the mental lattice should be a function of the payoffs for alternative outcomes. Further, it is likely that mappings are strongly influenced by experience and by expectation, which means that rare physical changes in the relations between elements are essentially unthinkable by an experienced human operator. In discussing the meaning of cognitive mappings, Moray suggests that the lattice may support more than static facts; it may embody rules for action. A particular form of graph capable of generating action is the Petri net, which was discussed above.

The lattice or diadic graph has been discussed here in relation to mental modeling. It has also been applied for various other purposes. Warfield (1974a,b), for example, demonstrated graph models by which groups of people could analyze their goals, by which organizations could analyze their structures, and by which manufacturers could analyze the time precedence of their manufacturing processes. He also showed how, given the diadic relation between every possible pair of elements in a system (the *reachability matrix*, including, e.g., the relative level of goals, relative power in an organization, relative time precedence of two manufacturing operations), one can determine the relation of adjacent elements on the graph (the *adjacency matrix*), and thus the whole graph can be drawn. (The reverse is trivial.)

Mental models in relation to other "internal" models in supervisory control systems

Before elaborating on the relation of mental models and decision aids to the plan-teach-monitor-intervene-learn functions, it is important to consider what other kinds of models are embodied within a supervisory control system, and where, physically, these are located. Figure 1.40 shows four loci of models in a telerobot system: (1) mental models (presumably resident in the supervisor's head), (2) software-based models in the computer, (3) representations of the telerobot-task in the configuration of the

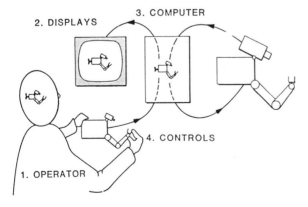

Figure 1.40
Four loci of models in the supervisory control system: (1) mental model; (2) display representation; (3) control configuration; (4) computer model. [Courtesy of W. Verplank.]

human's hand controls, and (4) representations of the telerobot-task in the graphics-text presentation on the supervisor's displays (including computer-generated, video, and other-than-visual displays). The latter two are not typically considered models, but they truly are. The arrangement of what the operator sees and what she does with her hands and how this corresponds with what she thinks is critical. Miscorrespondence (inability or difficulty in mapping from eye or other sensor to mind, and then to hand) is likely to cause delays and errors. The computer's internal models will run at their own speed and in terms of whatever the programmer decided, but these must bear correspondence to the mental and display-control models. All, of course, must correspond to the external reality.

Designing in this correspondence is not a trivial matter. In the parlance of conventional human factors, notions of *display-control compatibility*, *user expectation stereotypes*, *naturalness*, and *transparency* are often used.

The behaviorist challenge to mental models and cognitive science

In some sense, of course, cognitive science has existed ever since researchers began to test memory, visual perception, and similar topics of classical psychology. Thinking and problem solving were subjects of active research during the latter part of the nineteenth century and early in the twentieth. However, during the period of so-called *behaviorism* in psychology, best characterized by Skinner's (1938) *Behavior of Organisms*, mental events were accorded the status of convenient myths. Responses of animals of all kinds were determined by concurrence of stimuli with rewards. Introspective methods to study thinking were ridiculed, and serious questions were raised about what can be measured experimentally about mental activity and how. "Mental model" was not a term so often used then, but the concept was certainly there at the time and was included in the ridiculed "mental" category.

Today the computer metaphor seems to have provided renewed courage to talk about thinking and mind, and license to claim the existence of a science of mental events. Behaviorist ideas, while applied widely by educators and trainers, may be said to be moribund in research circles. One wonders if there will be a resurgence of behaviorist criteria in some form. If these comments seem to reveal a bias, it is only because as a student the author was exposed to Skinner and acquired some respect for his adherence to the operational criterion for science, namely that one can know (in the way of disciplinary science, exclusive of faith and other forms of experience) only what one can measure. Further, behaviorism seems to accord with the philosophical outlook of systems engineering, namely that one can analyze the behavior of a system by measuring inputs and outputs (stimuli and responses) and from these infer transfer relations which can then be used to generalize (describe and predict). Sometimes this is called "black-box" modeling. It does not require one to know the mechanism inside the box. In proceeding to discuss mental models and related topics the author has appeased his behavioristic conscience by rationalizing that mentalisms are insight-provoking metaphors—and furthermore they are fun!

The hermeneutic challenge to rationality in cognitive science

Engineering design has always been dominated by rationalistic ways of thinking, not only about technology itself, but also about human users of technology. Indeterminacy in human behavior is regarded by experimental psychologists, economists, and human-factors engineers as a probabilistic *noise* or *remnant* in otherwise observable behavior, for example as expressed in mathematical models of human tracking behavior (McRuer and Jex 1967). *Bounded rationality* as articulated by Simon (1969) has been widely accepted as a basis for systems design. Although the contrary idea that the observer influences the observation is common in experimental physics (i.e., the Heisenberg principle), and even experimental psychologists and sociologists recognize some equivalent of this (for example, the reason for double-blind experimental procedures), the effect has never been seen by engineers to be very significant. Certainly designers of human-machine systems have always assumed that what information they provide the human operator is what the human operator perceives—apart from minor random error and "noise" and lack of control.

Meanwhile, growing from philosophical questions concerning the interpretation of mythical and sacred texts like the Bible, a philosophical movement called *hermeneutics* (the art or science of interpretation) came into being. The question was whether a text has meaning independent of the act of human interpretation. An older objectivist school said yes. The other school, which currently seems to prevail (at least in philosophy), says no, that the interpreted and the interpreter do not exist independently, that understanding is a process of interaction between what is factually in the text and what the reader brings to the interaction from previous experience. Most closely associated with the latter view are Heidegger (1962, 1968) and Gadamer (1975, 1976). Winograd and Flores (1986) point out that, while Kant (the penultimate rationalist) thought it "a scandal of philosophy and of human reason in general" that no philosopher has given an acceptable answer to "How can I know whether anything outside my subjective consciousness exists?", Heidegger (1962) argued that the scandal is that "such proofs are expected and attempted again and again."

Winograd and Flores side with Heidegger and critique traditional rationality as applied to cognition, computers, and systems engineering on the basis of hermeneutics. On this basis they argue that human beliefs and assumptions cannot be made fully explicit, that practical intuitive understanding is more fundamental than theoretical understanding, and that humans do not relate to things by having stable mental representations (mental models) of them. They characterize Heidegger's ideas and terms (italicized below) with behavioral examples: By real-life circumstance one is *thrown* into situations and actions like hammering a nail without the need or the opportunity to be a detached observer. Hammering is what is known (*readiness-to-hand*), and the abstract idea of a hammer emerges only through a *breaking-down*, resulting in *blindness* to the full reality of *being*.

In the human-computer interaction, what Winograd and Flores describe as the normal ready-to-hand state of being corresponds to what Hollnagel called experiencing through the computer (or the hammer) to the task, and break down and blindness to experiencing the computer itself. According to Winograd and Flores, the effect of experience as understood in hermeneutics accords with the way Minsky's frames work:

In a way, frame-based computational systems approach meaning from a hermeneutic direction. They concentrate not on the question "How does the program come to accurately reflect the situation" but rather on "How does the system's preknowledge (collection of frames) affect its interpretation of the situation?" The meaning of sentence or scene lies in the interaction between its structure and the preexisting structures in the machine.

Human understanding, for Winograd and Flores, is "not a fixed relationship between a (mental) representation and the external objects represented, but a commitment to carry out a dialog...that permits new distinctions to emerge." They see organizations as "networks of commitments" in which conventional decision support systems "obscure responsibility" and "conceal commitment" and give an "illusion of objectivity." They prefer to see computers used as "tools for conversation to monitor such commitments, and to anticipate breakdown" and provide a space of action possibilities when this occurs.

Thus we see that ideas of mental models, mental workload, and cognition generally receive ample criticism from two rather different perspectives.

1.9   Extending the Paradigm of Supervisory Function

The plan, teach, monitor, intervene, and learn functions may now be elaborated in light of the foregoing discussion of mental models. Figure 1.41 lists the categories of human supervisor functioning in the order in which they normally would occur in performing a supervisory control task. Figure 1.42 presents the same sequence of functions in the form of a pictorial flow chart in which for each function the corresponding mental model is shown as a "thought balloon" of what the supervisor might be asking herself, and the potential computerized decision aid is shown as a rectangular box. Normally for any given task the planning and learning functions are performed mostly off-line relative to the automatic operation of the system. The teach, monitor, and intervene functions are done iteratively, and therefore are shown within an inner and on-line loop, as will be explained below.

1. PLAN means

1a. Understand controlled process. The supervisor must gain understanding of how the given physical thing, equipment, or system which is to be operated operates, how it works, and what are the relations by which inputs to it become outputs. This is usually the first consideration in training an operator—presumably to establish a proper mental model of the controlled process. The trainee needs enough knowledge of the appropriate variables and their input-output transfer relations to be able to control and predict what the process will do, but does not need details that are irrelevant to operation. The computer aid here is the conventional training simulator.

1b. Satisfice objectives. To control engineers the objective function is a closed-form analytical expression of "goodness" which is a scalar function

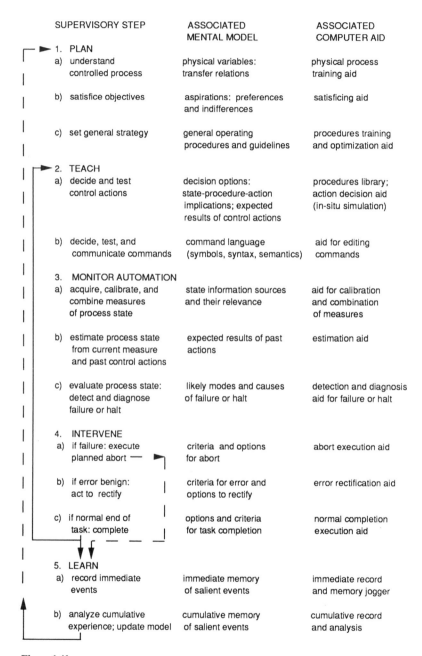

Figure 1.41
Extended supervisor functions with assumed mental models and computer aids. Nested
loop relations are indicated by lines at left.

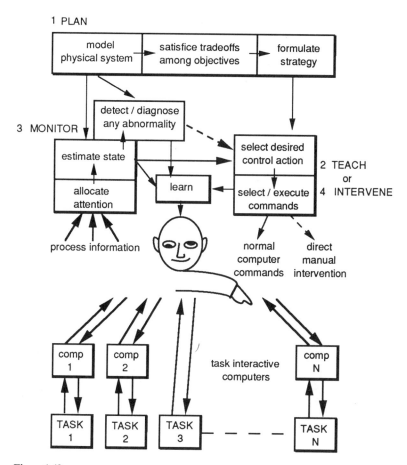

Figure 1.42
Extended paradigm for supervisor functions (which include both mental models and decision aids).

of all relevant variables or "performance attributes" or "objectives." To satisfice means to decide on such a function which is sufficiently precise for current purposes (March and Simon 1958). The computer, when properly programmed with appropriate known constraints and inter-attribute relations, may help the supervisor decide what goals and attribute tradeoffs are acceptable (see chapter 3 below).

1c. Set general strategy. The supervisory operator is usually given some procedures or operating guidelines which she is to follow generally (or to deviate from as required for the particular task at hand). This is the third function which is usually performed off-line, before the automatic system starts up. It is the second activity usually addressed formally in training programs (objective function setting is typically not addressed formally, though it might well be). The mental model here is that of the general operating procedures and guidelines which must be committed to memory (where detailed procedures can be accessed and read as needed). The corresponding computer aid here is one for procedures training. To help the supervisor relate the strategy planning to the satisficed objectives there might also be an aid for optimization in a broad sense, particularly when the general procedures are not already formulated and where certain goals are given and are not to be modified. Any of a number of common operations-research techniques might be applied here, depending upon the class of tasks.

2. TEACH means

2a. Decide control actions. On the first pass of stepping through the supervisory functions, this function would consist of the actions necessary to start up the automatic system, but on successive passes the specific control decisions must be based on feedback of state. The supervisor's job is then to decide what procedures are appropriate for the estimated state and what specific actions are implied, in consideration of process dynamics and satisficed objectives as mentally modeled in steps 1a, 1b, and 1c.

2b. Decide, test, and communicate commands. This is necessary in order that the computer be able to implement the intended actions. It is essential at this point to make a clear distinction between commands and control actions, since in normal control engineering practice (and indeed in normal activities of living) they may be taken to be the same. Commands are the operator's movements of analogic control interface devices such as joysticks, master manipulator arms, or computer screen cursor controls, and her stroking of symbolic alphanumeric and special function keys. Control actions are the responses the human-interactive computer makes to these commands to signal the task-interactive computer, activate motors or other actuators, and thereby force the controlled process to modify its state. The mental model in this case is the command language (the set of admissible symbols or words or movements, the syntax or rules for their combination, and the semantics or meanings of both individual symbols and combinations). The computer aid in this case is an editing aid, an interactive means to help the user say to the computer what it needs to hear in order to do what the operator wants done. This is not unlike an editing aid for word processing or for programming in general, where the computer informs the user what commands are not interpretable, and might come back and suggest what might be meant.

3. MONITOR AUTO means

3a. Acquire, calibrate, and combine measures of process state. This requires that the supervisor have a mental model of potential sources of relevant information, their likelihood of knowing about particular variables of interest, and their likely biases in measuring and reporting. There can be many sources which have something to tell about any one variable: real-time sensors, computerized data bases and "expert systems," human experts, and incidental sources which are likely to be unreliable but may provide some useful evidence. Some sources advertise themselves as being very precise but may not be; others may be much more precise than first expected. Some may be consistently biased, so that if only the bias could be removed they would provide very accurate measurements.

3b. Estimate process state from current measure and past control actions. Estimation theory provides a normative way to do this which is commonly used in modern control practice. This requires a good model of the physical process, which is not ordinarily available in complex systems controlled by a human supervisor. Presumably the human supervisor has some internal (mental) model of how past control actions should be affecting present process response, and tries to combine this with her best (but probably inaccurate) direct measurement data on the current process state in order to form a best overall estimate of current state. But this is not easy for a human, especially if the system is complex. However, for a computer, given a good model of the controlled process and a single best measurement of its state (which still is likely to be imperfect), it is relatively straightforward to calculate the best estimate of the current state. The problem then lies in displaying this to a human operator in a meaningful and useful way.

3c. Detect and diagnose failure, conflict, halt, or assignment completion. This means that the supervisor must detect and diagnose whether the process has failed (strayed sufficiently far from given objectives), whether some control activity is in serious conflict with some other control activity (in which case the conflict must be resolved), whether the process has prematurely halted (stopped before the commanded actions were all executed without getting into trouble), or finally, whether it has reached the normal end of its assigned program. The supervisor must diagnose where and how any abnormalities occurred. The mental model accordingly incorporates, in addition to the state estimate available from 3b, the likely modes and causes of failure, conflict, halt, or subtask completion.

4. INTERVENE means

4a. If failure, execute planned abort. When the state has deviated sufficiently far from what is desirable (or the control conflicts, or halt conditions are not rectifiable)—according to direct supervisor observations or computer-based failure detection—the supervisor promptly executes an already programmed appropriate abort command. Her mental model is of a relatively small number of preplanned abort commands and their criteria for use. A computer decision aid in this case can advise her which to use and how to use it.

4b. If there has been no failure and if an error or a conflict is rectifiable or a halt is benign, take appropriate action. The mental model includes a relatively small number of command options to resolve an error or a conflict. As in 4a, the computer decision aid can advise which to use and how to use it. This category includes small adjustments of parameters, or small additions to the control signal itself to "nudge" the controlled process.

4c. If the operation has reached the normal end of its assigned subtask, cycle back to 2a. If there is no failure, error, or conflict, the operator is not likely to have a simple preplanned open-loop command at the ready. In this case she must cycle back to 2a for a considered execution of the next subtask.

5. LEARN means

5a. Record experience. The recording of what was considered, what was commanded, and what happened cannot be left to informal chance. It may be helpful to have the computer aid provide some "memory jogging" display such as a chart of recent state trajectories, or a listing of alarms or other key events (as is commonly done in nuclear power plants).

5b. Update models. Especially when the task is terminated by abortion in response to failure or by normal completion, the computer aid should provide some cumulative record and analysis in a form that can be accessed and used later during the PLAN phase.

1.10   Fitting the Extended Supervisory Control Functions to the Elements of the Modern Control Paradigm

Figure 1.42 is a diagram of a supervisory control system representing the sequence of supervisory functions as they relate to the key system variables, the task-interactive computer and the controlled process. Figure 1.43 takes this same set of variables and interrelates them in the format of the canonical modern control paradigm—modified as necessary to include all the functions and additional variables that have been discussed above.

Figure 1.43 cross-references the functions of figure 1.41 with numbers and letters above or below certain blocks. At the top of figure 1.43 the three "off-line" PLAN functions 1a, 1b, and 1c are shown in sequence as in figure 1.41. At successive stages they generate the parameters of the process mental models $\mathbf{A}'$ and $\mathbf{B}'$ (models of natural process response $\mathbf{A}$ and forced process response $\mathbf{B}$), the mapping of estimated state to objectives $\mathbf{V}$, and the control (teach, 2a,b) law $\mathbf{L}$. $\mathbf{L}$ takes as input the state estimate $\hat{x}$

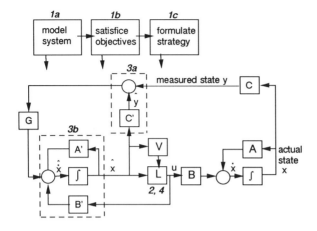

Figure 1.43
Extended supervisor functions in relation to canonical control model. Numbers indicate correspondence to figures 1.41 and 1.42.

from 3b. Evaluation function **V**, also dependent upon $\hat{x}$, provides the normal objectives evaluation for **L**, and also diagnoses conditions of failure, error or halt (the 3c function which forces **L** to perform the special intervene functions of 4a,b, and c).

C', in turn essential to feed 3b, represents the supervisor's internal model of **C**, the physical sensors attached to the process and the human and computer "expert" resources actively accessed, calibrated, and combined by the human supervisor and/or a computer aid. Hence **C'** is much more than just a passive measurement matrix. The 3a block, which includes **C'**, determines the discrepancy between **y** and **ŷ**, the degree to which expected results of past actions **u** (3b) are insufficient to completely predict **y**, so that there must be a correction through **G**. **G** may be said to represent part of the learning function, 5.

Together the parameters **A'**, **B'**, **C'**, **L**, **G**, and **V** constitute the fully internalized mental model of the supervisory controller operating in the iterative or "in the supervisory loop" mode much as they do in the Kleinman-Baron-Levison optimal control model of the human controller. (**V** is our explicitly added internal model.)

The 1a, 1b, and 1c blocks are add-ons needed to achieve the required meta-control or parameter generation. As yet no generic analytic expressions have been put in all of the blocks, even those in the closed-loop portion of figure 1.43 such that analysis, simulation, and modeling follow easily and naturally therefrom. This is the frontier research problem. Baron has assumed some such structure for his PROCRU program for procedure-driven aircraft landing, and Stassen has done it in his super-tanker models.

1.11   Factors that Limit Our Ability to Model the Supervisory Controller

Free will and inability to measure mental events

In simple direct manual control and other human-machine systems where the purpose of the task is relatively fixed and evident, mathematical modeling has been relatively successful. In contrast, supervisory control involves complex and flexible systems where operators have free will in planning, setting goals, and evaluating worth. Modeling free will seems a contradiction in terms, since the free-will aspect of the operator's response is generated from within, not determined by an input.

In modeling human motor skill the researcher can control experimental conditions and make direct observations of the variables of interest. This is not true of mental events. They can only be inferred. This is the basis for the ancient mind-body dilemma, as well as the rejection by earlier behavioral scientists of mental events as legitimate scientific concepts. Such "behaviorism," as was noted above, is out of fashion now. Computer science begat cognitive science and made computer programs admissible representations of what people think. However, the limits on direct measurement of mental events do not go away.

The most difficult (perhaps even impossible) aspect of supervisory control to model is how a decision maker sets goals and makes goal tradeoffs (objective functions, risk criteria, utility, etc.) in the first place—as contrasted to using a given objective function to make decisions, which is the traditional content of decision theory. (This topic is treated again in chapters 3 and 4.) The supervisor freely establishes what is good and what is bad *as part of the control task*. This makes it especially difficult for the outside observer. The underlying criteria for decision making are not directly available to the observer, which may make the observed decision behavior seem arbitrary. There seems little prospect for mathematical modeling of free, willful mental judgments of the human supervisory operator in the near future.

Ambiguity between own decision and dependence on decision aid

The human supervisor presumably uses both her own mental model *and* computer decision aids provided to her. If she chooses to follow the advice given by the decision aids, can it then be said that we are modeling the supervisor's decisions? If she claims to "know" certain facts or have a "plan" which happens to correspond to the knowledge or plan available in the computer, can the normative decision aid be considered a yardstick against which to measure inferred mental activity? Where there is free interaction between human and computer it is difficult to determine what is true human decision behavior and what is slavish following of the computer's advice. Mental and computer models are more easily treated as a combined entity which produces operator decisions. We will return to these issues again in chapter 4 to reflect on what, after all, is the purpose of having human operators in complex systems.

Ambiguity between experience of computer and experience through computer

It was stated above in the discussion of human-computer interaction that it is desirable that operators of telerobots perceive themselves as observing and controlling the task on the other side of the computer, as though the computer were transparent and they were working with a tool *through* that transparent medium. But often, and particularly in the case of a novice operator and/or a poorly designed system, the system is perceived to be opaque; i.e., the operator's perception and experience are *of* the computer. In place of the computer mediator one can consider any tool or instrument. The experienced carpenter experiences the task through the tool; the tool is merely an extension of her body. The novice carpenter experiences the tool in her hand. This fundamental orientation of the operator, whether *of* or *through*, and the degree of *transparency* or *opacity*, is believed to be an important determiner of behavior and always in question. The researcher tries to understand the operator's orientation and its degree by eliciting mental models, but this is difficult.

Sheer complexity

This is the most obvious factor limiting our ability to model supervisory control. The aggregation of hardware, software, and human behavior which we call a supervisory control system, taken together with the variety of task situations which such systems are designed to accommodate, tends to be extensive—more extensive than conventional man-made control systems in industry and government have been. The simple fact that supervisory control calls upon "higher levels" of human behavior makes modeling such systems at least as complex as modeling such human behavior without the accompanying technology. We cannot claim stupendous success in such behavioral modeling.

In spite of these difficulties, we must continue efforts to model and predict what we can about human behavior in this more and more prevalent form of control system.

2 Supervisory Control of Anthropomorphic Teleoperators for Space, Undersea, and Other Applications

After a brief historical review and some discussion of current needs and configurations of anthropomorphic teleoperators, this chapter takes up the supervisory functions of planning and teaching (command language) as introduced in chapter 1. Since the whole spectrum from direct teleoperation to high-level supervisory control is embraced, important aspects of more direct remote sensing (television, teleproprioception, force and touch feedback, time delay, and telepresence) are considered next. Then state estimation from a higher-level or computer-based perspective is covered, and finally the measurement of the performance of a teleoperator system. The supervisory functions of intervening and learning from error are left to chapter 3, where they are deemed more appropriate and where the examples fit better.

2.1 History of Teleoperators

Before 1970

Many of what some believe to be new developments in teleoperator technology actually had their beginnings long ago.

Well before the sixteenth century there were teleoperators in the form of fire tongs, animal prods, and other simple arm extensions. Early in the nineteenth century there were crude teleoperators for earth moving, construction, and related tasks. By the 1940s prosthetic limb fitters had developed arm hooks activated by leather thongs tied to other parts of the wearer's body. Around 1945 the first modern master-slave teleoperators were developed by Raymond Goertz at Argonne National Laboratory, near Chicago. These were mechanical pantograph mechanisms by which radioactive materials in a "hot cell" could be manipulated by an operator outside the cell. Electrical servomechanisms soon replaced the direct mechanical tape and cable linkages (Goertz and Thompson 1954), as shown in figure 2.1. Closed-circuit television was introduced, so that now the operator could be an arbitrary distance away.

By the mid 1950s technological developments in "telepresence" (they didn't call it that at the time) were being demonstrated (Johnsen and Corliss 1967; Corliss and Johnsen 1968; Johnsen and Magee 1970; Heer 1973; Vertut and Coiffet 1986a,b). Among these were force reflection simultaneous in all six degrees of freedom (DOF), coordinated two-arm teleoperators, and head-mounted displays that controlled the position of the remote

Figure 2.1
The E-1 electrical master-slave manipulator developed by Goertz at Argonne National
Laboratory. [From Johnsen and Corliss 1967.]

camera and thereby produced remarkable visual telepresence. Particularly
impressive was R. Mosher's development of the General Electric Handyman (Mosher and Wendel 1960; Mosher 1964), which had two electro-
hydraulic arms each with ten DOF (two DOF for each of five fingers). Both
master and slave are shown in figure 2.2.

By the late 1950s there was interest in applying this new servomechanism
technology to human limb prostheses. Probably the first successful development was that of Aaron Kobrinskii (1960) in Moscow, a lower-arm
prosthesis driven by minute myoelectric signals picked up from the muscles
in the stump or upper arm. This was followed rapidly by similar developments in the United States and Europe (in the mid to late 1960s), including
teleoperators attached to the wheelchairs of quadraplegics which could be
commanded by the tongue or other remaining motor signals (figure 2.3).

Figure 2.2
Mosher's Handyman electro-hydraulic manipulator developed at General Electric Co.
[From Johnsen and Corliss 1967.]

By that time research in remote touch sensing and display was already underway (Strickler 1966), though there was little interest in applying "teletouch."

From the early 1960s telemanipulators and video cameras were being attached to submarines by the US, USSR, and French navies and used experimentally. For example, the US Navy's CURV vehicle (figure 2.4) was used successfully in 1966 to retrieve from the deep ocean bottom a nuclear bomb that had been dropped accidentally from an airplane off Palomares, Spain. Offshore mineral-extraction and cable-laying firms soon became interested in using this technology to replace human divers, especially as oil and gas drilling operations got deeper.

In the early 1960s the race to the moon began. A particularly vexing problem was posed by the transmission time delay between Earth and

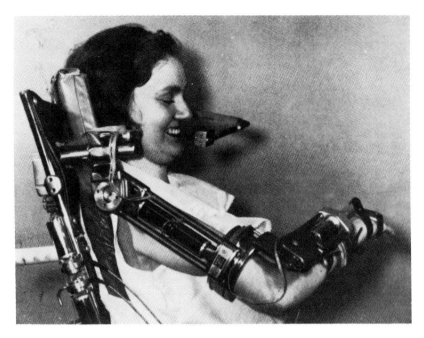

Figure 2.3
Early arm-aid for wheelchair patient. [From Johnsen and Magee 1970]

the moon. Closed-loop control from Earth to moon was impractical because of the resulting instability. By 1965 experiments in academic research laboratories had revealed the problems that time delay caused for telemanipulation and vehicle control (Ferrell 1965), in particular that the only way to avoid instability is to make an open-loop move without waiting for feedback, then to wait for confirmation before making the next open-loop move. Experimental results (figure 2.5) made clear why, with significant time delay, it takes intolerably long to perform even the simplest remote manipulation tasks.

The early lunar teleoperator called Surveyor demonstrated vividly the "move-and-wait" problems of time delay in an actual space mission. Soon thereafter supervisory control was shown to offer a way around the time-delay problem (Ferrell and Sheridan 1967). It immediately became apparent that supervisory control had advantages even when there was no time delay in the communication channel, where, in order to avoid collision or the dropping of grasped objects, quicker teleoperator reaction time was

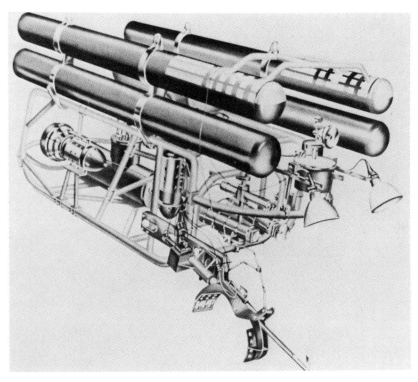

Figure 2.4
Early cable-controlled underwater research vehicle (CURV) developed by the Naval Ocean Systems Center. [From Johnsen and Corliss 1967.]

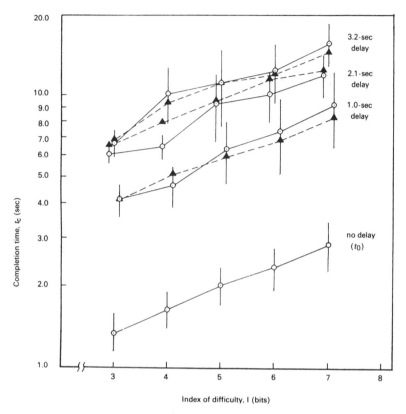

Figure 2.5
Ferrell's results for time-delay in telemanipulation. Experiments were performed in simple
two-DOF grasp-and-place tasks with various accuracy requirements (Fitts' index of
difficulty) and pure time delays. o: Measured t_c. ▲: Predicted t_{ca}. (Vertical lines are ± 1
average standard deviation. Averages of two subjects at each delay; averages of all six for
no delay.) [From Ferrell 1965.]

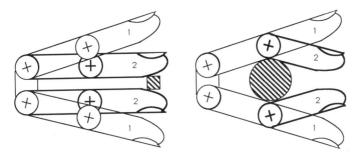

Figure 2.6
Tomovic's prosthetic hand, demonstrating simple hierarchical control. If touch is at the tips of the fingers, they close from the base joint and remain unbent, as in the left diagram. If touch is at the at the middle of the fingers, they close at the distal joint as in the right diagram. [After Tomovic 1969.]

needed than the distant human operator could provide. Closely related research by Crossman et al. (1974) had shed light on how humans allocate their attention when controlling multiple systems simultaneously.

Tomovic (1969) pointed out the hierarchical nature of human motor control, in which the higher level, once it gives commands to lower levels for implementation, has no influence for some time. Tomovic embodied a very simple form of hierarchical control in his hand prosthesis (figure 2.6). If the wearer, in grasping an object, first touched it at the distal end of a finger or thumb, the hand would automatically close with the fingers unbent. On the other hand, if contact was first made at the proximal end, the fingers would automatically curl around the grasped object as they closed.

Though the US space agency's nuclear rocket project mounted a major effort in teleoperator development in the 1960s, after that program was canceled and throughout the 1970s there was little US support for tele-operation or telerobotics in space. The Soviets continued to build on their successes with the Lunakhod (figure 2.7), the first remotely controlled lunar roving vehicle.

By 1970 the Western interest in teleoperation had turned to undersea applications, for there was great economic demand for offshore oil. The French developed their ERIC vehicle, the Americans the Hydroproducts RCV 150. These were small unmanned submarines with remotely controlled video and manipulation capability plus the necessary thrusters for maneuvering. Industrial (manufacturing) robotics was coming into full develop-

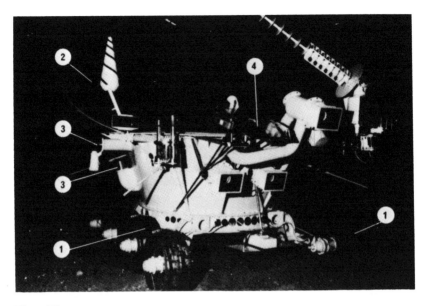

Figure 2.7
Soviet Lunakhod lunar rover. 1, eight wheels with metallic mesh tread, two bogies on each
side; 2, solar cell; 3. periscope camera; 4, laser reflector. [From Vertut and Coiffet 1986a; ©
Prentice-Hall.]

ment. Unimation, General Electric, and Cincinnati Milacron in the United
States, Hitachi, Fujitsu, and others in Japan, and many firms throughout both Western and Eastern Europe had begun using relatively simple
assembly-line robots, mostly for spot welding and paint spraying. By 1980
industrial robots had wrist-force sensing and primitive computer vision,
and push-button "teach pendant" control boxes were being used for relatively simple programming from the shop floor.

Since 1970

Since 1970 the pace of teleoperator development has quickened, but in
the eyes of many it has mostly been carried along by the more extensive developments of industrial robots. The principal developments in
teleoperation (including telerobotics) have been for undersea application
(driven in the 1970s by the oil industry in the US, Japan, France, the UK,
and Scandinavia , and in the 1980s by the navies of those countries) and for
space application. In specialized markets such as medical colonoscopy
(inspecting the colon) and arthroscopy (repairing damaged knees without

cutting them open), warehousing, and police sentry functions, there are now viable firms selling teleoperation products and services. Other industries such as construction, agriculture, and mining, have tended to shy away from "high-tech" devices, but there may now be signs of change.

Industrial robotics has been much less successful than was heralded by the grand predictions of 1970. Telerobotics, too, has progressed slowly. The pace of robotics in space has been held back by continual budget cuts and an emphasis on the manned space shuttle. The development of telerobotics in the oil industry slowed because the price of oil dropped and stayed down. Hazardous waste has been left largely unattended. Nevertheless, in the United States, NASA, the Department of Defense, and the Department of Energy have recently increased their interest in teleoperation and telerobotics significantly. Japan, in its quiet steady way, has continued to develop teleoperator and telerobot technology, and in many respects is the world leader.

The distinction between teleoperators and industrial robots

What is the relation of teleoperators and telerobots to factory or industrial robots, both as to the history of their development and as to the role of the human operator? With respect to hardware there are few differences. The essential differences lie in the conditions of the task and in the need for control by a human operator.

Industrial robots justify themselves by repetitively performing mostly predictable tasks in controlled environments with speed and accuracy. They are programmed by humans for large product batches, and reprogramming during a batch run is abnormal. In human teleoperation there is little or no repetition of the same identical task. Even in telerobotics the automatic execution of a program unfolds with new combinations of commands, objects in different locations, and circumstances always at least a little different from those in the past. Whereas an industrial robotic manufacturing operation can go unmonitored by a human for a long period, in direct teleoperation a human must remain in the control loop continuously. In telerobotic control the operator must make frequent observations to ensure that actions occur as intended, or, if they do not, to revise the instructions.

For these reasons human teleoperation for working in space, under the sea, or in other hazardous environments has followed a different course than industrial robotics. There has been surprisingly little interest in human supervisory control for industrial robots, and the availability of a nearby human operator to monitor, reprogram, maintain, and repair in "hands-on" fashion has been taken for granted. However, now that industrial robots are being treated as "work cells" and aggregated into larger "flexible manufacturing systems," this is beginning to change. Repeated-task factory robots will not be discussed below except for a brief section in chapter 3.

2.2   Current Needs and Activities

Space

The primary current example of a space teleoperator is the 20-meter-long remote manipulator system (RMS) built by the Canadian firm SPAR and carried aboard the US space shuttle (figure 2.8). It has six degrees of freedom and is controlled directly by a human operator viewing through a window or over video and using two three-axis variable-rate-command joysticks (one for three translations, one for three rotations). Weight considerations have dictated that this arm be very light; it will not support its own weight in earth's gravity. In space, using very low rates of motion, it can move hundreds of kilograms with ease. Master-slave control is not deemed appropriate for such low angular rates. Modest computer aiding exists in the form of resolved-rate control (coordinate transformation) so that the end point moves in a translational or rotational direction corresponding to the direction of force of the operator's joystick—whatever the values of the arm's intermediate joint angles (Whitney 1969b).

Until recently a new focus in the US space program was a "flight telerobotic servicer" (FTS), a general-purpose manipulation device that has two arms approximately the length of human arms. Initially the plan was that the FTS would be carried aboard the space shuttle at the end of the long RMS arm, much as human astronauts have been carried on past missions. Eventually the FTS would be attached to a free-flying thrust platform and would be provided with a modicum of computer intelligence beyond simple control laws or coordinate transformations. Figure 2.9 illustrates the design for the FTS, now canceled by NASA.

New telerobotic roving vehicles and manipulators are being designed for landings on the moon and on Mars and other planets. It would be highly desirable to control these directly from Earth, but the communication time delay poses a serious control problem, as has already been noted. (This

Figure 2.8
Two views of the space shuttle arm. Above, the 60-foot arm extending aft from across shuttle bay as viewed by astronaut operator; below, end effector supporting two astronauts as they prepare to repair the satellite seen beneath them. [Courtesy of NASA.]

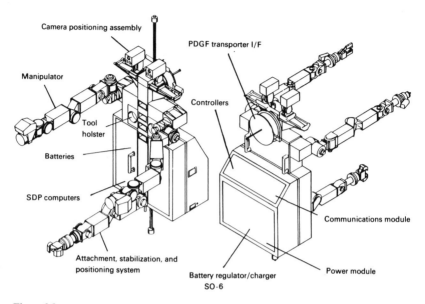

Figure 2.9
Design proposed for NASA flight telerobotic servicer (FTS). [Courtesy of NASA.]

problem and various partial solutions are discussed more fully near the end of this chapter.)

Possible uses for the major mission-oriented teleoperators (RMS, FTS, other space-station telerobots being developed in Europe and Japan, and planetary roving telerobots) are routine inspection, maintenance, and science experiments. The currently projected requirements for extra-vehicular activity (EVA) required to do maintenance on the space station have been declared unacceptable by the astronauts. Further, the astronaut (mostly mission-specialist) staffing requirements to perform all the jobs requested of space science principal investigators are excessive. In the latter case it is clear that the space science community does not appreciate what even today's telerobots can do—that a physically present astronaut is not always needed, for example, to make simple observations of instruments and throw switches, or to make geological observations on the lunar or the Martian surface. Even a simple telerobot or a dedicated miniature video-camera or remotely operated switch may suffice. Even within the narrow confines of space science and engineering, the potential users of telerobots are often not in good communication with the providers.

See Sheridan et al. 1987 for a review of the human-automation interaction needs associated with space systems.

Undersea oil and science (geology, biology) applications

By 1980 "remotely operated vehicles" (ROVs) had come into extensive use by the offshore oil and gas industry in well head completion operations, monitoring of pipelines, placing of sacrificial anodes and inspection of welds on subsea structures, and other tasks (Vadus 1976; Yastrebov and Stepanov 1978; Busby 1979). These developments were motivated partly by the high cost of human divers—which can exceed $10,000 per working hour at depths of 300 meters, both because of the time required for ascending and descending and because of the extensive support facilities required. Perhaps more significant is the risk to life—over fifty divers have been lost in North Sea oil operations. Both cost and risk factors also weigh in favor of ROVs over manned submersibles. Though the pace of offshore oil operations has slowed in recent years because of declining oil profits, development of ROV technology has continued.

Most current undersea manipulators are hydraulic, to withstand the high forces and rugged conditions to which they are exposed. Consequently they tend to be relatively clumsy. Direct master-slave and joystick-controlled teleoperators have been employed both on ROVs and on manned submersibles. In the latter case the teleoperator is controlled by a human operator only a few meters away through a window in the submersible. Since most wellhead assembly operations have been done above the surface, there have been few requirements for fine dexterity. Mostly only crude grappling has been required, plus a lot of inspection work. However, undersea operating companies insist upon high reliability. One rather interesting use of ROVs has been to monitor human divers, both for safety reasons and to ensure that they keep working.

ROVs can carry a variety of sensors—not only video cameras (often made to be sensitive at very low levels of ambient light), but also ultrasound, x-ray, laser and gyroscopic sensors for determining own-vehicle position and for examining other objects. In addition, pressure, temperature, conductivity, and various chemical sensors are used to measure conditions of the surrounding water column.

Communication arrangements for ROVs vary widely. Figure 2.10 shows a matrix of twelve possible systems; the columns are different arrangements for communications from support ship to subsea system and the rows are

LOCATION OF OPERATOR, COMMUNICATION FROM SHIP

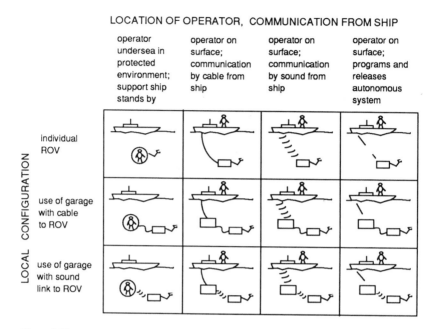

Figure 2.10
Matrix of communication configurations for undersea remotely operated vehicles (ROVs).

different arrangements for communications within the subsea system. Communications between human and telerobot become more difficult in going either down or to the right in the matrix. Because of limited bandwidth, sonic communications are not yet used for control, except experimentally. However, the unobtrusiveness of sound communication, such as freedom to maneuver around obstacles, even *given* the low bandwidth, makes it attractive for supervisory monitoring and control. Availability of power and cable dynamics are other tradeoff factors. Arguments can be generated favoring any of these arrangements, depending upon the task assigned.

Both marine geologists and marine biologists have become very interested in using ROVs for performing remotely their scientific investigations. The scientists have liked manned submersibles, which permit them a relatively unimpeded wide-angle view, but they have disliked the high cost and risk of such vehicles. Sometimes manned submersibles and ROVs are used together. For example, the expedition to the *Titanic* by the Woods Hole

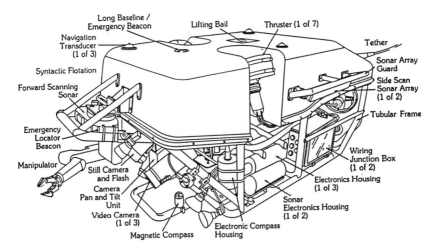

Figure 2.11
Woods Hole's remotely operated submersible, Jason. Jason incorporates several
supervisory control modes. [Courtesy of Woods Hole Oceanographic Institution.]

Oceanographic Institution utilized the three-person submersible *Alvin* plus
two unmanned submersibles, *Argo* and *Jason Junior* (Ballard 1986). *Argo*
is a heavy vehicle passively suspended on a long cable (3500 m in the case
of the *Titanic*) which carries mostly sonar, video, and photo equipment,
while *Jason Junior* is a tiny "swimming video camera" less than half a meter
in diameter. Its successor, *Jason*, is a somewhat larger ROV having multiple
control modes, including full supervisory control (figure 2.11). Unlike the
oil industry, the marine biologists need to be gentle and surreptitious, so
as not to destroy the very creatures they are studying. The required forces
are much less, and more dexterity and skill in maneuvering are needed than
in most oil operations.

Nuclear power plants and radioactive "hot cells"

The nuclear "hot laboratories" continue as the application most wedded
to force-reflecting master-slave systems. Vertut and his CEA Laboratory
near Paris have developed what has probably been the most extensive and
successful set of such systems, including the respected MA-23, which uses
pulleys rather than gears to reduce motor speed and increase torque but
yet make the manipulator back-driveable (figure 2.12). This and the current American counterparts, all direct descendants of the early Goertz

Figure 2.12
View of pulley system in Vertut's MA-23 mobile telemanipulator developed at CEA in
France. 1, moving drum (receiving about 10 turns of 0.2 mm thick tape; 2 and 3, opposing
tape; 4, mobile pulley blocks; 5, fixed pulley block; 6, tape fitting and tightening; 7, large
cable; 8, pulley with large torque for unit rotation; 9, shoulder casing; 10, shoulder pulley;
11, elbow pulley; 12, mobile pulley blocks in shoulder casing; 13, seven other tapes for
transmission of orientation and gripper movements. [From Vertut and Coiffet 1986a; ©
Prentice-Hall.]

machines, have had to be designed to remain inside of highly radioactive nuclear fuel reprocessing enclosures for many months; thus they must be extremely reliable. Nevertheless, such teleoperators are now becoming sufficiently mobile and dexterous for doing tube-repair work on steam boilers and other nuclear power plant maintenance tasks. The Japanese, for example, have developed a robotic device capable of crawling along the outside of a pipe while monitoring for leaks.

Teleoperators have been valuable in the cleanup of the nuclear power station accidents at Three Mile Island and Chernobyl.

Toxic waste cleanup

The US Department of Energy is faced with a massive cleanup of both nuclear and chemically toxic wastes and obsolete equipment which accumulated from almost 40 years of nuclear bomb building. During this period hundreds of large tanks were filled with toxic chemicals which are residues from plutonium processing. These tanks, buried underground at various sites around the country, are now beginning to leak. In addition, thousands of 55-gallon drums of chemicals and low-level nuclear waste have been plowed underground. Finally, several large processing factories must be dismantled—factories crammed with tanks and pipes which make it almost impossible for a vehicle to move around inside. The risks of radiation and chemical toxicity are considered too great for human workers, even with protective clothing. The work will have to be done by teleoperators and telerobots.

Construction

There are many types of teleoperator needs in construction, and they pose rather different technological demands (and have for many years, since this was an early teleoperator application). One need is earth removal: roughly specified displacements of material must be made while forces encountered may vary over a wide range. This is a problem where "impedance control" (see discussion below) may have potential. A second need is assembly of building components—not unlike assembly in manufacturing, except that the grasping, transporting, and positioning are on a large scale and are not exactly repetitive. Common assembly operations on bricks or other building components must be continually reindexed to new coordinates or performed relative to previous work, always at a new spatial location.

Also in this category are teleoperators for reaching up to repair power lines, cut limbs from trees, perform inspection or maintenance on bridges, or wash windows of high buildings. In many of these applications the end manipulation or inspection operation is not so exacting, but relatively large forces must be exerted at relatively long cantilever distances from a convenient base (such as the ground). Alternatively, local attachment receptacles may be "built in" at various locations in structures such that a second "holding arm" can attach near the work site and support local reaction forces.

Agriculture

Agricultural teleoperation is an attractive approach for large-scale farms and is just beginning. Typically this means remote driving of one or more tractors, as well as remote control of furrowing, planting, or picking attachments. Local intelligence may control speed to a set point, keep a vehicle on a straight course across a field relative to an infrared or other sensor/emitter, turn the vehicle at the end of a designated row and align it for the next row, and adjust height or other variables relating to the attachment.

Mining

Mines have always been hazardous environments, and over recent centuries mining accidents have resulted in thousands of deaths. Typically operators are located on or adjacent to the cutting and transporting machinery, the most hazardous location possible. There has been limited automation in the form of "longwall" and "highwall" semi-automated continuous coal mining systems. The US Bureau of Mines has experimented with direct teleoperation of a tractor vehicle with a manipulator/cutter arm controlled over a cable by a protected human operator located some distance back up the mineshaft. In addition to three closed-circuit video channels, operators were provided information about the cutting auger, including sounds, vehicle pitch and roll, hydraulic fluid and filter variables, methane concentrations, temperature, and electrical power loads. One general problem in coal mining is sensing where coal seams are and deciding where to cut. A second problem is that of communication. Dragging a cable is not satisfactory, because the cable is likely to get caught or abraded or broken; radio or sound waves are occluded, because mine shafts and tunnels are not straight. If operating energy can be stored on board the teleoperator, this could be a good application for disposable optical-fiber line unreeled and laid down as the vehicle moves into the mine.

Warehousing and mail delivery

Automated warehouses, wherein telerobotic vehicles are guided locally by optical or magnetic strips on the floor and programmed globally by remote human operators, have been in operation for years. When the vehicle reaches its designated location it stops, raises its grasping device (usually a specially designed fork-lift, two-jaw grasper or vacuum device sized for the particular packages or containers being used in that facility) to the height of the proper bin, retrieves the package or container located there, collapses down to its original height, and delivers its cargo to a dispatching location. Warehouses specially designed for such operations have bins much higher than the reach of a human worker, and thus much more can be stored and retrieved in a given amount of ground space.

Mail-delivery telerobots are similar, in the sense that buildings must be modified to accommodate them. They usually move down office corridors slowly to avoid accidents with human workers, beeping and flashing to call attention to themselves. Typically such vehicles do not have manipulators to handle the mail. Designated individuals must pick up the mail from the vehicle.

Firefighting and lifesaving

To build a firefighting telerobot is both an engineering challenge and a humane challenge. The telerobot must enter burning buildings at extreme temperatures, open doors and climb stairs, relay back to the human operator visual information about the location of persons or valuable property, and grasp and and carry incapacitated persons from the building. Possibly as well, this telerobot could sense the location of the most intense fire and/or smoke, and carry means to fight the fire itself. To the author's knowledge, the development of such a telerobot has been discussed but the funding has been negligible.

Policing

One policing function is that of sentry duty—guarding the security of factories, stores, or other buildings during non-working hours. There are now sentry telerobots that can be programmed to travel on preplanned courses and schedules. These carry both video cameras and microphones, but can also be manually controlled directly by the central human monitor. Many electromechanical sentries may be monitored and controlled by a single human sentry.

Military operations

Teleoperators have become very attractive to military technologists as means to extend a soldier's viewing or manipulation functions to some dangerous location without exposing the soldier to the danger. Examples of this are inspection and deactivation of mines and other explosives, observation of enemy operations without exposure to enemy fire, and remotely piloted aircraft. The current talk of "battlefield robotics" usually means teleoperators, since human operators are still very much needed. Even in "Star Wars" technology it is difficult to imagine that ultimate responsibility would be given over to a computer without capability for updating programs and direct human intervention when necessary. Further comments will be made below concerning military uses of teleoperator/telerobotics technology and the social implications.

Assistive devices for the disabled

New developments in arm prostheses include elegant digital processing of myoelectric signals and high-power-density mechanical actuators, augmented by impressively natural-looking hands. Motorized wheelchairs are available which climb stairs or have special wheel arrangements which can drive the wheelchair in any direction or rotation. For quadraplegics there are telerobots to aid in feeding or other simple assistive manipulation tasks which the patient controls with head, mouth, or tongue motion, or voice, or some combination of these. Such telerobots can be attached to a wheelchair or a bed, or are able to wheel themselves around the room. Because they are working in such close proximity to people's faces, they must be absolutely fail-safe.

All these systems must conform to a very special requirement for telerobots in this application area, namely that they must be cosmetically acceptable to the user, and not appear too awkward or call attention to themselves. Handicapped persons will often sacrifice function in order to avoid looking foolish.

Technology developments in this area are currently held back by economics. Such devices cannot be mass-produced to "fit" all patients. Different patients have very different needs, e.g., have different capabilities for communication with the device. Furthermore, research funding is limited, and users are dependent upon insurance companies or other third-party payers to purchase or maintain the devices.

Telediagnosis

The term *telediagnosis* refers to a physician diagnosing a patient by remote means, for example over a combined video-audio communication link. Such a link was set up in the late 1960s between the large hospitals of downtown Boston and Logan Airport after an aircraft accident in which ambulances were blocked by rush-hour traffic jams in the tunnel connecting the airport to downtown and many persons died for lack of medical attention. Trials with this telediagnosis communication link proved that with only a nurse or a paramedic physically present with the patient, adequate diagnosis of minor trauma could be rendered by a remote physician, and the nurse could then provide whatever therapy was immediately necessary. The evaluation experiments included controls whereby the physician could pan, tilt, and zoom the video camera, and in one experiment could teleoperate a six-degree-of-freedom positioning device by moving the display monitor to view the patient (figure 2.13). This was an early implementation of telepresence, to be discussed more fully later in this chapter. Experiments were also done with remote video viewing of x-ray pictures and with remote video psychiatric interviews. One psychiatrist commented to the author that his patients told him they felt "the TV provided an especially close relationship" between them and the doctor.

Experiments (unpublished) were also performed at the MIT Man-Machine Systems Laboratory to evaluate the use of a commercial force-reflecting master-slave manipulator to perform auscultation (e.g., positioning a stethoscope and listening for breath sounds) and palpation (e.g., feeling for enlarged organs). It was shown that stethoscope positioning was satisfactory, but palpation of organs was not. Presumably use of the telemanipulator masked the necessary tactile discrimination.

Telesurgery

Surgery is an application for teleoperators that offers great promise but at the same time poses severe demands.

One form of teleoperator is the endoscope, a coherent fiber-optic bundle with tubes for conveying fluids to or from the distal end point, wires for modifying its curvature so it can be maneuvered around corners, and

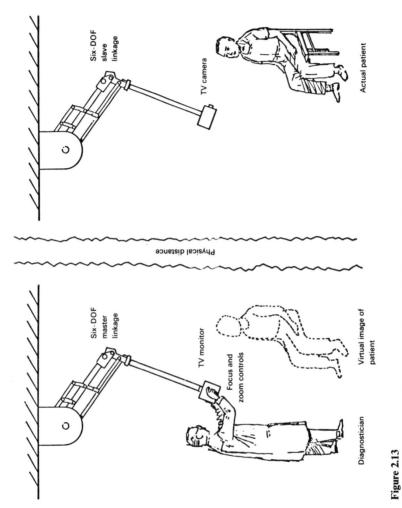

Figure 2.13
Medical telediagnosis using movable display with slave camera to provide telepresence.
User can position display to any viewpoint and thereby have sensation that remote patient
is on the other side of the TV monitor.

additional wires operating an end-point gripper or snare or cauterizer. Such devices, when inserted into the gastrointestinal tract (from either end),have proven very successful for inspection, biopsy, and simple surgery, often saving much cost and patient inconvenience over more radical surgical procedures. Similar devices are now routinely inserted into skeletal joints so that pieces of bone or other tissue can be cut and removed or other repair work can be done without laying open the inner tissue and exposing it to infection. Such teleoperators may be used in the near future in other surgery where sites to be diagnosed or treated are not accessible to the physician's direct vision.

In eye surgery, old equipment—an array of multiple optical mechanisms, separate lights and computer displays, switches, adjustment knobs, stop cocks, and foot controls—is being replaced by integrated displays and controls which are simpler to operate. Time-consuming and error-prone verbal communications with the nurse to perform various actions during surgery are eliminated. Six-DOF vitroretinal (retinal surgery) teleoperators with bilateral force feedback and adjustable gain from master to slave down to a resolution of a few microns are being designed.

Entertainment

The Sarcos Company has developed for the theme-park industry a rather impressive array of programmable anthropomorphic robots which can be dressed in human clothing, face masks, and skin-like gloves and made to mimic very realistically people dancing, singing, and gesturing (figure 2.14). Currently these are not telerobots, since once programmed they simply perform the same routines on cue; they have telerobot potential, however. For example, they could serve to perform improvisational dance or acting—a computer-mediated extension of the marionette (an early and pure form of manual teleoperator). They could be made to respond to voices or gestures of other people. There are many obvious applications to entertainment.

2.3   Teleoperator Configurations and Coordinates

Comparative requirements for anthropomorphic telerobotics

Table 2.1 compares various kinds of telerobots with respect to a number of criteria. These are classes of teleoperators. Within any class there are

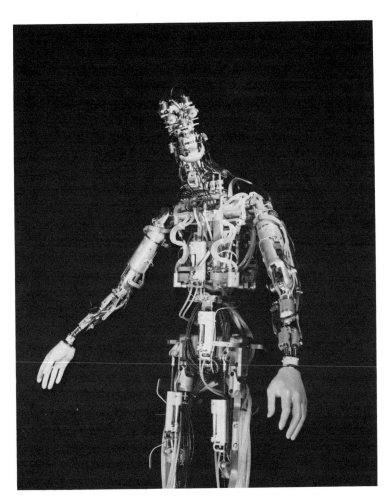

Figure 2.14
Sarcos programmable robot for theme parks. [Courtesy of Sarcos Corp.]

Table 2.1

Basis of comparison	Space (NASA/DOD)	Undersea (oil/science/DOD)	Nuclear, chemical	Police, fire, defense (land)	Discrete parts manufacturing
hostility to humans	vacuum, zero G, heat	high pressure	radiation, toxicity	fire, active enemy	none
hostility to hardware	vacuum, heat/cold	high pressure, salts	corrosion, radiation	fire, active enemy	dirt, heat
preprogrammability	high	medium	low to medium	low	high
level of production	low	low to med	medium	low	high
range of mobility	deep space	ocean bottom	100 m	1000 m	10 m
speed of mobility	wide range	5 m/s	2 m/s	10 m/s	1 m/s
obstacles to mobility	none	ocean bottom	complex structures	buildings, trees	factory floors
range of manipulation	10 m	2 m	10 m	2 m	2 m
accuracy of manipulation	0.001 m	0.002 m	0.002 m	0.005 m	0.0001 m
speed of manipulation	0.2 m/s	0.5 m/s	2 m/s	2 m/s	5 m/s
forces of manipulation	0.1 Kg	1000 Kg	5000 Kg	300 Kg	300 Kg
complexity of manipulation	low	medium	medium	medium	high
reliability	very high	high	very high	medium	medium

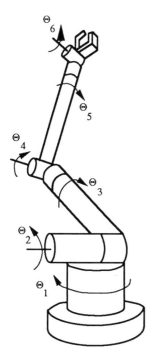

Figure 2.15
Alternating twist and bend arm links provide simplest kinematic equations.

tasks with widely varying requirements. It is evident that with respect to
these classes some requirements (such as range of manipulation) differ by
only one order of magnitude while others (such as manipulation force) differ
by four or five orders of magnitude.

Kinematics of serial-link manipulator arms

Teleoperator kinematics and dynamics is a very large problem area involving much current effort, especially since it is a problem shared with
factory robotics. Because the theory is well documented, it will not be
engaged here to any extent.

Most master and slave arms are serial-link kinematic chains with rotational joints. In several common serial arms (such as that shown in figure
2.15), bend and twist articulations alternate. Occasionally a sliding joint
has been used, as in the Salisbury/JPL master arm shown in figure 2.16.

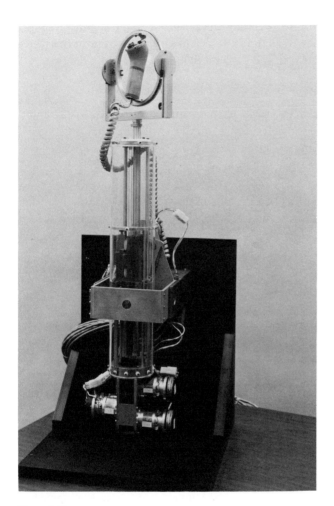

Figure 2.16
Salisbury/JPL six-DOF master arm. Operator's handle is at top in this view. All DOF are
rotational except one (shown in vertical direction here). [Courtesy of Jet Propulsion
Laboratory, California Institute of Technology.]

When **q** is a vector representing the positions (joint angles or sliding displacements) of the articulations, **x** is set of six end-point positions (three of which are orientations), and **f** is a set of functions relating the two,

$$\mathbf{x} = \mathbf{f}(\mathbf{q})$$

is the *direct kinematics*. In a series chain its solution amounts to a straightforward series of trigonometric operations. Determining what the articulations should be to obtain a given x, i.e.

$$\mathbf{q} = \mathbf{f}^{-1}(\mathbf{x}),$$

is called the *inverse kinematics*. Because of the trigonometric nonlinearities, the inverse kinematics is not trivial to solve. For six-DOF arms and special geometries there are closed-form solutions (Featherstone 1983). If the equations are linearized around an operating point for small changes in the variables with respect to time or another argument,

$$\Delta \mathbf{x} = \mathbf{J} \Delta \mathbf{q},$$

where **J** is called the Jacobian, and the elements $J_{ij} = \partial f_i / \partial q_j$, then there are much more robust techniques available to perform the inversion (Whitney 1969c). There are also a number of iterative solution methods (Uicker, Denavit, and Hartenberg 1964). Powerful new kinematic computational methods and associated nonlinear control techniques have extended the mechanical prowess of manipulator arms (Featherstone 1983; Asada and Slotine 1986).

Utah-NOSC arm

As of this writing, the most sophisticated and best performing force-reflecting master-slave arm/hand is the University of Utah developmental arm being built for the Naval Ocean Systems Center in Hawaii (Jacobson et al. 1989). It is pictured in figure 2.17. The master and slave arms have the same kinematics, each with seven degrees of freedom, while the hand control and the end effector each have three DOF. The latter include a two-DOF thumb and a one-DOF spreading finger. A second finger is fixed to the wrist.

Parallel-link arm

An alternative to the common serial-link kinematic configuration has been demonstrated by Landsberger and Sheridan (1985); see figure 2.18. This

Figure 2.17
Utah-NOSC electro-hydraulic teleoperator system. [Courtesy of University of Utah.]

cable-controlled six-DOF parallel-link configuration has the following advantages over serial-link arms: higher stiffness-to-weight ratio, because no bending members are required; higher end-point force capability, because links act in parallel; all actuators are mounted on the base, thereby reducing inertia by a large factor; inertial properties are relatively invariant with respect to position; cable capstan drive eliminates gear and joint backlash; all six cable actuator subsystems are identical, making manufacture cheaper; cable links and spine collapse to a small rest size; the compressive spine may be adjusted to any desired compliance; the forward loop specification of actuator position, given any desired end-point position, is an easy calculation and does not require inverting a Jacobian. Disadvantages are that the arm cannot "bend around" objects, that the arm's strength deteriorates at greater than 45° from the symmetric axis, and that wrist rotation is limited to about 50°.

Because proportional computer control was found to inflict large accelerations and hence sudden loads on the cables of this manipulator, Chao

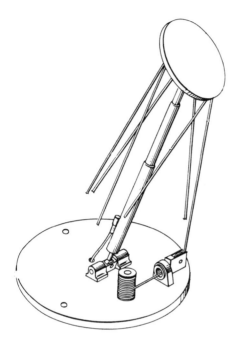

Figure 2.18
Landsberger's parallel-link manipulator. Central compressive spring is gimbal-joint-mounted on both upper plate (wrist) and lower plate (base). Six cables are independently controlled by winch motors on base to position wrist in six DOF.

(1989) developed an active "path smoothing" scheme which has advantages over passive filtering. The computer monitors the feedback signal and sends new commands to the controller only when such signals will not cause the manipulator to exceed given acceleration limits. Chao's addition reduced maximum cable accelerations tenfold, greatly enhancing smoothness, without seeming to affect the overall speed of operation.

Controlling redundant-link arms

An advantage of the conventional serial-link arm, and presumably a reason why animal limbs evolved as serial kinematic chains, is that the serial-link arm can reach around obstacles once the number of joints (or degrees of freedom) is greater than six. This principle of redundancy can be demonstrated in a thought (or actual) experiment with a planar three-link serial arm, where the two end points are fixed. The middle link is seen to be free to rotate.

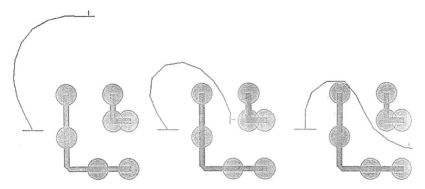

Figure 2.19
Das' computer simulation of shared control of redundant-link manipulator. Curved line is simulated 12-link arm fixed at one end. The human operator drives end-point of arm, while computer determines that configuration which best avoids contact with obstacles (shaded).

Whereas the direct kinematics are straightforward, as before, solution of the inverse kinematics in this case requires additional constraints; otherwise the solutions are infinite. Das (1989) reviews the literature for redundant solutions and proposes a new algorithm which is a hybrid of the generalized inverse and steepest-descent procedures. The problem was formulated as constrained optimization, where the end effector's position and orientation are set by the human operator and the intermediate links are constrained by a hypothetical set of springs connecting each joint to obstacles in the field of manipulation which one seeks to avoid.

Das demonstrated analytically and experimentally that this algorithm is stable with rapid convergence and thus operates nicely in real time. He then set up experiments with human subjects continuously moving the arm's end point through a field of fixed obstacles to a designated target (all portrayed on a computer display), while the computer took care that the intermediate structure did not collide with the obstacles. In a first case the arm had twelve DOF. (Figure 2.19 shows the idea with a stick-figure arm, spherical objects, and a succession of "snapshots" of the operation.) In a second (kinematically equivalent) case there was a six-DOF arm attached to a six-DOF vehicle, both to be controlled simultaneously. In the second case the human operator controlled the arm's end point with a six-axis track ball while the computer controlled both the arm joints and the vehicle position to circumvent the obstacles. Experimental results showed that, when compared with the situation where the human operator had to control all twelve DOF, computer-control of redundant DOF was much quicker and also better in terms of obstacle avoidance.

Teleoperator hands (end effectors)

Multi-degree-of-freedom general-purpose hands resembling human hands seem a most obvious need, but the sad fact is that these have not been developed beyond a few laboratory prototypes. Most commercial manipulators have simple parallel-jaw grippers. A few have claws, magnetic or air-suction gripping mechanisms, or attachment devices for welding, paint spraying, or other special purposes.

Interchangeable end-effector tools provide another way to accomplish versatility, much as carpenters, surgeons, and other craftsmen do interchange end-effector tools as they work. Future teleoperators may incorporate a great variety of interchangeable tools, for both modifying and measuring the environment, as well as general-purpose hands. It is not yet clear how to make the trade between special and general-purpose end-effectors, but this problem calls for research.

Experimentation with multi-DOF hands is still in its infancy. Two such hands widely used for experimental purposes are the Salisbury hand (figure 2.20) and the Utah-MIT hand (see Salisbury 1981; Jacobson et al. 1986).

Operator hand controls

The most popular operator hand controls are the articulated master arm and the joystick.

Most articulated master arms have been used for master-slave positioning. Usually these have been kinematically isomorphic to the slave in construction. They need not be, however, so long as they have the same number of DOF as the slave and as long as the end-point direction of motion of the master and the slave correspond—the computer can do the coordinate transformations. The master should be sized to the convenience of the operator—it need not be the same size as the slave. Its full range of motion must conform both to the available space and to the operator's reach; at the same time there must be enough movement that small random muscle movements do not produce significant command signals. These constraints on both ends limit the dynamic range. Master arms as small as 1 foot in total length are in use. Master-slave position control provides quick and natural repositioning, but relatively poor ability to

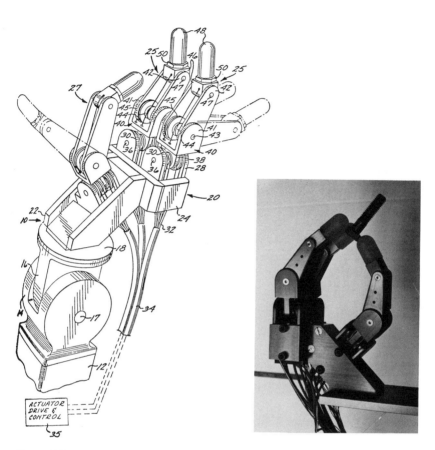

Figure 2.20
Salisbury hand. [Courtesy of K. Salisbury.]

move very slowly. Figure 2.16 shows a master arm designed by Salisbury for the Jet Propulsion Laboratory.

The joystick is commonly available in up to three degrees of freedom, is normally spring centered, and commands an end-effector (or vehicle) rate proportional to joystick displacement. It can also command acceleration. There is usually kinematic resolution by computer, so that end-effector movement direction corresponds to joystick movement independent of the arm configuration. A slight electrical dead zone is usually added to prevent inadvertent drifting of the arm in any particular direction. The joystick permits high positioning accuracy, but at the cost of relatively slow repositioning movements. In six-DOF applications two joysticks have typically been used: one to command translation in three DOF and one to command rotation in three DOF.

There have been several six-axis joystick designs, one of which (developed by the German firm DLR) uses optical transducers, and a similar device called the "Space Ball" in the US. Mostly these are isometric devices

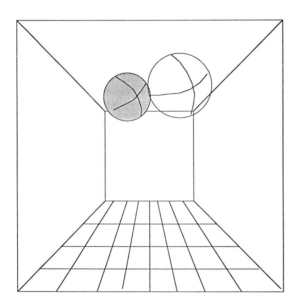

Figure 2.21
Roseborough's six-axis tracking display. Aligning the six-axis (white) cursor with the six-axis (shaded) target requires translation in z until the sizes of the circles are the same, translation in x and y to make the circles coincide, and rotation in three axes until the cross-hairs coincide.

(very stiff "force-sticks"). There has been some question about how well an operator can use such a device to control all six axes at once.

Massimino et al. (1989a) experimentally measured human tracking capability using such a six-axis "sensor-ball" and the tracking display shown in figure 2.21. The idea was to keep the two balls aligned horizontally and vertically and of the same size (front-back indication) and to keep the cross hairs on the cursor and the target together. RMS errors were measured and compared for tracking on one and three axes at a time as well as on all six, and where sensor-ball force commanded both rate and acceleration. Massimino found that translational movement perpendicular to the display screen produced significantly more RMS error than did horizontal or vertical translations. Performance in rotational DOF did not differ significantly from one to another. Rate control was better than acceleration control, as expected. With more simultaneous DOF, performance on any one axis deteriorated. Figure 2.22 illustrates the translation results.

Some newly developed commercial sensors that can be used to do six-axis positioning have the advantage over the conventional master-arm that they can be positioned freely in space without a mechanical link to a

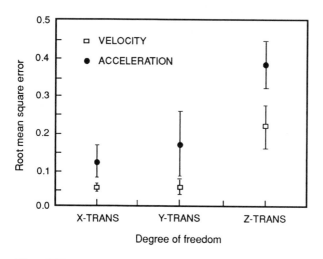

Figure 2.22
Massimino's results of tracking with six-axis sensor ball. Subjects simultaneously tracked in all six degrees of freedom, using the display shown in figure 2.21. The graph shows the component translation errors in x, y, and z. Data points are averages of six subjects. Vertical lines indicate one standard deviation.

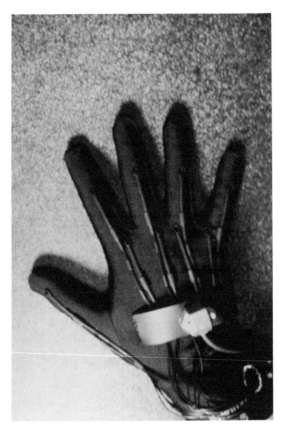

Figure 2.23
VPL DataGlove. [Courtesy of VPL Corp.]

fixed base. The Polhemus sensor is a six-DOF electromagnetic system consisting of a transmitter and a receiver, each slightly bigger than a cubic centimeter. When one is moved relative to the other, provided they are not separated by more than a meter and provided there is little interference from nearby metal objects, the change in their relative position is measured in all six DOF to within several millimeters in translation and roughly 1° in rotation.

The VPL DataGlove (figure 2.23) is a nylon glove worn by the operator. It has optical fibers embedded on the dorsal side of each finger and the thumb. When any joint flexes, light passing through the optical fiber serving that joint is reduced because of scattering, and this is a measure of the flexure of the optical fiber. Unfortunately the glove tends to slip on the skin, the bends of the fibers do not coincide one-to-one with the operator's finger-joint rotations, and both may have different kinematics from the teleoperator hand being used. Therefore the control of teleoperation is neither precise nor consistent, and it may be necessary to perform rather complex calibrations in order for satisfactory open-loop mapping from operator hand pose to teleoperator hand pose to be achieved (Hong and Tan 1989; Pao and Speeter 1989). The Exos articulated multi-DOF hand goniometer (figure 2.24) serves a similar function but consists of a pin-jointed multi-segment exoskeleton worn on the hand, with Hall-effect sensors to measure joint rotations. It is bulkier but more accurate than the DataGlove.

Using other motor outputs to signal the computer

Body limbs other than hands have been used as means of control, the most common example being the clutch, brake, and accelerator pedals of auto-mobiles. The lower limbs, because of their mass, are not the fastest means of control, but they do give the advantage of large force capability, which was a good reason for assigning them to operate brake and clutch pedals prior to the time of power assist.

Head motion and eye motion are other means for the operator to signal the computer. Head motion can be measured by mechanical linkages attached to helmets or by electromagnetic or optical trackers. Eye tracking instruments are now readily available and of high quality, and are widely used to measure eye scan paths. Mostly these follow a pattern of 50-msec saccades (rapid movements which are quite unpredictable in direction and extent of movement and which seem to depend on the information "of

Figure 2.24
EXOS hand goniometer. [Courtesy of Exos Corp.]

interest" in the image) followed by 200–500-msec dwell periods, during which the brain presumably reads in the information.

Using these for human output, however, constrains the use of head and eye motion to scan visual displays (especially with telepresence and virtual presence systems) and is not generally recommended for aiming or for cursor control. The military services once experimented with head and eye motion for aircraft and tank pilots to aim guns (and as a result came a number of jokes about inadvertent head scratching and random eye fixations on the gunnery range).

In the case of quadraplegics, where no motor output is available from the neck down, telerobotic devices have been commanded by head motion, eye motion and blinking, tongue motion, and voice. (Voice command is discussed further below under *supervisory command language*.)

Operator-resolved and task-resolved coordinates

Operator-resolved manipulation means that the operator can move or rotate her own hand and have the teleoperator end effector move or rotate in the same direction, independent of the kinematic configuration of the master or slave arm segments or joint positions. This is achieved by using the Jacobian (Whitney 1969b) for resolving the velocity of the slave in correspondence to the velocity of the master.

Task-resolved manipulation means that the operator can order the teleoperator end effector to move or apply force in a coordinate system referenced to a normal to the surface of a large object or environmental structure such as a ship or a pipe (Yoerger and Slotine 1987). This requires sensing that surface in the process of manipulating and continually performing coordinate transformations to update the axes with respect to which the operations are being done This is an extension of end-point resolution—ability to command the finger to move in a desired trajectory without having to worry about how to move all the joints between the finger and the shoulder.

Having the computer "nullify" known disturbances

It is sometimes useful to employ relatively straightforward and conventional feedback control to minimize disturbances that occur with respect to some variable while that same variable is being controlled in parallel or at a higher level by a human. This occurs, for example, in remote manipulation of objects undersea, where the manipulator base is sometimes a mobile

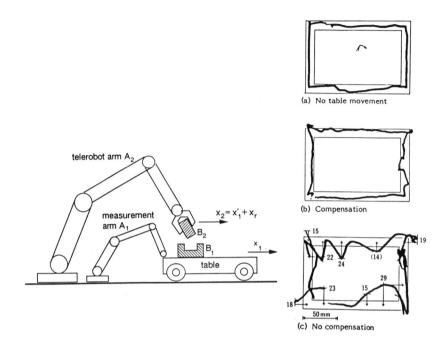

Figure 2.25
Tani's and Hirabayashi's experiments in manual telemanipulation with compensation of relative motions. On the left is shown the experimental setup. To position block B_2 relative to block B_1, when B_1 is subject to random table movement x_1 and there was no compensation, human controlling arm A_2 had to include both compensation for x_1 and the desired relative motion x_r. When x_1 was measured optically or mechanically (e.g., by measurement arm A_1) compensation x_1' could be provided automatically; the human needed only supply x_r. If the video camera was fixed, the human necessarily saw both x_1 and x_1' movements. In Tani's experiment both x_1 and x_2 were in three DOF, while in Hirabayashi's they were in six DOF. At the right are examples of Tani's results for path-tracing task for (a) no table movement, (b) compensation for table movement, and (c) uncompensated table movement.

submarine or vehicle which may move relative to the object being manipulated, so that either direct manual control or supervisory control is difficult. This relative motion occurs either because a manipulator is being supported by a vehicle which is hard to hold steady against a surge of ocean current or other unpredictable disturbances, or because the object being manipulated is being buffeted, or both. The same problem could occur in space during docking, or in terrestrial mechanical manipulation. One way to overcome this is to make some measurement of the relative changes in displacement and orientation between manipulator base and object, by optical, sonic, or mechanical means, and then to compensate for these changes by added motion of the manipulator end effector. Tani (1980) experimentally demonstrated the advantages of such compensation for three-degree-of-freedom tasks. Figure 2.25 illustrates his setup and results.

Hirabayashi (1981) also implemented a disturbance measurement and compensation scheme experimentally. He constructed a six-degree-of-freedom (all angular movement) measurement arm which was lightweight and flaccid (offered little restraint). A six-degree-of-freedom Jacobian matrix transformation then allowed determination of the relative displacement of any object to which the measurement arm was attached. Hirabayashi set up a continuous random positioning apparatus (three degrees of freedom, roughly 0.2 Hz bandwidth, 6 inches RMS amplitude) to move a task board into which pegs were to be inserted. He then attached the measurement arm to this task board, and used the resulting measurement of displacement to produce a compensatory displacement bias between the master and the slave. When the arm was under computer control it compensated to within 0.2 inches, even with a crude 3-foot-long measurement arm. Then computer compensation was added to manual master-slave control of actions relative to the moving object. It was found to be much easier for the operator to put pegs into the holes in the moving task board with the compensation than without it.

2.4 Supervisory Command Language

Currently there is great interest in how best to transfer knowledge from the human brain (knowledge representation, mental model) into a corresponding representation of procedures or model within a computer, and how best to transfer what the computer "understands" back to the human. The former is commonly thought of as the "teaching" problem. However, the latter—how confirmation of what has been taught is communicated back to the human teacher—is also a critical component.

There are several ways to teach a telerobot. One is by explicit programming (concatenation of symbols which the computer "understands"). This can be done by means of "low-level" code (e.g., "Move joint 5 at rate $+R$ until $\theta_5 = 374$"), or it can be done at a "high level" (e.g., "Put the large peg in the far hole" or "put *that* peg in *that* hole"). Alternatively, teaching can be done by space-force-time demonstration, where every aspect of the demonstration is recorded for precise playback at a later time, or more likely where only particular variables at particular times are indicated to be remembered and later used. There can also be combinations of these methods. Various methods and experiments are described below.

Manipulating objects and their representations

As mankind has evolved there are two ways in which the human body has affected its environment: by manipulation and by communication. Both can be called "tool using." In manipulation, humans have used their hands, or other parts of the body or mechanical tools in the hands, to apply forces and displacements to physically modify the environment. In communication, the vocal cords or other parts of the body have been used as tools to make representations for others to observe and understand. As we move toward computer mediation in performing tasks, we necessarily move more toward using our bodies more for communication than for direct manipulation.

The correspondence between human verbal language and digital computer language has been widely appreciated. Both are thought of as alphanumeric strings which have meaning as a function of their syntax and parsability. What seems not to have been so widely appreciated is the close correspondence between human verbal language and human manipulation of objects in the physical environment. This lack of appreciation is all the more surprising since the subject-verb-object sentence (with appropriate modifiers on each) corresponds rather directly to the hand-action-tool "sentence," or more generally the logic of hand/tool-action upon-external object. It has taken the artifact of the teleoperator to make us aware of this close relation. But we still do not have fully satisfactory representational languages for manipulation.

Symbolic and analogic command languages

Teaching or programming a manipulation or mobility task, including specification of a goal state and a procedure for achieving it, and including necessary constraints and criteria, can be formidable or quite easy, depending upon the command hardware and software. By *command hardware* is meant the way in which human motor action—hand, foot, or voice—is converted to physical signals to the computer. Command hardware can be either *analogic* or *symbolic*.

Analogic command means that there is a spatial or temporal isomorphism between human response, semantic meaning, and/or feedback display. For example, moving a control up rapidly to increase the magnitude of a variable quickly, which causes a display indicator to move up quickly, would be a proper analogic correspondence. Pointing to an object to identify it is another example of analogic command. Manual force or position tracking amounts to continuous analogic command.

Symbolic command, by contrast, is accomplished by depressing one or a series of keys (as when typing words on a typewriter), or uttering one or a series of sounds (as in speaking a sentence), each of which has a distinguishable meaning. For symbolic commands, a particular series or concatenation of such responses has a different meaning from other concatenations. Spatial or temporal correspondence to the meaning or the desired result is not requisite. Sometimes analogic and symbolic can be combined, e.g., where up-down keys are both labeled and positioned accordingly.

It is natural for humans to intermix analogic and symbolic commands or even to use them simultaneously. This happens, for example, when one talks and points at the same time, or plays the piano and conducts a choir with one's head.

Both analogic and symbolic commands may be used by a human operator for communication at any of Rasmussen's three levels—knowledge-based, rule-based, or skill-based behavior of the human supervisor. For example, demonstrating to a telerobot what the operator deems to be a "graceful" movement would be knowledge-based analogic command, done with reference only to complex criteria in the operator's head rather than to easily specified rules. Pointing to objects to identify them is clearly rule-based analogic instruction—rules being implemented in the operator's head which can be transferred through hand motions to the computer

Table 2.2
Examples of symbolic and analogic control at three behavioral levels.

Behavioral basis	Communication codes	
	Continuous analogic	Discrete symbolic
knowledge	play charades	write a computer program
rule	point to a named object	name an object pointed to
skill	draw an O	type an O

cursor. Guiding the robot in a straight line or at a constant speed is skill-based analogic command.

Alphanumeric symbols could also be used to instruct the telerobot to make a graceful movement, but they might better serve to communicate knowledge-based heuristics for avoiding obstacles or making tactile discriminations (which cannot be done so easily by analogic demonstration). Symbols might be better than analog demonstration for communicating to the telerobot how to draw given geometric figures like squares or triangles, since the figures might end up being more precise. This and naming of objects pointed to would be rule-based. Simply typing a well-learned sequence of letters or numbers would be a skill-based symbolic communication.

Table 2.2 illustrates these relationships.

Borrowings from industrial robot command language

Early industrial robots could be programmed by means of "teach pendants" (small hand-held switch boxes) by which the teacher, standing adjacent to the robot, could command its joint movements one DOF at a time, thus programming simple routines which could be refined and later replayed many times for assembly-line operations. More sophisticated teach-pendant command structures gradually allowed the teaching of commands for start, stop, speed, etc. between various reference positions, conditional branching conditions, and arbitrarily defined macros (Nof 1985).

The early robots also had explicit "mid-level" symbolic command languages, such as Ernst's MH-1 (1961) and Unimation's PAL and HAL (Snyder 1985; Nof 1985). Barber's MANTRAN (1967) was an early attempt to build a higher-level language useful for "one-of-a-kind-and-right-now" human-to-telerobot commands. Paul (1981) reviews the computational aspects of robot command language.

Brooks' SUPERMAN, and comparison of alternative supervisory teaching modes

T. Brooks (1979) developed a high-level command system he called SU-PERMAN which allowed the supervisor to use a master arm to identify objects and command elemental motions in terms of those objects. He showed that even without time delay such supervisory control—including both teaching and execution—often took less time and had fewer errors than manual control. In terms of figure 1.10, closed-loop control within loop 3, once initiated, often proved quicker and more precise than that over loops 1 and 6.

Brooks first developed software to enable the supervisor to teach the computer by performing a manipulation with the master arm of an Argonne E2 manipulator and simultaneously code the objects and the movements using a symbolic keyboard. Later, when the human operator required a particular already-trained manipulation, she simply "initialized" a new coordinate system relative to the old one by moving the teleoperator hand to the starting point of the task (e.g., grasping a particular nut or valve handle) and signaling for execution on "this" object. The computer auto-matically retransformed the old coordinates to a new coordinate system and performed the desired task, possibly also following commands to terminate the execution at a previously identified location or object.

Brooks' supervisory programs could, upon certain touch conditions' becoming true, branch into other programs. For example, the telerobot hand could grasp a nut, unscrew it half a turn, pull back to test whether it was off, and, if it was, place it in a (previously located by this demonstration procedure) bucket, or if it was not, repeat the operation.

Six manipulation tasks were identified for experimental investigation: retrieval of a tool from a rack, returning a tool to its rack, taking a nut off, grasping an object and placing it in a container, opening or closing a valve, and digging sand and putting it in a container. In addition, four manual control modes were employed: switch (on-off reverse, or fixed rate), joystick (variable rate), master-slave position control, and master-slave position control with force feedback. Both one-view and two-view (separate dis-plays, not stereo) video conditions were tested. For all these combinations of conditions both direct manual teleoperator and supervisory control were compared. Figure 2.26 plots typical results.

As would be expected, the time required by the computer to perform its portion of the task remained fixed regardless of the manual control mode

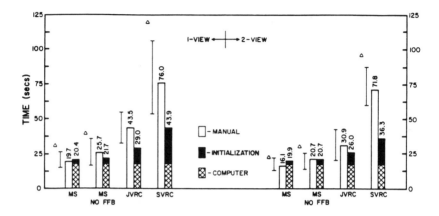

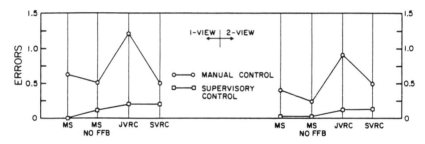

Figure 2.26
T. Brooks' results for SUPERMAN. Control modes: MS, master-slave with force feedback;
MS NO FFB, master-slave without force feedback; JVRC, joint variable rate control;
SVRC, switch variable rate control. The bars in the upper figure show the average time of
two trained subjects to perform a nut-removal task. Each Δ gives the average time for an
untrained subject. The capped lines represent the total range of data for the trained
subjects. The lower figure shows the average number of nut-removal errors (collisions or
dropping the nut) for the two trained subjects.

by which the human operator taught. As seen in figure 2.26, the initialization times increased with control complexity. Gains from supervisory control for any manual mode are seen to be most significant for tasks that do not require initialization procedures other than a button push (i.e., tool retrieval and tool return). The control mode columns clearly indicate that both forms of rate control can be aided by supervisory routines almost regardless of the task, that master-slave control without force feedback is worse than supervisory control in mating and related tasks in which there are force interactions with the environment, and that master-slave control with force feedback rarely benefits from supervisory control (assuming no significant time delay—see a later section concerning this special problem).

In all cases the error rates for supervisory control were lower than those for direct manual teleoperation. Theoretically there is no reason why master-slave control with force feedback should be any faster than supervisory control. Consider that the computer could simply mimic the human operator's best trajectory and hence be at least as fast. Unfortunately, in practice there is always a certain overhead associated with retransformation of coordinates, trajectory calculations, and sensor logic. Also, it was generally observed that the subjects were making adaptive motions, whereas the computer was limited to more rigidly defined trajectories and states.

Thus, even with no time delay, supervisory control was found to be more effective (as determined from the task completion times and manipulation errors) than switch rate control, joystick rate control, and master-slave position control. Bilateral force-reflecting master-slave control was found to be slightly faster than supervisory control but more prone to errors. Since the experiments were performed under "ideal" conditions, it could be predicted in 1979 that supervisory control would show an even greater advantage when used with degraded sensor or control loops (time delays, limited bandwidth, etc.).

Yoerger's experiments on teaching modes

Yoerger (1982) extended Brooks' work, developing a more extensive and robust supervisory command system that enabled a variety of arm-hand motions to be defined, called upon, and combined under other commands. In one set of experiments Yoerger compared three different procedures for teaching a robot arm to perform a continuous seam weld along a complex curved workpiece. The end effector (welding tool) had to keep 1 inch away, to retain an orientation perpendicular to the curved surface to be welded, and to move at constant speed.

Part of Yoerger's system was an on-line computer simulation and display that allowed motions of the manipulator to be simulated in all six DOF to test programs before they were actually executed. The operator could view the simulation from any angle, could translate or zoom the display, could run various simulations in faster than real time, and could then call for an actual execution of some already stored trajectory at some specified new location.

Yoerger tested his subjects in three command (teaching) modes using the simulation:

Continuous trajectory analogic demonstration. The human teacher first moved the master (with slave following in master-slave correspondence) relative to the workpiece in the desired trajectory. The computer would memorize the trajectory, and then cause the slave end effector to repeat the trajectory exactly.

Discrete point analogic specification with machine interpolation. The human teacher moved the master (and the slave) to each of a series of positions, pressing a key to identify each. The human supervisor would then key in additional information specifying the parameters of a curve to be fitted through these points and the speed at which it was to be executed, and the computer would then be called upon for execution.

Analogic specification of reference information and symbolic goal specification relative to the reference. In this mode the supervisor used the master-slave manipulator to contact and trace along the workpiece, to provide the computer with knowledge of the location and orientation of the surfaces to be welded. Then, using the keyboard, the supervisor would specify the positions and orientations of the end effector relative to the workpiece (e.g., to move along but 1 inch away from the designated surface at a given speed and a given angle). The computer could then execute the task instructions relative to the geometric references given.

Figure 2.27 diagrams Yoerger's task. Figure 2.28 shows the average results for three experimental subjects, based on running measures of both position error and orientation error in system performance after teaching in each of the three modes. Identifying the geometry of the workpiece analogically, and then giving symbolic instructions relative to it, proved the constant winner. It was further shown that the interface decreased the operator's dependence on visual feedback. The system decreased the vari-

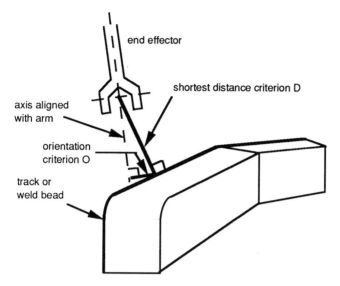

Figure 2.27
Yoerger's experimental task and measurement. Task was to guide end-effector (e.g., welding gun or x-ray inspection device) at constant velocity along a track (e.g., weld bead) curved in 3-space (e.g., heavy line in figure) while simultaneously keeping a constant distance away from and perpendicular to the track. Distance criterion (D) was the shortest distance to the track, orientation criterion (O) was the shortest distance between that line and the axis of the arm.

ability in performance between operators, and the computer graphic display helped the operator understand elements of the programming system without requiring a formal mathematical description of how the commands work.

Yoerger's results showed that analogic teaching can be especially useful when an operator does not know the exact coordinate values of a position but can see via the graphic or television display what she wants. Using analogic definitions in combination with symbolic commands simplifies the teaching of telerobotic tasks. Programs can be written in which the operator points (moves) to an object in the task environment and then describes an operation to be done on the object by specifying motions built on the previously defined positions. Using the relative commands, the arm may be moved relative to its current position and orientation. Such relative commands can be useful for describing tool motions, such as turning a valve or brushing a weld.

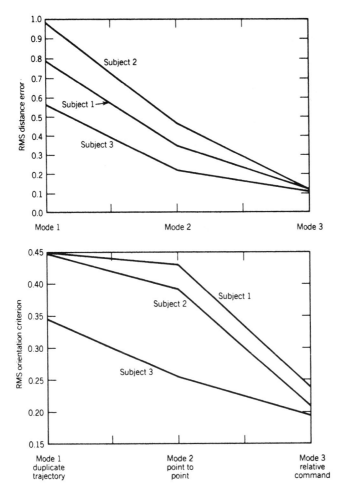

Figure 2.28
Yoerger's results for alternative methods of teaching. Mode 1: Human demonstrated full trajectory, computer reproduced it exactly. Mode 2: Human demonstrated series of discrete positions and orientations, computer connected them with smooth trajectory. Mode 3: Human indicated relevant surface of workpiece and specified trajectory relative to it with symbolic commands, computer executed as instructed.

The computer in Yoerger's setup could be instructed to make decisions during the control process using structured flow of control statements. Complicated tasks for the manipulator could be composed as a hierarchy of subtasks through the extensibility mechanisms of structured languages (this system was programmed in FORTH). Once the motions required for a particular task had been defined in a program and analogic data had been input regarding the environment, entire tasks could be accomplished with a single command.

Mouse-based object level control (S. Schneider and R. Cannon)

Using a planar three-DOF, two-arm manipulation task, Schneider and Cannon (1989) demonstrated a computer-graphic supervisory command interface that permitted the operator to move a mouse, click on an object to be moved, drag a "ghost object" to a desired new position, and then release the mouse button. The computer would then dutifully perform the operation. This was essentially similar to Brooks' method for identification by pointing at the object to be grasped and moved and to Yoerger's method of moving a computer-graphics-simulated manipulator to a point in simulated space as a means to specify the subtask goal for subsequent automatic execution.

Schneider and Cannon added two modes. In one the ghost object, when in proximity to a nominal target (say a peg in proximity to a hole), could be made to "snap" into a preprogrammed relation to the target (into the hole). In another mode, again using the mouse, the operator could attach one end of a ghost spring to an arbitrary point on a ghost object and the other end to a fixed point in the environment. The real object, when manipulated, would then assume the equivalent impedance characteristics. In general, equivalent stiffness, damping, and mass can be added in this manner in any independent direction. (See section 2.6 below.)

D. Cannon's experiments with "put that there"

D. Cannon (1992) conducted experiments in analogic task teaching in unstructured environments wherein the supervisor's role was limited to task conception and pointing, and the telerobot did the rest. (The phrase "put that there" was originally popularized by Bolt (1980) as a graphics interface technique.) Using a mobile robot with a six-DOF arm and two pan-tilt CCD video cameras mounted on a post (figure 2.29), the human

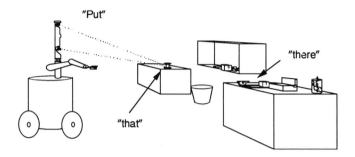

Figure 2.29
Cannon's ranging telerobot for "put-that-there" experiments. [Courtesy of D. Cannon.]

operator aimed camera reticles at the crucial objects and destinations to accomplish a real-world task. From camera angle triangulations, in concert with combinations of meaningful subphrases such as "put that...and that...there," the telerobot interactively built arm and mobile base trajectories for the immediate or delayed execution of tasks. The tasks involved objects and locations about which the robot had essentially no foreknowledge, such as putting tools in a tool box, items of trash in a wastebasket, and blocks on a pallet; all the items had been strewn randomly in a workspace. Cannon demonstrated that his technique reduced human supervisory control time and sped up task execution.

Such point-and-select and "ghost object manipulation" methods are a bridge between autonomous robotics and telemanipulation. Though point-and-select telerobots with autograsping and obstacle-avoidance systems can often operate in unstructured environments without any telemanipulation, a supervisor may be in a stronger position if she has hand/gripper telemanipulation and perhaps full robot telemanipulation (up to the number of DOF controllable) at times during or at the ends of some trajectories. Indeed, an operator may benefit from having a full set of options across the entire spectrum from autonomy to telemanipulation and using a point-and-select interface of some type to connect the two ends of the continuum. Perhaps this powerful combination can be achieved with very little overhead if the hardware and the software are chosen appropriately.

In cases involving significant time delays, the point-and-select approach eliminates the need for the move-and-wait stepping actions of telemanipulation. This is because destinations, rather than incremental motions, are prescribed so that the robot can move quickly and continuously between locations of importance. Task-specific criteria, such as proper welding speed and offset requirements, could be incorporated such that the phrase "weld from there to there" creates a routine that installs a welding rod and then, using proximity sensors, follows the contours of any curved surface between the two points while keeping the angle and the spacing of the rod correct for welding on that surface. The command "paint all but that" could become meaningful with advanced natural language systems. In all such cases, the role of the human remains at the highest level of supervisory control commensurate with defining tasks involving objects and destinations about which the robot has no specific foreknowledge.

M. Brooks' teaching of a finite-state machine

M. Brooks (1989) proposed a pattern-matching task controller for a telerobot which is taught by a human operator's demonstration of skill. Brooks' goal was to "replace statements like *IF force > 13, THEN* ... with statements like *IF match (data, pattern) THEN* ..., where *data* is the current multidimensional sensory state and *pattern* is learned during trial executions." Brooks visualized any given manipulation task as a network of a small number of component motions such as "grasp a tool," "move tool until touches workpiece," "use tool to clean," and "put tool back in rack." Each component motion had starting and stopping states which had sensory predicates attached, i.e., positions, velocities and forces which were likely to accompany those states in the context of doing that task. A task execution is a path through the network, which will not always be the same, but depends on what particular sensory predicates occur at any given termination state. Such a procedure is called a *finite-state machine*.

The system architecture is arranged as in figure 2.30. The human supervisor teaches by demonstration, signaling when a given motion starts and stops (i.e., when the start-termination states occur) and if she wants to give names to different states. During learning, the pattern-matching task controller records and correlates the motion states with the sensory data. Subsequently the supervisor can name a starting point and (presumably) the telerobot will perform the task from that point, generating the proper state transition when it recognizes the appropriate pattern of sensory data. Brooks notes that the human supervisor is teaching skill to the computer, not intelligence, and suggests that a scheme such as this is a good operational way to distinguish the two.

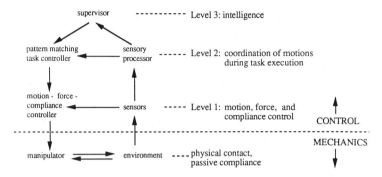

Figure 2.30
M. Brooks' telerobot architecture. [After M. Brooks 1989.]

Another of Brooks' stated goals was to construct sensor-based control
mechanisms that are unconditionally stable despite the use of *non-colocated*
sensors, where a *colocated* sensor measures a controlled state (actuator
position, velocity, or torque) *at* the site of actuation and the non-colocated
sensor measures it somewhere else. An example of the latter is a gripper
contact force sensor which is located in a wrist segment several inches and
one joint removed from the gripper point of contact. Non-colocated sensors
are unstable because physical dynamics intercede between the actuator and
the sensor. In Brooks' scheme sensor data are not used to close a servo-
feedback loop but merely to "trigger a finite-state machine at the rate of
at most one or two transitions per second." In this way non-colocated
sensors can be used without provoking instability. This issue is critical in
the case of force feedback for active compliance control, to be discussed in
section 2.6.

Dual-mode sensory-based teaching (Hirzinger and Heindl)

Hirzinger and Heindl (1983; see also Hirzinger and Landzettel 1985) proposed and experimentally implemented a technique by which the human
operator, either on or off line, could continuously specify a position trajectory to a telerobot in space, using an isometric "force joystick" or "sensor
ball" to control rate in six axes. Especially in cases where there was time
delay, a local computer simulation or duplicate hardware teleoperator
could be used to produce immediate and easily observable feedback. When
the telerobot sensed contact with the environment, or alternatively when
the operator chose, there was a switch to a force control mode, where the

forces applied to the six axes of the sensor ball served as reference signals to a force a control loop closed locally at the remote teleoperator.

The former (rate) mode presumably would be used in free space, and the latter (force) mode when contact with external objects threatens instability and/or the operator needs force feedback (e.g., in fitting a peg in a hole). Note that Hirzinger's system was not true force feedback. The spring restoring forces from the six-axis joystick were what was felt by the operator, and these were also giving reference signals to the local force control loops. Ranging sensors attached to the end effector could be made to act as pseudo-force sensors in contributing to the balance of end-effector forces to commanded forces.

Asada-Yang techniques for teaching force-position-time relations by demonstration

Asada and colleagues have experimented with a variety of methods for teaching by demonstrating. Asada and Yang (1989) demonstrated a system to capture the deburring skill of an experienced machinist and transfer that skill to a robot. The machinist taught the computer by repeated demonstrations, and at the same time a variety of sensor signals were recorded, such as forces, positions, grinding-wheel speed and torque, and sounds. Analysis of these data by means of discriminant functions determined an "average" mapping or control law from process state variables (inputs to the human) into control actions (human outputs).

The teaching process consisted of

(1) predetermining what single "feature" characterizes the data as read by each of the L sensors,

(2) transforming the data from each teaching run for each action A_i of N such control actions into a vector x in "feature space" whose elements are feature weightings,

(3) normalizing each axis of feature space by the standard deviation of all N blocks of data (one for each of N actions), and

(4) computing the mean and the standard deviation in feature space of all the vectors corresponding to each A_i.

The class w_i was then defined by a hypersphere in feature space centered on that mean and having a radius equal to that standard deviation. Later, when running the program, whatever x' occurred was then compared with all N hyperspheres in feature space, and the action A_i corresponding to the closest one (by mean square distance) was triggered.

Asada and Liu (1990) proposed similar teaching by means of neural-net conditioning.

Action, direction, agreement, negation, and delegation as bases for command

T. Brooks (1988) reports on experiments with five progressively graded levels of human supervisory control of a telerobotic vehicle, which he calls *action, direction, agreement, negation,* and *delegation.* By *action* he means either real-time direct and continuous control by the operator or continuous record and then playback. In either case the operator must "do" each and every step of the task. *Direction* means that the operator specifies each in a series of small incremental goals, and the computer interprets and executes these one step at a time. *Agreement* means that the computer selects an action but waits for the operator to agree to it; if she doesn't, another action can be selected, and so on. *Negation* means that the computer seeks to carry out a task autonomously but the human operator may override it. *Delegation* means that the human operator specifies overall goals, then turns over part or all of a task to the computer to perform as it sees fit. The computer in this case has no responsibility to inform the operator what it decides. At the time of this writing the implementation had not been completed.

These five levels of supervision correspond to five of the levels of Sheridan's ten-point scale of degrees of automation, which will be stated and discussed at the end of chapter 4.

Communication confirmation in command and display

It is easy to think that communication with a machine requires only giving action commands and getting back indications of state, where both command and state information are coded symbolically, analogically, or in combination. Indeed, that has been characteristic of most machines, from dishwashers to automobiles to aircraft. However, reflection on how humans communicate with one another reveals that something more is going on, something very important: there is intermediate feedback for both giving commands and getting state information, as shown in figure 2.31. If an assignment is given to an unsophisticated subordinate she may simply go off and act as best she understands, much as a simple machine would.

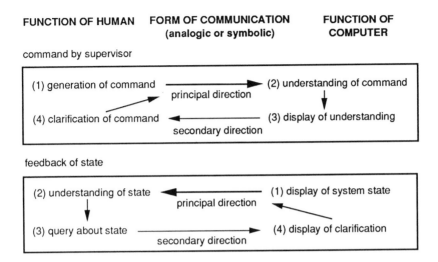

Figure 2.31
Intermediate feedback in command and display. Heavy arrows indicate the conventional understanding of functions. Light arrows indicate critical additional functions which tend to be neglected.

A more sophisticated human worker (or an intelligent machine) would respond at that point with something like "This is what I understand you have asked me to do; is that correct?", leaving the supervisor the opportunity to clarify, and not have to guess whether the subordinate has understood. Similarly, when one person reports on the state of objects or events, the intelligent listener is likely to nod or otherwise indicate what she understands, or to ask for clarification. The human supervisor of an intelligent machine should be given the opportunity to do the same, with the machine then confirming, clarifying, or providing more detail as necessary. This is the essence of human dialog, and it should be built into supervisory control systems.

Voice command

Voice-recognition systems (for voice command by human operators) are now widely available at reasonable prices. They all must be trained by one or more speakers on a limited vocabulary. Naturally there are tradeoffs involving size of vocabulary, speaker training, speaking speed and style, number of different speakers to be accommodated by the same algorithm (one speaker is always preferred), recognition reliability, and cost. If speech consists of disconnected words, recognition is much more straightforward than if words are connected as in natural speech. Further, a single speaker will modify the sound of his or her voice as a function of stress, fatigue, and attention.

Speech-recognition algorithms are of various sorts, ranging from rule-based techniques and template matching more probabilistic or self-learning approaches such as hidden Markov modeling and neural networks. Probabilistic algorithms generally store contingent probabilities based on the two previous words spoken. Measures of the vocabulary such as *perplexity*, defined as $2^{(entropy)}$, or an equivalent number of equally likely events to be distinguished, are commonly used.

It is important that the designer of speech command formats consider not only speech-recognition reliability and speed, but also the acceptability and naturalness of use by the speaker. For example, moving a cursor by using the speech commands "Up, up, up, left, left" would be easy enough for the computer but time-consuming for the operator, whereas "Go to the top right corner of the rectangle" should be understandable by the computer and much more natural for the operator.

Voice command for teleoperation has been considered for at least a decade (Bejczy, Dotson, and Mathur 1980), but thus far its acceptance has been limited.

2.5   Television, Telephony, and Teleproprioception

The whole world has been exposed to television, and the technology is inexpensive and highly developed. In resolution, contrast, frame rate and color quality it is quite adequate for most teleoperation tasks. However, there remain some problems which, while not critical in ordinary TV programming, are critical for teleoperation. Telephony (generally, sound transmission over a distance) is a much older technology, not applied much as yet to teleoperation. Teleproprioception (sensing where things in the remote environment are in relation to one another) is more complex, involving the "remoting" of seeing, hearing, and some other senses, and has less well-developed technology associated with it.

Teleoperation with video vs. direct vision

For some teleoperation tasks which are not too distant, e.g., viewing radioactive objects through leaded glass windows, peering out through manned submersible portholes, viewing near space telemanipulations from within pressurized space vehicles, direct viewing has been preferred over video. Whether or not this is wise depends upon how close the video camera can be brought to the objects of interest, whether camera has pan, tilt, or translational capability, what are its contrast and illumination ranges and frame rate, how well it reproduces color, and how important any of these factors is for the job to be done.

Massimino and Sheridan (1989) compared telemanipulation capability for direct vision vs. video in simple block-insertion tasks. They found that mean task-completion times dropped off dramatically as the subtended angle of the effective visual field dropped below 3° and the frame rate below 30 frames per second (figure 2.32). However, for broadcast standard resolution there was no significant difference between direct viewing and video when the total visual field of objects to be manipulated was the same.

The importance of color is obviously task dependent, and may be over-played. In this regard it is interesting to note that Murphy et al. (1974) found that experienced dermatologists could diagnose skin lesions as well over black-and-white video as over color video.

Bandwidth limitation in telemanipulation: The tradeoff among frame rate, resolution, and grayscale

One reason for using supervisory control in space, the deep ocean, or elsewhere is because of a specific constraint on the bandwidth of communication between a human operator and a remote system. This can be due, for example, to dissipation of radio or audio or to limited speed of electronic switching. Another reducing factor may be that the operator may have to time-share her attention. Thus one is left asking, for a given fixed communication bandwidth, how best to trade off the three variables of frame rate (frames per second), resolution (pixels per frame), and grayscale (bits per pixel), the product of which is bandwidth (bits per second).

These tradeoffs were studied by Ranadive (1979) in the context of master-slave manipulation. Experimental subjects were asked to perform two remote manipulation tasks using a video display as their only feedback while using the Argonne E-2 seven-degree-of-freedom servo manipulator (in this case with force reflection turned off). The first task was to locate a nut on a fixed bolt or knob and take it off by unscrewing it. The second task was to pick up a cylinder and place it sequentially within the bounds

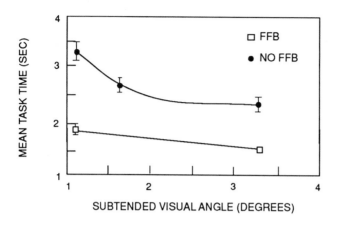

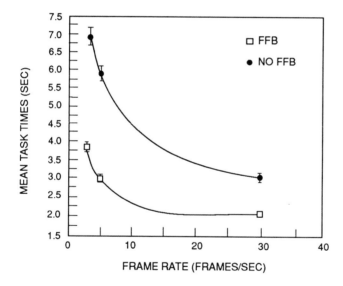

Figure 2.32
Massimino's results showing decreasing completion time of block insertion as (above) visual angle and (below) frame-rate increase. Force feedback and no force feedback conditions are compared. Bars indicate standard error of the mean.

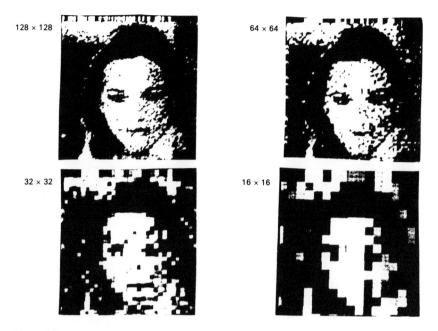

Figure 2.33
Effects of resolution reduction in Ranadive's experiments. Pixel resolution is indicated at upper left. [After Ranadive 1979.]

of three fixed squares on the table. Performance on each task was defined as the inverse of the time required to do that task correctly.

The video display was systematically degraded with a special electronic device that allowed the frame rate to be adjusted to 28, 16, 8, or 4 frames per second, resolution to be adjusted to 128, 64, 32, or 16 pixels linear resolution, and grayscale to be adjusted to 4, 3, 2, or 1 bits per pixel (i.e., 16, 8, 4, or 2 levels of CRT intensity). Figure 2.33 shows the effect of resolution reduction. When subjects first saw the video pictures with which they had to perform remote manipulation tasks, they refused to believe that they could succeed. Much to their surprise, however, they discovered that they were able to perform with a considerably degraded picture.

The data-collection runs were ordered so that two of the three video variables were kept constant while the third was varied randomly among the levels for that variable. Figure 2.34 shows the results. On the top row are shown the performance effects of frame rate, resolution, and grayscale while the other variables are held constant. Note that for frame rates

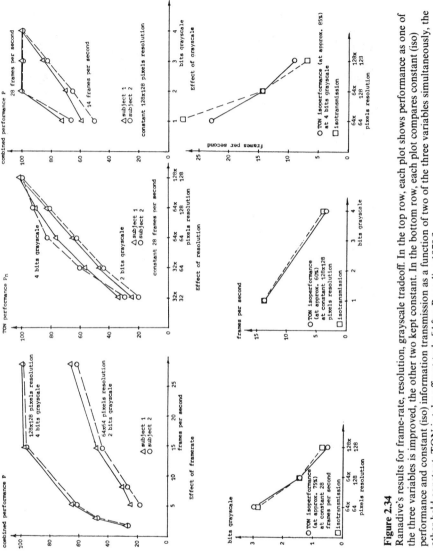

Figure 2.34
Ranadive's results for frame-rate, resolution, grayscale tradeoff. In the top row, each plot shows performance as one of the three variables is improved, the other two kept constant. In the bottom row, each plot compares constant (iso) performance and constant (iso) information transmission as a function of two of the three variables simultaneously, the other held constant. TON is take-off-nut task. [After Ranadive 1979.]

beyond 16 frames per second improvement depends on resolution and grayscale; performance improves smoothly for increases in resolution; for grayscale there is no improvement beyond 2 bits if the frame rate is high enough.

On the bottom row, constant-level-of-performance tradeoffs (in this case using the take-off-nut task only) are shown for each of the three pairs of video variables. These iso-performance curves (solid lines) are compared to iso-transmission lines, i.e., combinations of the two parameters which produce constant bits per second. It is seen that there is a remarkable correspondence. This means that, for this experiment, and within the range of video variables employed, human-and-machine performance corresponds roughly to bits per second of the display, regardless of the particular combination of frame rate, resolution, and grayscale.

Operator-adjustable F-R-G tradeoff

If a limited-bandwidth channel must be used as the means for communication between human operators and teleoperators, it seems reasonable to allocate these fixed channels as required by the task at each moment. That is, frame rate, resolution, and grayscale would not each have fixed bandwidth allocations; rather, provision would be made to trade off among these as needed, keeping their product as close as possible to the maximum.

To make this idea more understandable, assume that a given human operator of a teleoperator needs to get an accurate picture of a static object. She would like high resolution and sufficient grayscale, but the frame rate could be anything. In contrast, suppose the operator needed to monitor the speed at which a well-known object moved against a background. Only enough resolution and grayscale would be necessary to get a good definition of what is object and what is background, but the frame rate would have to be high. Either condition could be obtained by adjustment.

Deghuee (1980) used an experimental computer-based aiding device which allowed the operator to make this three-way adjustment in situ, i.e., she could adjust the F-R-G tradeoff herself while performing a master-slave manipulation task of the type performed in Ranadive's experiments. In particular, the same master-slave manipulator was used with the force feedback turned off, and the same take-off-nut task, but a many-peg-removal task was chosen instead of the task Ranadive used. Scoring was inverse time, the same as in Ranadive's experiments, and the video variables were the same.

Two maximum bit rates (products of frames per second, pixels per frame, and bits per pixel) were used: 11,500 bits per second and 23,000 bits per second. The subject used three keys to call for any F-R-G combination, up to the maximum. When one factor was increased the other two were automatically decreased to keep the product at the constant maximum. Performance was compared with and without this adjustment capability. As might be expected, by use of the tradeoff control performance was significantly better ($p < 0.05$), though there was much variability in performance because the means of making this adjustment were not so well "human engineered" and the visual interpretation time was extensive.

This study confirmed that, with some training and some patience and with no force or tactile feedback, an operator can remove a nut with a remote manipulator using video of only 104 bits per second. An important special use of the adjustment became apparent in this case, namely to periodically but briefly increase resolution and grayscale at minimum frame rate in order to get confirmation that the peg was in the hole. This device demonstrates an important aspect of supervisory control—the computer assisting the operator to control the display. In figure 1.10 this is loop 8 working in conjunction with loop 2.

Stereopsis and other depth cues

To recreate in teleoperation the sense of depth obtained when viewing a real object with two eyes, different 2D images must be obtained from two horizontally separated viewpoints, then presented to the corresponding left and right retinas. The brain recreates the 3D information from a variety of cues, of which binocular disparity is but one. In direct viewing, other strong 3D cues are accommodation, shadows, prior knowledge of relative size and of what object is behind what other object, and motion parallax (i.e., the ability to move the head from side to side and gain a different viewpoint). None of the latter cues requires two eyes. In televiewing accommodation is not available, and motion parallax is available only with head-mounted or other head-position-measuring display techniques (see section 2.8).

For teleoperation the images can be obtained by two separate video cameras, or by a single camera outfitted with two optical paths sharing the video field in time or space, or by a geometric model run in a computer. Presentation of the images can be by means of two separate optical paths (one to each eye) or by a single display which provides two images in parallel. The latter can be separated for each eye by color filtering (wearing red and green glasses) or by temporal shuttering (alternate presentation to each eye of each corresponding image). Image transmission must maintain proper size, shape, brightness, and color (if color is displayed as such and not used for binocular channel separation).

In an early study on the effect of stereo in a teleoperated peg-in-hole task, Kama and duMars (1964) found little effect as compared to mono video. The fact that force feedback was available may have made the stereo less important than it might have been otherwise. However, Chubb (1964) subsequently used the same subjects and apparatus and found that well-practiced subjects reduced their task-completion times by 20% when they viewed the task directly with two eyes rather than one. Smith et al. (1979) confirmed this finding using stereo TV (electronically switched PLZT glasses). Surprisingly, Dumbrek et al. (1990), in a simulated nuclear plant teleoperation, and using a color polarized-light stereo display technique, report a 23% reduction in task completion time as compared to conventional mono TV.

It is possible to achieve the sensation of stereo by direct viewing of a special graphic image on a plane—what is called an autostereogram. Figure 2.35 (from Tyler 1982) is such an image. By viewing it with slightly crossed eyes the viewer should see six horizontal ridges uniformly separated by five valleys.

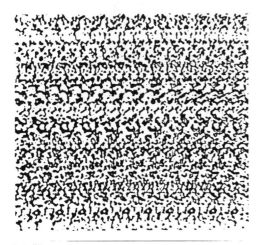

Figure 2.35
Autostereogram from Tyler 1982. View at normal reading distance with eyes slightly crossed; six horizontal ridges separated by five valleys should appear. © Butterworth-Heinemann.

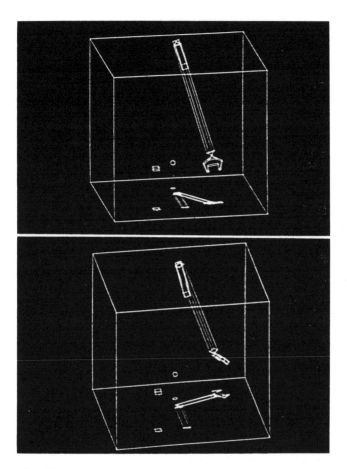

Figure 2.36
Winey's displays. Projections of arm and hand, ball and block, are "shadowed" on lower face of wire frame.

Monocular display aids for depth

Stereopsis is not always practical; even when it is, depth perception continues to be a major reason why performance of direct manipulation is not matched by that of telemanipulation.

Winey (1981) evaluated three means to provide depth cues on a video or computer display: front plus side views (orthographic projection), artificially generated shadows projected on an imaginary horizontal floor (shown in Figure 2.36), and an analog proximity indication of the distance between the gripper and the manipulated object. The operator's task was to operate a computer-simulated six-DOF manipulator so as to reach out and grasp a simulated sphere or block, which was stationary in some cases and moving in others.

How much each depth indicator helped is summarized in figure 2.37. The analog proximity indicator with no additional display (the experimental control) gave such poor results that it was omitted from subsequent statistical tests. A three-way analysis of variance showed significant differences between subjects, display types, and tasks. On both stationary and moving tasks, the front and side orthographic projections showed the best performance. The use of shadows yielded the second-best response times. All the subjects felt the shadow gave them the best perception of the object's position in the environment. The main difficulty with the shadow depth cue was that the manipulator's shadow tended to obscure the object's shadow when the two were in close proximity. Based on the experimental results, Winey suggested that the front and side views be combined with the shadow, where the shadow is used to provide an intuitive perception, while the side and front views provide the detail. An alternative in practical applications would be to allow the operator to select the view with which she is most comfortable.

Kim et al. (1985) showed that superposing in the video display some computer-generated perspective grid lines, with equi-depth reference lines drawn from the reference grid to important objects, makes it easy for the observer to comprehend the relative depth of the objects. Superposing other essential graphics onto the video picture, much as the aircraft pilot's "head-up" display is superposed onto the windscreen, is a convenient way to save the human operator from having to keep accommodating from computer displays to video and back again. Computer-generated components of a display can be made to look realistic and then become "virtual displays." The latter topic will be discussed in section 2.8.

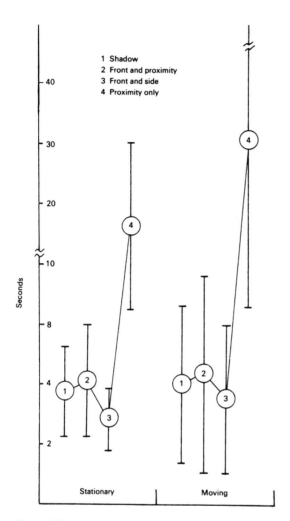

1 Shadow
2 Front and proximity
3 Front and side
4 Proximity only

Figure 2.37
Winey's results. The task was to control with the wire frame manipulator in figure 2.36 to reach out and grasp the ball or block. Numbers indicate display aids used: (1) front view and shadow, (2) front view and numerical proximity indication, (3) separate front and side views, (4) proximity indication with no other view. Circles are averages across subjects; vertical bars indicate + and − one standard deviation.

Telephony in teleoperation

A physician routinely does telephonic teleoperation when she moves her stethoscope around on a patient's body. Telephonic teleoperation is similarly performed when an underwater ROV positions an accelerometer at various places on an undersea structure to test for vibrations excited by currents and waves. However, "remoting the ear" has not been done much in teleoperation. This may change as research on acoustical signatures permits remote inspection of bridges, remote internal inspection of piping in industrial plants and the body's cardiovascular system, or acoustical monitoring of building cleaning, mining, earth moving, or other sound-producing teleoperations.

Binaural localization can fairly easily be remoted, and experiments have been performed to accentuate this capability by steering pairs of large exponential horn-microphone pickups which are separated at distances much greater than the two ears. The pinna (outer ear appendages) are now much better understood in terms of the way they change the frequency spectra as a function of where the sound source is located (front-back and upper-lower as well as lateral position).

What is teleproprioception, and why is it important?

Proprioception, from the Latin, literally means "sense of self," and commonly refers to one's awareness of the position and orientation of one's own limbs and body relative to the surroundings. Gravity provides a strong vestibular cue and a directional static loading on one's own body, so that muscle reflexes are driven automatically to maintain posture and body-position awareness. With a teleoperator these cues are normally missing, or at least there is a severe problem of establishing anything approaching the tight coupling between proprioceptive sensors and brain. Hence the importance of *teleproprioception*. (See the definition in the introduction.)

Kinesthesis is literally sense of motion. Kinesthesis and proprioception are terms often used together by psychologists, at least in part because the same receptors in the human body's muscles and tendons mediate both. For that reason we lump them together in our discussion.

Telekinesthesis and teleproprioception are particularly critical because, as telemanipulation experience has shown, it is very easy for the operator to lose track of the relative position and orientation of the remote arms and hands and how fast they are moving in what directions. This is particularly aggravated by one's having to observe the remote manipulation through video without peripheral vision or very good depth perception, or by not having master-slave position correspondence, i.e., when a joystick is used. Potential remedies are multiple views, wide field of view from a vantage point which includes the arm base, and computer-generated images of various kinds (the latter will be discussed further below). Providing better sense of depth is critical to telemanipulation anywhere.

Display-control correspondence and anthropomorphic design

Closely related to teleproprioception and telekinesthesis is the question of whether there should be a one-to-one correspondence between displays (of whatever sensory modality) and the control devices upon which the operator directly acts with her hands (or feet or body). A fundamental principle of human-factors engineering is to design the controls and displays, insofar as possible, so that a control action and a resulting change in the display are in the same relative location with respect to the other controls and displayed variables, and move in the same direction. One way to ensure that this condition obtains is to design the teleoperator anthropomorphically—having the same form as the human operator—and then arrange at least the analogic controls (e.g., a master arm or joysticks), and perhaps even some of the symbolic controls, with geometric correspondence to what they control on the teleoperator. Of course a conventional identical master-slave system fulfills this condition.

Figure 2.38 shows the complexity of teleproprioceptive relations to be kept track of by the operator. Hopefully these would be isomorphic as shown. Vectors in the diagram above represent positions and orientations of vehicle V, sensor S (e.g. video camera), arm of manipulator A, and object manipulated O at the remote site. Vectors in the diagram below represent the operator's body B, head H, control lever C (master), and display of remote arm A' and object manipulated O' relative to display D, all at the local site. Perfect isomorphism may require that

$$D - B = S - V,$$

$$C - B = A - V = A' - D,$$

$$O' - B = O - V,$$

$$S = H, B = V.$$

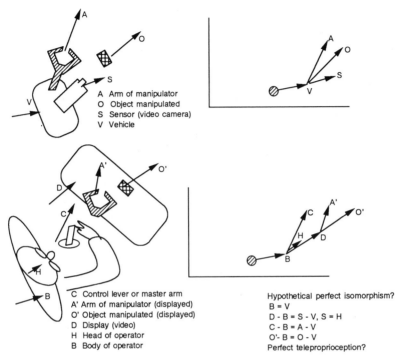

A Arm of manipulator
O Object manipulated
S Sensor (video camera)
V Vehicle

C Control lever or master arm
A' Arm of manipulator (displayed)
O' Object manipulated (displayed)
D Display (video)
H Head of operator
B Body of operator

Hypothetical perfect isomorphism?
B = V
D - B = S - V, S = H
C - B = A - V
O'- B = O - V
Perfect teleproprioception?

Figure 2.38
Hypothetical isomorphisms important for teleproprioception. At left, human operates a control lever and views a display, thereby controlling a remote manipulator. Vectors indicate position changes (assumed for this example) of salient elements. At right, vectors are connected to indicate important changes in relative positions of the the elements at both local and remote sites. What vector relations are the best isomorphisms, or produce the best telepresence, remain open questions for research.

The operator often must orient the teleoperator arm at a fixed location and orientation, for example a peg adjacent to and aligned with a hole. How well can this be done using a 2D video display? Yoerger (1982) tested the operator's ability, viewing both directly and through video, to orient the slave hand normal to a plane when the plane was at different angles to the view direction. He found that there were significant orientation errors as a function of plane's orientation relative to view direction, and that for both direct and video viewing subjects consistently underestimated the angle between the view and the plane. A 45° angle between the view direction and the plane was found to be best.

If there is a 90° or greater rotation between hand movements and (lagged) displayed movements of the controlled object, performance in tracking and manipulation deteriorates. Bernotat (1970) showed that adding an indicator of hand position to the rotated display improves tracking performance, but that the performance reverts when the hand-position cue is removed. Cunningham and Pavel (1990) used an even more difficult 108° rotation of the display in a discrete aiming task, adding a novel "wind indicator" to the display which provided a virtual causation of the rotational bias. Subjects were instructed to oppose the virtual force represented by the indicator. This enhancement reduced aiming error by 70 percent in the first 10 minutes of practice, and aiming error did not rise after removal of the cue. This suggests that biases caused by display-control rotations can be overcome with proper cueing.

Specialized proximity sensing and display

Proximity sensing (sensing that objects are close by without seeing or touching them) is not something humans normally do except by vision, but cats do it by whiskers or olfaction (smell), and bats and blind persons do it by sound cues or vibrations felt on the face. Electromagnetic and optical systems can be used for measuring proximity (close-in ranging) to avoid obstacles or decide when to slow down in approaching an object to be manipulated. Bejczy, Brown, and Lewis (1980) built such a system for experimental evaluation in space (figure 2.39). Short-range sonar, commonly used in photographic ranging, can also be used. Such auxiliary information can be displayed to the eyes by means of a computer-graphic display, or, if the eyes are considered overloaded, by sound patterns, especially computer-generated speech.

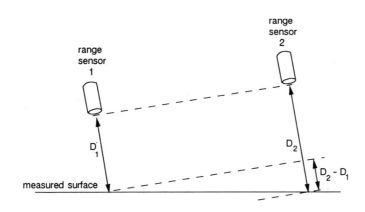

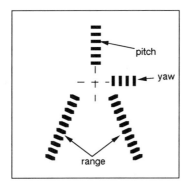

Figure 2.39
Bejczy's proximity scheme for simultaneous measurement of pitch, yaw, and range relative
to a surface. Above, a pair of range sensors measures angle as a range difference (thus to
measure either pitch or yaw). The corresponding display is shown below. For range, a pair
of indicator bars (of equal length) is set at an angle as shown to convey a depth perspective.
[After Bejczy, Brown, and Lewis 1980.]

Teleproprioception: Viewing a computer-modeled virtual environment

One of the most promising ways of achieving teleproprioception is through computer aiding. In this case the computer, when given the positions and orientations of teleoperator vehicle (base), arm and hand segments, environmental objects, and video camera view, can provide a synthesized view from any position and orientation selected by the operator. The viewpoint is no longer restricted by where the video cameras happen to be. The operator is free to "roam" arbitrarily to get a vantage point she likes, or to compare the views from several different points, perhaps using a joystick or other controller to "fly" her viewpoint around in simulated space.

Das (1989), in the context of his above-mentioned experiments with computer-simulated telemanipulation, systematically compared this free selection technique with three other views. A second view was fixed just above the manipulator base, as though the operator were viewing through a window from inside the vehicle. A third view was fixed in space to one side of the task and some distance away. And a fourth view was selected by a "best view" algorithm. The algorithm assumed the operator wants a true projection of three relative distances: from manipulator end point to the target and to the two closest obstacles. For any one of these distances, an equally good viewpoint was anywhere on the plane bisecting the line drawn between the two objects, e.g., the end point and the target. Thus there were three planes to consider. The intersection of the three planes was taken the "best" viewpoint. Figure 2.40 illustrates the idea.

Das' results showed that, in terms of speed and obstacle avoidance, performance was best when the operator could select the view. The automatically selected view and the fixed point beside the task were less good for most subjects, but one novice did best with the automatic view. The view "out the window" was worst.

2.6   Force Feedback and Impedance Control

The nature of force feedback

Resolved force sensing is what the human body's joint, muscle, and tendon receptors do to determine the net reaction force and torque acting on the hand, i.e., the vector resultant of all the component forces and torques of the hand acting on the environment. Various limbs can perform this

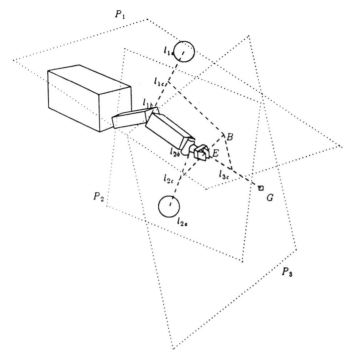

Figure 2.40
Computer-controlled "best view" of telerobot used by Das. Lines l_1, l_2, and l_3, respectively, are the distances from the teleoperator to the two closest obstacles (circles) and to the goal, G. Planes P_1, P_2 and P_3 are perpendicular bisectors of these lines. The "best" viewpoint is taken to be at the intersection of these planes (at B in the case shown) because it provides an orthogonal projection of these distances to the obstacles and to the goal. [From Das 1989.]

measurement over a wide dynamic range and with a just-noticeable difference of 6–8 percent in the 2–10 newton range.

In force-reflecting master-slave systems such resolved forces are measured at the slave end either by strain-gauge bridges in the wrist (so-called wrist-force sensors), by position sensors in both master and slave (which, when compared, indicate the relative deflection in six DOF, which in the static case corresponds to force), or by electrical motor current or hydraulic actuator pressure differentials.

Display of feedback to the operator can be straightforward in principle; in force-reflecting master-slave systems the measured force signals drive motors on the master arm which push back on the hand of the operator with the same forces and torques with which the slave pushes on the environment. This might work perfectly in an ideal world where such slave-back-to-master force tracking is perfect, and the master and slave arms impose no mass, compliance, viscosity or static friction characteristics of their own. But not only does reality not conform to this dream; it can also be said that we hardly understand what are the deleterious effects of these spurious mechanical characteristics in masking the sensory information that is sought by the telemanipulation operator, or how to minimize these effects. At least, thanks to computer coordinate transformation, it has been shown that master and slave need not have the same kinematics if force reflection is to be used. Corker and Bejczy (1985) used the Salisbury/JPL master arm (figure 2.16) to show this. It has also been shown that force reflection can be applied to a rate-control joystick (Lynch 1972), but it is not altogether clear what the advantages are.

Force feedback and instability in teleoperation

There are several factors in master-slave teleoperation which contribute to insensitivity to contact or other forces. These can result in instability because the operator may not feel the forces imposed on the slave by the environment and will keep moving the master when force feedback should signal him to stop or to reverse direction.

There is effective masking of forces felt by the operator because the mechanism of the force-reflecting hand controller may have significant coulomb friction ("stiction") force F_c, viscous friction force F_v (F_c and F_v would not occur at the same time), inertial force F_i, and gravity force F_g between the force feedback actuators/sensors and the handgrip, all of which can cancel or, because they might be larger than feedback forces from the slave, confuse the operator as to what is their source. These masking forces add to the operator's own sensory threshold F_s for force detection. This effect is multiplied by whatever ratio R obtains for force feedback transferred to the master relative to forces applied to the slave by the environment. Combining these factors results in a net force threshold F_T:

$$F_T = R(F_c + F_v + F_i + F_g + F_s).$$

F_c and F_s are usually the major culprits.

Linear analysis of force-position relation for mechanical coupling

A linear, lumped-parameter model of the force-position relation is shown in figure 2.41 and detailed below in the case of fully mechanical coupling of the hand through a manipulator "master" to the environment. It is

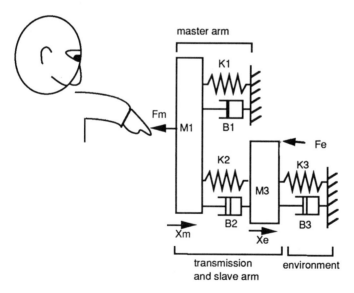

Figure 2.41
Linear, lumped-parameter model of force-position relations for mechanical coupling. F_m is the force applied to the human arm. M_1, B_1, and K_1 are the mass, damping, and stiffness of the master (control handle) relative to the base reference. B_2, and K_2 are the damping and stiffness between the master and slave environment. M_3, B_3, and K_3 are the mass, damping, and stiffness of the slave environment relative to the base reference. X_m and X_e are displacements of the master and slave environment. F_e is the unbalanced force from the slave environment.

assumed that the manipulator master imposes on the hand some spring-mass damping relative to the base reference and that other spring-mass damping is interposed between the hand and the manipulated object. Manual position X_m and applied force F_m form an energy couple at the human end, while manipulator position X_e and force F_e form the corresponding couple at the environment end.

Even though most teleoperator systems include active electrical or hydraulic control and are not of the direct mechanical coupled variety, such a model may serve as a baseline against which to gauge other systems. It may help to answer questions about the degree to which sensation is masked or impeded by the equivalent characteristics of the master arm and/or similar slave arm. From a model such as is shown below one can predict F_m/F_e force sensitivities for given filter parameters and also model experimental results. We then may study the effect of various parameters on performance. Where S is a Laplace argument or a time derivative,

$$F_m = (M_1 S^2 + B_1 S + K_1)x_m + (M_3 S^2 + B_3 S + K_3)x_e + F_e$$

and

$$(B_2 S + K_2)(x_m - x_e) = (M_3 S^2 + B_3 S + K_3)x_e + F_e.$$

Solving for x_e in the second equation and substituting for x_e in the first yields

$$F_m = (M_1 S^2 + B_1 S + K_1)x_m + F_e$$

$$+ \frac{[M_3 B_2 S^3 + (B_2 B_3 + M_3 K_2)S^2 + (B_2 K_3 + B_3 K_2)S + K_2 K_3]x_m - (M_3 S^2 + B_3 S + K_3)F_e}{M_3 S^2 + (B_2 + B_3)S + (K_2 + K_3)}.$$

If all terms are finite, this means that the feeling of every environmental force component is modified by properties of the intermediate teleoperator mechanics and filtered through a damped oscillatory filter.

For K_2 large (i.e., a rigidly connected master and slave),

$$F_m + [(M_1 S^2 + B_1 S + K_1) + (M_3 S^2 + B_3 S + K_3)]x_m + F_e,$$

and so the local and environmental damping and stiffness terms simply add. There is no way to distinguish slave from master forces in this case.

For K_3 and B_3 both equal to 0 (i.e., the slave has no contact with the environment),

$$F_m = (M_1 S^2 + B_1 S + K_1)x_m + F_e$$
$$+ \frac{(M_3 B_2 S^3 + M_3 K_2 S^2)x_m - (M_3 S^2)F_e}{M_3 S^2 + B_2 S + K^2}.$$

In this case, if $B_2 = 0$,

$$F_m = (M_1 S^2 + B_1 S + K_1)x_m + F_e + \frac{(M_3 K_2 S^2)x_m - (M_3 S^2)F_e}{M_3 S^2 + K_2},$$

which means that environmental mass and stiffness are felt in combination and through an undamped oscillation, and so too are the unbalanced forces.

If for the no-contact situation $K_2 = 0$, then

$$F_m = (M_1 S^2 + B_1 S + K_1)x_m + F_e + \frac{(M_3 B_2 S^2)x_m - (M_3 S)F_e}{M_3 S + B_2},$$

which means that environmental mass and damping are felt in combination and through a first-order lag, and so too are the unbalanced forces.

Evaluation of conventional force-reflective telemanipulation

Force reflection was inherent in the original direct mechanical cable-connected master-slave manipulators of Goertz, and was designed into the early electrical and hydraulic master-slave systems as noted earlier. Numerous studies have been performed over the years to evaluate whether, and under what circumstances, force feedback helps performance. Brooks 1979, Hill 1977, Vertut and Coiffet 1986a,b, and Bejczy and Handylykken 1981 are relevant.

Massimino and Sheridan (1989) found that force feedback in an Argonne E2 master-slave system made a consistently significant difference and cut task-completion times almost in half.

Computer-graphic display of force-torque information

Force-torque information is easy to provide visually. Figure 2.42 shows a computer-graphic force-torque display developed by Bejczy (1980). The bars at the center provide a pseudo-perspective view of hand coordinates X, Y, and Z. The diagonal bar represents the F_x translational forces (in and out of screen). Bars at upper, right, and lower edges represent the moments around the X, Y, and Z axes, respectively. The two vertical bars on the left show finger opening and clamping forces.

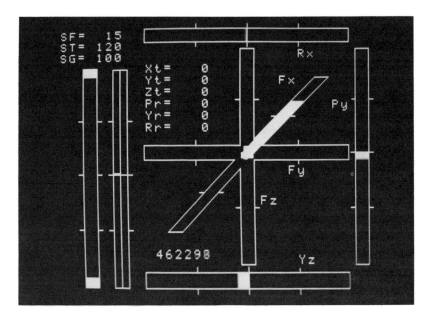

Figure 2.42
Bejczy's force-torque display. [Courtesy of Jet Propulsion Laboratory, California Institute
of Technology.]

Sharing control between teleoperation and computer autonomy to achieve force control

In chapter 1 mention was made of trading and sharing of control between
human and computer. Hayati and Venkataraman (1989) developed an
architecture for a flexible telerobot which shares control by a human
operator using a full multi-degree-of-freedom position master and a semi-
autonomous computer. Their scheme allows command signal vectors from
both on-line teleoperator and computer to be weighted and added, where
the weighting coefficients depend on factors such as time delay and whether
the telerobot is operating in "free motion, guarded motion, fine motion,
free force application, guarded force application or fine force application."
For example, when in free motion, teleoperator inputs do not affect system
stability, and thus can be allowed to dominate. However, in any force
application or in guarded motion (i.e., where a contact surface is nearby)
contact-force instability is likely, and thus teleoperator weighting is re-

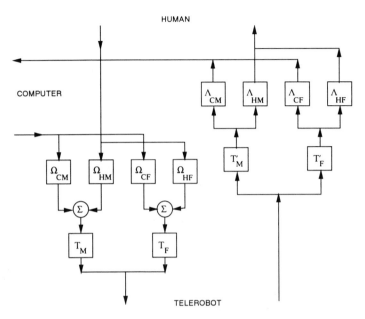

Figure 2.43
Weighting scheme of Hayati and Venkataraman (simplified by author) for sharing control between computer and human. Inputs from both computer C and human H are transformed by weighted control matrices for both the movement M and force F, then appropriately combined and subjected to Jacobian transformations T as shown. The reverse is done to provide feedback to the computer and human. [After Hayati and Venkataraman 1989.]

duced. During fine motions teleoperation weighting is allowed along motion directions, but suppressed along other direction which may involve contact forces. The position and force feedback vector from the telerobot is similarly subjected to weighting matrices, where the coefficients are determined by criteria of stability and the separation of error contribution from each separate input agent.

Figure 2.43 illustrates the weighting scheme. The weighting matrices are defined relative to the (preplanned) task space; each of six degrees of freedom can be set in one of ten modes independently, resulting in 10^6 combinations. (Note the similarity of this to Hirzinger's telerobot, described above, wherein when contact with the environment is made the operator's joystick control ceases to be a rate master and becomes a nominal force input to a loop closed locally at the slave.)

Comparison of task sharing with alternative control and force feedback modes

Hannaford et al. (1989) performed an experimental evaluation of several command and sensory feedback modes including task sharing as just described above (one of the many combinations of control modes), using the Jet Propulsion Lab (Salisbury) positional master arm and a Westinghouse Puma 560 robot arm serving as a slave. The five modes were (1) position control with visual feedback only, (2) position control with visual display of position and force (as described above in the subsection on graphical force display), (3) bilateral force feedback to the master arm (which they termed "kinesthetic control"), (4) shared control (based on the scheme just described above), and (5) direct bare-handed control. In this case of "shared control" the operator's force commands were added to those of automatic force accommodation for orientation axes and fine position control, while conventional force feedback to the human was used for free translation. They used four tasks in their experiments: attaching and detaching blocks covered with velcro, a matrix of peg-in-hole tasks with different size pegs and different size chamfers, mating and unmating several standard electrical connectors, and unmating, mating, and locking an electrical bayonet connector.

Some of the results are shown in figures 2.44 and 2.45. In figure 2.44, two of the tasks the shared control proved significantly better than kinesthetic control, and the force levels (actually a sum of squared force integrated over time) even approached those for bare-handed ("manual") manipulation. A second shared mode was also tried, wherein orientation was solely under control of local automatic force accommodation and translation was solely under position control of the operator. Results for this mode, not shown here, were not so good, and lay on the average somewhere between results for modes (1) and (2). Figure 2.45 shows averages across three of the tasks for completion time, force level (squared), and errors, plotted against three of the control modes. Results from these experiments underscore that shared teleoperation and computer control is promising, but the number of arrangements (not simply limited to the 106 of the JPL system) yet to be evaluated is staggering.

Grasp requirements and manipulation theory

Abstract theory of manipulation and of mechanical tool-using has been surprisingly lacking. Control engineering, as it developed from 1940

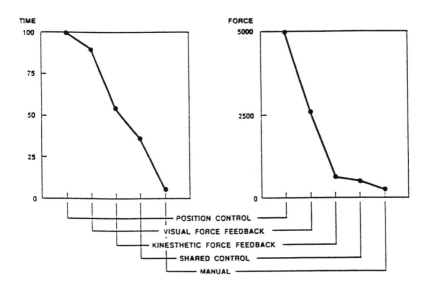

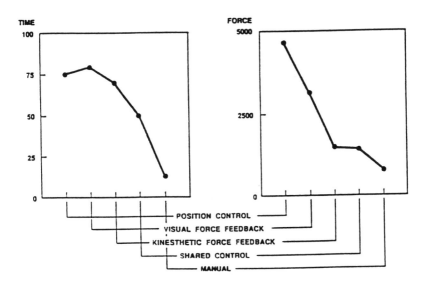

Figure 2.44
Hannaford's time and force results for task sharing with alternative control and force feedback modes.
(above) Averaged completion time and force performance for peg-in-hole task.
(below) Averaged completion time and force performance for electrical connector attachment task.
[From Hannaford et al. 1989.]

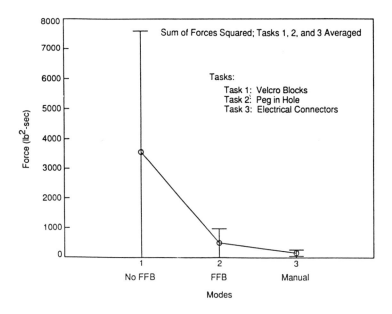

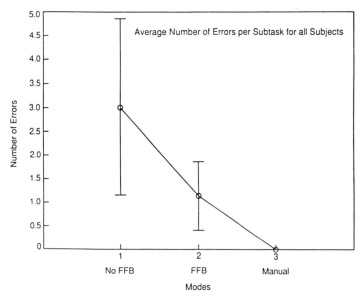

Figure 2.45
Hannaford's force and error results for task sharing with alternative control and force feedback modes.
(above) Sum of forces squared averaged over three tasks
(below) Errors averaged over subjects.
[From Hannaford et al. 1989.]

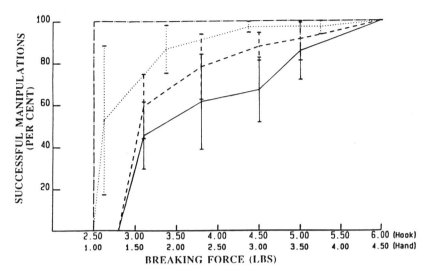

Figure 2.46
Meek's results comparing prosthetic hand without force feedback (open loop) and with force feedback (closed loop) and natural hand in grasping breakable objects. Data are averages of 10 subjects. Bars indicate + and − one standard deviation. (———) Open-loop control; (−−−−) closed-loop control; (····) natural hand; (−·−·−) theoretical curve. [From Meek et al. 1989.]

through 1960, never really coped with the complex sequential dependencies of coordinating sensory and motor activities to perform mechanical multi-DOF manipulation tasks.

Grasp requirements have been of interest to engineers who design prosthetic arms and hands. For example, Meek et al. (1989) compare abilities to grasp and lift various breakable objects using the normal hand and using a prosthetic hand with and without force feedback. Figure 2.46 shows how force feedback improves capability to grasp and lift without exceeding breaking force over the no-force-feedback case, but does not match bare-handed capability. The force feedback in this experiment did not improve task-completion times, while bare-handed times were roughly half those of the prosthetic hand.

Recently there have begun a number of theoretical studies of grasp by multi-fingered robot hands (see, e.g., Yoshikawa and Nagai 1991).

Impedance control

Impedance is normally defined as the relation between applied force F and velocity V. For a linear system impedance Z is commonly defined as

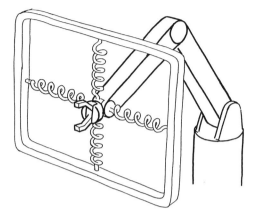

Figure 2.47
Hypothetical end-point compliance frame (equivalent to impedance felt by externally imposed forces).

$$Z = F/V = Ms + B + K/s,$$

where M is mass, B is viscous damping, K is stiffness, and s is the Laplace argument or time-derivative equivalent in the time domain. This implies a common null point for all terms.

Impedance control for a telerobot may be thought of in terms of a hypothetical "compliance frame" (figure 2.47) attached to the end point of the teleoperator arm (master or slave side, whichever one chooses to consider). In this case it becomes clear that the compliance null point can be moved in position, while the compliance and/or viscosity parameters (mass is usually neglected) can be adjusted independently. Thus a relatively constant force may be applied to an object in spite of small arm motions relative to it by commanding the end point compliance to be soft and adding a large equivalent position bias in the desired force direction. Alternatively, a relatively constant position may be imposed on an object by a stiff spring (what we usually think of as position control). In fact, subject to constraints of stability and actuator limits, any desired end point impedance to motion (or admittance of forces) may thus be programmed to mimic the desired compliance, viscosity, and mass parameters of the end point. These parameters may even be different in different directions, or change with time—which seems to be what we do with our own limbs in catching balls, threading needles, and other ordinary manipulation tasks (Hogan 1985; Kazerooni et al. 1986).

Local automatic impedance control for a telerobot

Customarily local impedance control is used in robots to improve both stability and tracking performance. Hannaford et al (1989) showed that if local force feedback on the slave side of a master-slave teleoperator is used, a price must be paid in terms of fidelity of telemanipulation from the human through to the task. He demonstrated this by means of a hybrid two-port representation. More will be said below of such a model.

The best impedance for a master-slave manipulator

There is a diversity of opinion about what constitutes the "best" impedance for a master-slave teleoperator. One argument (Handylykken and Turner 1980) is that an ideal teleoperator is one that is transparent, i.e., the equivalent of an infinitely stiff and weightless mechanism between the end effector of the master arm and the operator's hand assembly of the master arm. Vertut and Coiffet (1986a,b) have suggested instead that operators get tired when holding their arms in fixed and awkward positions and/or applying constant forces (as master-slave systems often require), and the author's experience confirms this. Bejczy and Handylykken (1981) report that there seems to be different best combinations of force-feedback gain (from slave to master) and feedforward gain (from master to slave) for different tasks.

Providing for the operator to adjust the impedance of the master and/or the slave may be a promising way of making a master-slave teleoperator more versatile than if the compliance-viscosity-inertance parameters remained fixed. A carpenter may carry and use within one task several different hammers, and a golfer many clubs, because each different tool provides an impedance characteristic appropriate for particular task conditions which are expected. Carrying many teleoperators into space, for example, may be avoided by making the impedance adjustable between slave and task and/or between human and master.

Should the impedance of the human arm serve as a model? The human arm has amazing capability. Also, as we shall see below, the impedance seen at the master port of a master-slave manipulator is to some extent dependent on the human operator's arm impedance. As Hogan (1985) reports, much evidence supports the notion that the human arm can be modeled as having passive impedance. This model does not imply that the human arm is passive. However, the active part of the human arm dynamics can be considered as a state-independent force source that, at least in the linear case, does not affect the system's stability. At the same time, there is evidence that the human arm's impedance varies over a wide range, though the rapidity of adaptation may be limited. Perhaps the lesson from traditional manual control (McRuer crossover model) could be applied to the human arm and manipulation task, namely that the combination of the arm and the task are much less variant than either by itself, and therefore the simplest and probably most useful model should be a model of the combination.

Raju's and Chin's analyses and experiments on master-slave impedance relations

Raju (1986; see also Raju, Verghese, and Sheridan 1989) modeled a master-slave manipulator system as in figure 2.48. Z represents compliance-viscosity-inertance (impedance), T represents joint torque, and Ω represents joint velocity (for master m or slave s), all in the frequency (Laplace) domain. Z_h and Z_t are the given impedance characteristics of the human neuromuscular system and of the task, respectively, and Z_m and Z_s are impedances looking into the master side and into the slave side respectively of the master-slave manipulator. If

$$Z_{11} = T_m/\Omega_m \text{ for } \Omega_s = 0,$$

$$Z_{12} = T_m/\Omega_s \text{ for } \Omega_m = 0,$$

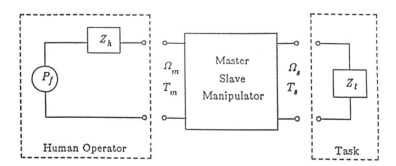

Figure 2.48
Raju's two-energy-port model for master-slave impedance adjustment. Z_h and Z_t are human and task impedances respectively, and Ω and T are velocities and torques respectively of both master and slave. P_f is the power (energy) source. [From Raju 1986.]

$Z_{21} = T_s/\Omega_m$ for $\Omega_s = 0$,

$Z_{22} = T_s/\Omega_s$ for $\Omega_m = 0$

are necessarily functions of feedback gains, the impedances of the two ports of the master-slave manipulator are

$$Z_m = T_m/\Omega_m = Z_{11} - [Z_{12}Z_{21}/(Z_{22} + Z_t)]$$

and

$$Z_s = T_s/\Omega_s = Z_{22} - [Z_{12}Z_{21}/(Z_{11} + Z_h)].$$

If active feedback control is implemented such that

$$T_m = Z_{ma}\Omega_m - U_m$$

and

$$T_s = Z_{sa}\Omega_s - U_s$$

where Z_{ma} and Z_{sa} are impedances looking into master and slave arms without the influence of feedback control on the respective actuators, and if the control law for the dependent signals $U(t)$ which drive the actuators at master and slave ports is

$$\begin{bmatrix} U_m(t) \\ U_s(t) \end{bmatrix} = \begin{bmatrix} -k_{11} & -k_{12} & k_{13} & k_{14} \\ k_{21} & k_{22} & -k_{23} & -k_{24} \end{bmatrix} \begin{bmatrix} \Theta_m(t) \\ \Omega_m(t) \\ \Theta_s(t) \\ \Omega_s(t) \end{bmatrix}$$

Then

$$Z_{11} = Z_{ma} + k_{11}/s + k_{12},$$

$$Z_{12} = -k_{13}/s - k_{14},$$

$$Z_{21} = -k_{21}/s - k_{22},$$

and

$$Z_{22} = Z_{sa} + k_{23}/s + k_{24}.$$

Note that Z_{11}, Z_{22} contain the dynamics of both the hardware (Z_{ma}, Z_{sa}) and the feedback gains, while Z_{12}, Z_{21} only contain the dynamics of the feedback gains. Raju showed that the k_{ij} can be manipulated to ensure that the master-slave manipulator system is passive, thus stable for any passive termination Z_h at the master port and any passive termination Z_t at the slave port. Chin (1991) further explored the two-port structure of the master-slave system where Z_h only interacts with Z_{11} and Z_t only interacts with Z_{22}, and showed that a special class of active master-slave manipulator systems called *structured passive* systems are also stable for any passive terminations Z_h and Z_t. Among other things, k_{ij}'s now can be selected from a wider range of values for stable teleoperation.

Under stability and other constraints, Raju showed that Z_m and Z_s can be adjusted by manipulating k_{ij} to match desired characteristics. Unfortunately, for the operator to feel the task stiffness perfectly and the task to feel the operator stiffness perfectly, k_{11} and k_{23} must be infinite.

An important experimental problem is to determine what admissible master-slave manipulator impedances work best for various given Z_t and Z_h. (Admittedly the human can change Z_h to some extent at will.)

Based on his model, Raju conducted experiments with a single-DOF master-slave teleoperator. He used a task diagrammed in figure 2.49, a series of spring-loaded detents which required some applied force to move from one detent to the next, but with too much force the slave could easily go three or four detents before it could be stopped. The subjects were to move the master arm so that the slave repeatedly moved one detent forward and one back, using only the force feedback provided (they had their eyes closed and were presented with white noise in their ears so that there were

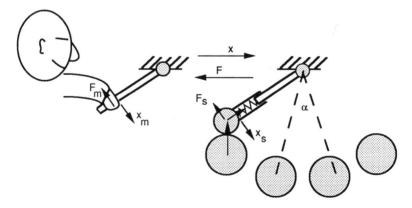

Figure 2.49
Raju experimental task for impedance adjustment evaluation. Human subject felt, through force F_m reflected to handle, the force F_s increase to local maximum as slave arm indexed by angle α over successive "bumps" (scale exaggerated). Vision and hearing were blocked. Task was to move by single steps without overshoot.

no auditory cues). Raju used both high-force detents with large separation and low-force detents with small separation. He systematically varied the stiffnesses at both master and slave in various tests. He then measured both successes (moving one detent but not overshooting) and time to complete a fixed number of cycles.

Raju found that for both tasks the success rate was unaffected by master stiffness, but when slave stiffness was low the slave consistently overshot. For both tasks, completion times were relatively unaffected by master stiffness, while low slave stiffness increased completion times especially in the task with stiff and more separated detents. This result was further substantiated by Chin. Using a similar experimental setup, Chin went on to show that Z_m and Z_s can also be adjusted by changing the length of master or slave arm linkage, and that master stiffness did affect the performance of the operator up to a point. He pointed out that in Raju's experiment the master arm linkage is about 4 times longer than the slave arm linkage. Thus, Z_m is only one-fourth of Z_s even when feedback gains k_{11} and k_{22} are equal to k_{23} and k_{24}. He suggested that since this low master stiffness has already put the human operator in a comfortable operating condition, performance will not be further improved through further reduction of the master stiffness. However, if a given hardware cannot provide a comfortable master impedance to a human operator, reducing master stiffness through adjusting feedback gains does help to improve the performance of the operator.

From all his experiments Raju concluded that adjustable impedance is desirable when a master-slave manipulator is to be used in tasks made up of subtasks with differing characteristics. Before contact with the task object, he suggests, the slave port impedance should be low and the master port impedance high, so that contact can be sensed but not result in imposition of excessive force on the task object. Upon contact, however, he suggests that the slave port impedance be increased so that the task can be executed, and the master port impedance reduced to provide a comfortable but adequate level of force feedback to the operator.

2.7 Touch Sensing, Display, and Use

The human touch senses

Touch is a term used sloppily to refer to various forms of force sensing, but more precisely to refer to the sense of differential forces (or, equivalently, displacements) on the skin in time and in space, both normal and tangential to the skin surface. The skin is a poor sensor of absolute magnitude of force, and it adapts quickly.

Five types of nerve fibers mediate touch (Sherrick and Cholewiak 1986; Corker et al. 1987):

(1)   Slowly adapting type I fibers terminate at the base of the epidermis in Merkel cells, are distributed densely (one per square mm), respond to temporal stimuli in the range 1–100 Hz, have a sensitive range of 0.03–3.0 mm skin indentation, and are acutely responsive to edges and regions of curvature.

(2)   Rapidly adapting type I fibers terminate at the base of the epidermis in Meissner corpuscles, are also distributed densely (one per square mm), have a bandpass of 2–200 Hz with peak sensitivity near 50 Hz, have a sensitive range of 0.001–1 mm indentation, and are less spatially and temporally acute than type 1 above.

(3)   Slowly adapting type II fibers terminate in deep Ruffini structures, are less densely distributed (10 per square cm), have low-pass temporal response (0–10 Hz), and are primarily responsive to horizontal skin stretch.

(4)   Rapidly adapting type II fibers terminate in deep Pacinian corpuscles, have a temporal bandpass of 20–1000 Hz with peak sensitivity at 300–400 Hz, and are extremely sensitive (100–1000 angstroms peak to peak) to skin amplitude vibrations generally, much less at the receptor ending.

(5)   Hair follicle receptors should also be added, which respond to light axial or bending forces, with spatial discrimination from 0.1–3 cm.

Touch sensing contexts and quantitative theory

Touch sensing may be considered in three different sensorimotor contexts:

(1)   Forces are imposed on the skin by the environment without any overt intentional movements made relative to the source of those forces. This may be called *passive* or *non-haptic* touch.

(2)   The movements of the touch sensor are made voluntarily in order to explore some portion of the mechanical environment, and to achieve touch identification of one or more objects and their positions and orientations. This may be called *pure active* or *haptic* touch, where kinestheic sensation may be correlated with cutaneous sensation to infer patterns in time and space.

(3)   Touch sensing is done as an integral part of actively manipulating with the hand or moving the body to perform some task not primarily one of touch sensing.

Context 1 may seem to be the equivalent of visual and electromagnetic image recognition and understanding. A great deal of quantitative theory has been applied to this problem for applications in robot vision, space photography of the earth and the heavens, biomedical imaging, etc. Unfortunately, cutaneous patterns do not seem to be perceived with enough resolution and memory to make much of this available theory applicable.

Context 3 has produced little research that is coherent, not because it is not recognized as being an important problem, but because it is so difficult, and because the modes of "touching in the precess of doing" are so many and varied. To this writer's knowledge no generally accepted theoretical or experimental paradigms have emerged.

Context 2 is now seeing some research in telerobotic applications, which may also offer a way into context 3. Haptic production of forces may be modeled as production of skin deformation $s(x, y, t)$, where x and y are displacements tangential to the skin surface and t is time. This becomes a mechanical stimulus to the skin over spatial variables x and y and time t. Stimulus s may be convolved with a spatio-temporal impulse response $h(x, y, t)$, to produce a response $r(x, y, t)$, where the locus of response r (whether it is skin receptor deformation or a locus farther into the neural processing chain) is left open. This relation can also be Fourier-transformed. Such an approach, of course, makes first-order linear assumptions, but such assumptions have served well for hearing research and may well do the same for touch research. Much remains to be done to provide instruments to measure s (or generate it in a controlled way) and to measure either r or h.

For larger haptic movements, Schneiter (1986) and Schneiter and Sheridan (1984) considered the baseline case of a contact-only sensor which touches at a point and thereby establishes both the contact position and the normal to the surface (face) at the point of contact. They assumed that the sensor can be moved freely in space (except through objects); they also assumed a world of objects whose shapes are completely known but whose positions and orientations are unknown. The problem was to determine the identity, position, and orientation of each object, after it is first contacted, with the smallest average number of moves. They claim to have solved that problem by a strategy which consists of rules for trying to intersect the object boundary by straight-line movements from different far points, and narrowing down a space of alternative models as to which object it is and where on its boundary the cumulative contacts have been made.

Touch perception

Though "labors in these lower vineyards of the sensory domain" (Sherrick and Cholewiak 1986) have not provided neat quantitative paradigms, the literature on tactual perception is extensive. An excellent review is that provided by Loomis and Lederman (1986), which includes determination of absolute and differential thresholds as a function of force magnitude and direction relative to the skin, time, frequency, body locus, two-point separation, stimulus size and shape (including texture), recognition among previously learned patterns, and the effects of masking on all of these.

When discrimination and recognition are sufficiently large that multiple fingers and reshaping of the hand are required, that is called *stereognosis*.

A classical experiment of Gibson (1962) illustrates the differences among various modes of tactile perception. Subjects attempted to recognize shapes of cookie cutters having mean diameter of 2.5 cm by passive touch, by what Gibson called sequential touch (rocking the cookie cutter around while pressing it into the subject's palm), and by haptic touch. Recognition accuracies were 49%, 72%, and 95% respectively. Replications have verified this order and the clear superiority of haptic touch. Shapes drawn passively on the forehead, the abdomen, a hand, and other relatively flat skin surfaces are reported as though observed from the same vantage point as the person drawing.

Touch-sensing devices

There are now a few devices for artificial *teletouch* sensing. Most of these have much coarser spatial resolution than the skin, such as the very first touch sensors for telerobots (which consisted of a few microswitches placed at gripping surfaces or where obstacle collisions might occur). Various devices have now been marketed (e.g, by the Lord Corporation) which are relatively coarse arrays of magnetic, resistive, capacitive, or optical continuous force/displacement elements.

A series of touch sensors developed in the author's laboratory used light reflected off a flexible mirror, which has the potential for very small active elements and high resolution. The first such teletouch system was built by Strickler (1966). It worked as follows (see figure 2.50): The reverse side of the elastic "skin" of the gripper was an inward-facing mirror mounted on a transparent elastic polymer. Light from a source inside the gripper was passed through a ruled grid and reflected off the deformable mirror on the back side of the gripper, thereby producing a deformation in the grid pattern. This deformation was picked up optically by a coherent optical-fiber bundle, then by a closed-circuit video system, and was displayed directly to the human operator. Strickler's system was adapted to an E2 master-slave manipulator and tested without force feedback. After a little practice it was easy to distinguish where on the gripping surface objects were being grasped, how tightly they were being grasped, and what was their general shape.

Following some experiments by Cicciarelli (1981), Schneiter (1982) (see also Schneiter and Sheridan 1984) built a touch sensor in which the localized variations in the intensity of light reflected from the deformable mirror are brought through a coherent fiber bundle to a video sensor and thence to a computer, as illustrated in figure 2.51a. Bejczy (1983) built a version of this with isolated cells to prevent "crosstalk." Following a slightly different principle, Moses (1984; see also Sheridan and Schneiter 1986) used opaque rubber with tiny holes instead of transparent rubber. In this case as the external object deformed the skin and pushed the mirror closer to the emitting and receiving fiber pairs; the pressure made the hole smaller, so that light return was reduced rather than enhanced (figure 2.51b).

At about the same time, experiments were being conducted with rubbery conductive materials (using suspended carbon or other materials) that changed their electrical resistance as a function of mechanical deformation between conductors (Whitney 1968). Another refinement was made by Hillis (1981). This same principle is applied in a recent commercially available touch sensor by Interlink, a 16×16 array packaged in a one-inch square of polyethersulfone 0.25 mm thick, reasonably linear within a pressure range of $0.1-10 \, kg/cm^2$. One exotic resistive material, called Pressistor, is a piezoresistive semiconductor powder suspended in an organic polymer which can be painted onto porous materials or electrode arrays. Research is now underway to integrate electrically and optically conductive materials directly into VLSI chips, so that logic can be local (as is established to be the case in the retina), thereby obviating the need for many wires from the skin surface to the computer logic.

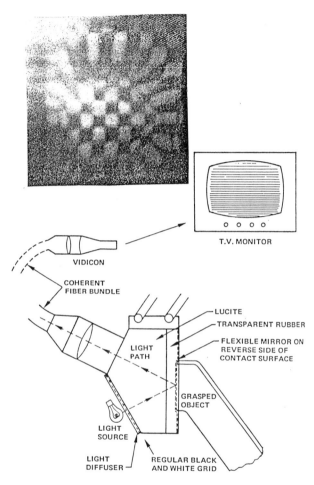

Figure 2.50
Strickler's telemanipulation touch-sensor. Visual display (top) shows how regular pattern of small white squares from light source (bottom) is distorted by deformable mirror in teleoperator "skin" as object is grasped. [From Strickler 1966.]

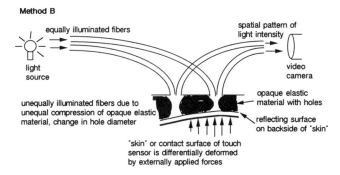

Method A

equally illuminated fibers

spatial pattern of
light intensity

light
source

video
camera

unequally illuminated fibers due to
unequal distance of optical fibers
form reflecting surface

tranparent elastic
material

reflecting surface
on backside of "skin"

"skin" or contact surface of touch
sensor is differentially deformed
by externally applied forces

Method B

equally illuminated fibers

spatial pattern of
light intensity

light
source

video
camera

unequally illuminated fibers due to
unequal compression of opaque elastic
material, change in hole diameter

opaque elastic
material with holes

reflecting surface
on backside of "skin"

"skin" or contact surface of touch
sensor is differentially deformed
by externally applied forces

Figure 2.51
Principles of Sheridan-Schneiter optical touch sensors. Above, method A: transparent
elastic material compresses with increasing applied force, resulting in decreasing scatter
of reflected light. Below, method B: opaque elastic material compresses with increasing
applied force, resulting in closing of holes and decreasing light return. For each sensor only
two locations are shown from a large array.

Harmon's (1980, 1982) reviews of the state of tactile sensors for robots are surprisingly current.

Touch display devices

The most difficult problem for teletouch is not sensing but display. How should artificially sensed pressure patterns be displayed to the human operator? One would like to display such information to the skin on the same hand that is operating the joystick or master arm which guides the remote manipulator. This has not been achieved successfully, the major reason being that the skin receptors are masked by the forces of gripping the handle as well as the reaction forces of inertia, friction, and spring-centering (if any) of the master. An option is to display to the skin at some other location than at the handle-gripping surfaces.

Much of the early research in tactile displays was directed toward aiding the blind. One type of aid was for converting text (for example, from newspaper teletypesetter tape) to braille. Another was for conversion of video to crude tactile images. Arrays of vibrotactile vibrators have been commonly used in tactile displays such as the Optacon, which, when scanned line by line over printed text, will produce vibration patterns on the skin which an experienced user can "read."

The piezoelectric bimorph principle has also been used (Hill and Bliss 1971). In this method, a sandwich of two oppositely polarized sheets of lead zirconate (fixed at one edge and free at the other, with conductors between sheets and outside) bends as a beam when voltage is applied across the sandwich, and vibrates with alternating voltage. Up to 64×64 such bimorph vibrators have been packaged into a 7×7-inch array. The bimorph vibrator arrays proved the most successful for blind character-by-character reading; however, no one has produced a sufficiently satisfactory "picture" for mobility or other general image recognition, as was earlier hoped for.

Another tactile display method is direct electrical stimulation of the skin with alternating currents, but this has proved to be quite variable as a function of electrode attachment, moisture, etc., and can produce pain and other undesirable side effects. An array of modulated air jets presented to the skin can produce vibrations similar to the bimorph (Bliss 1967). Such air jet arrays do away with the "tickle" of vibrators, but produce instead an undesirable skin cooling effect and cannot be valved at rates greater than 200 Hz.

Most of the success in teletouch has been achieved by displaying remote tactile information to the eyes using a computer-graphic display (Schneiter 1982; Bejczy 1983).

The above problems for tactile teleoperation are in spite of the fact that without vision one can easily track a randomly moving tactile stimulus almost as well as a visual one. This was shown by Weissenberger and Sheridan (1962), who used a handle lightly gripped between the thumb and the index finger to equalize the pressure, and by Jagacinski et al. (1983) with a similar display.

Building up a visual display of touch as an accumulation of independent point-contacts

Fyler (1981) developed a novel means for tactile probing and discovery of the shape of an unknown object or environment. This technique offers promise for undersea teleoperations where the water is so turbid that video is useless (and because high-resolution acoustic imaging is as yet unavailable). It is the analog of a blind person probing in the dark by repeatedly touching at different points on an object or environmental surface in front of her and gradually building up a "mental image" of what is there, continually guiding her touching activity on the basis of what she discovers.

In performing "tele-touch" with a master-slave remote manipulator, if there were no dynamics and if force feedback were perfect it might be asserted that building up the necessary "mental image" would be no different than direct manual groping in a dark room. However, every manipulator operator knows that is not reality; the master-slave manipulator itself is sufficiently cumbersome that one quickly loses track of where contact has recently been made and what the arm's trajectory has been. In performing tele-touch where a computer is determining the trajectory rather than a human operator's hand movements guiding a master, building up the "mental image" is still more difficult.

Fyler designed a unique touch-probe, a mechanical device that closes an electrical contact when it encounters a slight force from any direction. Then he programmed the computer to determine and store the cartesian coordinates where any contact (touch) is made. He displayed on the computer screen, along with an arm simulation, a projection of cumulative touch points so stored.

The operator could make no sense of such a display so long as the points were fixed. But the instant the image of points and arm simulation was rotated (slowly, say 20° per second) the shape and orientation of the one or more surfaces on which the contacts were established became immediately evident. What was a "mental image" in the case of direct manual grasping or touching became an explicit visual image.

As more points were added, the definition of the surface or object became more apparent. Fyler developed an algorithm to have the computer connect adjacent points with lines so that the best available "image" in three dimensions was a polyhedron and its planar projection was a polygon (or, if both front and back surfaces of an object are touched, two overlapping polygons). With rotation the polyhedron immediately became evident even more quickly than with just points. Rotation was at a constant rate—usually around an axis near to or transecting the surface or object of interest; alternatively it could be controlled manually by a trackball.

Since Fyler's system worked in real time, as contacts were made, points were added to the display, and what started out to be a polyhedron with

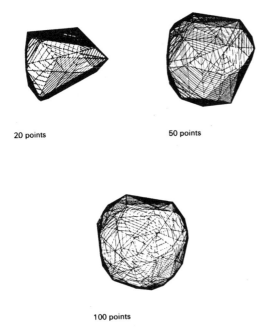

20 points
50 points

100 points

Figure 2.52
Successive examples of Fyler's display for touch perception in turbid water as adjacent contact points are connected and planar facets are drawn. Rotation of the image helps operator identify shape, in this case a sphere. [From Fyler 1981.]

few vertices and faces became a smooth surface, or a recognizeable object. The first few contacts between the manipulator probe and the environment were made more or less at random. As the polyhedron took on form, it became evident to the operator where to place the next few probes to provide the most discrimination and not waste effort and time by probing in the wrong places. Figure 2.52 illustrates the building up of an image or a sphere as points are added.

Another display trick Fyler demonstrated was to put the touch-defined polyhedron into a raster-graphic display generator's lookup table in such a way that the orientation of any facet of the polyhedron was determined. Then by use of the lookup table he "illuminated" different facets of the polyhedron on the raster display as a function of the orientation of each facet—as if the sun or light source were at one angle shining on a polyhedron. Again the operator was provided a trackball, in this case to let him move the apparent light source to any radial position surrounding the object (the polyhedron in this case being fixed in orientation, not rotating).

2.8   Telepresence and Virtual Presence

Background of telepresence

Goertz (1965) and Chatten (1972) showed that when a video display is fixed relative to the operator's head and the head's own pan-and-tilt drives the camera pan-and-tilt, the operator feels as if she were physically present at the location of the camera, however remote it is. (The term *telepresence*, defined in the introduction, is much more recent.) This technique has now been used not only to achieve telepresence but also to provide an equivalent wide angle of view (by turning the head and moving the video camera field) without incurring the cost of more pixels. In contrast, some flight simulators achieve a wide view by projecting a very-high-resolution image through cylindrical or spherical optics to a wrap-around screen (requiring many more pixels on both video camera and display and comcomitant higher bandwidth required for communication).

Telepresence is commonly claimed to be important for direct manual telemanipulation. It has yet to be shown how important is the sense of "feeling present" *per se* as compared to simply having high resolution, a wide field of view, and other attributes of good sensory feedback. Further, although telepresence is usually identified with direct manual teleoperation, it may be just as important to be able to "feel present" when supervising a semi-autonomous telerobot.

In addition to visual telepresence, there are auditory telepresence (binaural localization and spectral correspondence to the real world), resolved force (muscle force) telepresence, tactile (skin sense) telepresence, and vestibular telepresence (achievable through a motion platform driven by the same disturbances the operator would be subjected to were she at the remote, or virtual, location).

Many of the mechanical-force or other disturbances which might contribute to one's sense of telepresence are the very things one seeks to avoid. For example, one often seeks to avoid vibration or sudden unexpected mechanical forces which interfere with visual-motor skills. One seeks to avoid extremes of temperature and pressure, explosions, and other hazards which might contribute further to telepresence but which may be the very reasons for teleoperation in the first place. Therefore, "full" telepresence is a questionable goal in many situations.

Tachi's experiments in telepresence using a helmet-mounted display

Tachi et al. (1989) developed and evaluated the hardware components to implement teleoperator telepresence (their term is *tele-existence*). At last report their head-mounted display was binocular, with 4-inch color liquid-crystal displays (320 × 220 pixels) and eyeglasses used to achieve close focus on the LCDs. The system was helmet mounted and weighed 1.7 Kg in all. An earlier system (Tachi and Arai 1985) used 3-inch CRTs in a 5-Kg assembly mounted in a five-DOF head-following servomechanism. With both systems they achieved good subjective report of telepresence. With the latter system they also did a quantitative test for stereopsis in which they made use of Helmholtz's (1925) horopter. In this test the subject, seated in darkness with head fixed, arranges three light points so that they lie in an apparent straight line symmetric with and perpendicular to the median plane. The expected form of horopter curves, borne out by Tachi's experiment in direct viewing, is that at some distance to the viewer the line is straight, at closer distances it is concave to the viewer, and at farther distances it is convex to the viewer. When viewing was through the binocular video system, after proper allowance for the focal length object lens, the horopter curves closely matched those for direct viewing.

The second component of Tachi's system was a six-DOF electromagnetic sensor similar to the Polhemus sensor described above. It had three ortho-

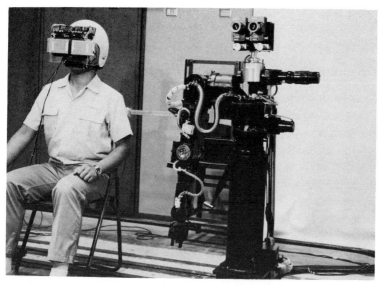

Figure 2.53
Tachi's experiments with head-mounted display for telepresence. Head position, measured
in six DOF electromagnetically or mechanically (six DOF boom not shown), drives camera
position, so that human's video display corresponds to viewpoint in remote environment.
[Courtesy S. Tachi, Ministry of Trade and International Industry, Japan.]

gonal 10-KHz fields, and he achieved accuracies of 2.5 mm in translation
and 0.5° in rotation within a 1.5-m^3 workspace. This drove a specially
built seven-DOF slave robot which was purposely anthropomorphic in
design to permit easy "tele-identification" with it. It also had a one-DOF
torso rotation for slaving to the operator's waist twist. Figure 2.53 shows
the operator with helmet-mounted display and the anthropomorphic
teleoperator.

The third component was a three-wheeled remotely driven vehicle on
which a pan-tilt-stereo video system was mounted (Tachi et al. 1988b). The
vehicle was driven by a manual joystick and the video driven by a head-
mounted display, which also, of course, received the video signals. Auditory
signals from microphones on either side of the vehicle were fed binaurally
to the operator's ears. Actually the vehicle was also part of an autonomous
vehicle navigation project. One of the justifications given for telepresence
in such a vehicle was the need for the operator to help out the autonomous
system when it runs into trouble and/or asks for assistance. In experimental

evaluations with the vehicle it was found that many collisions occurred when a conventional video display was used, whereas the head-controlled stereo display improved performance significantly.

Synthetic window display

In contrast with conventional stereo systems, where each eye's focus remains fixed and where the image does not respond to head movements as it would in normal viewing, in principle a head-mounted (and head-position-driven) display can provide normal parallax in response to head motion as well as true focus-convergence relations. Crane and Clark (1978) report a technique which can vary the apparent visual distance without changing the image's size and brightness, and which can be adapted for telepresence display.

The head-mounted or helmet-mounted display is not the only way to achieve "geometrically correct" visual telepresence. The virtual window is another technique. Schwartz (1986) describes a fixed high-resolution stereo-video system with head tracking, corresponding camera positioning, and image reproduction to each eye to correspond to what the viewer would see were she looking through a fixed window. Merritt (1987) reports ongoing research to utilize both of these techniques in a sophisticated telepresence viewing system.

Background of virtual presence

When a computer-generated picture is substituted for the video picture and similarly referenced to the head orientation, the viewer can be made to feel present within an artificial world, which in addition to displays can include controls (which one actuates by moving one's hand to the corresponding locus in body-referenced space). The term *virtual presence* is used to describe such an arrangement. Synonyms, some of which seem self-contradictory, are *virtual environment, artificial reality*, and *virtual reality*. It may be said that systems to create virtual reality are now a reality. This can be attributed to the availability of computer graphic systems which are able to generate compelling object representations sufficiently fast, greatly improved head-mounted displays and optics, and position sensors such as the Polhemus, the VPL DataGlove, and the EXOS exoskeleton (figures 2.23 and 2.24) which can translate head and free limb movements into corresponding apparent movements of the computer-generated objects. Figure 2.54 illustrates the idea.

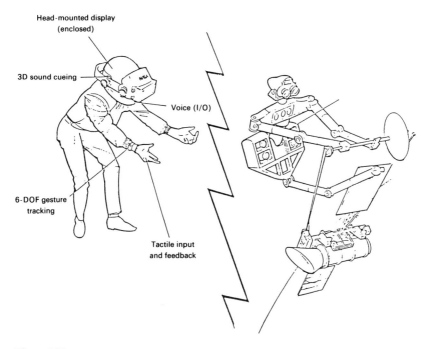

Figure 2.54
Operator wearing head-mounted visual and auditory display and instrumented gloves,
experiencing virtual presence in fictional space environment generated by computer.
[Courtesy NASA.]

Of course the idea of virtual presence is not new. The original idea of
Edwin Link's first flight simulators (developed early in the 1940s) was to
make the pilot trainee feel as if she was flying a real aircraft. First they were
instrument panels only, then a realistic out-the-window view was created
by flying a servo-driven video camera over a scale-model terrain (this would
properly be called *telepresence*), and finally computer graphics were put in
to create the out-the-window images. Now all commercial airlines and
military services routinely train with computer-display, full-instrument,
moving-platform flight simulators. Similar technology has been applied to
ship, automobile, and spacecraft control. One important lesson emerging
from the years of flight training experience is that for initial training
purposes it is not necessary to create the full virtual reality, and indeed this
causes sensory overload and inhibits early training. Only at latter stages,
after part-task trainers have been used for component skills, is the full
virtual reality simulator employed to "put it all together."

Ellis (1991) provides a sampler of recent research on pictorial displays for both virtual and "tele" environments.

Early experiments with virtual presence

Winey (1981) demonstrated virtual force feedback in a teleoperation task by modifying a seven-DOF force-reflecting Argonne E-2 master to interact with a computer simulation rather than its normal slave mechanism. Two environmental objects, a sphere and a stepped rectangular peg, were defined by "touching conditions" which described whether or not the object was in the manipulator tong's grasp. Various dynamic and static properties for the objects, such as gravity, viscous drag, elasticity, and conservation of momentum, were included in the simulation and could be modified. The manipulator and the objects could be enclosed in a rectangular room. When a moving object collided with a wall of the room, it rebounded. This served to keep the objects within reach of the manipulator, as well as demonstrating conservation of momentum. The simulation could be displayed from any viewpoint, and the viewpoint could be either stationary or in motion. The display could also be scrolled and zoomed so that any portion of the display could be observed in detail.

Two applications of force feedback were introduced in the simulation. When a simulated object was gripped by the simulated manipulator, force feedback was sent to the actual master. This was sufficient to keep the simulated slave tongs open to the width of the object. The resulting sensation felt by the operator was that of an actual object within the tongs. The second application used force feedback on all joints of the manipulator:

A three-dimensional elastic surface was also defined (figure 2.55). The neutral surface (no force applied) was assumed to be relatively flat, eliminating the need to calculate the surface normal. Instead, the surface normal was assumed to be vertical. Different elastic coefficients were assigned to various locations on the surface. Force feedback to the master was generated proportional to the penetration distance beyond the neutral surface and the stiffness, so that the compliance of the surface could be felt when it was compressed. To provide a visual indication, a gridwork approximation of the surface was displayed on the graphics terminal. To aid the operator in perceiving depth, the contour directly under the manipulator was displayed in darker linework. As the manipulator compressed the surface, the contour deflected. If the surface was soft, deflection occurred only in the neighborhood of the penetration. If the surface was stiff, a larger

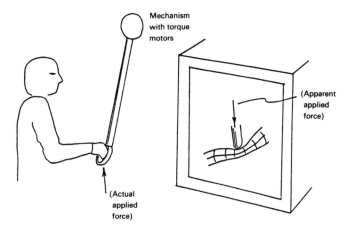

Figure 2.55
Winey's early virtual presence setup. Through a force-reflecting master arm coupled to a computer simulation, the human felt as well as saw the slave hand deforming the object.

portion of the surface deflected. Surfaces ranging from extreme rigidity to a consistency approximating foam rubber were simulated. Subjective evaluations of these simulations indicated that a strong sense of telepresence was achieved.

Early experiments with virtual dataspace

Virtual images, instead representing objects one might see during manipulation in a physical space, can represent abstract data. Bolt (1984) demonstrated a system for exploring a three-dimensional data space, using a large-screen projection of computer-generated objects to which the user could point with a Polhemus sensor and give simple verbal commands— e.g., "put that there," or "move forward" (to next layer of information). Barrett (1981) explored means to provide a system by which a user can browse through a continuous "non-physical" data space of five dimensions. He considered a standard catalog of spur gears which vary according to diameter, bore, thickness, tooth pitch, and material, and had his experimental subjects look for gears to match given needs by "flying" in the data space in one attribute direction at a time and thereby making corresponding changes in an image of a gear. In this way subjects could easily observe what gears were available, and how the various attribute combinations looked. Knepp (1981) performed similar experiments with a five-dimensional data space in which only three dimensions were represented (in perspective) at any one time. She learned experimentally that users have a very difficult time "rotating into another dimension" (i.e., substituting one dimension for another in the dataspace so that the entire perspective image changes). It was impossible to retain a sense of relation between the two dimensions which did not change. (See also Knepp et al. 1982.)

NASA Ames and USAF Wright-Patterson virtual presence demonstrations

Over the last decade two virtual environment demonstrations were mounted simultaneously—one at NASA's Ames Research Center by Fisher and McGreevy and their colleagues (see Fisher et al. 1987), the other at the Wright-Patterson Air Force Base Aerospace Medical Research Laboratory by Furness and his colleagues (see Furness 1986). NASA's development of a virtual environment workstation was justified as an experimental and developmental tool for eventual control of teleoperators with telepresence, as a control device for access and manipulation of data, and as a means to visualize physical flow and other computer-simulated phenomena in three dimensions. The NASA development concentrated on achieving a visually correct and comfortable head-mounted display and convincing computer graphics. The Air Force project was explicitly intended to investigate head-mounted display of real-time computer-generated images to a fighter pilot, who, instead of looking out at the (possibly weather obscured) real environment, could look around to see a clear virtual environment of mountains or other terrain (labeled as necessary), command trajectory, threat locations, etc. The Air Force project also concentrated on miniaturizing the head-mounted display system.

Virtual acoustic displays may play an important role in virtual presence. This is largely due to the "cocktail party effect" (Cherry 1953), the ability to resolve and identify meaningful sound patterns spatially even though their signal strength is but a fraction of the total sound energy entering the ear. On the basis of power spectral transfer functions for sounds reaching the eardrum from sources at different external locations (distortions due to head and pinna structures as well as room configuration and damping characteristics), an electronic device called the Convolvatron can produce in earphones a realistic experience of multiple sound sources as a function of head position and orientation (Wenzel et al. 1988).

Brooks' experiments on docking molecules

One of the most interesting applications of virtual environments is the work of F. Brooks and his colleagues using force-feedback master arms with computer-simulation-driven displays (both visual and force) of molecules (Brooks 1988). In building synthetic drug compounds the organic chemist cannot predict exactly how molecules will fit together. Binding energy is a complex function of atomic positions, involving Coulomb and Van der Waal nuclear, hydrogen bonding, and thermodynamic forces. In addition to the six-DOF of molecular docking provided by the simulation geometry, there are twelve twistable bonds in the drugs, for a total of eighteen dimensions to an energy space pockmarked by local minima. The aim is to find global minima. Brute-force optimization would require years of computation to explore the space. Experience has shown that an experienced operator, using knowledge of chemistry, feedback of forces, and trial-and-error control, can achieve such a dock in about 25 minutes on Brooks' simulation.

In another ongoing experiment, Brooks is using a head-mounted display together with magnetic resonance images of patient anatomies to help radiation oncologists visualize alternative radiation therapies by determining the shape, intensity, and direction of multiple beams to burn the target tumor without damaging vital organs.

Still another experiment enables observers to "walk around" inside a virtual building by walking on a treadmill to determine speed and turning bicycle handlebars to determine direction.

Other experiments on interacting with virtual environments

Tachi's head-controlled stereo display was tried together with the six-DOF electromagnetic hand positioning control on a computer-generated virtual environment (Tachi et al. 1988a) described above. This display was also tried with a virtual environment consisting of both wire-frame and solid-model computer-graphic images. Tachi et al. experimentally evaluated several aspects of the system. One experiment compared their binocular stereo viewing to monocular viewing on a task to align two wire-frame objects drawn in perspective. They found binocular viewing to be significantly better than monocular. A second experiment compared wire-frame objects to solid-model objects in the computer-graphic display, both examined under the binocular condition, in a task requiring the subject to remember and then reproduce various poses of objects. The results indicated a preference for the solid models. A third experiment compared the electromagnetic position sensor to a joystick in a task of three-orientational-axis tracking. The calculated transfer functions were essentially the same for both hand controllers.

Patrick (1990) added a tactile buzzer to a VPL Data Glove and programmed it so that the wearer can "reach out out touch something"—in this case, when the index finger or the thumb or both are correctly positioned they feel a vibrotactile stimulus. Such a tactile display, however, gives the impression of touching a tuning fork, not an inert object. Kramer (1991) has done a similar experiment with a mechanically servoed plate which pulls against the fingertip as the fingers close to create a virtual touch of a virtual object.

One interesting application of virtual reality is surgical training, and a specific example of that is simulation of arthroscopy (surgery on bones and joints by using surgical instruments and fiber optics inserted through the patient's skin). In such a simulation, the arthroscopist trainee sees on a computer screen (as though through an optical fiber bundle inserted in, say, a knee joint) a knife or tweezer or both (as though inserted from another direction) as well as cartilage, muscle tissue, and bone. The trainee holds a simulated surgical instrument and makes a cut, at the same time seeing the knife cut through cartilagenous tissue and feeling the viscous reaction forces. When the "knife" hits the bone she sees it stop and at the same time feels it up against a hard surface. The mechanical design of such a multi-DOF virtual environment tool and the generation of high-bandwidth forces which correspond accurately to real force feedback is a difficult problem, as is the algorithmic modeling of impedance characteristics for various kinds of animal tissue. Kan-Ping Chin explored this mixture of visual and tactile virtual environments in unpublished experiments performed at the MIT Man-Machine Systems Laboratory.

New research by VPL Corp. allows two people to share the same virtual space. Each person, wearing a VPL Data Glove to drive the image of her own hand, can touch or shake hands with the other person. Alternatively the hand images can be given animal form (e.g., a lobster in one impressive demonstration) and interactively dance.

Design criteria for visual telepresence and virtual presence

High-quality visual telepresence or virtual presence requires that the viewed image follow the head motion with no apparent lag or jitter (this is a servo-control problem and has been hard to achieve in existing systems), that an object in the display subtend the same retinal angle as it would in direct vision, and that motion parallax and other head-motion cues also correspond to direct viewing. Other problems are in achieving sufficient field of view (it should be at least 60°), depth of field, correct focal length, image separation for stereoscopic fusion, and luminance, resolution, color, and other image-quality factors, particularly at the fovea. When the image is computer-generated, additional problems lie in achieving sufficient image-generation speed and frame rate, grayscale, and variable accommodation (in contrast to fixed focus at infinity). As one might expect, there are also serious problems of cost, size, and weight.

It is natural to seek an objective measure or criterion that can be used to say that telepresence or virtual presence have been achieved. However, telepresence (or virtual presence) is a subjective sensation, much like mental workload, and it is a mental model—it is not so amenable to objective physiological definition and measurement. Some might assert that a subjective report from the person having the experience is the only measure. An objective criterion might be a test analogous to that for computer intelligence attributed to Alan Turing: if the observer cannot reliably tell the difference between telepresence (or virtual presence) and direct presence, then the telepresence (virtual presence) has been fully achieved.

A practical criterion of telepresence proposed by Held and Durlach (1987) is the degree to which the observer responds in a natural way to unexpected stimuli—e.g., by blinking her eyes or ducking her head when she sees that an object is about to hit her. We are far from meeting this strict criterion in most applications. Elsewhere, Held (1990) suggested that conditions for the perception of presence (and telepresence) include the sensor's (visual, auditory, tactile, etc.) ability to discriminate figure from background; perception of the sensor's independence of the world, based on independence of positional and other changes in the sensor and in the world; and perception that the sensor is able to access the world at will, based on an ability to move the eyes and move the limbs at will.

Three independent determinants of the sense of presence

In consideration of what Held and others have suggested, I propose that there are three principal and independent determinants of the sense of presence: *extent of sensory information* (the transmitted bits of information concerning a salient variable to appropriate sensors of the observer), *con-*

trol of relation of sensors to environment (e.g., ability of the observer to modify her viewpoint for visual parallax or visual field, or to reposition her head to modify binaural hearing, or ability to perform haptic search), and *ability to modify physical environment* (e.g., the extent of motor control to actually change objects in the environment or their relation to one another).

These determinants may be represented as three orthogonal axes (see figure 2.56a), since the three can be varied independently in an experiment. Perceived extent of sensory information is sometimes regarded as the *only* salient factor. Sometimes the other two are lumped together as "user interaction" (Zeltzer 1990). Figure 2.56a shows "perfect presence" as the maximum of all three, though it is far from clear by what function "presence" is determined by combinations of the three. It surely is not a simple vector sum. Lines of constant information communicated are suggested in the figure to indicate that the "extent of sensory information" is a much greater consumer of information (bits) than the two control components, "control of sensors" and "ability to modify environment."

I am not implying that the three principal determinants of presence operate alone. They are surely task-dependent. It seems to me there are two major properties of tasks which affect behavior, both subjective and objective: task difficulty and degree of automation. Task difficulty may be defined in terms of entropy measures, such as Fitts' *index of difficulty* (Fitts 1954). Degree of automation is the extent to which the control of the task (the ability to modify the environment) is automatic rather than manual. Intermediate levels of automation are included within supervisory control.

Given the three independent determinants of presence, I see the larger research challenge to be the determination of the dependent variables: sense of presence (as measured by subjective rating and by the objective measures suggested above), objective training efficiency, and ultimate task performance. This mapping is illustrated in figure 2.56b.

Jex's criteria for "feel" of hand controls and time delay in simulators

The above discussion of telepresence and virtual presence was based primarily on visual considerations. What can be said of proper telepresence conditions for force feedback? There is considerable experience with force feedback in aircraft and automobile simulators, where reproducing the feel of hand controls' feedback is a high priority.

Jex (1988), based on much experience with aircraft and automobile simulators, posited the following four critical tests for achieving virtual

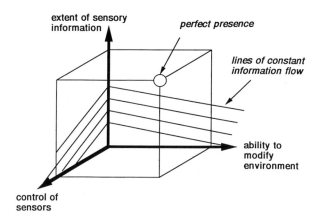

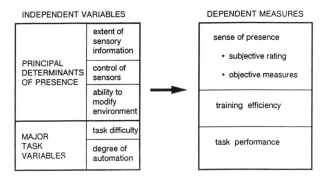

Figure 2.56
Determinants of the sense of presence.
(above) Three components of presence. Hypothetical lines of constant information suggest that for purposes of providing a sense of presence, information channels are better used for control of sensors and modification of the environment than for higher resolution displays. (below) Salient independent and dependent variables, the relations of which are yet to be understood.

reality in the "feel" of hand controls (control sticks in aircraft, steering wheels in automobiles—what Jex calls "manipulanda"):

• With all other simulated forces set to zero, when the mass or inertia of the simulated hand control is set to zero, it should feel like a stick of balsa wood (i.e., have negligible lag, friction, jitter, or forces) up to the highest frequency that a finger grip can impose, or about 7 Hz.

• When pushed against simulated hard stops, the hand control should stop abruptly, with no sponginess, and it should not creep as force continues to be applied.

• When set for pure Coulomb friction (i.e., within a non-centering hysteresis loop), the hand control should remain in place, without creep, sponginess or jitter, even when repeatedly tapped.

• When set to simulate a mechanical centering "detent" and moved rapidly across the detent, the force reversal should be crisp and give a realistic "clunk" with no perceptible lag or sponginess.

Jex has also concluded that for a wide range of simulations in which operator steering of a vehicle is involved, in order to keep mental workload and performance within acceptable bounds, any simulation delay artifact must be less than about one-fourth of the effective operator response delay.

2.9 Special Problems Caused by Time Delay in Master-Slave Teleoperation

Why there is a problem

Continuous teleoperation in earth orbit or deep space by human operators on the earth's surface is seriously impeded by signal transmission delays imposed by limits on the speed of light (radio transmission) and computer processing at sending and receiving stations and satellite relay stations. For vehicles in low earth orbit, round-trip delays (the time from sending a discrete signal until any receipt of any feedback pertaining to the signal) are minimally 0.4 seconds; for vehicles on or near the moon these delays are typically 3 seconds. Usually the loop delays are much greater, approaching 6 seconds in the case of the earth-orbiting space shuttle because of multiple up-down links (earth to satellite or the reverse) and the signal buffering delays which occur at each device interface. A similar problem is encountered with remote control in the deep ocean from the surface if acoustic telemetry is employed to avoid dragging miles of heavy cable. Because sound transmission is limited to around 1700 m/sec in water, communicating over a 1700-m distance poses a 2-sec round-trip delay.

Continuous closed-loop control over a finite time delay is not possible, because any energy entering the loop at such a frequency that half a cycle is equal to the time delay will result in positive feedback rather than negative, so that if the loop gain exceeds unity at this frequency (which it normally would at low frequency) there is an inherent instability. Of course in the case of supervisory control, wherein commands are sent by the human operator through the time delay to a computer, the computer then implements the commands by closing loops local to itself, reporting back to the supervisor when the task is completed. The computer's local loop closure has no delay in it and therefore causes no instability. Nor, because of the intermittent nature of the supervisor's control, does the delay in her command-feedback loop cause instability.

Early experiments by Ferrell and others

With such delays in a continuous telemanipulation loop, it has been shown experimentally that the time for a human operator to accomplish even simple manipulation tasks can increase manyfold, depending upon the time delay and the complexity of the task. This is because the human operator, in order to avoid instability (which is quite predictable from simple control theory), must adapt what has come to be called a "move and wait strategy," wherein she commits to a small incremental motion of the remote hand or vehicle, stops while waiting (the round-trip delay time) for feedback, then commits to another small motion, and so on.

Ferrell (1965) was the first to demonstrate experimentally the predictability of teleoperation task performance as a function of the delay, the ratio of movement distance to required accuracy (see the discussion of Fitts' law in section 1.5), and other aspects of delayed feedback in teleoperation. Ferrell's results (figure 2.5) are for simple two-axis-plus-grasp manipulations on a table. Black (1971) performed similar experiments with a conventional six-axis-plus-grasp master-slave manipulator (figure 2.57). Thompson (1977) showed how task-completion time was affected not only by time delay but also by degrees of constraint (see figure 1.25). (Thompson's experimental results are shown in figure 2.58.)

This problem has discouraged control of space vehicles from the ground. However, as more and more devices are put in space, the requirements

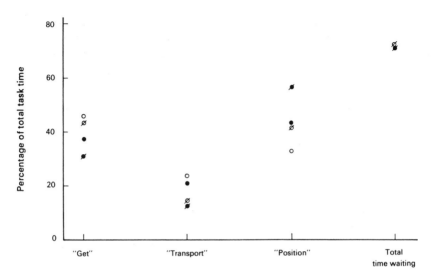

Figure 2.57
Black's six-axis time-delayed telemanipulation results (average of three subjects). The task, to transfer a $\frac{1}{2}$-inch-diameter peg from one hole to another, was broken into segments: "get," "transport," "position," and "wait," using both subjective and objective criteria. Percent-of-task-time data suggest that "position" is most sensitive to delay, "transport" least. (●) Small hole (diam. 0.63 inch) without delay; (o) large hole (diam. 1 inch) without delay; (ϕ) small hole with $3\frac{1}{2}$-sec delay; (ϕ) large hole with delay.

increase for humans to perform remote manipulation and control, and if this can be done entirely from earth there are great savings in dollars and risk to life.

Predictor displays

"Predictor displays," where cursors or other indications driven by a computer are extrapolated forward in time, are of two types. A first is based upon current state and time derivatives—i.e., Taylor-series extrapolation. A second involves inputting current state and time derivatives, as well as expected near-future control signals, into a model (Kelley 1968). Such displays have been employed in gunsights, on ships and submarines, and as "head-up" optical landing aids for aircraft pilots. When there is significant transmission delay (say more than 0.5 sec) and a slow frame rate (say less than one frame per 4 seconds), a predictor display can be very useful. Both of the latter conditions are likely to be present with long-distance acoustic communication.

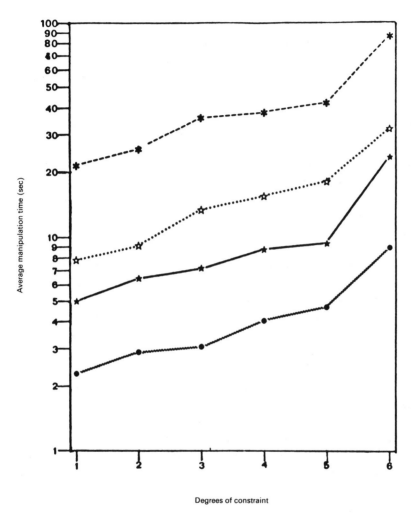

Figure 2.58
Thompson's results for time delay and degrees of constraint (defined in figure 1.25).
Averaged times include transport of peg to hole, positioning, and inserting. The four curves
represent (from top to bottom) delays of 3 seconds, 1 second, 1/3 second, and 0 seconds.
[From Thompson 1977.]

Verplank (see Sheridan and Verplank 1978) implemented an experimental predictor of the second type for a simulated planetary rover. A computer model of the vehicle was repetitively set to the present state of the actual system, including the present control input, then allowed to run at roughly 100 times real time for a few seconds before it was updated with new initial conditions. During each fast-time run, its response was traced out in a display as a prediction of what would happen over the next time interval (say several minutes) "if I keep doing what I'm doing now." A random terrain was generated and displayed in perspective, and was updated every 8 seconds (figure 2.59). A predictor symbol appeared on the terrain, continuously changing as the experimental subject controlled the motion of the vehicle, through a one-second time delay. Front-back velocity control was accomplished through corresponding position adjustment of a joystick, and turn rate by the left-right position of the joystick. Also superposed on the static terrain picture was a prediction of the viewpoint for the next static picture, and an outline of its field of view. This reduced the otherwise considerable confusion about how the static picture changed from one frame to the next, and served as a guide for keeping the vehicle within the available field of view. By using the above two display symbols together, relative to the periodically updated static (but always out of date) terrain picture, subjects could maintain speed with essentially continuous control. By contrast, without the predictor they could move only very slowly without going unstable.

Such techniques are adequate for continuous control of single-entity or "rigid body" vehicles, but not for telemanipulation, where it is necessary to predict, relative to the environment, the simultaneous positions of a number of parts—i.e., a spatial configuration in multiple degrees of freedom, not just a single point.

Noyes (1984) built the first predictor display for telemanipulation, using newly commercially available computer technology for superposing artificially generated graphics on to a regular video picture. The video picture was a (necessarily simulated) time-delayed picture from the remote location, generated as a coherent frame (snapshot) so that all picture elements in a single scan were equally delayed. (Otherwise the part of the screen refreshed last would be delayed more than the part refreshed first.) As shown in figure 2.60, the predictor display was a line drawing of the "present" configuration of the manipulator arm or vehicle or other device. The latter was generated by using the same control signals that were sent to the remote manipulator (device) to drive a kinematic model of it. The

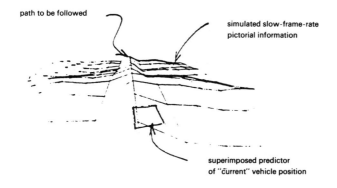

path to be followed

simulated slow-frame-rate
pictorial information

superimposed predictor
of "current" vehicle position

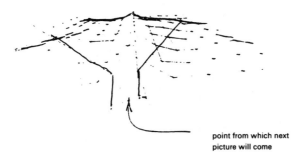

point from which next
picture will come

Figure 2.59
Verplank's lunar roving vehicle predictor display. Slow-frame-rate pictures (8 seconds per
frame) were simulated by a computer-generated terrain. The path to be followed was a
ridge. A moving predictor symbol (perspective square) was superposed on the static
picture of the terrain. The point from which the next picture was to be taken and the
corresponding next field of view were also indicated. [From Sheridan and Verplank 1978.]

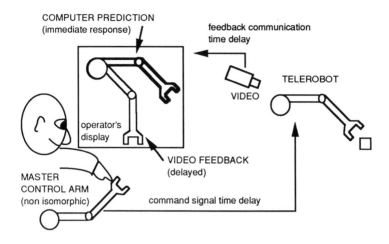

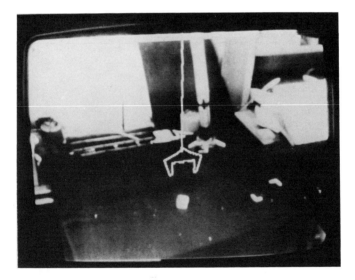

Figure 2.60
Noyes' telemanipulation predictor display. Diagram illustrates experimental setup; photo shows stick figure arm superposed on video screen. [From Noyes 1984.]

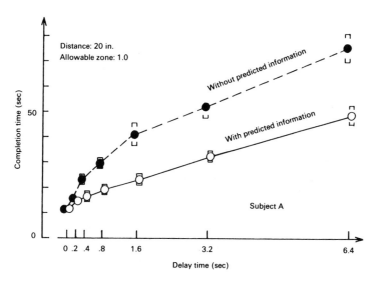

Figure 2.61
Hashimoto's results for predictor display evaluation in simple task of repositioning a block
20 inches to within a one inch tolerance. Data shown are for one subject. Brackets are
standard error of the mean for repeated trials. [From Hashimoto et al. 1986.]

computer model was drawn on the video display in exactly the same
location where it would actually be after a one-way time delay and where
it would be seen to be on the video after one round-trip time delay. Since
the graphics were generated in perspective and scaled relative to the video
picture, if one waited at least one round-trip delay without moving, both
the graphics model and video picture of the manipulator (device) could be
seen to coincide. The effectiveness of these techniques was demonstrated
for simple models of the manipulator arm and simple tasks (Noyes 1984;
Noyes and Sheridan 1984; Mar 1985; Hashimoto, Sheridan, and Noyes
1986). With such a display, operators could "lead" the actual feedback and
take larger steps with confidence, reducing task performance time by 50%
(figure 2.61).

Two more elaborate predictor instruments

When the motion of vehicles or other objects not under the operator's
control can be predicted, e.g., by the operator's indicating on each of several
successive frames where certain reference points are, these objects can be
added to the predictor display. With any of these planning and prediction
aids, the display can be presented from any point of view relative to

the manipulator or vehicle—which is not possible with the actual video camera.

A prediction architecture proposed by Hirzinger et al. (1989) includes this notion (figure 2.62) as well as dynamic prediction. The stick-figure overlay on the delayed video is driven by a dynamic model (whereas Noyes et al. used a kinematic model). In the figure this is constituted by the sum of the A and/or B feedback coefficients operating on correspondingly delayed commands. In the middle of the diagram is the implementation of the canonical first-order $x(k + 1) = Ax(k) + Bu(k)$, where k corresponds to what is going on instantaneously with the space telerobot. The $x(k + 1)$ estimate is corrected in the usual way by Kalman gain-multiplied discrepancy between estimated $y(k - nd)$ and the corresponding actual downlink signal. The delay line on the right side is required to estimate $y(k - nd)$. By estimating $x(k)$—i.e., what is happening in space—activities such as rendezvous and docking can be coordinated with clock-determined events which are not under the control of this human operator.

Another predictor instrument was developed by Cheng (1991) as an aid to human operator control of the Woods Hole Oceanographic Institution's remotely operated submersible *Argo*. Essentially the latter is a heavy vehicle suspended and passively towed by a very long cable (up to 6000 m) from a support ship. The time constant for changes in control from the ship to become manifest in the position of the submersible is of the order of 10 minutes. To predict the submersible's trajectory in latitude and longitude from steering control actions performed on the ship, the model for the predictor must include the submersible, the cable, and the ship (all fairly nonlinear), and must account for both wind and water current disturbances. The cable was the most difficult to model, but it was found that a relatively simple linear model whose parameters are continuously updated (see figure 2.63) does a rather good job. In simulation trials, such a model cut the error in following a given trajectory to one-third. With the predictor display, human operator control actions were at significantly lower levels of thrust than without the predictor, a result consistent with theoretical analysis which suggested that the predictor effectively lowers the gain and increases damping.

Van de Vegte et al. (1990) employed a modified version of the Kleinman et al. (1970) optimal control model (OCM) to predict human control of a teleoperated submersible. In essence, having an external predictor allowed them to eliminate the pure delay and the predictor which are internal to the OCM.

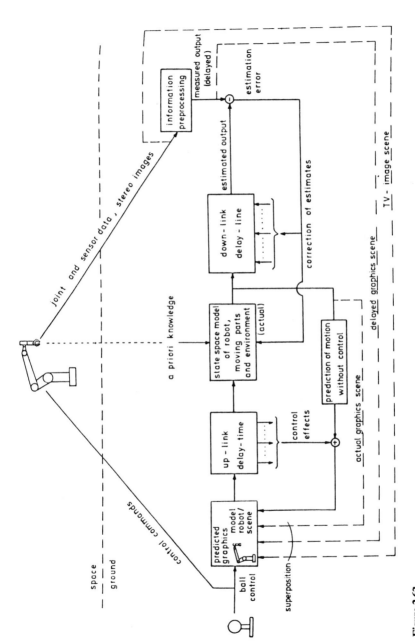

Figure 2.62
Hirzinger's predictor incorporating adaptive model. [After Hirzinger et al. 1989.]

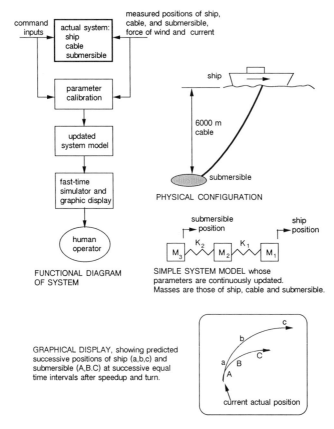

FUNCTIONAL DIAGRAM
OF SYSTEM

PHYSICAL CONFIGURATION

SIMPLE SYSTEM MODEL whose
parameters are continuously updated.
Masses are those of ship, cable and submersible.

GRAPHICAL DISPLAY, showing predicted
successive positions of ship (a,b,c) and
submersible (A,B,C) at successive equal
time intervals after speedup and turn.

Figure 2.63
Cheng's adaptive predictor for towed submersible.

Time-delayed force feedback

All the discussion above dealt with time delay of visual feedback in tele-operator control. Force feedback with time delay is a different problem. Ferrell (1966) showed that it is unacceptable to feed resolved force continuously back to the same hand that is operating the control. This is because the delayed feedback imposes an unexpected disturbance on the hand which the operator cannot ignore and which, in turn, forces an instability on the process. With visual delay the operator can ignore the disturbance and can avoid instability by a move-and-wait strategy or by supervisory control (Ferrell 1965).

Since Ferrell's experiments there have been various proposals, the simplest of which is to display force feedback in visual form on a computer display. Alternatively the force feedback can be to the hand that is not on the master hand or joystick. Another suggestion has been to feed back disturbances greater than a certain magnitude to the controlling hand for a brief period, at the same time cutting off or reducing the loop gain to below unity, and subsequently to reposition the master to where it was at the start of the event. Finally, there is the possibility of predicting the force feedback to compensate for the delay, and feeding the predicted force but not the real-time force back to the operator's hand.

Buzan (1989; see also Buzan and Sheridan 1989) evaluated the latter approach experimentally. He employed an open-loop model-based prediction to drive both a visual predicted-position display and a force exerted back on the operator through a master positioning arm. He did his experiments with a one-DOF teleoperator system, a 3-second time delay, and two challenging computer-simulated tasks. The first task was to extend the arm to make contact with (and unavoidably accelerate) a floating mass, then grasp it with a discrete action (an additional "half" DOF) before it "got away." The second task was to push an object into a "stiff slot" with enough force to get it in and have static friction hold it there, but not so much force that it goes right out the other side. Figure 2.64 illustrates both tasks.

Buzan tried three force-feedback-display techniques. In one, which he called *direct force feedback*, he simply presented the predicted force (but not the delayed "real" force) to the active hand, the hand commanding the teleoperator position. In a second method, which he called *dual force feedback*, he presented the delayed force to an inactive hand and the

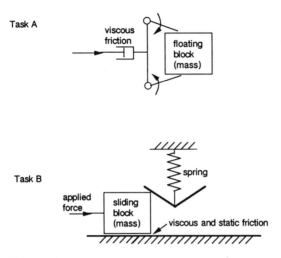

Figure 2.64
Buzan's tasks for time-delayed force feedback experiments. In task A, human subject was
to reach out and grasp block (which was freely floating in space) without inadvertently
accelerating it out of reach before grasp could be achieved. In task B, human was to push
block to center of spring-clamp until light static friction held it there and not let it pop out
the other side. Models used to generate predictor displays were simplifications of
(simulated) real-time tasks (e.g., no static friction in task B).

predicted force to the active hand. In the third display technique, which he
called *complimentary force feedback*, he presented to the active hand the
sum of a low-pass-filtered delayed force feedback and a high-pass-filtered
predicted force feedback.

Buzan's results showed, among other things, that end-point impedance
made a big difference in these tasks. The contact-and-grasp task was easiest
with a soft end-point compliance, while the slot task favored a stiff end-
point. These results accord with Raju's results, reported above. Buzan also
found that the complementary force feedback proved difficult to use. When
the visual predictor was used and was perfect, the predicted force feedback
had a negligible effect on performance. When telemanipulation was blind,
both the direct and the dual force feedback worked quite well, enabling the
operator to do the tasks where he otherwise could not.

Impedance control under the condition of a pure time delay within the
control loop was studied by Anderson and Spong (1987). They were able
to validate a control law that compensates for time delay and ensures
asymptotic stability of manipulator joint velocities under the special circumstance of contacting arbitrary passive environments (thus coping with

the problem of contact instability). Their result accommodates nonlinearities in all DOF and allows for power to be gained between the human and the environment. This suggests that force feedback can be turned on automatically after contact is made, and that (apart from the problem of helping the human operator to achieve good closed-loop control) at least stability can be maintained.

Time and space desynchronization in a predictor/planning display

The use of computer-based "internal" models for planning and control has been discussed in numerous contexts. Chapter 1 discussed the Kalman filter for state estimation, and later the idea of different computer-based operator aids for various supervisory functions. Chapter 2 thus far has discussed computer-based models for coordinate transformation, for goal-setting and satisficing, for language interpretation, for teleproprioception, for building up a touch display, for producing a virtual environment, and as the basis for a predictor display to compensate for time delay.

Conway, Volz, and Walker (1987) extended the predictor idea of Noyes and Sheridan (1984) and combined it with a planning model in what they call "disengaging time-control synchrony using a time clutch" and "disengaging space control synchrony using a position clutch." In their scheme, the *time clutch* allows the operator to disengage synchrony with real time, to speed up making inputs and getting back simulator responses for easy maneuvers and to slow down the pace of such commands and simulator responses for hard maneuvers where more sample points are needed. The computer buffers the command samples and later feeds them to the actual control system at the real-time pace, interpolating between sampled points as necessary. (This is not unlike the "speeding up on the straightaways and slowing down on the curves" example previously cited as an advantage of preview control, and in fact is what anyone would do in making best use of planning time.) The only requirement is that the progression of planned actions must keep ahead of what must be delivered "right now" for real-time control (and also take into account any time delay).

Disengaging the *position clutch* allows one to move the simulator in space without committing to later playback, this for the purpose of trying alternative commands to see what they will do. Disengaging the position clutch necessarily disengages the time clutch and creates a gap in the buffer of command data. Reengaging the position clutch may require path interpolation from the previous position by the actual telerobot controller.

Conway et al. offer the following scenario as an example:

We perform a complex maneuver with clutches engaged. We then disengage the time clutch to quickly hop over a series of simple manipulation movements, such as pushing a series of switches. A faint "smoketrail" superimposes the forward simulation path over the return video display, helping us to visualize our progress along the chosen path. Having saved some time, we then disengage the position clutch, and by trial and error movements position our manipulator in simulation to begin a complex maneuver. During this phase, the simulation-generated manipulator image moves on the display, but leaves no "smoketrail" of a committed path. Upon reaching the correct position and orientation to begin the next maneuver, we reengage both clutches (the "smoketrail" will now be the new interpolated path segment) and wait for the remote system to catch up. We then begin the next maneuver. In this way we (1) save some time, (ii) use the time saved to later preposition for another action, (iii) avoid taking the actual system through complex, manipulatively unnecessary prepositioning movements, and (iv) do this all in a natural way through simple controls.

Conway et al. tested these ideas experimentally using a Puma robot arm, a joystick hand controller, and a simple two-dimensional positioning task. They compared teleoperation under three conditions: without any predictor display, with predictor display, and with predictor display plus time clutch. Plots of task-completion time as a function of task difficulty ratio (distance moved divided by diameter of target) yielded results for the first two conditions which confirmed the Hashimoto-Sheridan results that the predictor by itself made significant improvement (they found up to 50% shorter completion times for some subjects). They also found that adding the time clutch could make further improvement (of up to 40%) if the slewing speed of the robot arm was constrained to be very slow and if the operators used finesse and were careful not to overdrive the system. Various other researchers have adopted versions of the "time clutch." These ideas deserve further development.

Forward-backward editing of commands for prerecorded manipulation

At the extreme of time desynchronization is recording a whole task on a simulator, then sending it to the telerobot for reproduction. This might be workable when one is confident that the simulation matches the reality of the telerobot and its environment, or when small differences would not matter (e.g., in programming telerobots for entertainment). Doing this would certainly make it possible to edit the robot's maneuvers until one was satisfied before committing them to the actual operation. Machida et al. (1988) demonstrated such a technique by which commands from a master-slave manipulator could be edited much as one edits material on a video tape recorder or a word processor. Once a continuous sequence of movements had been recorded, it could be played back either forward or in reverse at any time rate. It could be interrupted for overwrite or insert operations. Their experimental system also incorporated computer-based checks for mechanical interference between the robot arm and the environment.

2.10 State Estimation, Decision Aiding, and On-Line Planning

Applying state estimation to decision aids for supervisors of telerobots

As was discussed in chapter 1, state estimation has potential where all information about what is going on "right now" is not available in convenient form, or where measurements are subject to bias or noise, or where multiple measurements may conflict. In the earlier discussion, Kalman filters were used to provide optimal base lines for modeling human decision making. What about using state estimation as a basis for giving advice to the human operator, to provide the human operator a best estimate of the current situation or state? This may include where the telemanipulator end effector is relative to reference coordinates, to environmental objects of interest, or to limits on joint angles or joint angle velocities, or use of energy or other critical resources. The state must be displayed to the human operator in a way which is meaningful and and which enables the controller to use it for purposes of control.

A complete state estimate yields a "best" probability density distribution over all system states. This requires that the same signals which were inputs to the actual controlled dynamic process also be inputs into the best available model of the process. The output of the model is then combined in a Bayesian way with the best current measurements of state, and the result is the best state estimate (see figure 2.65). In the literature there has been surprisingly little application of state estimation to directly advise human operators. The tendency has been either to automate the control using optimal state estimation or to leave the operator on her own to infer whatever she can from available displays of direct measurements.

Roseborough (1988) describes experiments wherein human controllers of partly deterministic, partly stochastic processes (which is characteristic of

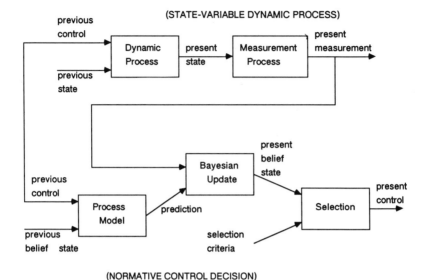

(STATE-VARIABLE DYNAMIC PROCESS)

(NORMATIVE CONTROL DECISION)

Figure 2.65
Component operations in control by state estimation.

real supervisory control systems) are provided with such normative decision aids. Results show that operators cannot assimilate cognitively all of
the state information which a full formal estimate makes available. They
perform their control tasks better if they are given only averages and some
simple index of dispersion, and not the full distribution. In the case of
joint distributions over two or more variables, they do better by considering only the marginal distributions, or just point averages on the independent variables. Figure 2.66 illustrates examples of such reduced state
information.

Planning by trying it out on a computer simulation first

The trend in supervisory control is toward explicit goal or objective function specification, aided by computers. This is for helping the decision
maker clarify her own goals, for communicating goals to other people, or
for communicating goals to a computer controller. But currently, more
often than not, supervisory operators make control decisions without
explicating objective functions. In this case the computer may simply serve
as a means of trying out decisions before committing them to action—i.e.,
"What would happen if—?" Commands (supervisory or direct) can be

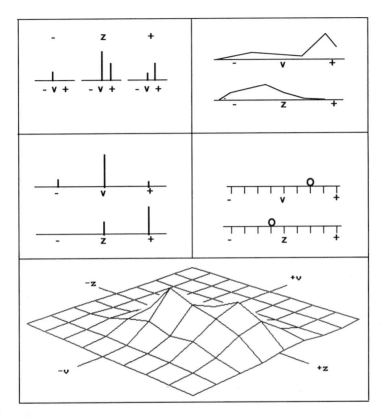

Figure 2.66
Alternative displays of reduced state information used by Roseborough in simple control experiment. A process had 81 possible states: any combination of nine positions (z) and nine velocities (v). The true state was not displayed, only reduced state information according to one of the five displays shown above. The subject could apply unit +, −, or 0 change in velocity. A random disturbance did the same. [After Roseborough 1988.]

given to the simulation model but not to the actual process. Then the model results can be observed, and the process can be repeated until the operator is satisfied that she knows what commands are best to commit to the actual process.

Yoerger (1982) implemented such a test capability in a supervisory manipulation interface whereby the operator could see a graphic display of just where a manipulator arm would move relative to a workpiece on the basis of given commands.

Another example of such a simulation tool is the NASA Ames space orbital maneuvering aid (Ellis and Gruenwald 1989), shown in figure 2.67. This is useful, since it is not easy for a human operator to predict the results of her own thrust commands on the resulting trajectory. Hypothetically a human planner also exercises an internal or mental model to predict

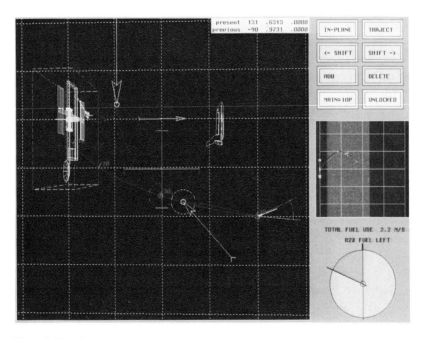

Figure 2.67
Ellis and Gruenwald's space orbital planning aid. Its purpose is to enable operators to visualize orbital trajectories despite counterintuitive, nonlinear dynamics and operational constraints such as plume impingement. Violations of the constraints appear as circles and arcs. An accompanying "geometric spreadsheet" allows users to manually optimize their maneuver plans by satisfying interacting constraints. [Courtesy of S. Ellis, NASA.]

expected results of potential control actions. Early models of supervisory control embodied this idea (Sheridan 1976a). Rasmussen (1976) included a dynamic world model in an early version of his multilevel model of behavior.

When the controlled process response is slow or delayed, commands can be given to a simulator (responding essentially instantaneously) and to the actual process at the same time, so that a discrepancy between what was mentally predicted to happen when the control actions were decided upon and what the computer simulator indicates will happen can be used as a basis for refining the next control action. More specific use of this technique will be described later for the time-delay case. There are also possibilities for having the simulator "track" the movement of the actual process so that any on-line tests start from automatically updated initial conditions. The idea of testing commands before committing them to action has had many antecedents in computer control.

Cannon (1992) mentions how point-and-select programming can help build up missing structure in a simulated or virtual-world model. For example, a telerobot could enter a new environment about which there is limited or no foreknowledge. The human operator could then quickly point out obstacles and name potential items of interest. Focusing on these named locations, machine vision and other sensing systems could do a reasonable job of building a meaningful virtual-world model. This can simplify a world-apprehension task, which could be overwhelming for a totally autonomous robot. By overlaying the resulting model simulation views on real-world video displays, a human operator might quickly see discrepancies, such as a door frame mistaken for a table leg or a hole perceived as a shadow. Editing the resultant model could be performed by a second round of point-and-select operations, for example by pointing out correct edges of previously named but incorrectly modeled objects. Or a graphic editor could be used to redraw lines until the virtual world had been corrected from various viewpoints. Once constructed, an accurate model environment could allow an operator to perform a variety of planning and cross-checking activities before risking real action.

Computer-graphic aids for avoiding obstacles

Park (1991) developed a computer-graphic control aid by which a supervisor could plan and essentially try out an anticipated telerobot arm movement in a simulation, again before committing to the actual move. He

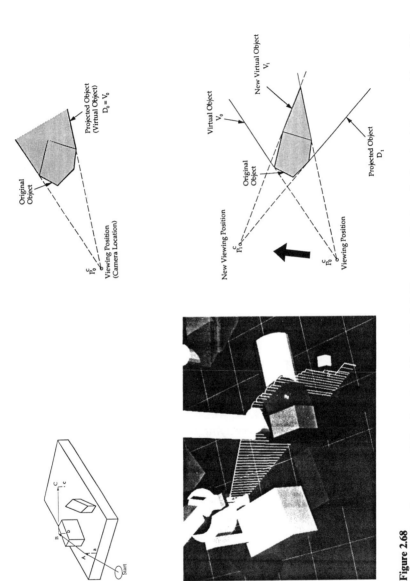

Figure 2.68
Park's display of computer aid for obstacle avoidance. Top left: Human specification of subgoal points on graphic model. Bottom left: Computer display of composite planned trajectory with lines to floor to indicate heights. Right: Generation of virtual obstacles for single viewing position (above) and pair of viewing positions (below). [From Park 1991.]

assumed that for some obstacles the positions and orientations were already known and represented in a computer model. The user commanded each straight-line move to a subgoal point in three-space by designating a point on the floor or the lowest horizontal surface (such as a table top) by moving a cursor to that point (say A in figure 2.68a) and clicking, then lifting the cursor by an amount corresponding to the desired height of the subgoal point (say A) above that floor point and observing on the graphic model a blue vertical line being generated from the floor point to the subgoal point in space. This process was repeated for successive subgoal points (say B and C). The user could view the resulting trajectory model (figure 2.68b) from any desired perspective (though the "real" environment could be viewed only from the perspective provided by the video camera's location). Either of two collision-avoidance algorithms could be invoked: a detection algorithm which indicted where on some object a collision occurred as the arm was moved from one point to another, or an automatic avoidance algorithm which found (and drew on the computer screen) a minimum-length no-collision trajectory from the starting point to the new subgoal point. Park's aiding scheme also allowed new observed objects to be added to the model by graphically "flying" them into geometric correspondence with the model display. Another aid was to generate "virtual objects" for any portion of the environment in the umbral region (not visible) after two video views (figure 2.68c). In this case the virtual objects were treated in the same way in the model and in the collision-avoidance algorithms as the visible objects. Experiments with this technique showed that it was easy to use and that it improved safety greatly.

Chiruvolu (1991) experimented with the idea of superposing on the video model-based images allowing the operator to "see through" the teleoperator arm and hand. This allows for peg-in-hole or other assembly operations which otherwise are not possible with limited camera views.

2.11   Measuring Performance of Teleoperation

Categories of performance measures and tasks

The standard performance measures for teleoperation are essentially the same measures that have been used by production-line industrial engineers and motor-skill psychologists for many years—namely, time to complete given tasks and arbitrarily devised scores for how well they are completed (accuracy and error). The tasks used might be classified as follows:

Calibration tasks For manipulation or vehicle mobility, examples are tracking a straight line in a given direction, or a complex curved path; pointing or positioning the end effector relative to an external reference in one or many degrees of freedom; moving away from and returning exactly to a given position; or simply holding steady, with or without an externally applied force. These are components which are in themselves easily measurable and parameterizeable, and which when strung together make up real tasks. There might also be visual or tactile or force-discrimination tasks of various kinds. Note that motor activities (manipulation and mobility) necessarily involve sensing, and sensory activities necessarily require the muscles to move the sensors around.

"Laboratory toy" tasks This class includes manipulation tasks such as positioning or stacking blocks, putting pegs in holes and removing them, starting nuts on bolts, and tying knots in ropes. These are tasks that involve grasping and ungrasping, free movement as well as movement near obstacles, and fine adjustments and force interactions. Comparable mobility tasks might be climbing stairs and maneuvering through an obstacle field. Inspection tasks might be to find and identify given objects. Tasks in this category can be calibrated to some extent: the sizes of blocks, pegs and holes, and nuts and bolts, their fits relative to each other, their weights, and other characteristics can be varied.

Actual tasks These, of course, depend upon the application, including assembly and disassembly of actual connectors or machines, mobility in actual space, undersea, mine or surface environments, or inspection of actual structures. They are not easily calibrated, and they tend to be one-of-a-kind.

For purposes of testing any of the above, tasks can be self-paced (the subject is instructed to do the task at a "comfortable" pace) or self-paced within a total time constraint (after T seconds effort must stop whether or not the task has been completed). Some special tasks, such as tracking a randomly moving target, can be continuously forced-paced.

Standards for characterizing and assessing performance

No suitable scheme exists for notating and interrelating manipulation, mobility, and inspection events. Time-and-motion analyses used by production engineers for specifying standard assembly and inspection times and methods have been crude taxonomies at best. Notation for other sensorimotor skills performed in space and time either lacks full description of what to do, leaving much to "interpretation" (as in the case of music scoring), or is too qualitative (as seems to be true for labanotation, the scoring of dance, an example of which is given in figure 2.69. See Hutchinson 1961). In the case of telemanipulation, dynamic description of the trajectory in time, space, and force of every relevant vehicle, manipulator, and task object—i.e., the full trajectory in complete state space as explored by Whitney (1969a)—is clearly impractical. AI researchers have taken to using structured list relations (in software, using language such as LISP) individually and arbitrarily devised to fit the problem of each researcher.

At the moment there are essentially no accepted standards for asserting that one telemanipulator system (of hardware or software or both) is better or worse than some other. Of course to some extent this is necessarily context dependent, and the success will depend upon specific mission requirements. But there should be an effort to develop some generic and commonly accepted indices of performance which could be used to profile the capabilities of a teleoperator vehicle/manipulator system, including factors of physical size, strength, speed, accuracy, repeatability, versatility, and reliability. The idea of standardized task boards have been suggested by various government user agencies. Engelberger (in Sheridan 1976b) once proposed a standardized intelligence test for industrial robots.

Furthermore, terms such as *accuracy*, *repeatability*, and *linearity* are often not used in a common way within the technology community. In behavioral science, for example, *error* has many meanings, while in control science its meaning is much more limited. No one is asking for rigid standardization, but some commonality across tests and measures appears necessary to avoid great waste and bureaucratic chaos.

The question may be raised whether the teleoperator's human operator, either in direct manual or supervisory control mode, can be evaluated separately from the performance of the entire man-machine system. Separating out the man from the man-machine system is not a new question, but the answer has remained elusive. Clearly, given the same physical teleoperator, some human operators can do better, just as any one human operator can perform better with one teleoperator than with another.

Direct experimental comparisons of humans and telerobots

Direct experimental comparisons between humans performing "hands-on" and teleoperators performing either in direct or supervisory-controlled

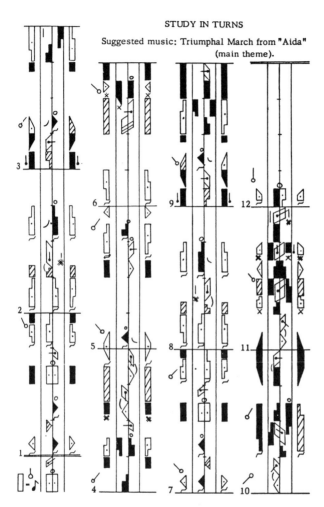

Figure 2.69
Example of labanotation, scoring of a dance. Time sequence is from bottom to top, starting at left. Within each segment (see numbers adjacent to horizontal lines) left-and-rightmost symbols refer to left and right arms, inner symbols refer to left and right legs. [From Hutchinson 1961; © New Direction Books.]

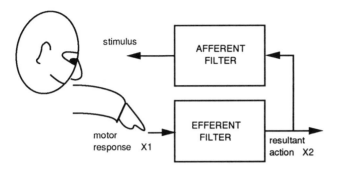

Figure 2.70
Human efferent and afferent "filters," including all those factors external to the human that modify the signals going from human to the intended action in the environment, and those which modify the signals from the actual resultant action back to the human.

fashion must be made on a much more extensive and scientifically controlled scale, making use of both manipulation theory and the generic performance measures called for above. One sees the need for space teleoperation performance experiments, for example, to be done first on the ground in laboratories or in neutral buoyancy tanks, much as Akin (1986) has begun doing, then in space on shuttle flights (e.g., the NASA EASE/ACCESS experiments in assembling structures in space), and eventually on the space station. The same should be done for divers, nuclear power equipment maintainers, surgeons, miners, construction workers, firemen, policemen, and soldiers in developing teleoperators corresponding to their specific needs.

Sensory, cognitive, and motor filtering

It is surprising that in closed-loop human-controlled systems such as teleoperator systems we still have relatively little idea whether overall performance limitations are due primarily to the sensory, cognitive, or motor limitations of the human operator, to the processing and display of sensory information (call this an "afferent filter"; see figure 2.70), or to the processing and implementation of control action (call this an "efferent filter"). In other words, for which of the three components does limitation or distortion have the greatest impact upon performance, and with respect to which component will a given investment produce the greatest improvement?

When touch and kinesthesis are involved, unlike vision and hearing, there is a significant energy-port couple relation between force and velocity (or displacement) so that what constitutes input to and what is output from the human is arbitrary. In any case, if one is considered input the other must be output. In such a case it is probably more appropriate to resort to a filter model in which what is forward and what is feedback are determined by the governing equations for the coupling, and in which there is an arbitrary assignment of causality between force and position. A model such as that illustrated in figure 2.41 is useful for such analysis.

Inferring human intention

Performance of teleoperation tasks (i.e., achievement of assumed overall task goals) consists not only of implementing a series of subtasks, but also of *selecting* those subtasks (subgoals). Thus, performance measurement, apart from measurement of sensorimotor performance of each intended subtask, can be said to be determination of whether proper subtasks or subgoals were properly selected and organized. It is natural to consider subgoal selection in analysis of high-level human behavior (e.g., management science or psychiatry), but this is rare in analysis of skill behavior.

The problem is precisely that of inferring intended subgoals from observation of actual skill behavior. At a higher level of behavior, what a person intends often becomes apparent and can easily be analyzed into steps and verbalized. By contrast, analysis of visual or haptic inspection and manipulation into discrete intended steps seems far more difficult. Yared and Sheridan (1991) have offered a procedure for doing this based on computer linguistic analysis.

3 Supervisory Control in Transportation, Process, and Other Automated Systems

This chapter deals with systems which the new mix of automation and human supervisory control is turning into "non-anthropomorphic telerobots" (systems which operate autonomously for periods and which do not have human form). Aircraft, automotive vehicles, and nuclear power plants will be discussed as primary examples. Flexible manufacturing systems will be discussed only briefly, partly because of the complexity of this application and partly because only a few researchers have explored supervisory control in this context. Other developments in such diverse fields as petroleum, chemical and pharmaceutical process control, space systems, patient monitoring in hospital operating rooms, and automatic teller machines will be mentioned only briefly as examples. Some of the above systems may subsume a number of anthropomorphic telerobots, but control at an aggregate level poses different kinds of problems than were considered in chapter 2.

The supervisory functions of *planning* and *teaching* were discussed already in chapter 2 with respect to anthropomorphic teleoperators. In this chapter the component of planning that may be called *goal setting* or *satisficing of objectives* is treated more extensively, as it seems to be a more critical factor for the type of application treated here. The function of *monitoring* is then discussed under the three headings of "supervisory monitoring displays," "failure detection, diagnosis and location," and "mental workload." *Learning*, for systems of the kind dealt with in this chapter, occurs through analysis of "human error."

The direct sensory modes of remote control (television, teleproprioception, force and touch feedback, time delay, and telepresence) are not discussed in this chapter, since these topics are less critical to automation in transportation vehicles and process control (non-anthropomorphic telerobots), or their essentials have already been covered in chapter 2.

3.1 Aviation Automation

Airplanes can now automatically adjust their throttle, pitch, and yaw damping characteristics. They can take off and climb to altitude autonomously, or fly to a given latitude and longitude, and can maintain altitude and direction in spite of wind disturbances. They can approach and land automatically in zero-visibility conditions. To do these tasks, airplanes make use of artificial sensors, motors, and computers, programmed in

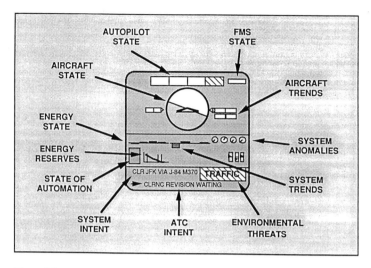

Figure 3.1
Pilot information requirements. [Courtesy C. Billings, NASA.]

supervisory fashion by pilots and ground controllers. In this sense airplanes are telerobots. In aviation the supervising pilot is called a "flight manager." Figure 3.1 provides a metaphoric summary of pilot information requirements for performing this task.

American commercial aviation can be considered as one very large supervisory control system which includes many pilots, ground controllers, and other operational personnel, as well as all the aircraft, radar, communications, computers, and display equipment required to provide air traffic control and air navigation for the nation. This system in now being modernized, partly to improve performance capability (to meet increasing traffic demands and to reduce human error and equipment failures), partly to standardize hardware, software, and procedures, and partly to reduce staffing and the costs of operation and maintenance.

Driving forces for aviation automation

Safety   A principal reason for adding automation to aircraft is to make them safer, and there is agreement that this effort has succeeded. At the same time, there is the obvious and continuing need to reduce human error in the cockpit and to make flying even safer. According to Chambers and Nagel (1985), "pilots are implicated in well over half the accidents which occur." According to international civil aviation authorities, because of refinements over the years the number of accidents caused by the machine has declined, while the number caused by humans has risen proportionately. Though more people travel by automobile, and safety per passenger mile continues to be better for commercial aircraft, aviation accidents tend to be dramatic and visible—more newsworthy than auto accidents, and perhaps more readily blamed on someone or something.

Economics   Commercial aviation is a very competitive industry. Flight crews have been reduced from three to two in many modern aircraft, on the basis of the alleged ability of automation to reduce crew workloads. Autopilots are present in essentially all commercial and military aircraft and are gradually making their way into private aircraft. Coping with the cost of fuel, especially as air traffic congestion increases, is a challenge which automation can help meet.

Technology   One might presume that technology would be adopted only insofar as it improves safety and economy, but it seems that often technology is adopted so that an airline can claim to have the latest equipment, or so that pilots and airlines can become familiar with the new technology in anticipation of future refinements in economics and safety. Computer technology, radar and optical sensors, and the soft technologies of control theory and artificial intelligence have been drivers in themselves.

What forms has the new technology taken?

New aviation technology (Billings 1991) includes TCAS (traffic alert and collision avoidance system), ARTS (automated radar terminal system), SSR (secondary surveillance radar), and ILS/MLS (instrument or machine-aided landing systems). The "glass cockpit" came in several years ago with Boeing's 757 and 767, in which integrated computer-graphic CRT, LED, and LCD displays integrate information heretofore presented on separate displays. These have replaced the multiple independent mechanical flight instruments and have permitted simplification of the instrument panel. Autopilots have been provided with multiple control modes, e.g., for going to and holding a new altitude, flying to a set of latitude-longitude coordinates, or making an automatic landing when the airport has the supporting equipment. In the new Airbus A320 a primary flight mode is fly-by-wire through miniature side-sticks, in dramatic contrast to the old control yokes. In the cockpit, computer-generated and computer-

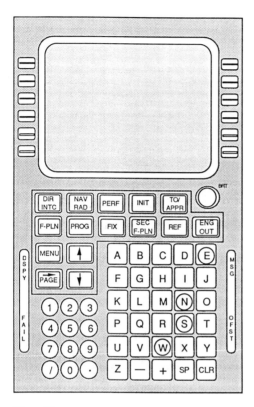

Figure 3.2
Flight management computer display of MD11. [Courtesy C. Billings, NASA.]

based expert systems give the pilot advice on engine conditions, how to save fuel, and other topics. Performance management systems are now available to optimize fuel and time.

The most exotic recent addition to the flight deck is the flight management system (FMS). The FMS is the aircraft embodiment of the human-interactive computer illustrated in figure 1.6. In the MacDonnell-Douglas MD11 version it appears as shown in figure 3.2, having a CRT display and both generic and dedicated keysets. 1400 software modules provide maps for terrain and navigational aids, procedures, and synoptic diagrams of various electrical and hydraulic subsystems. A proposed electronic map that would show flight plan route, weather, and other navigational aids is illustrated in figure 3.3. When the pilot enters a certain flight plan, the FMS can automatically visualize the trajectory and call attention to any way-

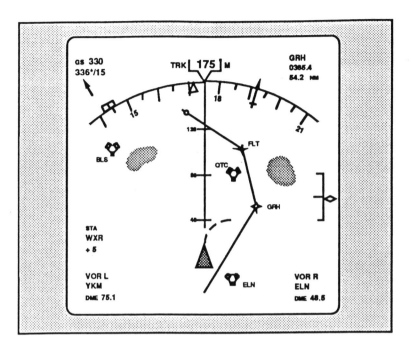

Figure 3.3
Computer-generated map display showing weather, flight plan route and navigation aids. [Courtesy C. Billings, NASA.]

points which appear to be erroneous on the basis of a set of reasonable assumptions. (This might have prevented the programmed trajectory that allegedly took KAL 007 into Soviet territory.) A proposed synoptic display for some electrical power components in the B747-400 is shown in figure 3.4. Such displays indicate numerically the values of the key variables, and call attention to any variable that is in an abnormal state. With some abnormalities, the subsystem is automatically reconfigured by opening or closing switches or valves; the pilot is informed afterward what has been done.

Pilot error

Pilot errors anonymously reported to the Federal Aviation Administration's Aviation Accident Reporting System are correlated with various causative factors. The behavioral factors are distraction, forgetting, failure to monitor, use of non-standard procedures, and complacency; the system-

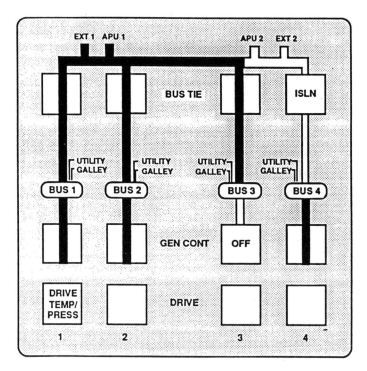

Figure 3.4
Synoptic display of AC electrical system of B747-400. [Courtesy C. Billings, NASA.]

related factors are lack of traffic information, degraded information, ambiguous of absent procedural guidance, environmental distraction, high workload levels, and equipment failures. Setup or data-entry errors are becoming more common. Interestingly, the human-factors problems of display interpretation, which were principal concerns 20 years ago (Grether and Baker 1972) are nowadays proving to be rare.

"Pilot error" is a controversial term. The issue is whether the pilot is a perpetrator or an agent. Many blunders can be directly attributed to the interface between the pilot and the autopilot system. In this regard, Bergeron and Hinton (1985) comment: "Forget some key step, set the automation into operation, trust it, and discover the error too late.... The problem appears to be almost as if the pilot thinks of the autopilot as a copilot and expects it to think for itself.... The pilot stores simultaneous inputs in short term memory for future processing. An overriding important piece of incoming information tends to wipe out large portions of his short term memory."

Wiener and Curry (1980) list the following causes of pilot error: failure of automatic equipment, automation induced error compounded by crew error, crew error in equipment setup, crew response to a false alarm, failure to heed automatic alarm, failure to monitor, and loss of proficiency.

In regard to the second-listed cause they cite the following example:

A Swift Air Lines Nord 262 departed Los Angeles International westbound. Shortly after gear retraction, its right engine autofeathered. Autofeather is a device common on advanced twin-engine propeller-driven planes. It senses a loss of power in an engine and feathers the propeller automatically. It is armed only on takeoff and initial climbout. The purpose of the autofeather is to preclude the possibility that a crewmember will shut down the wrong engine in the event of a power failure on takeoff. It remains for the crew to secure the dead engine, increase power on the operating engine, make trim adjustments, and continue climbing for a safe altitude for return to the field. Immediately after the right engine autofeathered the crew shut down the *left* (operating) engine. The result was a fatal ditching in the Pacific Ocean. Examination of the right engine showed there had been no power loss, and the autofeather had been due to to a broken hydraulic hose in the sensing mechanism. Later investigation revealed that inadvertent autofeathers on Nord 262 aircraft were not unusual. Thus, a device designed to automate human error out of the system had triggered a chain of events that was compounded by the very human error that it was supposed to prevent.

In regard to the sixth factor, it is often said that errors committed by the automation take longer to discover than those committed by humans. As noted earlier, the crew of KAL 007 allegedly failed to notice the aircraft's significant departure from the flight plan.

Other issues related to pilot-automation interaction

Complexity of the new technology   The number of independent warnings presented in the cockpit has grown from 188 in the B707 and 172 on the DC8 to 455 on the B747 and 418 on the DC10. Now there are efforts to reduce the number of warnings and reduce complexity. The ground proximity warning system, introduced by congressional mandate in 1974, has been denounced by pilots for frequent false alarms. Warnings on the newer B767 prioritize information, indicate severity, and in some cases present appropriate action. The TCAS makes a once-per-second survey of the relative positions of all other aircraft equipped with transponders within 15 miles, and only when altitude, distance, and closure rates are within certain ranges will it trigger the alarm. However, there still is said to be a problem with the mixing of TCAS-equipped and non-TCAS-equipped aircraft in crowded terminal areas.

Pilots' acceptance of new technology   The majority of pilots seem to like and use automated aircraft systems, but to be concerned about erosion of their skills. They have an interesting phrase to characterize the surfeit of new displays, controls, and decision aids: "killing us with kindness."

Out-of-the-loop monitor vs. in-the-loop controller   Even a decade ago it was apparent (Wiener and Curry 1980) that there was a dilemma between the pilot's being a continuous in-the-loop controller and being a monitor (supervisor) of automation. Figure 3.5 poses the dilemma. If the pilot does all the controlling she becomes overloaded and fatigued, while if the pilot is switched to a monitor of automatic systems there is the danger of

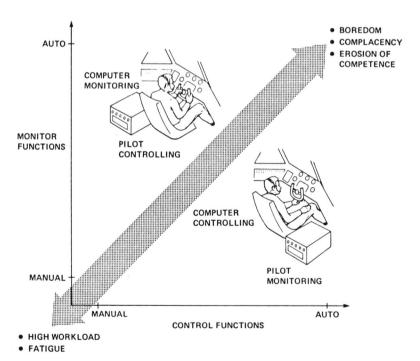

Figure 3.5
Pilot continuous control vs. monitoring of automation. [From Wiener and Curry 1980.]

becoming bored, complacent, and inattentive. Somehow active monitoring seems the ideal, but how to achieve that? New TCAS and windshear advisory systems offer examples.

The subproblems here are several:

• Is the human a better or worse failure detector when acting as an out-of-the-loop monitor than when acting as an in-the-loop controller? Experimental evidence on this is mixed.

• How serious is the "warmup delay" during the transition from monitor to active controller?

• Should the computer take charge automatically and inform the operator afterward, or make the change only after the operator's acknowledgement?

• Is an intermediate level of reliability worse than either of the extremes? The pilot may trust the equipment but not be experienced at handling a failure when it does occur. With intermediate reliability, she doesn't know whether to trust and ignore the prospect of failure or to mistrust and carefully monitor. In-between monitoring, it seems, is confusing.

In the Defense Advanced Research Projects Administration's Pilot's Associate Project, the pilot remains an active system monitor/manager while the electronic copilot flies the airplane and performs routine control tasks.

Inner loop vs. outer loop: Computer as helper vs. commander Most automation is in inner loops, with the pilot supervisory mode in outer loops. The flight director is a contradiction to this; the outer-loop decisions are automated and the plot is given the inner-loop steering commands for response. The Europeans have favored warnings and other information that provide helpful data rather than command information. In a similar vein, NASA has developed a rule-based "smart" checklist for the pilot.

Trading vs. sharing This is another variant of the problem of degree of automation. *Trading* means the pilot intermittently hands control off to the computer and later actively takes it back, but either one or the other is in the loop at any particular time. *Sharing* means both the pilot and the computer do different aspects of the control task in parallel, at the same time. These alternatives were diagrammed, in a generic way, in figure 1.34.

In aviation these are sometimes seen as mutually exclusive modes of control, but they need not be. In operating the autopilot, the pilot is trading. But even while the autopilot is holding altitude, the pilot may wish to change heading, thereby sharing.

Workload management   There has been a great concern about pilot workload in recent years, and the prospects of automation have fueled a debate over workload and whether, with new automation, the flight crew can safely be reduced to two. There is also concern about underload during periods of dull straight-and-level flight on autopilot; can the pilot wake up to a sudden demand, a sudden increase in workload? And is there an optimum level of workload (Verplank 1977) which could ever be sustained with the help of automation?

Flexibility of displays   There are many possibilities for how information should be displayed, given that computer-graphic displays allow for almost infinite flexibility. This is especially true when "soft" keys are used on CRT overlay touch screens, which are capable of being reconfigured to suit the phase of the mission or other circumstances. Should the pilot have the option to reconfigure some displays to suit his taste? Should reconfiguration of some displays, for example the primary flight displays, not be allowed? This is the policy of the MD11 design.

Dependence on the head-up display   Use of the head-up display (HUD) provides an example of a current controversy in the field of man-machine design philosophy (Naish and Von Wieser 1969). HUD protagonists want crew members to "head-up" during bad weather to see the runway as soon as it becomes visible. Antagonists prefer that the automatic landing system be employed all the way to the ground, with the pilot acting as a monitor. A middle ground would be to do an "autoland" approach monitored by means of a head-up display, a technique currently operational on some European carriers.

Communication between crews   Precise verbal communication is critical. This is especially true for international flights, where spoken communications may not be in the participants' native languages. Confusion and ambiguity in spoken communication is alleged to have caused the Tenerife accident between two fully loaded B747s. Heretofore we have depended on ordinary natural-language radio communication. Should this be supplanted with computerized tower-to-aircraft and inter-aircraft communication and display?

Ultimate authority   The problem of authority is one of the most difficult. Popular mythology is that the pilot is (or should be) in charge at all times. But think about it. When a human turns control over to an automatic system, it is with the expectation that she can do something else for a while (as in the case of setting one's alarm clock and going to sleep). It is also recognized that there are limited windows of opportunity for escaping from the automation (once you get on an elevator you can get off only at discrete floor levels). People are seldom inclined to "pull the plug" unless they receive clear signals indicating that such action must be taken, and unless circumstances make it convenient for them to do so. Examples of some current debates follow:

•   Should there be certain states, or a certain envelope of conditions, for which the automation will simply seize control from the pilot? In the MD11 it is impossible to exceed critical boundaries of speed and attitude which will bring the aircraft into stall or other unsafe flight regimes. The pilot can approach the boundaries of the safe flight envelope only by exerting much more than the normal force on the control stick.

•   Should the computer automatically deviate from a programmed flight plan if critical unanticipated circumstances arise? The MD11 will deviate from its programmed plan if it detects windshear.

•   If the pilot programs certain maneuvers ahead of time, should the aircraft automatically execute these at the designated time or location, or should the pilot be called upon to provide further concurrence or approval? The A320 will not initiate a programmed descent unless it is reconfirmed by the pilot at the required time.

•   In the case of a subsystem abnormality, should the affected subsystem automatically be reconfigured, with after-the-fact display of what has failed and what has been done about it? Or should the automation wait to reconfigure until after the pilot has learned about the abnormality, perhaps been given some advice on the options, and had a chance to take initiative? The MD11 goes a long way in automatic fault remediation.

Automation guidelines

Wiener and Curry (1980) offer some guidelines for design of cockpit automation and use of human pilots in conjunction with automation:

With respect to autopilot monitoring:

- Make displays easily visible, interpretable, and understandable.
- Ensure that the automation does the task the way the user wants it done. Allow for different operator styles, but make sure automation is insensitive to these choices, i.e., it works just as well with one as with another.
- Try to prevent peaks in workload. Have the automation work in such as way as to smooth out the peaks and valleys with respect to time.
- Since it is difficult for the computer to understand when the task's demands on the operator are too high, train the operator to recognize and to use automation as a resource.
- Give pilots training in monitoring and in otherwise working with automation (something they normally didn't get in flight school).
- Make pilots' duties meaningful, not busywork.
- Have the automation check for errors in setup (programming) when possible.

With respect to alarm monitoring:

- Keep false alarms within acceptable limits.
- Make alarms specify which failure mode caused them.
- Provide information so that the operator can make quick validity checks
- Have alarms indicate the degree of time urgency.

Future research and modeling

Research and modeling are needed to predict demands on pilots and equipment at all levels, and to get a better idea what worst-case transients might occur. Analyses should specify criteria by which pilots' requests are honored or refused, criteria for aircraft separation under different weather and facilities considerations, and what weather information should be sent by data-link to pilots. In any model it probably makes little sense to include more than a very small number of aircraft and pilots or ground controllers, since we now know so little about how to model multi-person human-machine systems. Two particularly difficult long-range research issues for aircraft automation concern the use of expert systems and the idea of "pilot-automation mutual models":

Use of expert systems; advice and consent   One tends to think of automation as a way to perform control once some human has told the computer what is to be done. However, that is only part of it. In fact, by analogy to the human nervous system, this may be the smallest part. After all, the lower brain does most regulation and feedback control, while the larger upper brain assesses sensory information and does planning. Future automation may in time develop more in the direction of advice-giving expert systems and data-fusion than automatic control as we have known it. For example, the pilot may need help in multi-attribute decisions, such as the selection between alternate airports under conditions of weather, type of instrument approach available, passenger facilities, maintenance facilities, runway length and conditions, fuel available and fuel cost, surrounding terrain, etc. The computer can weigh multiple factors more quickly than the pilot or the ground controller, but must then offer a convincing explanation of how it has developed its advice. The difficult human-factors question concerning how much advice is too much probably will remain. That is, at what point, as an advice-giving system becomes more reliable and more user-friendly, does the operator accede to its advice perfunctorily, in effect abandoning responsibility for critical independent thought?

Mutual models of the other   Well known to practitioners of control engineering and artificial intelligence is the usefulness of having, within the computer, a model of the process being controlled, or a model of the "outside world" with respect to which decisions are being taken. In cognitive psychology the idea of a "mental model" is also well established (though our ability to measure experimentally and understand such a mental model still leaves much to be desired). It has been variously proposed that when a human and a computer are working together each should have a dynamically updated model of the other. Presumably, if these mutual models could be made explicit, there would be a better basis for human and computer to monitor and understand one another, and to mutually confirm assumptions and intentions. Some wags go so far as to suggest that each should have a model of the other's model of itself, and possibly so on in infinite recursion. Unfortunately, the discipline is very far from providing effective mutual models. Not only does cognitive science offer little as yet that the engineer can work with for measuring the operator's mental model of the computer, but it is far from clear what overt human behavior should form the basis of a dynamic computer-based model of the human.

3.2   Automobiles: Intelligent Vehicle-Highway Systems

In terms of the trend toward non-anthropomorphic telerobotics, the automobile has not progressed nearly as far as the aircraft. Automation in automobiles is a just-emerging field, discussed here because of its future economic potential and because eventually it may touch everyone.

If the present trends continue to 2020, highway traffic in America will double (US Department of Transportation, May 1989). Sharp increases will occur in urban congestion, air pollution, and economic losses due to delays, stress, and accidents. 80,000 fatalities per year are projected in the year 2000 if the current rate stays the same and if Federal Highway Administration (FHWA) projected travel growth applies.

Dramatic improvements have occurred recently not only in microelectronics and software but also in radar, sonar, infrared, laser scanning, video imaging, and other means of detecting and measuring environmental objects. Vehicle detection by electromagnetic inductive loops buried in the highway has been somewhat unreliable, owing to ice and other conditions. New optical and infrared sensors mounted on the vehicle or on structures adjacent to the highway may be used in the future for detecting, identifying, and communicating between vehicles and local or central communication nodes. Global positioning satellites in synchronous orbit can, through triangulation, allow automobiles to locate themselves to within a few meters. All of this has led to plans for "intelligent highway vehicle systems (IVHS) for private automobiles, trucks, emergency vehicles, and taxicabs.

Past and current IVHS projects

Europe   In Germany, where the IVHS idea first caught on, ALI-SCOUT provided for routing information interchange between roadside infrared transceivers and specially equipped vehicles along a 60-mile stretch of the Autobahn. LISB is a later version being tested in Munich and Berlin. A project called AUTOGUIDE set up similar tests between London and Heathrow Airport. Two large projects have been set up under European Community auspices. One is PROMETHEUS, a consortium which began in 1986 among many European automobile companies, supplier companies, electronic firms, and university research institutes. It has an 8-year $800 million budget to develop a uniform Europe-wide traffic system incorporating IVHS technology. Three levels of driver communications are intelligent driver aids self-contained on-board the vehicle, communication networks between vehicles, and communications between vehicle and roadside. The second large program is DRIVE, which began in June 1988 with a budget of roughly $150 million over three years. It adds pollution prevention and standardization of products and services throughout Europe, and emphasizes information transfer between vehicle and highway.

Japan   The Japanese have two IVHS projects. One is AMTICS, a joint project involving the National Police, the Ministry of Posts and Telecommunication, the Japan Traffic Management and Technology Association, and 59 private companies. Eleven cars and a bus in central Tokyo receive traffic congestion information from a central location. Initial tests were completed in June of 1988. The second is RACS , which uses somewhat different technology and is sponsored by the Public Works Institute of the Ministry of Construction, the Highway Industry Development Organization, and 25 private companies. Navigation, traffic information, roadside information, and individual messages are disseminated from 74 roadside beacons in a 350-km^2 area of downtown Tokyo.

United States   A project called ETAK has demonstrated map matching augmented by dead reckoning to track vehicle location on a CRT map display. PATHFINDER is a cooperative demonstration project of the Federal Highway Administration, the California Department of Transportation, and General Motors. A number of specially outfitted vehicles operating in a 12.3-mile corridor of the Santa Monica Freeway in Los Angeles and on adjacent arterial roads receive real-time traffic information from a control center to help drivers avoid congestion and delays. TRAVTEK is a new collaboration between GM and the American Automobile Association to demonstrate navigational aids in Orlando. PATH is a six-year, $56 million program for the development of automation, electrification, and navigation technologies. As part of this effort, the University of California at Berkeley is developing advanced technology for automated vehicle control, longitudinal control based on a doppler radar, lateral control using preview sensing of magnets in the highway, and other control technology to support platooning, on-board electrical propulsion, and IVHS navigation and traffic management.

Mobility 2000 was a national study and discussion of IVHS concepts and needs convened by FHWA, with participants from a variety of government agencies, automobile and other industrial firms, and universities. It began in 1986 and has recently been transformed to become IVHS America. What follows is a brief overview of a number of issues gleaned from the author's participation in those discussions. These are grouped into the same four categories used in the Mobility 2000 and IVHS America meetings.

IVHS technology

Advanced traveler information systems (ATIS)   Advanced driver information systems technologies are being planned to reduce congestion through electronic pre-trip and en-route planning and navigation aids. These include on-board generation of maps, signs and speech messages to locate destinations and tell how best to get there, supplemented by continuous en-route guidance (continuous advice about weather, congestion, and what to do at each forthcoming choice point in the highway to reach a designated destination). ATIS should also provide electronic vehicle identification for toll debiting, and electronic "yellow pages" which may be scanned to determine availability, desired features, and location of fuel, food, medical, or other services. A computer-generated map display for navigational aiding is shown in figure 3.6.

At the first stage of development, most of the information provided the driver (in addition to what she sees through the vehicle windows) will come from digital storage within the vehicle. Such a CD-ROM or other digital store would be updated periodically by a digital area traffic information receiver. At a second stage (to about the year 2000) it is anticipated that vehicles will receive continuous area-wide dynamic information (e.g., current traffic conditions and traffic network link times, "Mayday" messages) from an electronic communications infrastructure (the so-called Advanced Traffic Management System, or ATMS). Plans are that by 2005 each vehicle will automatically exchange information (on local traffic conditions and best routes to the indicated destination) with the ATMS.

Advanced vehicle control systems (AVCS)   To some technologists the ideal transportation system is full automation, portal-to-portal transportation without human intervention. The path to such a goal is likely to be long, and some would say essentially unreachable. However, more modest AVCS attainments can have high payoff for traffic efficiency as well as safety. It has been claimed that, whereas the best current estimates indicate

Figure 3.6
Map display for automobile navigation. [Courtesy Toyota Motor Co.]

that ATIS and ATMS functions can produce improvements of no more than 10% to 20% in recurrent congestion (which is negated by 2–3 years' normal traffic growth in major metropolitan areas), AVCS can increase the capacity of a bridge or freeway by several hundred percent (Shladover 1990). At early stages, with the driver in full control, AVCS technology is expected to include obstacle detection for objects in front of or at the side of the vehicle (with appropriate warning of driver), driver vigilance monitoring and warning, vehicle status monitoring, infrared imaging to enhance night driving, head-up display to provide special information in a virtual image located in front of the vehicle, anti-lock braking, and four-wheel steering. Later AVCS will include adaptive cruise control to automatically maintain headway relative the vehicle in front, automatic braking if there is potential for collision, and automatic lane-keeping. Eventually, AVCS should enable platoons of up to 20 vehicles to move fully automatically between cities at high speeds at one-meter headways. In the latter case, joining and unjoining platoons will require new technology as well as new driver skills.

Commercial vehicle operations (CVO) This category includes heavy trucks, public safety vehicles (police, fire, ambulance), and taxis. Because these vehicles represent greater dollar investments and are also more heavily regulated than private automobiles, they are expected to adopt ATIS and AVCS technology more quickly and extensively. They are likely to have automatic vehicle identification and location, more extensive vehicle and driver status measurement (including tires, load balance and stability, alcohol, and drowsiness), and more extensive "yellow pages" to include information on where particular kinds of repairs can be obtained, where a truck can be pulled off the road for rest or maintenance check, etc.

Advanced traffic management systems (ATMS) As planned, advanced traffic management systems will make use of in-highway and in-vehicle sensing, measurement, and communication technologies to determine loci of congestion or hazard, best routings and speeds, and vehicle/driver status. This system will communicate appropriate information back to drivers through traffic signals, highway signing, or in-vehicle displays. ATMS can also close and open lanes and ramps. The human factors of the ATMS are not unlike those of those of the air traffic controller or the operator in a process control plant.

Issues of driver interaction with the new IVHS automation

Interaction with the ATIS computer while driving: Distraction and confusion There is little safety hazard if *before a trip is initiated* the traveler interacts with an on-board CD-ROM to indicate desired routing and be shown alternatives on a computer-generated map, or communicates with ATMS sources over home or vehicle-based telephone/computer to get updated traffic, weather or other information or routing advice, or consults "yellow pages" on availability and location of services. Clearly, doing this (reading and interpreting computer-generated maps, text, and symbolic displays, operating buttons, switches, and cursor controls to initiate programs to enter desired destinations or route choices) while simultaneously driving in traffic *can* seriously distract attention from the road and compromise safety. This is especially true if the driver does not see out the window what she expects, and suddenly becomes confused, delays too long in making required control actions, and exacerbates a predicament.

Reading and interpreting computer-generated maps, text, and symbolic displays Map reading is a capability not shared by all members of society. Some people are more "visual thinkers" and some have had much more training in visualization (e.g., artists and engineers) than others. Airplane pilots and others who must use maps in their work and for their survival may be said to be largely self-selected. Putting maps into automobiles, where they become a semi-requirement to driving, can pose a serious problem of human engineering. Map displays will have to be observed a longer time than a glance, in contrast with the speedometer and other existing instrument panel displays. The driver must repetitively glance from roadway to map and back. With each glance she must reaccommodate, which itself may take considerably longer than one second, especially with older drivers. It is well established in the human-factors literature on visual monitoring and visual-motor control that glance frequency is proportional to the rate at which salient image patterns are changing. Thus we have the easily foreseeable scenario of an older person struggling to read a map to determine what maneuver to make as she is driving into a complex traffic situation, not knowing whether to make a turn or continue, not able to take her eyes off the road for very long, yet experiencing difficulty reaccommodating with each glance, and not having time to dwell on either display long enough to take in all of what she needs!

Add to this the fact that many drivers will not be good map readers. The computer map should probably remain oriented so that the actual vehicle orientation corresponds with the vehicle's orientation on the map. But the difficulty with that is that the general orientation of the map will continually change, so the driver who has a hard time with spatial relations may lose her sense of location when the map orientation changes after she makes, say, a 90° turn, and will have to spend considerable time getting reoriented.

Increased hand control complexity   In comparison with an aircraft cockpit, the automobile instrument panel has been blessed by having relatively few buttons, switches, and hand controls to be operated while driving. (Most drivers now learn to operate only the most important radio controls while driving—e.g., station-selection and volume—and ignore the others.) IVHS threatens to increase the number of controls significantly. A challenge will be to keep the number of additional controls down. Each manufacturer will want to include many options, some of them not particularly essential, to help market its equipment. Having more controls will make it more difficult to design controls for easy selection by location and touch, to ensure that they are reachable, and to uphold stimulus-response compatibility (meaning controls are located appropriately relative to each other and relative to displays, and direction of operation is consistent with direction of display and with expectation).

Ignored and too-complex warnings   Whatever the technology, radar, sonar, infrared, or laser, the collision warning is meant to draw the operator's attention to imminent events that require instantaneous attention (e.g., rapid closing speed with a vehicle in the same lane, a vehicle converging from a different direction on a collision course with one's own, or one's own vehicle heading off the road). It is likely to be a relatively simple auditory alarm since a visual alarm may not be seen in time. Directionality (indication of where to look) can be provided by using two or more sound sources. However, a particular collision warning may not be expected. If the threshold is too sensitive, a high occurrence of collision warnings for fully expected traffic situations may be "crying wolf" so often that the driver's response is inhibited (or, to use a somewhat out-of-fashion behavioral psychology term, extinguished).

Announcement of route-following information is different. This requirement results from having preplanned and prespecified a route to the ATIS navigation system. The announcement must not only indicate that a turn is imminent but must also indicate in which direction to turn, in which lane to be, and to what speed to slow to—quite a complex of information. It therefore is likely to be an attention-getting auditory signal plus a visual or synthetic speech message. Use of synthetic speech and/or graphical signals or both in this context raises the obvious but interesting question of standardizing speech and visual symbol formats across manufacturers. In the air traffic control world many accidents have been attributed to lack of insistence and adherence to standard speech communication formats.

Excessive dependence and false alarms   The warnings described above could create excessive dependence and condition the driver to become less attentive to the highway and what's coming. If a warning malfunctioned by not alerting the driver when she had come to depend on it, there could be a serious result. If such a warning system malfunctioned by indicating impending collision when there was none, and the driver responded by a sudden, inappropriate braking and/or steering maneuver, something an immediately trailing vehicle was not expecting, a serious accident could occur . Thus, the requirement for reliability is high.

Head-up displays   The head-up display (HUD) mentioned in conjunction with aircraft is now being tried in automobiles. It is a computer-generated graphics, symbol, or text presentation of warning or other urgent information. It is optically projected onto a partially reflecting segment of the windshield directly in front on the driver and focused at near-infinity, so the driver in observing it while driving need change her glance only slightly and need not reaccommodate. One special problem in the automobile is that the HUD image will seldom be seen against a clear visual background, as in aviation. More likely the background is cluttered with moving and distracting patterns.

Dynamic display of surrounding "traffic situation"   In aviation the "cockpit display of traffic information" (CDTI) provides a "plan view" of traffic not only in front but also in back and on both sides, with relative speed information, and simple prediction (based on speed difference extrapolation) to indicate who is closing on whom. In the highway situation such a system might show vehicles overtaking on either right or left, vehicles remaining at the same speed as one's own vehicle at "blind" locations on either right or left, vehicles tailgating one's own, as well as safe or unsafe distances/speeds relative to vehicles immediately ahead. But would it over-load the driver? Is it better that she just turn her head or use the rear-view mirrors?

Automatic speed, headway, braking, or steering control imposed on other-wise conventional human control   This automation assumes: (1) the driver will take control back when appropriate or continue in the manual control mode when an "automatic control event" has ended; (2) successful transi-tion from human to automatic control when entering a platooned, high-speed automatic control mode, or transition back to fully human control; (3) unanticipated emergency takeover by the human driver from the auto-matic control system. Automatic speed control is simply an extension of what we now know as cruise control, and assumes the driver will stay attentive, will take control back when she should, and/or will resume control when the computer decides the need for the automatic control takeover has ended and hands control back. Clearly the driver must know what to expect from the automatic system—under what circumstances it will give back control, and under what circumstances the human driver must actively take back control. Automatic headway control is determined largely by sensed distance to the vehicle ahead plus ATMS information about traffic congestion farther ahead. In this case automation-human control transitions occur with much shorter headways than with speed control. Questions such as whether at any instant of time control should be automatic *or* human (with the other quiescent), or control should be automatic *plus* human (actions superposed) must be researched in this context.

Automatic braking of the vehicle when the driver does not expect it could prove difficult for the driver to accept, and may have some serious safety consequences. One such consequence could be that the driver will be thrown off balance (foot will inadvertently depress brake because of body inertia, even though in a seat belt). The problems of criteria for transition-ing control and getting it back, as well as the question of trading vs. sharing of control between human and computer are particularly critical here.

Of various proposed driving control enhancements, automatic steering takeover may be the least acceptable to drivers and have the most serious safety consequences. Were this to be used, e.g., for avoidance of obstacles, it is far from clear how to give steering control back to the human or how to continue automatic steering.

Anticipated transients from human to fully automatic control in platoons or special guideway lanes, and vice-versa Typically, to enter a platooned, high-speed lane, the driver will drive her vehicle into a special ramp, perhaps slow or even stop her vehicle, and signal that she wishes to enter a high-speed platoon. If the vehicle is within the proper position and speed range, automation will take over, add the vehicle to a platoon, and accelerate the platoon when it is properly formed. If the vehicle is not within proper range, control will be given back and the driver will be expected to drive more or less in the same direction back onto the regular highway. To leave a platoon such a procedure would be reversed. In the case of either transition to automatic control or back to human control, the computer would act to prevent the change unless certain key conditions were fulfilled, otherwise allowing for "graceful" removal of the vehicle from the queue. This component of AVCS, though highly capital intensive, would be fairly predictable, and therefore may not have such serious safety implications as automatic control imposed or superposed on conventional driving.

IVHS proponents suggest that once the vehicle is safely ensconced on the automatic highway the driver can relax, read, sleep, or do whatever she chooses. Others insist that the driver must remain alert, positioned properly and monitoring the highway ready to take over control should the automation fail. There is serious question whether this last would be realistic to expect. Once the vehicle is on "automatic" for any period of time, and if the driver is not expecting to take over, experimental literature in manual control and vigilance suggests that there is little likelihood that she can be counted upon. However, the question deserves further investigation in the IVHS context.

The ever-busier high-speed office One compelling safety concern in this category is the image of the ever-more-sophisticated in-vehicle office, operating full-tilt even while moving at highway speeds. We all know the commuter with her cellular telephone, and evidence from Stein et al. (1987) already suggests that there are safety hazards due to the workload imposed by the cellular telephone. The cellular telephone is a status symbol, and having a fax machine, computer E-mail, and other such modern electronic appendages in one's vehicle may become even richer status symbols. As traffic jams become more prevalent, it may become more and more common to see the business or professional driver attending almost fully (eyes, hands, and brain) to business communications.

Exacerbation of the above problems because of age, education, culture, or physical handicap   The fraction of older drivers on the highway may be expected to increase dramatically in the coming decade. This means a decrement in the average driver's vision capability (uncorrected acuity, accommodation range, accommodation time, color discrimination at night, and ability to turn head and move body to obtain depth cues or to attend to what is to the side of or behind her vehicle). Average age increase will also mean longer reaction time for finding and operating controls, for remembering procedures for making requests of ATIS, and for making maneuvering decisions. Those with poor education may find particular difficulty with map reading and interpretation, and reading and understanding text messages such as route guidance. Non-English-speaking drivers may be expected to have somewhat the same difficulties as those with limited education. Vision handicaps are likely to affect map reading the most. The hearing impaired will naturally have problems with an auditory collision warning. Perhaps the more serious problem is the devotee of eardrum-shattering rock music, to whom the auditory alarm may simply be masked out. Motor and body movement handicaps may limit ability to perform some high-dexterity data-entry functions (e.g., directing a cursor on the map with a trackball).

It may be expected that the older and/or less well educated driver will adapt to automation technology less readily and understand less well its requirements and procedures. In entry to and exit from automated guideways there may be critical signs and symbols required which demand taking account of cultural differences. A physically handicapped person might have an especially difficult time with automatic braking and steering because of being thrown off balance. The most serious concern in this category has to do with combinations of negative factors occurring simultaneously.

Risk homeostasis   There is an often-espoused theory that drivers seek a fixed risk level, and as safer vehicles and highways are provided the driver will simply speed up, until the risks are again at the same level as before the "safer" capability was introduced. Will IVHS technology have that effect?

Social interactions on the highway   Today's drivers have little chance to interact socially, except to exchange anonymous glances or in some cases (e.g., in Boston traffic) to try to create the impression they don't know the other is there. Tomorrow's IVHS technology can change all that. Not only could there be communication between vehicles and the ATMS, but there could also be communication between the vehicles themselves (there already is with cellular phones and CB radio). Suppose (as a thought experiment) that, as one is moving down the highway in one's car, one can selectively direct spoken comments to different surrounding vehicles much as one does in a small group discussion. It is entirely within audition technology art to receive properly coded incoming signals displayed by two or three sound sources in such a way that the "location" of the virtual source is clearly identified, and in the context of conversations with surrounding vehicles the driver has little doubt about which vehicle a message directed to him is coming from. Direction of an outgoing message to a vehicle could be accomplished by pointing a hand- held wand (directly or through the rear-view mirror).

While the skeptic might consider such communications to be foolish (or, worse, a facilitated means of hurling insults), I believe this could improve and enrich social interactions on the highway from the present state of anonymity and uncertainty about one's neighbor and how she will respond. One could say to a selected car "Pardon me, I need to turn here, do you mind if I break in?" or "Did you know your right tail light was out?" or "Excuse me, but is this New York City?" In order to stay awake, one might try to strike up a conversation: "Hello there, this is a boring stretch of highway isn't it? Where are you from in Kansas?" It seems to me that potentially such conversation makes the highway not only more humane but also safer.

Driver error and design guidelines

IVHS is so new that not enough error data have been collected, nor have significant design guidelines evolved. Many of the problems are not unlike those of aviation, and in many ways what happens on the highway will follow naturally from what is proven in aviation. On the other hand, the highway is a much more democratic and free-for-all place, and it is unlikely that either the technology or the human operators will ever be as constrained, reliable, and well regulated as in aviation.

3.3 Nuclear Power Plants

The nuclear power plant is a third example of a non-anthropomorphic telerobot. The use of the term *telerobot* may seem even farther from the conventional notion of "robot" here, since the plant itself does not move. However, the definition of *telerobot* given in the introduction still applies. The plant machinery under direct control by the computer and under supervisory control by the human moves relative to its environment— which in this case amounts to the environment (water, steam, oil, etc.) moving within the stationary plant. The sensors, the actuators, and the control structure all meet the same criteria as the other telerobots discussed above.

Status of the technology

In some sense the typical nuclear power plant is not as advanced a tele-robot as is a typical modern chemical or pharmaceutical plant, petroleum refinery, or fossil-fuel electrical power generating plant. The latter tend to have advanced faster and farther in use of computers and automatic control, and in terms of computerized control rooms and decision aids. This is because the nuclear power plant, on which much more public attention is focused than the others, is highly regulated, and therefore likely to be more conservative about change—especially when it appears that human employees are being relieved of control in favor of computers.

The physical process of nuclear power generation begins with nuclear fuel rods, which, when placed in close proximity to one another, generate a fusion reaction accompanied by heat. In the *pressurized light-water reactor*, ordinary water under high pressure is pumped past these rods in the *reactor vessel* and then circulated through a heat exchanger, called a *steam generator*. In the exchanger's secondary loop other water is thereby converted to steam, which drives a turbine and is then cooled back to water and recirculated. The turbine shaft is coupled directly to the electrical generator. In the *boiling light-water reactor* the operation is similar except that the cooling water is converted to steam in the reactor vessel by passing the fuel rods, and this steam goes directly to the turbine—there is only one cooling loop and no steam generator. In Canada, deuterium (heavy water) is used in place of ordinary water. In some British plants inert gas is used as the coolant. Some modern plants use liquid sodium and have three successive cooling loops.

This seemingly simple process, in a sense the inverse of the heat pump or refrigeration, is implemented in an extremely complex way. There are thousands of sensors and hundreds of indicators, controls, and alarm lights. Clearly the control room of a nuclear power plant is a prime candidate for the same kind of computer-augmented simplifications that have been implemented in the flight decks of modern transport aircraft.

Just before the Three Mile Island accident, Westinghouse, General Electric, Combustion Engineering, and Babcock-Wilcox, the four major manufacturers of nuclear plant equipment, had advanced control room designs. However, these were never implemented, because new plant construction essentially ceased after the accident. The accident resulted in the Nuclear Regulatory Commission (NRC) mandating a number of human factors improvements:

• detailed control room redesign;

• improved "symptom-based" emergency procedures which specify what operators should do based on what the instruments say—even though the operators may not understand the cause;

• improved emergency training;

• the continuous availability of a *shift technical advisor* who has more theoretical understanding of the regular plant operators; and

• the installation of a *safety parameter display system* (SPDS) designed to give the operators an overview of the health of the plant (the many alarm lights having proven sometimes confusing to interpret and therefore useless in a major emergency).

Current issues regarding automation and supervisory control

The following are some of the issues which particularly involve automation and the new roles of the operator:

Flexible computer-based displays and controls vs. dedicated instruments and switches   Traditional nuclear plant control rooms are large and cumbersome, with their benchboards and backboards and side panels covered by many rows of switches and indicators. Three reasons for this are the size of the standard hardware instruments, the requirements for protection against earthquakes, and the requirements for redundancy coupled with the requirements that wires for such redundant subsystems be physically separated from one another so as maximize the survival of at least one channel in case of fire. As in aviation and other applications, the computer enables the traditional control panel to be greatly simplified. Many alternative displays can be provided in the same space, such as fluid flow and wiring diagrams, trend plots (as key variables against time), and bar charts formatted to indicate the proper ranges of variables for the particular plant condition or maneuver being undertaken. Instead of dedicated switches and knobs, control can now be made by touch-screen or mouse or track-ball to select pull-down menus or "soft keys" on the computer display. The old seismic, redundancy, and fire requirements have to be reconsidered in light of the new technology, which promises more efficient and friendly coupling with the human operator.

Unfortunately, again as in the case of aviation, not all is perfect about the new computer-based displays and controls. Some evidence has been forthcoming that operators like to be able to turn to fixed, remembered locations for particular kinds of information, especially in emergencies. If certain information is needed in a hurry, it can be frustrating not to remember how to bring it up on the computer screen.

There is room for a few dedicated computer-based displays. A good example is the safety parameter display system mentioned above, which was mandated after the Three Mile Island accident to provide at one location, and in an integrated way, a display of the "health" of the plant. If the plant isn't completely healthy, the SPDS indicates generally where the trouble lies. Typical designs have provided, for 6–12 key variables, simple bar graphs indicating deviation from normal, or light-boxes labeled with abbreviations, which turn color or flash as a function of the degree of abnormality. Figure 3.7 gives an example. An alternative display shows an overview flow diagram for whole plant, elements of which turn color or flash or show warning messages in text. The computer-generated flow diagram is perhaps most useful for second-level (somewhat more detailed) information about a subsystem of the plant which is abnormal. The information is displayed either automatically or at the operator's request. Some other summary display systems have been offered and have been bought by individual plants, including systems for monitoring radiation, fire, or toxic fumes. The point of such systems is to obviate the need for the operator to scan a large number of individual displays to detect whether anything is abnormal and to indicate generally what it might be.

Use of computers for advice-giving and automatic control as well as display Thus far it has been assumed that the human operator is there to decide what control actions to take and to take such actions on the basis of the information displayed to her. Expert systems, which draw conclusions and give advice, go a step further. Having the computer decide what

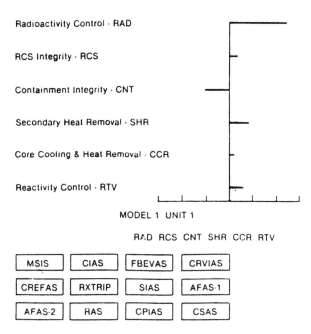

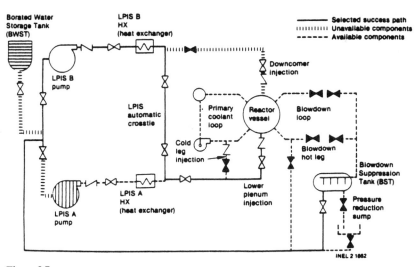

Figure 3.7
Three safety parameter display systems (SPDS). Above, six variables represented by bars indicating deviations from normal; middle, twelve light boxes to indicate class of abnormality; below, diagram of a plant, components of which flash or change color to indicate abnormality.

to do and do it without human intervention goes even further. The question is how far to go. The NRC and US nuclear power industry have been extremely conservative in adopting the advice-giving decision aids and the automatic control systems already available.

To be sure, simple automatic control loops have been in nuclear power plants for many years. These have been single-variable proportional-integral-derivative (PID) regulator controllers to hold levels and flows and other variables to operator-specified set points. What is in question are the more sophisticated computer-executed algorithms and control techniques based on many variables simultaneously. So too, there have been paper documents available for years to explain the meanings of particular alarm lights, what might have caused them to come on, and what immediate procedural steps are recommended. However, the use of computer displays to provide such information, or the use of computers to inhibit the display of some alarms which are totally redundant when other alarms are triggered, is controversial. A principal concern, whether well founded or not, is simply whether computer hardware and software can be as reliable as the old analog instruments.

Rasmussen (1986) has gone further and suggested that the computer might well provide explanations of "reasons why" various hardware and procedures were designed as they were. Then the operator, when tempted to conclude that current conditions call for circumventing established procedures or uses of hardware systems, can have the benefit of the designer's thinking. Often such information is inaccessibly filed away or long since lost.

The use of computer-based advice-giving raises the same questions in the nuclear power context as were raised earlier regarding the human operator's becoming over-dependent on such advice and abdicating responsibility. The use of computer-based automatic control brings up the same questions for nuclear power that were considered earlier about the human operator as a monitor versus an in-the-loop controller.

Selection and training of operators Nuclear power plant control room operators in the US must be licensed by the NRC, and those in other nations must be licensed by their governments. Regular control room operators are examined at one level; senior operators are examined at a higher level. A senior operator must be on duty at all times. This person, called a *shift supervisor*, is the equivalent of the captain of a ship or a transport aircraft. Maintenance personnel and operator assistants, who often work in the control room, are not licensed.

Many questions have been raised concerning the proper qualifications for regular and senior control room operators. One of these questions concerns level of education; another concerns age. A third and perhaps more interesting question concerns the relative emphasis on practical vs. theoretical training. Some assert, especially as control rooms become more sophisticated and control becomes more automatic, that operators should have a profound theoretical understanding of how the plant works, so that they can "see beyond" the control room instruments and anticipate physically what is happening or is about to happen. Others assert a quite different view, namely that expert theoretical advice is always available but that in an emergency a "contemplative scientist" is not what is needed so much as a skilled practical person who can respond instantly and "buy time," and that the theoreticians can came in later.

Another interesting question is that of limiting selection with respect to body size. Traditionally, nuclear plants have been built with the expectation that the operators would be men. Small women often need stepladders to reach the controls. Current control room design guidelines suggest the need to accommodate the 5th-percentile to 95th-percentile person, without specifying the reference population. However, the 5th-percentile woman is very much smaller than the 5th-percentile individual of a mixed population consisting mostly of men.

These days much operator training is accomplished with full-scale high-fidelity control room simulators. Much as airline pilots, operators are trained initially and in refresher courses in these simulators, using some of the worst imaginable accident scenarios. One of the mistakes that has been made, however, is to overemphasize disastrous "design-basis accidents" and not put enough emphasis on small accidents with compound abnormalities which have a tendency to grow gradually and insidiously. In real life, the latter pose the more serious threat.

Human error and probabilistic risk analysis In order to justify nuclear power to the public and the Congress, the NRC and the nuclear industry have resorted to probabilistic risk analysis (PRA). This is an application of combinatorial statistics to calculate the relative likelihood of safety-related events, such as radiation releases of a certain magnitude outside the plant, and economics-related events, such as plant "availability" (i.e., that it is not shut down). As part of this analysis the probability of human error must be specified for each step in the execution of each emergency procedure. "Performance shaping factors" such as time on shift, training, and whether operators are distracted by radios (or, conversely, annoyed because management will not allow them) are also being acknowledged as having a significant effect. The subject of human error and some of the techniques used in human reliability analysis (HRA) are discussed more below.

HRA and its relation to PRA continue to be controversial. There are fundamental questions about what human errors are, what causes them, and whether the human operator can be treated for risk-analysis purposes in the same way as pumps, valves, and computers. Automation and supervisory control will not make these problems go away, but will require new efforts to yield reasonable reliability numbers.

Traditionally PRA has considered only hardware and control room operators. Now plants are being forced to quantify the reliability of software. There are many other human beings performing safety- and economics-related functions in power plants, such as those doing maintenance and management. The effects of these additional sources of human error are also discussed below.

New plant-design philosophy: Simplicity vs. defense in depth   Traditional nuclear power plants are built on a philosophy of "defense in depth." This means there are multiple systems providing a series of protective barriers to keep radiation from the public. A few such barriers are automatic systems to "scram" the plant (drop neutron-absorbing control rods between the fuel rods to inhibit the nuclear fission reaction), systems to pump borated high-pressure water into the reactor vessel to further inhibit the reaction, and a steel-reinforced reactor containment structure designed to withstand the combination of a transport aircraft engine colliding at cruising speed and high overpressure inside, and still keep the radioactivity from leaking out. There has been a cost to this defense in depth, not only in dollars but also in complexity. Having safeguard on top of safeguard calls for more pumps, valves, pipes, sensors, wires, and instruments to control and monitor the multiple layers of safety systems. Some would say this has resulted in plants that are less safe than if designs were simpler.

New designs being considered tend to be smaller, passive (e.g., depending on gravity rather than pumps to flood the reactor in emergencies), and much less inherently complex. Greater simplicity of basic design does not preclude the use of computers); the claim is that a simpler plant can be run by a single operator monitoring a small number of computer screens in a control room the size of an airplane's flight deck.

Standardization of plants vs. the free market In the US every nuclear power plant is different. The local utility hires an architectural engineering firm (of which there are many) to design and build a plant, and buys the reactor vessel, the major pumps, the steam generator, the turbine-generator, and other major components from various suppliers. There are few requirements for standardization, only that the plant be shown to the NRC to be safe. The two plants on Three Mile Island, even though the major components were from the same vendor, had different architect-engineers and turned out to look quite different both inside and out. (Unit 2, where the accident occurred, was the newer and more complex of the two.)

Plants designed and built in such a free-market manner have proven to be costly to build and maintain (every plant must maintain an independent engineering staff), difficult to regulate (failures and weaknesses that arise in one plant cannot be "fixed" in other plants), and even more difficult to learn and generalize from (the statistical sample is one). For this reason, the precedent set by France, Germany, and Japan, where successful plant designs are built in multiple copies at far less cost than in the US), will probably be followed for the next round of US nuclear plants. This should be true of control software, procedures, training and management policies, and other hardware aspects in addition to all the hardware.

3.4   Flexible Manufacturing Systems

The phrase *flexible manufacturing system* (FMS) refers to the combination of many discrete parts-manufacturing operations under some combination of automatic (computer-based) and human control within a single factory. An FMS may include one or many computer-controlled machines used to perform individual metal-forming operations (rolling, stamping, extruding, casting, etc.), cutting operations (milling, drilling, boring, reaming) surface-finish operations (grinding, painting, heat-treating, etc.), and the transfer of raw materials for in-process parts between workstations. Any one such machine can be considered to be a telerobot, anthropomorphic or not. In the aggregate, the problems of automation and supervisory control resemble those of vehicles in traffic or those of process control.

The importance of FMS might seem to warrant more extensive treatment than it will be given here. The fact is that, although FMS technology is undergoing very active development, and both operations-research and optimal-control modelers have been contributing to this development since it began, there seems to be little recognition that the fully automatic factory (sometimes referred to in the popular media as the "lights-out factory") is just as far off as the fully autonomous robot in any other application—not withstanding the fact that a few demonstrations of combined automatic operations have succeeded in running for days at a time. Parts break or become defective. Tools wear. Machines have to be maintained and repaired. Manufacturing objectives change, and the FMS must be reprogrammed from time to time. Realistically, both humans and computers are required.

Important supervisory functions of the FMS supervisor are scheduling of production changes, constraints of limited resources, monitoring of system flows and outputs, scheduling of maintenance, and intervention in the case of failure. Ammons, Govindaraj, and Mitchell (1988) discuss these problems.

The purpose of production scheduling is to reduce item flow times, reduce work-in-process inventory, increase machine utilization, guarantee product quality, and meet promised due dates. There are physical constraints on the rates and accuracies of materials handling and transfer (with some important tradeoffs), and constraints on parts feed and cutting or processing speed (more tradeoffs). There are economic constraints on dollars and on time, safety constraints, and accuracy (quality) constraints.

Mathematical models have addressed only a few variables and issues, and artificial intelligence and advanced control can accommodate only those factors that are well defined. The numbers of variables, possible configurations, and salient qualitative factors in FMS are immense. Thus, the human operator must plan and manage. Carefully designed displays and controls and computer-based simulation, prediction, and decision support are essential. Sharit et al. (1987) and Sanderson (1988) review the literature.

Sanderson (1991) proposes a model of human supervisory scheduling of FMS. Her model, which she calls the "model human scheduler," superposes 27 production rules on the Rasmussen (1986) human decision ladder (from signals-in at the foot of one leg, to goal criteria at the apex, down the other leg to actions-out, with short-cut transitions at various levels). It includes skill-based, rule-based, and knowledge-based scheduling components. Her model, as yet not fully implemented, also draws upon the "model-human-processer"of Card et al. (1986) to implement some cognitive steps.

3.5 Other Examples of Non-Anthropomorphic Telerobots

Other kinds of process control

In just about every one of the process-control industries (i.e., where some product is more or less continuously pumped or otherwise moved through a plant) there has been extensive automation with human supervision. This includes petroleum, chemicals, and pharmaceuticals, and injection molding in manufacturing, to name a few such applications. The need for operators to move about the plant opening and closing valves and switches has been reduced greatly—control is either done remotely from a central control room or executed by a computer according to a program, and usually both are possible.

Space systems

The space applications of telemanipulation were discussed in chapter 2. There are many remote control functions to be performed on spacecraft which are not on telemanipulators (the latter being categorized in this book as anthropomorphic telerobots) but rather more resemble process control. This includes continual monitoring of engines, fuel, computers, and other instruments, life-support systems, and payloads, including scientific experiments in which ground-based personnel perform non-manipulative tele-science. The human supervisory operators in this case typically sit in front of consoles at NASA's "mission control" centers at Houston and Cape Canaveral.

Monitoring patients in hospitals

Another form of supervisory control is carried out on the continuous process that is a human patient. Sensors can be set to continuously monitor heart rate, oxygen or other chemical properties of the blood, respiration rate, chemical properties of respiratory gases, EEG, EKG, and so on, in or out of the operating room. Monitoring and supervisory control of anesthesia is where most closed loop control has been focused. There are good prospects for using predictor displays (such as were mentioned in chapter 2) as aids to the anesthesiologist or in other patient-monitoring situations.

Automatic teller machines

In the ATM what is being processed is cash and paper printouts. The user programs her request, and the computer responds on the basis of its data and does the local control required to deliver the cash, print the statement, and debit or credit the account. There may be lots of options, and in the future there will be more elaborate dialog with the customer and a wider range of services.

3.6   Goal Setting and Satisficing

In chapter 1, *planning* was asserted to be the first of four principle functions of the supervisor, and the "satisfice objectives" aspect of planning was presented. Some specific examples of teleoperation planning aids were given in chapter 2. Here we deal more fully with the issue of decision making and valuation (satisficing of objectives) as it applies to supervisory control.

According to Johannsen and Rouse (1979), rational planning can be broken down into (1) generation of alternatives, (2) imagining the consequences, (3) valuing (or evaluating) the consequences of the alternatives, and (4) choosing one alternative as a plan. These four steps correspond nicely to the supervisory *plan* function of the supervisor set forth earlier. Johannsen and Rouse also include "initiating execution of the plan, monitoring plan execution, and debugging and updating the plan," which in the present context belong to the teaching, monitoring, and learning supervisory functions.

Task analysis

Step 1 (generating feasible alternatives) and step 2 (imagining the consequences) are creative acts, but are constrained by what either nature or other people (or circumstances) have determined for us.

Putting these constraints down on paper is called *task (function) analysis*. It is a topic that has caused much confusion in communications between human-factors professionals and engineering designers. While the engineering designer might easily see that a detailed specification of machine and operator functions could be written down *after* the system hardware and software have been designed (and in that case one might call the task statement a *procedure*), the human-factors person sees task analysis as where the human-machine system design begins.

Task analysis for designing any machine results in a statement of what information and/or energy should be (is expected to be) sent from the machine to its environment, and vice-versa, under what circumstances. In the case of a human-machine system, task analysis is a specification of what information and/or energy should be communicated from the machine to the human (before the particular display, or method of communicating is designed), and what information should be communicated from the human to the machine (before the particular control is designed), both as a function of the time, space, or contingent circumstances surrounding their interaction. Task analyses commonly take the form of tables, where for each person and/or major machine subsystem there are different columns indicating time, place or other independent condition, information (energy) in, information (energy) out, and criterion of success or failure. They can also take the form of flow charts. Another form is a matrix, where different human or machine elements are indicated on the vertical and horizontal margins, and information/energy flows are indicated in the cells, along with time, spatial location, or circumstances. One can conceive of other ways to render the same information.

Usually, at least in designing a human-machine control interface, enough of the machine and its intended form of interaction with its environment are already specified so that the designer is not starting from nothing.

Objective function and satisficing

Step 3, valuation of the consequences of the various alternatives is a problem which shall be dealt with in some detail below. Choosing one alternative as a plan is essentially trivial once the first three steps are complete: one chooses that alternative having consequences with the greatest net positive value (which implies consideration of probabilities and constraints of what is possible, etc.)

One could say that completion of the chosen plan, and the equivalent realization of the accompanying consequences, constitute reaching a *goal* (or, synonymously for present purposes, an *objective*). Thus, steps 1–3 are equivalent to goal setting. Can one have a plan without having a goal? I don't think so. An aimless plan is a contradiction. Can one have a goal without having a plan? Perhaps not a detailed plan, i.e., one with subplans. The overall plan must necessarily be to able reach the goal (and if it is proven not able, a new plan must be formed or a new goal set). Subplans, if one has them, are simply to reach subgoals, and so on.

Even for a machine that all could agree is "completely automatic" some human being, whether system designer or operator, is called upon to evaluate the relative worth of alternative decisions (actions) in terms of their consequences. In controlling a telerobot this is likely to occur repetitively and often. Thus planning or goal setting (and the updating of such plans or goals as circumstances change) is obviously an important function that the human supervisor performs.

Formally, in a control system, the end consequences which have value are the controlled process state variables (e.g., position, orientation, velocity, force, length, reliability, or color) and the resources spent (time, energy, dollars, subjective effort). Rarely is the goal, the objective, to achieve the greatest possible value of a single state variable (e.g. speed) or the smallest possible value (e.g. dollars), where nothing else matters. In most real-world situations there are many variables that matter and that one would like to maximize or minimize simultaneously.

Is it goal setting, then, to specify the ideal values of many system state or resource variables? No, because real systems unfortunately cannot attain the ideal values of all the state and resource variables at once. Having the greatest possible speed, the greatest accuracy, the least energy consumption, and the lowest dollar cost simultaneously, all with 100% safety and reliability, is clearly not possible—in spite of the claims of some advertisers or politicians. The human valuer is left to specify the conditions for *compromising* among the objectives—the relative goodness (or badness) of all salient combinations of state variables and resources. The latter, a scalar function of many variables, is called the objective function. The simplest *objective function* is a sum of weighted variables.

In practice, not all the state variables need be arguments of the objective function, since the decision maker may not care about some components of the state vector. Normally system performance is judged in terms of a subset of the total state vector.

If the objective function can be specified and the system can be operated so as to achieve the maximum value of this function, given certain physical or economic constraints, we say that the system's performance has been *optimized.* If the human operator cannot quite specify a global objective function (one that covers all conceivable circumstances) and/or can be satisfied with system performance that comes "close enough," we speak instead of *satisficing.*

Multi-objective optimization: An elusive goal

To optimize anything—to find a "best" combination of salient variables—one needs to solve simultaneously two sets of equations: those that determine the physical and economic constraints and relations of the controlled process and those that specify relative goodness or badness of various states of the controlled process (the objective function).

In most so-called optimization done by control engineers and "operations research" analysts, the physical and analytical constraints are carefully considered in a model. All too often, the objective function is merely assumed by them to be of some convenient mathematical form, e.g., a sum of squares of time, error, and energy to be minimized with weighting coefficients arbitrarily assumed and "able to be adjusted later."

If the objective function were in terms of only one variable, e.g., cost in dollars to be minimized, then clearly one could optimize by evaluating various decision alternatives and determining which was of lowest cost—without considering other factors. Unhappily, in complex systems involving many objectives, determining real objective functions from real people has proven to be very difficult and very context-dependent. Hence optimization is correspondingly difficult. People all too often claim that they are "optimizing" a system when the most they can legitimately claim is that they are making it better with respect to an arbitrarily assumed criterion.

But these difficulties don't make rational decision making impossible. In fact, with some understanding of basic concepts plus a little humility, a decision maker can be quite rational. First let us look at decision among discrete alternatives, and introduce the ideas of *risk* and *criterion.*

Risky choice among discrete alternatives in terms of discrete objectives

Most real-world decisions involve the element of *risk* and the selection of a *probabilistic decision criterion. Risk* means that for any alternative decision (control action that might be taken) the ensuing benefits (in terms of some desired objectives) depend upon uncontrollable and uncertain events or system states. What the system analyst usually does is infer from histori-

CIRCUMSTANCES

		x p(x) =0.7	y p(y) =0.3	expected value	min	max
ACTIONS	A	6	4	5.4	4	6
	B	5	5	5.0	5	5
	C	7	0	4.9	0	7

Figure 3.8
Payoff matrix. Number in cell shows payoff for taking action (*A*, *B* or *C*) under
circumstance (*x* or *y*).

cal data or otherwise estimate the probability of each uncontrollable system state, and the benefit or cost resulting from control action in combination with each uncontrollable system state. For example, figure 3.8 shows
a payoff for the joint occurrence of each of two objectives *x* and *y* for each
of three actions *A*, *B*, and *C*. Marginal probabilities for the occurrences of
x and *y* are also given.

How one uses such a decision or payoff matrix depends on the *probabilistic decision criterion* selected. The most conservative decision maker
would select action B, using the *minimax* (minimize the maximum loss) or,
equivalently, *maximin* (maximize the minimum gain) criterion, since with
B the worst outcome would be that *y* would occur and her payoff would
be 5, whereas with *A* or *C* worse outcomes (4 or 0) could occur. The
expected-value decision maker would select action *A*, since if she repeatedly played such games (as do insurance companies) she would be quite
sure to win the most with this strategy in the long run. The gambler might
select *C* in hopes that *y* would not occur and she then would earn the
greatest possible amount. Thus, selection of a *probabilistic decision criterion* is necessary when making risky decisions. Even if one had a precisely
specified global objective function and physical constraints, if benefits were
partially a function of uncontrolled state variables it would be impossible
to optimize without the probabilistic decision criterion. If such a criterion
is not explicitly specified, it is implicit in any decision.

Von Neumann utility

To understand human specification of objective functions it is first necessary to understand the classical ideas of *utility*, the transformation from
conventional physical units of a state or objective variable into units

(utiles) which express relative worth or value to a decision maker or a system user. The roots of utility theory go back to the English philosophers of the nineteenth century, primarily Jeremy Bentham and John Stuart Mill, who first wrote about an individual and hedonistic (private) objective function which all people carry in their heads—but they offered no credible means to quantify utility. John von Neumann (von Neumann and Morgenstern 1944) set the foundations for modern utility theory by his axiom that the utility of an event multiplied by its probability of occurrence equals the effective (subjectively expected) utility, and thus the utility of any event (or object) can be established in terms of a lottery on other events for which the utility has already been established. This is explained below.

Mathematically, the utility U of any event is defined as a lottery of the utilities of two other events (which serves primarily to set the numerical scale for utility). Initially these are chosen as the events of maximum and minimum worth, and typically defined as having utilities of 1 and 0 respectively. The following one-variable example uses dollars as the objective variable and determines a decision maker's utility in the range from \$0 (taken as 0 utiles) to \$1000 (taken as 1 utile).

The experimental subject (decision maker) is faced with a 50–50 chance of receiving \$1000 or \$0, then asked for what value \$x received with certainty would she be indifferent between that \$x and the lottery. Figure 3.9 illustrates the procedure. Von Neumann utility assumes in this experiment

$$U(\$x) = 0.5\ U(\$1000) + 0.5\ U(\$0) = 0.5(1) + 0.5(0) = 0.5.$$

Only rarely would the decision maker select $x = \$500$. Usually the subject would be "risk averse" and settle for x closer to \$300 or \$400. This then becomes a point on the utility curve $U = f(\$)$ between points $[\$0, U(\$0)]$ and $[\$1000, U(\$1000)]$. Having determined what intermediate x has $U(x) = 0.5$, one could then use that x as the minimum in a lottery with \$1000, or use that x as the maximum in a lottery with \$0, and thus determine points on the utility curve intermediate between \$0 and x, and between x and \$1000. And so on.

An alternative experimental procedure is to ask the decision maker for a probability p such that she is indifferent between a given intermediate \$x and a chance p of \$1000. In this case the assumed underlying equation is

$$U(\text{of the given } \$x) = pU(\$1000) + (1 - p)U(\$0) = p(1) + (1 - p)(0) = p.$$

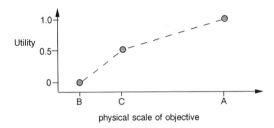

Figure 3.9
One-objective utility determination. Above, subject's indifference between experimentally
discovered certainty-equivalent C and a lottery {A with probability p and B with
probability (1 − p)} is equivalent to defining equation shown at right. Below, utility curve.
When (by assumption) utility of A = 1, utility of B = 0, p = 0.5, then utility of C = 0.5,
which fixes C on the utility curve. By finding new indifference points between A and C and
between B and C, and using the defining equation, additional points on the curve can be
identified.

Multi-objective decision making

The steps in determining a multi-attribute utility function are illustrated
by a two-attribute (two-objective variable) example:

(1) Define a space of two or more variables, say safety s and cost c (figure
3.10) where the minimum and maximum utilities are given as 0 for [min
s, max c] and 1 for [max s, min c] respectively. Figure 3.10 illustrates a
two-objective utility space.

(2) Determine the other two corner utilities of [min s, min c] and [max
s, max c] by the second method above (since the values of s and c are given).

(3) Determine the marginal utility for s, using the now-available values
of U(min s, max c) and U(max s, max c) as extremes on U(s, max c).
Likewise determine the marginal utility for c using the now-available
U(min s, max c) and U(min s, min c) as extremes on U(min s, c).

(4) Now assume that the utility curve of U(s, min c) has the same proportional shape as that of U(s, max c), though its extrema will be different.
Likewise assume the utility curve U(max s, c) has the same proportional
shape as U(min s, c). If it is further assumed that this proportionality of
U(s, c) holds throughout the [s, c] space, the utility of any point in that

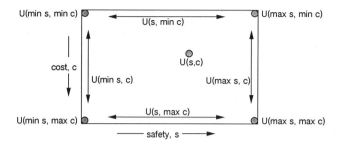

Figure 3.10
Hypothetical two-objective utility space (for objectives safety s and cost c). Assuming
$U(\min s, \max c) = 0$ and $U(\max s, \min c) = 1$, one can obtain $U(\max s, \max c)$ and
$U(\min s, \min c)$. Then marginal one-objective utility functions can be obtained for s and c,
for both max and min values of the other variable. Then, by interpolation, any $U(s, c)$ can
be obtained.

space $U(s, c)$ is determined. This key proportionality assumption is called
quasi-separability.

Similar methods have been applied (Yntema and Klem 1965; Keeney and
Raiffa 1976) to objective spaces in three or more dimensions, and computer
programs are available to assist in performing the experiments and interpolating. Resulting utility functions have been applied to a number of real
decision problems, with success in some cases.

Unhappily, Tversky and Kahneman (1981) and others have shown that
experimental subjects have difficulty with lotteries, especially lotteries of
events with which they have had little experience. Further, even when
subjects give consistent results, their actual choice behavior may not correspond to what the von Neumann utility model would predict, particularly
in multi-objective decision situations. This change in appreciation of the
difficulty of specifying the system objective function is exemplified by
recent trends in the way decision theorists have begun to abandon the
concept of global goodness or multi-objective utility in favor of *local utility*
and satisficing.

Assessing relative worth when one is not sure what objectives to consider

Conventional methods of multi-objective utility assume a fixed set of
objectives for rating the worth of a state (event, condition, situation).
Sometimes, however, the problem is more that of deciding what set of
objectives to use than of deciding how to rate the worth of the object or

action with respect to any one objective. Terano and Sugeno (1974) provide a method, based on fuzzy logic, to accommodate this problem. The method assumes that the ratings on objectives are independent of one another.

Suppose a decision maker can easily give a rating V_i on each of N individual objectives, and can also judge the relevance R_k of every possible combination of the N objectives, taken one at a time, two at a time, and so on up to all N at once. Sugeno's method then states that

worth $W = \max_{k} \{\min[R_k, \min_{i} (V_i \text{ in } k)]\}$.

In words, this says to consider each combination k of objectives: take the worst rating V_i of all objectives in that subset and compare that rating to the relevance rating R_k for that subset, then take the worse of the two. Do that for all combinations, and take the best of these. By the minimax criterion, that combination is the most appropriate one for evaluation, and its V_i rating is the appropriate net worth rating for whatever state is being judged.

This procedure is analogous to a set of chains (figure 3.11), one chain for every subset of objectives considered, where the strengths of the links are the worth ratings with respect to individual objectives and the mounting to the ceiling is the relevance rating for that set of objectives. One chooses

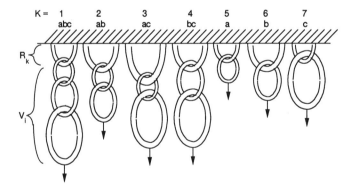

Figure 3.11
Chain analogy to Sugeno's fuzzy integral for comparing sets of decision criteria. Breaking strength of a given chain's ceiling attachment is degree to which corresponding subset of objectives is complete and appropriate. Strength of each individual link in that chain is degree to which reference object or event satisfies corresponding individual objective.

the strongest chain (determined by its weakest link), and its strength is the appropriate worth.

Other methods for rating worth

Von Neuman utility and Sugeno's method are but two of many methods for rating relative worth. Other scaling methods to elicit such worth judgements are Delphi methods (Turoff 1975a), cross-impact analysis (Turoff 1975b; Dalkey 1975; Kane 1975), and multi-dimensional scaling (Carroll and Wish 1975). Other methods are reviewed in Linstone and Turoff 1975.

Satisficing with the help of a computer

The techniques described above are closed-form techniques. They make implicit assumptions about how a person decides, require the person to conform to an information- elicitation procedure, and impose a final decision from a computer-based algorithm. What now appears much more acceptable to real decision makers is to provide a computer-based means for her to "dialog with herself," where the computer does not "second guess" and makes no assumptions at all about how she decides. In this case the computer only provides "book-keeping" on tentative ratings she has already made, and points out what decisions are unattainable in terms of hard physical or economic constraints given *a priori*.

In such a system the decision maker iteratively specifies an "aspiration" point in the objective hyperspace, i.e., says what combination of salient variables she would like that she thinks might possibly be achievable. The computer then returns an indication of whether that point is achievable or not, and, if that point is not at the limit of what the decision maker can have, suggests what point(s) she might like better. If, on the other hand, the decision maker's aspiration is not attainable, the computer suggests points nearby in objective space which are attainable.

Point 1 in figure 3.12 might be such a point in a two-objective-variable space. Say A is the ride quality or comfort of a trip and B is the speed. Then, by successive interactions with a computer, all neighboring points (combinations of the objectives) might be considered to find a point that is satisfactory in all respects. A computer, properly programmed with system constraint equations, can return a judgement of the feasibility or infeasibility of an initial aspiration—for example, in figure 3.12, letting the person know that a closest allowable point is 2, assuming a rough equivalent weight on the two objectives. Then the subject might decide that if this is

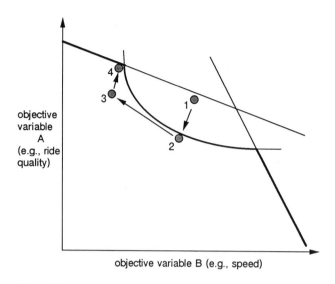

Figure 3.12
Satisficing in two-objective space. Computer is programmed with constraints which combine to define the Pareto frontier (limit to feasible or attainable points). Human specifies aspiration point (1), computer responds to suggest "nearest" feasible point on Pareto frontier (2), human then decides to try another aspiration point (3), computer responds with nearest point on Pareto frontier (4), and so on until user is satisfied.

the case she would prefer more of attribute *A* and less of *B*, as represented say by point 3. The computer can then point out that she can do even better, e.g., point 4—and so on in iterative exchange until the individual is satisfied with the tradeoff. This procedure has come to be called "satisficing" (March and Simon 1958; Wierzbicki 1982).

Charny's experiments on computer-aided satisficing

Charny and Sheridan (1989) implemented the satisficing techniques described above with a novel extension they called the *dynamic range tradeoff technique*. This computer-graphic tool allows the decision maker to specify a range rather than a point in objective space. On a graphic scale for each objective she sets an "acceptable" limit ("minimum acceptable" of a beneficial objective, "maximum acceptable" of a cost objective) and an aspiration level. The computer, already programmed with physical and economic constraint equations, then returns a combined "attainability range." Figure 3.13 illustrates the idea (though one would normally not bother with such a technique for an objective space of only two dimensions).

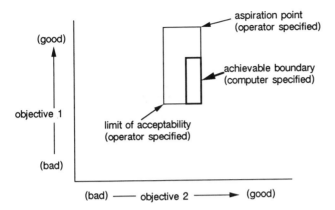

Figure 3.13
Charny's dynamic range tradeoff technique for satisficing.

The dynamic range tradeoff technique is particularly appropriate in supervisory control situations where, after goals have been set and execution is underway, there are unforseeable disturbances which then make the original goals unattainable. In such situations a supervisor may have to revise the goals (specify objectives) repeatedly on the basis of new circumstances. Charny and Sheridan evaluated the technique in the context of a problem designed to be both realistic and challenging to the human subjects. Viewing a display such as that shown in figure 3.14, subjects controlled a ship carrying a refrigerated cargo. The limited fuel had to be allocated between the refrigerator and the ship's thrusters, and the market return on the cargo was dependent on how far the ship got along a chain of islands before running out of fuel. Control could be entirely manual, with no computer assistance. Alternatively, an optimal automatic controller could be used for the given fuel allocation; however, the optimal controller, if and when it encountered significant disturbances (which might make the decision maker's goal unattainable), had no basis for updating itself once it started its execution. A third mode was manual control with the dynamic range tradeoff (DRT) satisficing aid. Experimental data showed clearly that in this experiment the control using the DRT was best.

Modeling multi-objective utility on line by tracking the operator's decisions

Freedy et al. (1985) review a number of experiments in which a different approach was taken to derive a decision maker's multi-objective utility. In

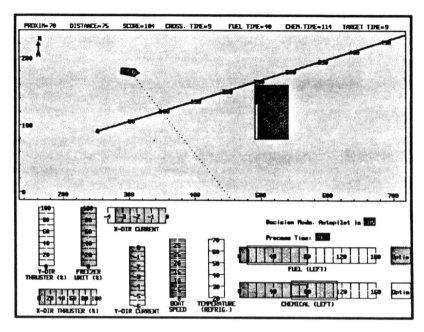

Figure 3.14
Charny's experimental display in ship control task. The task was to get the ship (symbol
shown) to the rightmost point along an island chain (line) to achieve the highest market
price for its cargo, without running out of fuel (to power ship) or refrigerant (which
prevented cargo spoilage), and given unpredictable ocean currents in X and Y directions.
Aspiration is indicated by dark rectangle, feasibility by small light rectangle inside. [From
Charny 1989.]

this case, operators' decisions were automatically monitored during the
process of system operation, and machine-learning techniques were employed to continuously derive best-fit parameters to a multi-objective
model of her preference structure. Once such a model converged, it could
provide on-line feedback to the operator to signal consistency discrepancies, could be used as a reference for behavior modification, or could
be used to train novice decision makers.

Figure 3.15 shows a simplified form of such a dynamic utility estimator.
At the left are multiple sensors (or groups of sensors), each indicating the
degree to which some one of R mutually exclusive features i is true of the
environment. The outputs of the sensors are weighted by corresponding
utilities, to yield expected utilities EU_i. The maximum utility is chosen
(which assumes that the operator being modeled makes whatever decision

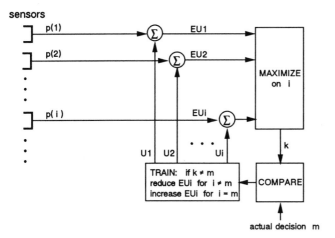

Figure 3.15
Dynamic utility estimation scheme. [After Freedy et al. 1985.]

yields the maximum possible utility), and the corresponding decision (feature) k is compared to the decision the operator actually makes at that point in time. If the decisions differ, the utility of sensor k is reduced and the utilities of the other sensors are increased. This process, which is actually based on use of discriminant functions for pattern classifiers (Nilsson 1965), will converge on correct pattern classification (a correct utility model) insofar as the features are linearly separable.

From many experiments (their feature classifiers and error correction training procedures were somewhat more elaborate than the simple one described here), Freedy et al. conclude that "(1) user models perform better on the average than the individuals they model; (2) user model-based recommendations minimize the chance of extremely bad choices; (3) user model-generated feedback provides real-time reference for behavior modification and training; and (4) user models reenforce normative response decision."

3.7 Supervisory Monitoring Displays

Information overload

In traditional control rooms and cockpits the common design practice has been to provide the human operator with an individual and independent display of each and every variable from each and every subsystem, and for a large fraction of these to provide a separate additional alarm display which lights up when the corresponding variable reaches or exceeds some value. This practice has resulted in part from the fact that different subsystems are designed and manufactured by different companies, and this is a way for each company to protect itself from claims that full information to operate its equipment is not provided.

Thus, a modern aircraft may have over 1000 displays, and a modern chemical or power plant over 5000. But monitoring becomes a travesty when the number of alarms is so excessive. In the author's experience in one nuclear plant training simulator during the first minute of a "loss-of-coolant accident" 500 displays were shown to have changed in a significant way, and in the second minute 800 more.

Clearly no operator or team of several operators could be expected to know all of what occurred on that panel. Recognition of this fact has motivated rethinking of display systems for human control of complex processes, particularly with regard to information overload (see also section 3.9). The availability of computer generation of displays has not automatically eased this problem, and could even exacerbate the information overload. The technology allows information to be packed almost up to any density, and multiple computer pages may be packed onto a single CRT. There is a kind of display imperative: "If the information is available electronically, make it available on the display."

Display intercorrelation and redundancy

The multiple signals displayed for almost any real operating system are highly correlated. This is not surprising in view of the tendency mentioned above for different manufacturers to specify requirements for display of all variables relevant to their equipments. Clearly many different equipments are tapped into the same pipes or electrical power busses, and differences in temperatures, pressures, flows or voltages from one point to another often are quite predictable functions of one another. In other words, the different variables tend to be correlated.

This is much as in ordinary life situations in which we move among people, animals, plants, or buildings and where our eyes, ears, and other senses easily take in and comprehend vast amounts of information—just as much as in the power plant. Our genetic makeup and experience enable us to integrate the bits of information from different parts of the retina and from different senses from one instant to the next—presumably because the information is correlated.

Experienced operators claim that they perceive "patterns" even in independently displayed signals, but don't pretend to understand how they do it. They affirm that it takes considerable experience as well as effort to do so. This is true whether displays are analogic (e.g. diagrams, plots) or symbolic (e.g. alphanumerics) or some combination. The challenge is to design displays to integrate the information and thus enable human operators to perceive patterns in time and space reliably and without great effort or experience. While some redundancy is helpful, there can easily be too much, to the point where the operator is wasting time observing the same information from multiple sources and missing other information that is critical.

One answer to redundant information is simply to actively inhibit one display when another display showing the same information has a higher priority in the procedure. The problem is that, for any two displays which are correlated most of the time, there may be times when they are not correlated, and the operator really should have access to both displays. This, it seems, is a job for the computer.

The "keyhole problem" with computer-generated displays

The term "keyhole problem" refers to the fact that many different displays are presented at the same location (in the form of different pages, which the operator must select one at a time). In other words, the world of interest can be seen only through the "keyhole" of the computer screen. If the information sought is not currently displayed, serious problems can arise if the operator does not happen to remember how to access the needed information. If the information is displayed but the operator glances elsewhere for a moment and then back again only to find the expected display gone (e.g., if some scrolling operation has moved it elsewhere), that too can be disconcerting. In contrast, the traditional control panel dedicates a particular space to each particular variable, and the operator makes use of this location sense in remembering and quickly accessing (scanning) the panel.

Dedicated overview displays

The keyhole problem for a single computer display can be resolved by dedicating at least certain portions of the computer screen to an overview of information in standard format, no matter what is being displayed elsewhere on the screen. The Apple Macintosh "desktop" and the IBM "windows" are based on this principle.

On a large instrument panel it is not a bad idea to have at least one dedicated display. The safety parameter display system now required in some form in all nuclear power plants was mentioned earlier (figure 3.7). The idea of the SPDS is to select a small number (e.g. 6–10) of variables which tell the most about the overall "health" of the plant, and to display them at a dedicated location, so that the human operator can see at a glance whether something is abnormal, if so what, and to what degree.

Equivalent overview displays were mentioned for aviation supervisory control systems (figures 3.3 and 3.4). In these cases the designer is entrusted to decide on what small subset of variables will suffice, and the computer is entrusted to filter the low-level raw data in real time and decide what information it is essential to pass up to the human supervisor. Dedicated "real estate" can be an asset, if it is affordable.

Integrated displays

Display integration means to combine representations of multiple variables in a meaningful relationship. For example, in a nuclear power plant both temperature and pressure are important properties of the cooling water at various locations. Traditionally, the operator has had to examine indicators for both variables and deduce whether the water is in the form of liquid or steam, with the help of a printed steam table. However, a simple two-dimensional plot of temperature and pressure can represent the combination as a point, and this can be displayed relative to a fixed phase-change line (figure 3.16), which relation is what the operator really wants to know.

One novel display technique for integrating variables is the "Chernoff face" (figure 3.17), in which the shapes of the eyes, ears, nose, and mouth systematically differ to indicate different values of variables, the idea being that facial patterns are easily perceived. The proponents claim that since facial recognition is such a well-established human skill, such displays would provide more reliable discrimination of important combinations of variables than more abstract displays. (The Nuclear Regulatory Commission, fearful that some enterprising designer might employ this technique before it was proven, formally forbade it as an acceptable SPDS.)

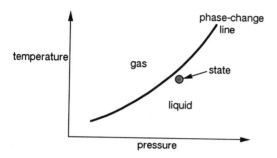

Figure 3.16
Integrated display of pressure and temperature for nuclear power plant.

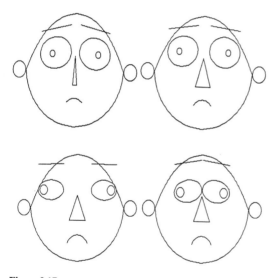

Figure 3.17
Chernoff faces. Different features of computer-generated faces represent different system variables. In upper figure note change in nose from left to right, then (lower left) change in both eyes and eyebrows, and finally (lower right) further change in eyebrows.

Display format adaptivity

The discussion of aircraft automation in section 3.1 mentioned format adaptivity—the ability to change both the format and the logic of the display as a function of the situation. Displays in aerospace and industrial systems now have fixed formats (e.g., labels, scales, and ranges are designed into the display). Alarms have fixed set points. However, future computer-generated displays (even for the same variables) may be different at various mission stages or in various conditions. Thus formats may differ for aircraft takeoff, landing, and en-route travel, and be different for plant start-up, full capacity operation, and emergency shutdown. Some alarms have no meaning, or may be expected to go off when certain equipment is being tested or taken out of service. In such a case adaptive formatted alarms may be suppressed (a different reason from that of redundancy, discussed above), or the set points may be changed automatically to correspond to the operating mode.

Future displays and alarms could also be formatted or adjusted to the personal desires of the supervisor, to provide any time scale or degree of resolution necessary at the time. Ideally, some future displays could adapt on the basis of a running model of how the human supervisor's perception was being enhanced. There are hazards, of course, in allowing emergency displays to be too flexible, to the point where they cause errors rather than prevent them.

Displays to aid with procedures

Part of monitoring is to maintain a running correspondence between the system state and the operating procedures. Normal operating procedures are mostly committed to memory by nuclear power plant operators and aircraft pilots, but there may be questions of whether one is correct, especially if abnormality is suspected.

"Smart checklists" are already being developed for aircraft in which the computer checks to see whether the operator really took the action called for in the procedure and, if not, calls attention to the discrepancy. Other computerized systems have been developed which, upon their own estimation of both past and present process states, display to the operator the procedures that best fit that plant condition (e.g., what to do in response to an alarm, or what to do at a particular time or stage in the plan). These procedures are not implemented automatically, though in some cases they could be. Usually it is deemed important to give the human supervisor some room for interpretation in light of her knowledge about the process or the objectives that the computer does not share.

Interaction with displays through icons, menus, and voice

Monitoring is not only a matter of displays but also a matter of enabling the operator to interact in a "user-friendly" way. There has been much development of interactive tools for computer workstations for word processing, spreadsheets, and drawing. A example closer to supervisory control of telerobots is NASA's Multi-Satellite Operations Control Center, which requires supervisory monitoring of many highly automated satellites. Bugs in new software, difficulties with communications, and weather often prevent scheduled photography or RF tests and operations.

Mitchell (1987) developed a simulator of this task and an associated "operator-function model," and studied human capabilities and computer-based aids in this context. Mitchell and Saisi (1987) developed qualitative graphic icons and adaptive windows as workstation interface aids and showed that they improved performance in satellite monitoring and reconfiguration. A related experiment (Mitchell and Forren 1987) suggested that augmenting keyboard commands by voice (recognition) was not a good idea in supervisory control at the time. When intent recognition and context-dependence decision making are further advanced, voice recognition as a component in supervisory control is likely to fare better.

3.8   Failure Detection, Diagnosis, and Location

Computer-based aids for failure detection, diagnosis, and location are particularly important—these functions are the ultimate reason for monitoring. In a complex semiautomated system the operator may have great difficulty knowing when some component has begun to fail. This can be because the component's deteriorating performance is being compensated by the automation, and hence no abnormality is indicated. Alternatively, variables that are abnormal could have resulted from a failure in a component well upstream. Finally, the operator can simply be overloaded. Many new failure measurement techniques have been developed in recent years, some involving Bayesian and other statistical inference, some involving multiple comparisons of measured signals to on-line models of what normal response should look like, and so on. In failure measurement the operator may depend heavily on help from the computer; however, she is the ultimate judge.

The subject of failure detection in human-machine systems has received considerable attention (Rasmussen and Rouse 1981). Moray (1986) regards such failure detection, diagnosis, and location as the most important human supervisory role. The problem is particularly difficult because the supervisory controller tends to be removed from full and immediate knowledge about the controlled process. The physical processes she must monitor tend to be large in number and distributed widely in space (e.g. around a ship or a plant). The physical variables may not be immediately measurable (e.g. steam flow and pressure) and may have to be derived from remote measurements of other variables. Sitting in the control room or cockpit, the supervisor is dependent upon artificial displays to give her feedback of actions taken or indications of disturbances.

Detecting failure by likelihood-ratio test

Assume x is a measure or indicator that has different probability densities under two mutually exclusive hypotheses or underlying circumstances H_0 and H_1, where H_0 is a no-failure condition and H_1 is a failure condition. Suppose the goal is to sample x and decide whether H_0 or H_1 is true. Actually, the goal is to maximize a net gain for making the "right" decision, where V_{00} is the payoff (normally positive) for deciding H_0 when it is true, V_{10} is the payoff (normally negative) for deciding H_1 when H_0 is true, V_{11} is the payoff (normally positive) for deciding H_1 when it is true, and V_{01} is the payoff (normally negative) for deciding H_0 when H_1 is true.

The likelihood ratio $L(x) = [p(x)|H_1]/[p(x)|H_0]$ was introduced in section 1.5. From that earlier discussion (or from reference to the Neyman-Pierson decision criterion in texts on decision theory—see, e.g., Sheridan and Ferrell 1974, chapter 19), H_1 was shown to be the proper (maximum-payoff) decision favoring condition 1 (failure) when the following criterion was met:

$$\text{Decide } H_1 \text{ iff } L(x) = \frac{p(x)|H_1}{p(x)|H_0} > \frac{p(H_0)}{p(H_1)} \frac{V_{00} - V_{10}}{V_{11} - V_{01}}.$$

Otherwise H_0 is the proper decision (or there is indifference if the left and right hand terms are equal).

For multiple samples of x, i.e., $(x_1, x_2, x_3, \ldots, x_n)$,

$$L(x = 1, 2, \ldots, n) = \frac{p(x_1, x_2, x_3, \ldots, x_n)|H_1}{p(x_1, x_2, x_3, \ldots, x_n)|H_0}.$$

By Bayesian analysis (Sheridan and Ferrell 1974, pp. 45–53) one can show that this result becomes the product of the individual likelihood ratios:

$$L(x = 1, 2, 3, \ldots, n) = L(x_1)L(x_2)L(x_3) \cdots L(x_n).$$

This general formulation applies easily to typical failure-detection situations. Curry (1981) discusses the application of such a criterion to complex failures in aircraft.

Although $x_1, x_2, x_3, \ldots, x_n$ can be successive measures of the same kind, they can also be different kinds of measures. This raises the question of whether the different indicators can be treated as independent. Brehmer (1981) has suggested that humans treat cues independently, which does not mean that they actually are independent.

Detecting failure by use of a Kalman filter

When a model of a dynamic system (of, for example, the mapping from some measure x to some other measure y) is available, it seems logical to drive the model by x and compare the measured y to the model output y'. A sufficiently large and long-lasting discrepancy between y and y' is indicative of either a poor model or a change in the actual system from what was initially modeled.

The model can take the form of a Kalman filter or observer, which calibrates itself over a period of time (as described in chapter 1). If there is a sudden failure in the actual system, y will change but y' will not, and the discrepancy (which amounts to the Kalman filter residual) will signal the failure. This acts as a kind of high-pass filter on process abnormalities.

Curry and Gai (1976) (see also Gai and Curry 1976, 1978) explored the criteria for detecting failures by this method, combined it with the notion of sequential analysis, and applied the result as a model of human failure detection. After n observations, if $L(x = 1, 2, 3, \ldots, n)$ is greater than some criterion C, a "failure" decision was made. If $L(x = 1, 2, 3, \ldots, n) < 0$, L was reset to zero (integration started over). They used as parameters of their model (all of which helped determine the value of C) the mean x for a "failed" process, the signal-to-noise ratio of the observation noise in the

Kalman filter, and the probabilities of the two types of error (missed detection of actual failure, false-alarm detection of a normal process). They tested this model with experiments in detecting the change in the mean of the width of a horizontal bar, and later in detecting instrument failures in simulated aircraft landing. They claimed good agreement between the model and the experimental results.

Wewerinke (1981) employed a similar method to successfully predict detection time for subjects monitoring four displays (figure 3.18). He employed a model more elaborate than Curry's, in this case the full "optimal control model" of Kleinman, Baron, and Levison (1970). Running estimates of the mean and the variance of each variable were updated by a Kalman filter to estimate the true state in spite of observation noise. The best estimates were used to compute the likelihood ratio described above. Using some model parameters of Kleinman et al., Wewerinke fitted the model to the experimental data and determined the one remaining free

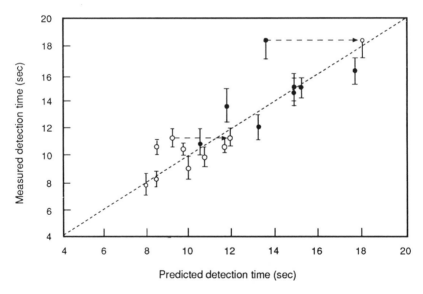

Figure 3.18
Wewerinke's results for prediction of system failure detection by optimal estimation model (line). Experimental subjects monitored four four displays of either high (o) or low (•) failure rates. Arrows for two points show "correction", under one set of display conditions, for bias due to prior knowledge of impending failure. r is the correlation between predicted and experimental values. For • and o, $r = 0.86$; for broken o, $r = 0.95$. [After Wewerinke 1981.]

variable, the length of the memory window over which the operator aggre-gated observations. He obtained a value of 4 seconds.

Disaggregated on-line computer simulation (DOCS)

The author and his colleagues (Sheridan 1981; Tsach, Sheridan, and Tzelgov 1982; Tsach Sheridan, and Buharali 1983) experimented with detecting and locating failures by continuously driving multiple-subsystem models with corresponding measured plant variables, then comparing the model outputs to corresponding measurements from the plant (figure 3.19). Then a computer-graphic display focused the operator's attention on any discrepancies between model outputs and measured variables, which indi-cated abnormalities.

Effort and flow variables (e.g., fluid pressure and flow, shaft torque and speed, and electrical voltage and current, all of which pairs are called "power bonds") were measured at various key points in the plant, at least one such pair for every state variable. The segmentation for component models occurred these points, with the effort forcing the submodel on one side and the flow forcing the submodel on the other side (as determined by causality in the real system). The model covariables were then compared to the actual measured covariables, and any significant discrepancy indi-cated a failure somewhere in the submodel from which the discrepant covariable was an output. By cuts and comparisons at different places in the system, a failure could be located to any degree of precision. Though the energy covariables afford one basis for model disaggregation, causality is the only necessary condition.

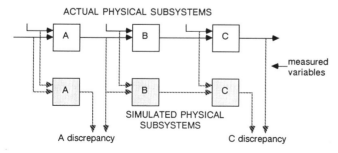

Figure 3.19
Disaggregated on-line computer simulation (DOCS).

A human operator could set thresholds for automatic operation of this system, then confirm or countermand the computer's detection and location decisions on the basis of raw signal data. Figure 3.20 shows one type of iconic display developed for this system—a polygon whose vertices indicate the degree to which each variable (of one subsystem in this case) is below or above a normal range (torus). The display therefore "points" to corresponding discrepancies between the measured and model variables as they evolve in time.

Tzelgov, Tsach, and Sheridan (1985) applied Bayesian updating to this problem. They assumed that both system and model outputs had Gaussian-distributed noise components. They compared the operator's behavior when an optimal Bayesian decision aid (in the form of a failure-to-no-failure odds ratio) was continuously available against the situation where only the raw discrepancy between a model and an actual process could be monitored. They also compared human performance when both model and process outputs were displayed as raw unsmoothed signals, when both were smoothed, and when only the model was smoothed. The results made it evident that the operators performed better when provided with the failure odds, and also that smoothing the model while leaving the actual process signal in raw form was best.

Fuzzy-logic models of failure detection

Fuzzy logic, described in chapter 1, can be applied quite directly to failure detection. For example, Laritz and Sheridan (1984) reported experiments in which subjects observed the values of two random inputs and two outputs of an otherwise black box under given conditions of "failure" and "normal." Actually the "black box" was a simple resistor network in which one or another resistor had opened. After some training, the subjects stated their own fuzzy rules for the input-output relations and also graphed their membership functions for the natural-language terms they used to state their fuzzy rules. Of course each subject used different words and therefore had different membership functions. Each subject's rules and membership functions were then used by the computer to predict future failures of the "black box." The computer could do quite a reasonable job on this basis; in fact, using the best subject's rules and membership functions, it performed much better than did some poorer subjects deciding for themselves.

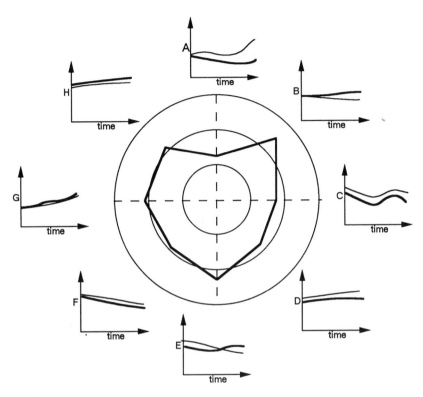

Figure 3.20
Iconic display, in which vertices of polygon indicate positive and negative discrepancies of measured variables from corresponding modeled variables, and thereby "point" to relevant time history for further examination.

Fuzzy logic seems to correspond with what Bainbridge (1981) calls "conditional leaning... conditional propositions about general aspects of process behavior." Bainbridge is critical of the notion that the human operator has as an internal model of the controlled process anything nearly so exact as mathematical equations.

Detecting failure during active vs. passive monitoring

Various investigators have questioned whether removal from active participation in the control loop makes detection and diagnosis of abnormalities more difficult. Curry and Ephrath (1976) compared monitoring an autopilot-controlled system in simulated aircraft landings with actively controlling by means of both a "spring-stick" and a "free-stick" (no force). Passive monitoring and spring-stick proved about equal in detection performance, and better than the "free-stick" condition. Ephrath and Young (1981) later tested the simple single-variable tracking and multi-variable control of airline pilots in a realistic simulation of instrument landing. Detection was significantly better during active controlling in the first experiment, and was significantly better during monitoring in the second. The difference seemed to be that the workload was much higher in the second task.

Detecting failure by symptomatic and topographic search

Rasmussen (1981) has made the interesting comparison between what he calls "symptomatic" search and "topographic" search. The first is what happens when a person presents to a doctor with specific symptoms and the doctor makes an evaluation of which, if any, disease is represented by that set of symptoms. The second is what happens when a person gets an annual medical checkup, going through a battery of screening tests to help a doctor focus on anything that may be abnormal.

More generally, in the case of symptomatic search, a set of symptoms characterizing the observed real system is used as a template to search through a database of alternative sets of symptoms, looking for a matching set. Functionally, pattern recognition is the mode of diagnosis.

In topographic search, one searches using a template representing the normal or planned operation and observes mismatches from this norm represented at locations in the template. The combined screening tests, done with tactical rules, result in stepwise limitation of the field, and point to what, if anything, has failed.

3.9 Mental Workload

The roots of the concept of workload go back to the early time-and-motion studies in factories, and to the "scientific management" of F. W. Taylor (1947). Mental workload has been a popular topic in human-machine systems research for the past two decades. Much of this research has been focused on pilots, partly to resolve disputes about whether the commercial aircraft flight deck should have a crew of two or three, partly to decide on the limits of what can be assigned to fighter and helicopter pilots flying nap-of-the-earth combat missions. But it has also been of concern in nuclear power plant control rooms and other settings where overload and concomitant deterioration of operator performance poses a serious threat

It is not mental workload *per se* that is of ultimate concern. It is whether the pilot (or other operator) can perform her job, with any margin of attention for unforeseen circumstances, stress, or complexities which may be infrequent but certainly do arise from time to time. Thus operator performance, which translates to system performance and safety, is the ultimate concern. As "objective" workload factors (i.e., variables such as number of tasks, complexity of tasks, urgency, and cost of not doing the task properly and on time) mount, mental workload (whatever it is) surely increases. But, unfortunately, until these objective loads reach a high level, operator performance (as measured by system performance) may show little, if any, decrement. Then, with a slight further increase, performance may decrease precipitously. (At that point subjective mental workload is particularly hard to measure, but may also decrease.) The hope has been that physiological and even subjective indices of mental workload can provide a better predictor of performance breakdown, well before the latter occurs, than direct measures of performance. Figure 3.21 illustrates the point.

Mental workload and automation

Aircraft piloting, nuclear power plant operation, and military command and control can involve long periods of boredom punctuated by sudden bursts of activity, without much demand for activity at the much-preferred intermediate levels. To some extent this is true even if no automation is present (e.g., long periods of manual piloting to maintain course), but automation only exacerbates the problem. It is not that the operator is

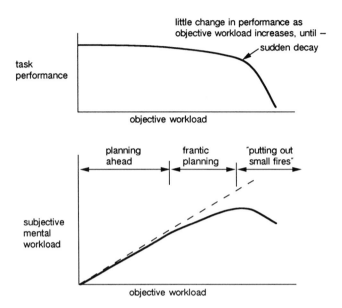

Figure 3.21
Relation of task performance and mental workload. With increasing objective workload, task performance breakdown can be anticipated much better from mental workload than from task performance itself.

simply bored doing a manual task. She may not be involved at all for long periods, and may become "decoupled" even from feeling responsible for control, knowing a computer is doing the job. But then, when problems arise that the automation cannot handle, or the automation breaks down, the demands on the operator may suddenly become severe.

Such transients—"coming into the game cold from the bench," so to speak—pose serious risks of human error and misjudgment. Experienced operators will react instinctively and usually be correct, or if the situation is novel may try to "buy time" to collect their wits. Operators have been known to accommodate to information overload by bypassing quantitative input channels (e.g., instruments) and going instead to *ad hoc* qualitative channels (e.g. voice messages), which may not be reliable.

Moray (1979) provides a number of views of mental workload, including both its definition and its measurement. Hart and Sheridan (1984) review the definition and measurement of workload as regards automation. They point out that automation has been motivated in some measure by desire to reduce workload, in some cases by people oblivious to the fact that the requirement for human monitoring of the automation itself creates workload (hence the pilot's term "killing us with kindness"). Mental workload is seen as a function of many factors, some of which have nothing to do with the operator: task objectives, temporal organization and demands (pacing, urgency, selectability of subtasks), hardware and software resources available (including automation), and environmental variables (workstation geometry, ambient temperature, vibration, lighting, etc.). Other factors are operator dependent: operator perception of task demands (which may be quite different from what is nominally assigned), operator qualifications and capacities, operator motivation (both *a priori* and in terms of accessing feedback during the task), and actual operator behavior.

Definitions and measures of mental workload

Physical workload is the energy expended (e.g., in calories) by the operator in doing the assigned task, measured by the heat given off or by the conversion of respired oxygen to carbon dioxide. Alternatively it can be the net mechanical work done on the environment (e.g., lifting a 10-pound weight 5 feet produces 50 foot-pounds of work). But physical workload is essentially different from mental workload, sometimes contributing to it (heavy physical demands can produce mental stress) and sometimes reducing it (exercise can be relaxing).

Task performance, as explained above, is what we seek to predict by measuring and modeling mental workload. However, it is best not to regard task performance as a legitimate measure of mental workload. An experienced operator is likely to be able to perform a task well with little mental workload, while an inexperienced operator may perform poorly with great mental load. In fact the very knowledge of performance can affect the mental workload. Therefore, task performance and mental workload should be kept distinct from one another.

Task complexity is a property of the task independent of the operator or the operator's behavior. Examples of task complexity are number or variety of stimuli (displays, messages) or actions required, rate of presentation of different displays or required pace of actions, time urgency before a deadline, improbability of the information presented or the actions re-

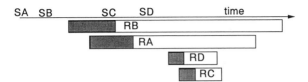

Figure 3.22
Example of overlap of multi-task memory demands. SA, SB, SC, and SD indicate time of
stimulus for responses RA, RB, RC, and RD respectively. Horizontal bars indicate time
interval during which responses are appropriate. Shaded portions indicate required
response duration. Assuming operator can do only one task at a time, the overlap and
order pose an interesting planning challenge.

quired, and degree of overlap of multi-task memory demands. The latter
notion is illustrated in figure 3.22. Measures of task complexity are properties of the task, not of the person. Hence they can be called measures of
"objective workload," "imposed workload," or "taskload," but not of
"mental" workload. The remaining three measures can be associated with
the operator's mental workload.

Subjective rating is by definition a non-objective measure, but interestingly it is the standard against which all objective measures are compared.
This can be done according to a single-dimensional or a multi-dimensional
rating scale. A single-dimensional scale in the form similar to the test pilot's
Cooper Harper rating (see figure 3.23a) is most commonly accepted and
has been widely used in commercial aviation (Cooper and Harper 1969).
A multi-dimensional scale, first suggested by Sheridan and Simpson (1979),
is illustrated in figure 3.23b. A more elaborate such technique, developed
at Wright-Patterson Air Force Base, is called the *subjective workload assessment technique* (SWAT) (O'Donnell and Eggemeier 1986).

It is important to consider that an operator's rating of workload will not
necessarily be the same as her experience of workload. There are factors
which drive the rating to differ from the conscious experience, and there
are aspects of the experience that are not conscious. Automation, if it has
no other effect, certainly changes the nature of the experience.

Physiological indices used for mental-workload assessment are many.
Some of these are heart rate, heart-rate variability, changes in the electrical
resistance of the skin due to incipient sweating, pupil diameter, formant
changes of the voice (especially increases in mean frequency), and changes
in breathing pattern. Great variability has been found in these measures;
no single measure has been accepted as a standard.

Secondary task performance measurement requires that the experimental subject do a secondary task at the same time she is performing the primary task. Examples of secondary tasks are backwards counting by threes, generation of random numbers, and simple target tracking. The better is performance on the secondary task, so the argument goes, the less is the workload of the primary task. The problem has been that airplane pilots and operators performing actual critical tasks sometimes refuse to cooperate, although in simulators (where they know there are no real dangers) they may be cooperative.

Experimental studies of human operators' mental workloads

Experimenters have tried to understand how workload builds up as operators undertake multiple tasks, and how workload is affected by manual, perceptual, and mental components of behavior. Moray (1979) and Williges and Weirwille (1979) review the earlier literature.

Common sense dictates that if a human operator is given too little to do she will become inattentive and her monitoring performance will decline. The classical literature on vigilance generally supports this claim (Buckner and McGrath 1963). If there is too much workload, as was discussed above, performance also declines. Thus there must be an optimum somewhere between the extremes of task load. The so-called inverted U-curve hypothesis (figure 3.24) is not a bold hypothesis at all. However, finding just where such an optimum exists for any particular task has been an elusive goal, and many factors other than task load seem to be at work. Verplank (1977) explored this question in the context of manual control and found little support for a usable inverted "U hypothesis" in any simple form.

Wierwille et al. (1985) reported a series of evaluations of the sensitivity and intrusion of mental workload estimation techniques. In simulated aircraft piloting they imposed psychomotor tasks (wind disturbances to be nulled), perceptual tasks (detection of instrument failures), cognitive tasks (wind triangle navigation problems), and communication tasks (execution of commands, response to queries). They measured subjective workload ratings, several attributes of primary task performance, several aspects of secondary task performance, and various physiological indices. They found that subjective ratings were highly sensitive to changes in imposed workload. Primary task performance measures (e.g., aircraft response) were not sensitive, except for those measures that corresponded to the

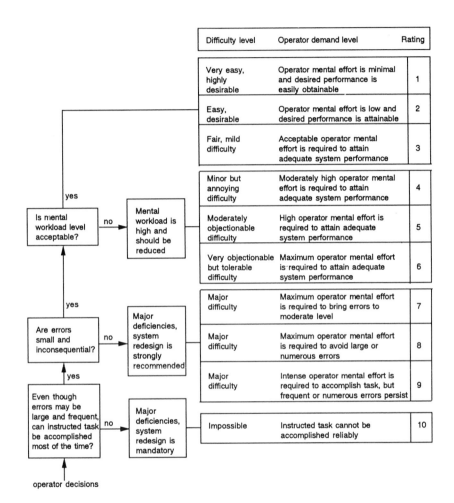

Difficulty level	Operator demand level	Rating
Very easy, highly desirable	Operator mental effort is minimal and desired performance is easily obtainable	1
Easy, desirable	Operator mental effort is low and desired performance is attainable	2
Fair, mild difficulty	Acceptable operator mental effort is required to attain adequate system performance	3
Minor but annoying difficulty	Moderately high operator mental effort is required to attain adequate system performance	4
Moderately objectionable difficulty	High operator mental effort is required to attain adequate system performance	5
Very objectionable but tolerable difficulty	Maximum operator mental effort is required to attain adequate system performance	6
Major difficulty	Maximum operator mental effort is required to bring errors to moderate level	7
Major difficulty	Maximum operator mental effort is required to avoid large or numerous errors	8
Major difficulty	Intense operator mental effort is required to accomplish task, but frequent or numerous errors persist	9
Impossible	Instructed task cannot be accomplished reliably	10

Is mental workload level acceptable? — no → Mental workload is high and should be reduced

yes

Are errors small and inconsequential? — no → Major deficiencies, system redesign is strongly recommended

yes

Even though errors may be large and frequent, can instructed task be accomplished most of the time? — no → Major deficiencies, system redesign is mandatory

yes

operator decisions

TIME LOAD	RATING
Often have spare time. Interruptions or overlap among activities occur infrequently or not at all.	T1
Occasionally have spare time. Interruptions or overlap among activities occur frequently.	T2
Almost never have spare time. Interruptions or overlap among activites are very frequent, or occur all the time.	T3

MENTAL EFFORT LOAD	RATING
Very little conscious mental effort or concentration required. Activity is almost automatic, requiring little or no attention.	E1
Moderate conscious mental effort or concentration required. Complexity of activity is moderately high due to uncertainty, unpredictability, or unfamiliarity. Considerable attention required.	E2
Extensive mental effort and concentration are necessary. Very complex activity requiring total attention.	E3

STRESS LOAD	RATING
Little confusion, risk, frustration, or anxiety exists and can be easily accommodated.	S1
Moderate stress due to confusion, frustration or anxiety noticeably adds to workload. Significant compensation is required to maintain adequate performance.	S2
High to very intense stress due to confusion, frustration or anxiety. High to extreme determination and self control required.	S3

Figure 3.23
Left: single-dimensional subjective mental workload scale developed by Wierwille and Casali (1983) and patterned after the Cooper-Harper aircraft handling quality scale. Right: three-dimensional subjective mental workload scale, developed by Reid et al. (1981) following Sheridan and Simpson (1979).

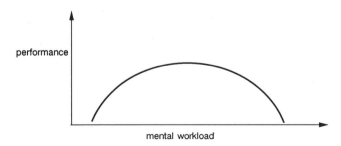

Figure 3.24
The inverted U hypothesis for performance vs. mental workload.

operator's control movements. Time from presentation to response was sensitive for the perception and cognitive tasks, even better than the subjective ratings (complex demands simply took longer to fulfill). Conversely, communication response times were shortened for increased task load. Most secondary task measures fared poorly (e.g., mental arithmetic, memory scanning, regularity of tapping), except for the standard deviation of time estimation. Secondary task measures cannot be used simultaneously with subjective ratings, as the latter are affected by both primary and secondary tasks. Physiological indices (pulse rate, respiration rate, pupil diameter, eye blinks, and eye fixations) were mostly insensitive to imposed taskload.

Wickins et al. (1985) did extensive workload-related experiments in one-axis and two-axis tracking (two hands in the latter case). The instructions were to pay special attention to the designated primary axis, but never ignore the secondary axis. Scores based on simple tradeoff functions were communicated to subjects after each trial. The investigators found that subjects' allocation of attention was distinctly non-optimal. Apparently, as tracking on the secondary axis became more difficult (the dynamic order increased), resources were allocated to it disproportionately to what was optimal by the scoring function. The investigators comment that their subjects had a hard time reallocating their efforts among concurrent tasks of different and changing difficulty. Also, there seemed to be an added "overhead" cost of time sharing among multiple tasks.

Berg and Sheridan (1985) performed a piloting simulation experiment with different approach and landing scenarios which differentially emphasized the effects of manual and mental activity separately and in combination. They measured altitude and speed deviations of the aircraft, and subjective ratings of "activity level," "task complexity," "task difficulty," "stress," and "mental workload." Their results indicated that, relative to a baseline scenario of low manual and mental activity, the high-manual-workload scenario most affected subjective ratings, whereas the high-mental-workload scenario most affected aircraft performance. Subjects seemed more conscious of the effects of manual activity than of those of mental activity. The increase in workload ratings proved more different from each other as manual activity increased, less so as mental activity increased. Relative to the baseline, the increase in workload ratings for the high-manual-workload scenario and the increase in ratings for the high-mental-workload scenario were approximately additive for the combined manual and mental scenario.

Ruffell-Smith (1979) studied pilot errors and fault detection under heavy cognitive load and found that crews made approximately one error every 5 minutes.

3.10 Intervention

The supervisor intervenes when the system state has reached the designated goal and the computer must be retaught, or when the computer decides the state is sufficiently abnormal and asks the supervisor what to do, or when the supervisor decides to stop the automatic action because the system state is not satisfactory.

The point of intervention

The following factors influence the point of intervention:

Criterion of abnormality of observed system state   In the nuclear power industry, regulations require that, when certain specified conditions occur, specified interventions must be made (e.g., the plant must be shut down).

Availability of the tools required to improve the situation   A fireman, when called to a fire, is helpless if water or a sufficiently long hose is not available. The supervisor of a complex process cannot effectively intervene until she has the proper tools available for control action.

Criterion of risk-taking   This can change, even during a task. If the supervisor uses a risk-averse criterion, such as minimax (minimize the worst outcome that could happen), her decisions (and hence the point of intervention) will be quite different from when she uses a more risk-neutral criterion, such as expected value (minimize the subjectively expected loss).

Tradeoff between collecting more data and taking action in time   The more data collected from the more sources, the more reliable is the decision of what, if anything, is wrong, and what to do about it. Weighed against this is the fact that if the supervisor waits too long the situation will likely get worse, and corrective action may be too late. Different operators will make different tradeoffs, which determine different intervention points.

Mental workload   This problem is aggravated by supervisory control in the following sense. When a supervisory control system is operating well in the automatic mode, the supervisor may have little concern. When there is a failure and sudden operator intervention is required, the mental work-load may go considerably higher. The supervisor may have to undergo a sudden change from initial inattention, moving physically and mentally to acquire information, make a decision, and act. The transient itself can destabilize and delay intervention, and render it ineffective.

The intervention stage as apparently the most error-sensitive

During the periods when the supervisor plans, teaches the computer, or learns (after the fact), there is no apparent system action, so human errors made during these periods are not apparent. When the computer is then committed to automatic control, any abnormality may be blamed on the automation.

At the intervention stage, however, the human operator is fully expected to fix things. It is at this stage that human error is most apparent. All eyes (and record-keeping) are focused on her.

The log-normal law for human intervention

Experience has shown that human response times for a broad class of emergency responses (interventions) are distributed in log-normal fashion. Figure 3.25 shows an example for time to read and perform procedural steps in a large-break loss-of-cooling accident (LOCA) in a nuclear power plant (a manned simulation exercise). The data are from Kozinsky et al. (1982). Most of the responses occur within a very short time of the initiating event; a few require a long time. Clearly the cumulative probability (that response will have been made before the time on the ordinate) will slope from the hypothetical origin at lower left to 1.0 at upper right for very long response times.

Crisis intervention by multi-person distributed decision making

As systems become larger and more complex, the people in the systems become separated by greater and greater distances from the other people with whom they are supposed to communicate and from the machines they are supposed to be controlling. Communications and actions necessarily become mediated by computers. When the communication channels have predictable constraints and delays, as in air traffic control, good procedures and regulation keep the system functioning reliably. When the functions to be performed at the remote site are sufficiently simple, the human operator can send a batch of commands in properly verified code and

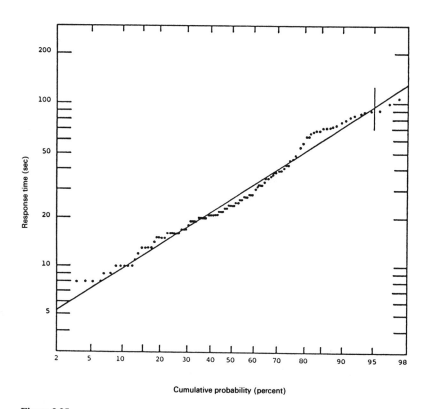

Cumulative probability (percent)

Figure 3.25
Log normal curve for time to read and perform a procedural step in a simulated
large-break loss-of-coolant accident in a nuclear power plant. [From Kozinsky et al. 1982;
© Electric Power Research Institute.]

expect a "telerobot" to execute the task, or send back reasons why it can't.
However, real situations are seldom so orderly, and various factors of
"distributed decision making" militate toward disorder.

We define the "distributed decision making" paradigm as having seven
sine qua non attributes: (1) There are multiple decision makers (DMs). (2)
The DMs jointly control a common pool of resources which they must
allocate to task demands (inputs). (3) Task demand inputs occur at unpredictable times, and indicate varying times available to satisfy them and
varying rewards if they are satisfied. (4) Any one input may be seen by one,
some, or all DMs. (5) There are insufficient resources to satisfy all demands.
(6) Communication between DMs may be constrained by noise or delay.
(7) DMs are trying to cooperate to maximize total reward.

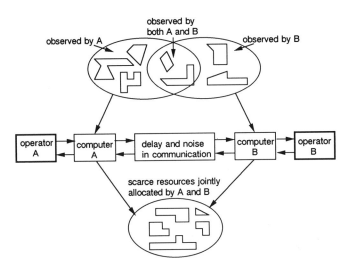

Figure 3.26
Distributed decision paradigm.

Figure 3.26 diagrams the distributed decision-making (DDM) paradigm.

This set of attributes appears to be common to many police, firefighting, and military operations. Until recently, there has been little formalization of this particular problem in the open literature, either experimentally or theoretically. As may be expected, some of the attributes have been studied in isolation or in combination with one or two of the others. Much of the decision literature is concerned with allocating insufficient resources to multiple demands to maximize reward—that is one view of what life is all about. There is a highly sophisticated body of theoretical literature on group decision making in econometrics (usually called "social choice")—but surprisingly little corresponding experimental literature, especially on attribute 4, nonuniformity of available data among decision makers (or different people seeing different sides of the elephant). There is much theory and some experimentation on communication over noisy and delayed channels, and on social isolation and breakdown resulting from communication constraints. (An example is the use of Petri net models by Levis and his colleagues, as described in chapter 1.)

There have been many studies of the relative effects of centralized versus distributed authority (March and Simon 1958), span of authority (or how many subordinates per supervisor), how long the supervisor can let the subordinate work on her own (Sheridan 1970a), how communication channels should be set up for particular kinds of problem solving (Chapanis 1975), and other factors. Bureaucratic activities within organizations can cause delays, add noise, and in a crisis make matters worse.

3.11 Human Error

There has always been been great interest in human error at the political, legal, and everyday levels. Somewhat surprisingly, however, there is a dearth of scientific literature on human error. Most effort in behavioral science has been focused on *correct* behavior, and not much on *incorrect* behavior. The nuclear power industry has been particularly interested in human error in recent years, and has produced a number of reports on the subject (for example, Rassmussen 1982). The US commercial aviation sector is also very interested in error at present because of massive overhaul of the air traffic control network. There are a few excellent books on human error generally, including Reason and Mycielska (1982), Norman (1988), Reason (1990), and Senders and Moray (1991). This section draws heavily on the generalizations stated by Senders and Moray, who summarize the concerns raised by a 1983 workshop on human error in Bellagio, Italy, in which the the author participated. Salient questions raised there should be engaged in any discussion of human error:
What is an error? How should error be defined?
Are errors always, or even ever, caused? If so, are there only a few, or are there an infinity of causes? What are the causes?
Is the central nervous system in a particular state just before an error?
Do errors occur at random, or can they be predicted? Can there be an error theory?
Would it be desirable to eliminate all errors, or are errors part of creativity? Can the least desirable errors be reduced? How, and by how much?
What is the relationship of an error to an accident? To a fault or a failure? To sin?
   It is easy and common to blame operators for accidents, but investigation often suggests that the operator "erred" because the system was poorly designed. Testimony of an operator of the Three Mile Island nuclear power plant in a 1979 congressional hearing makes the point: "Let

me make a statement about the indications. All one can say about them is that they are designed to provide for whatever anticipated casualties you might have.... If you go beyond what the designers think might happen, then the indications are insufficient, and they may lead you to make the wrong inferences. In other words, what you are seeing on the gage, like what I saw on the pressurizer level—I thought it was due to excess inventory—I was interpreting the gage based on the emergency procedure—hardly any of the measurements that we have are direct indications of what is going on in the system." (U.S. Congress Oversight Hearing 1979)

There is consensus among man-machine systems engineers that we should be designing our control rooms and cockpits so that they are more "transparent" to the actual working system, so that the operator can more easily "see through" the displays to "what is going on." *Situational awareness* is the term used in the aviation sector.

Often the operator is locked into the dilemma of selecting and slavishly following one or another written procedure, each based on an *a priori* anticipated causality. The operator may not be sure what procedure, if any, fits the current not-yet-understood situation. This makes her response quite unpredictable. In this regard Rasmussen (1978) commented: "In the analysis of accidents, the human element is the imp of the system.... The variability and flexibility of human performance together with human inventiveness make it practically impossible to predict the effects of an operator's actions when he makes errors, and it is impossible to predict his reaction in a sequence of accidental events, as he very probably misinterprets an unfamiliar situation." In a similar vein, Adams (1982) stated: "There is no possibility for a definition of units of behavior whose reliability can be determined.... Put simply we do not know how the reliability of a behavioral sequence can be synthesized from the reliability of its parts."

Theoretically, anything that can be specified in an algorithm can be given over to the computer, so the reason the human supervisor is present is to add novelty and creativity—precisely the ingredients that cannot be prespecified. This means, in effect, that the best or most correct human behavior cannot be prespecified, and that variation from precise procedure must not always be viewed as errant noise. The human supervisor, by the nature of her function, must be allowed room for "trial and error" by the system design (Sheridan 1983).

Many reputable analysts of human behavior have thought hard about human error and human reliability, and have been frustrated and discouraged by the problems. There is persistent skepticism about whether the human operator can be treated as just another element in an otherwise mechanical system. Yet the discipline of human-machine control and decision systems has progressed precisely because engineering models have been adapted, through experimental calibration, to human behavior.

Definitions

A usually acceptable definition of a human error is: an action that fails to meet some implicit or explicit standard of the actor or of an observer.

Some are not satisfied with such a definition, since it begs the question of what is the standard. The point here is that "error–no error" is the simplest possible (binary) categorization of complex human behavior, and that it depends on an arbitrary standard. Any behavior can be relegated to "error" or not by modification of the standard. It seems that a lack of consensus on a definition is the greatest source of variability in both modeling and empirical measurement of human error (Sheridan 1980).

A comparison with other forms of human endeavor is interesting. Ordinary human discourse tolerates infinite variation and shades of inference about human behavior. Psychiatry seeks at least qualitative categories of behavior. Psychometrics requires continuous quantitative scales of behavior. In contrast, human reliability analysis reduces behavior to a single binary discrimination. Varying degrees of human error are usually disallowed.

"Operator error" may be more a function of the measurement criterion of the analyst than of the behavior of the operator. For example, it is common in nuclear power plants that operators perform procedural steps within certain groups in an arbitrary order because they know that "the order of steps within these groups doesn't matter." Some steps may be delayed, or omitted altogether, or performed to a different criterion, because that's the way a particular operator was trained or understands her task—but these can be scored as errors.

Depending on the set point of an alarm, or a threshold of performance used for scoring and never explicitly revealed, a human-controlled continuous variable may make a single slow excursion just across the limit and back and be counted as one error (figure 3.27), or it may cross just over and back several times and be counted as several errors, or it may hover

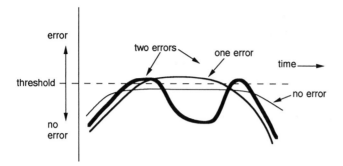

Figure 3.27
Three responses that to the operator are likely to appear similar, but by a given error criterion are scored very differently.

just short of the criterion and not be counted at all. To the operator, these three behaviors are imperceptibly different. An operator may allow a variable to trigger an alarm knowing full well she can easily recover, but nevertheless she is scored with an error.

It is clear that an error and an *accident* are not the same. A definition of an accident is an "unwanted and unwonted exchange of energy" (Senders and Moray 1991).

One sometimes speaks of "good errors." The engineer would assert that there can be no feedback control without an error signal—a measured deviation, however small, from a desired reference. The learning psychologist would assert that error is part of learning and skill development. The artist would claim that error is essential to creativity. Darwin claimed that error (he called it "requisite variety") is an integral part of evolutionary improvement of plants and animals.

Taxonomies

Generic distinctions   Many and varied distinctions and taxonomies or classification schemes for human error have been proposed by various investigators (Rasmussen 1981). Common distinctions are the following:

errors of *omission* vs. errors of *commission*

errors in *sensing, memory, decision, response*

errors in deciding what one intends (an incorrect intention is called a *mistake*) vs. errors in implementing those intentions (An execution not in accord with one's intention is called a *slip*; see Norman 1981.)

forced errors (in which task demands exceed physical capabilities) vs. *random* errors (which can be slips or mistakes).

Senders-Moray taxonomy   An error taxonomy proposed by Senders and Moray (1991) distinguishes the following:

the error in context of the environment, the associated stimuli and responses—whether it was an omission, a substitution, an unnecessary repetition, etc.

the cognitive or behavioral mechanism: attention, perception, memory, strength, or control capability

different kinds of bias: anchoring, overconfidence, confirmation bias, cognitive lockup, or tunnel vision

the level of behavioral complexity—whether the error occurred as part of
    simple sensing, detecting, identifying, or classifying,
    rote sequencing,
    estimation with discrete or continuous responding, or
    logical manipulation, rule using, problem solving

whether the error was endogenous (caused by events within the actor) or exogenous (caused by events in the actor's environment).

Levels of query and diversity of needs   Senders and Moray (1991) assert that there are many taxonomies, and that which one is appropriate depends on the level of the query and the purpose of the error investigation. Many different persons may be involved: police, lawyers, politicians, statisticians, engineering designers, behavioral scientists. Their queries (What error? What actor? Where and when? Which object was involved? Why did it occur?) are aimed to fit their diverse needs:

assignment of responsibility

design and assessment of systems

understanding of human behavior, estimate error rates

understanding of psycho/pharmacological agents.

Causes

That errors have causes seems obvious. Yet investigations of errors or accidents seldom come up with neat explanations of causality (unless they expediently truncate their investigation with simplistic explanations like

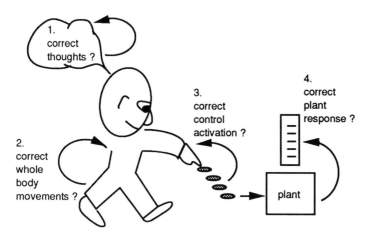

Figure 3.28
Hierarchy of ways feedback can be lacking.

"driver drunk" or "inattention"). Consider the typist who has hit an incorrect key. What is the cause? Most behavioral scientists would assert there is no one absolute cause, but something closer to a causal chain leading to the error. And in accident situations there is likely to be a causal chain leading from error to accident. Our hope, then, is to be able to intervene in the chain, preferably before the error but certainly before the accident. It has been said that whereas causes somehow may make errors happen, "reasons" are how people rationalize later. The following are some of the popular causes—or "reasons":

Lack of feedback   The idea is that, as in machines which have closed-loop or feedback control, human error is simply an epiphenomenon of inadequate feedback (measurement or sensitivity) that the system state has wandered into an unacceptable region of the state space. That is, humans are multi-dimensional feedback control systems, continually moving off track and correcting themselves in a progression of feedback loops encompassing thoughts, whole-body movements, manipulation of controls and system feedback (figure 3.28). If the appropriate feedback is lacking, because of sensory limitations or lack of training, or because the task or the environment is poorly designed, then the organism will tend to wander off course to the point where an "error" is made. Since the human operator

well practiced sequence: A ⟶ B ⟶ C ⟶ D

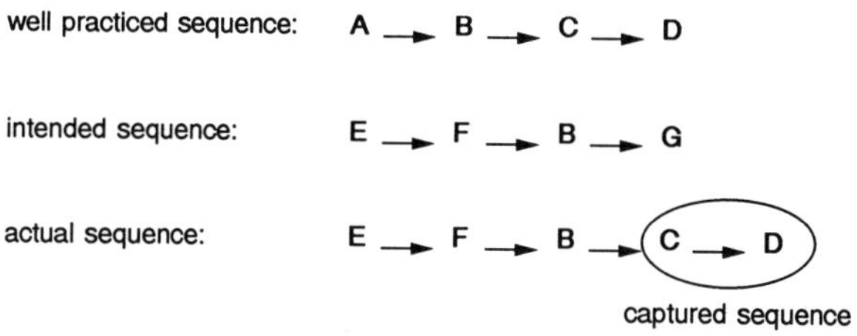

intended sequence: E ⟶ F ⟶ B ⟶ G

actual sequence: E ⟶ F ⟶ B ⟶ (C ⟶ D)

captured sequence

Figure 3.29
Capture error.

often anticipates or previews her upcoming tasks, that "course" of tasks must be evident to her.

Capture   In supervisory control a frequent cause of a slip error is *capture*. Let us assume that the operator is well practiced in some task sequence ABCD but occasionally intends to do EFBG. Both sequences require the common element B. The operator does EFBCD and then discovers her error (figure 3.29). Somehow her conditioning to do C after B was overwhelming. The correct but abnormal B–G course was not sufficiently compelling at the critical time.

Invalid internal models   One emerging theory of error causation appeals to the idea of an "internal model"—an input-output cognitive simulation of the controlled process or task which, when forced by process input, can be used to "observe" variables that are not convenient to measure directly. As was shown earlier, the computer internal model can also be repetitively updated with initial conditions and run in fast time to predict "what will happen if" any particular input is used. Presumably errors occur not only if the wrong mental model is used, but also if the parameters are miscalibrated relative to reality. This theory implies that not only training but also the design of displays and controls should correspond to an appropriate mental model of the task.

Hypothesis verification and the law of small numbers   Much laboratory research on individual decision-making has shown that subjects work to verify hypotheses they hold, searching for and retaining confirming evidence and ignoring or forgetting contradictory evidence and knowledge of what has not failed (Rouse and Hunt 1984). This has been observed in aircraft maintenance and in nuclear power plant failure diagnosis. It corresponds in everyday life to our common tendency to want to read what we know will agree with our preconceptions and to avoid what will not, or to find ways to explain away disconfirming experimental data—"selective filtering." Unavoidable noise and disruptions, of course, help provide an additional basis for such rationalization.

Closely related to this irrationality in human decision behavior is the tendency to infer more from small samples of data than is warranted—"the law of small numbers"—and to rely on anecdotes and isolated cases, possibly because such anecdotes provide good mnemonics. Subjective judgment of risk can be extremely fallacious, and the relative effects of probability and magnitude of consequences may be treated in irrational and even bizarre ways (Tversky and Kahneman 1981), especially for rare events.

It would be better if the supervisor could keep in mind a number of alternative hypotheses and let both positive and negative evidence contribute symmetrically in accordance with the theory of Bayesian updating (Sheridan and Ferrell 1974). Norman (1981), Reason and Mycielska (1982), Rasmussen (1982), and Rouse and Rouse (1983) discuss this problem from their different perspectives.

Stress and perceptual narrowing Stress is a construct which the non-behaviorist sometimes invokes to account for human error. From everyday experience this term has meaning, but its scientific use is plagued with difficulty. It is sometimes defined operationally in terms of time constraints, high risk, or problem complexity, which are not properties of the behavioral response. By that definition even a robot would be "stressed."

Stress usually implies time limitations, potential for serious undesirable consequences, and some degree of uncertainty. A commonly observed concomitant of stress is *perceptual narrowing*, also called *tunnel vision* or *cognitive lockup*, meaning the tendency to limit one's physical or mental attention and action to what is most immediate and familiar, being unable or unwilling to avail oneself of a broader set of options. Sometimes a stressed operator of a complex machine can be seen repetitively pushing the same button and looking at the same display, even though she is obviously not getting the information she expects and wants, whereas if she stepped back and observed other displays or considered other actions she could resolve her problem. A stressed operator performing a non-routine activity will also be more subject to procedural capture error.

Risk (error) homeostasis This is the notion that people inherently tend toward some level of risk (for whatever genetic or psychological or sociological reason) and therefore actively subject themselves to disturbances to their (otherwise) condition of stability. These disturbances are likely to result in at least small error. For example, it has been observed that when safety features or increased steering or braking capability are added to automobiles, drivers tend to drive faster or otherwise take increased risks to the point (so the theory goes) where the risk level remains as before. Perhaps somehow this is Darwin's *requisite variety* emerging on the highway.

In contrast to this is the *operant conditioning* of the psychologist B. F. Skinner, who asserted that error is unnecessary if behavior is properly shaped. His idea was that if "better" behavior is selectively rewarded, behavior will gradually improve and "error" will be reduced. Skinner's theories are mostly out of fashion today except in animal training and in some educational circles.

Error proneness Accident statistics lend little credibility to the idea that some individuals are "error prone." Some people clearly are subject to greater exposure to risk than others, however. An actor can be the agent but not the cause of an error. For example, the actor can be forced to decide on the basis of inadequate information.

State of the nervous system Senders and Moray (1991) assert that "there is no reason to believe there is such a thing as a recognizable state of the nervous system which occurs just before an error is made." At the same time we know full well that blood alcohol level, drowsiness, emotional stress, and other correlates of human error are also correlated with "states of the nervous system." Perhaps the problem is that we have an inadequate definition of "state" in this case.

Clearly at present there is no acceptable unified theory of causation of human error. There are many partially developed theories.

Difficulties of modeling and predicting human error

It would seem that insofar as error can be defined, one can simply count the number of errors in different categories, divide by the number of opportunities for that error to occur, and have an estimate of the probability of error. Then one can experimentally determine what factors increase or decrease that error, thus deriving error models. This is precisely what the nuclear power industry has been trying to do in recent years. However, this approach is not without serious problems.

First, with regard to the numerator of the estimate, many events that one would most like to predict—the events having the most serious consequences, such as nuclear plant meltdowns, dam breaks, or airplane crashes—do not happen often. Even if serious accidents (and the error chains leading to them) were to occur often enough to provide reasonable statistics, and automobile accidents fit this category, they happen in so many ways that there still are very few data in any one error-causation category. This fact of life frustrates the frequentist statistician, who depends wholly on empirical counts.

The Bayesian statistician, however, is not so discouraged by small samples, for she can start from subjective estimates and refine these on the basis of whatever data are available. The subjectivists have rules of thumb called *performance shaping factors*, which they apply to modify estimates of human error probability on the basis of subjective appraisal of surrounding physical, procedural, and organizational circumstances. There is active debate between the frequentist (or objectivist) and Bayesian or (subjectivist) approaches to treating error data.

Then, with regard to the denominator, it is not always clear what to assume for "number of opportunities." Should it be units of time, number of times a nominal procedure is repeated, physical limits on how often an error *could* be repeated, or what? Thus error rates and predictions demand thorough specification of assumptions of how both the numerator and the denominator were defined and measured. The choice of taxonomy and the criterion of "error" vs. "no error" have major effects upon the numbers obtained.

To try to increase the number of errors available for analysis, rather than sit back and wait for real errors to occur by chance, the experimenter forces the situation by using an operator-in-the-loop simulation. However, the simulation may differ from the true situation in that the experimental subject is likely to be conscious of being observed, and is likely to be trying to please the experimenter. In any case, in a simulation or an actual life situation, many human errors go unobserved, since operators detect their own errors and correct them before the observation can be made. Of course actual error (and accident) data should be used wherever it is available, and it has been shown that the collection of such data can be enhanced by providing certain protections for voluntary reporting.

What can be said for error prediction is that at best it is a matter of stochastic prediction, and mostly it is art and not science.

Given these caveats, we now examine the conventional approaches to human error analysis, data acquisition, and remediation.

Common approaches to modeling human error and reliability

Subject to the difficulties discussed above, there are four common approaches to modeling error and reliability of human-machine systems: the discrete failure combinatorial model, used to derive point estimates of human error probability (HEP); HEP sensitivity analysis; the time-continuum failure model, and the Monte Carlo failure simulation.

Discrete failure combinatorial model: THERP   Discrete failure combinatorial modeling, which includes human error probabilities (HEPs), is best described by THERP, the Technique for Human Error Rate Prediction (Swain and Guttman 1983; Meister 1964). THERP is based on standard combinatorial mathematics plus artful use of tabled human error rates. This is the method currently being used by the Nuclear Regulatory Commission. Mostly these techniques are used to characterize *event trees* such as that shown in figure 3.30.

Assume that estimates can be made (by subjective judgment or empirical records) for the probability q_i of human error on operation i, and for the probability f_i that such a human error will not be corrected in time to avoid a system error. For two independent error events A and B the probability of their joint occurrence, q_{AB}, is equal to $q_A q_B$. Then $Q_j = 1 - (1 - f_i q_i)^n$ is the probability of failure in n independent operations i in class j. The total system failure probability is then

$$Q_T = 1 - [(1 - Q_1)(1 - Q_2)\cdots(1 - Q_i)\cdots(1 - Q_k)]$$

for k independent classes. In dealing with multiple error events one must be particularly concerned about the dependence of one error, say B, on another, say A. With zero dependence, $\text{prob}(B|A) = \text{prob}(B)$ and the above combinatorial equations are true. With complete dependence, $\text{prob}(B|A) = 1$. In general, $\text{prob}(B|A) = \text{prob}(A, B)/\text{prob}(A)$.

The steps for conducting a human reliability analysis of a nuclear power plant based on THERP have been stated by Bell and Swain (1983):

Visit the plant, survey the control room, interview the operators.

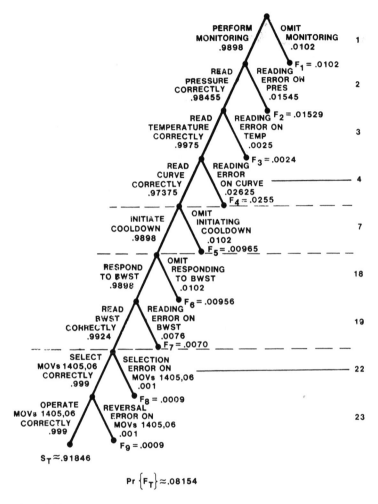

Figure 3.30
Event tree (sequence of events is from top to bottom). [From Swain and Guttman 1983.]

Review information available from systems analysis about critical operator interactions with plant systems.

Talk or walk through various critical procedures step by step with a trained operator in the control room or a simulator or a mockup.

Do a task analysis for various critical situations, formally listing, diagramming, and interrelating task components on paper.

Develop initial event trees.

Assign from tabled values appropriate nominal human error probabilities (HEPs) for component events.

Estimate the relative effects of performance shaping factors, such as stress, training, motivation, and fatigue, and adjust HEPs (see Embry 1976).

Assess dependence factors and adjust HEPs. Usually these are considered only for adjacent events on the trees; higher-order dependencies are neglected.

Determine success and failure probabilities for whole sequences of events, neglecting probability of recovery (discovery and correction of error in time).

Determine effects of recovery factors. If the failure rates are sufficiently low without the recovery factors, those sequences can be ignored anyway, so there is no need to bother with recovery factors which would decrease failure rates further.

Normally the HEPs for human operator sequences are turned over to reliability systems analysts, who incorporate those results into still more complex analyses (including equipment failures, weather and seismic conditions, etc.) using what are sometimes called *fault trees* (figure 3.31). If warranted, sensitivity analysis may be done for individual or combined HEPs, i.e., to get a ratio of the partial derivatives: change in probability of core melt or other calamitous "top event" divided by change in probability of some component "base-event" human error.

HEP sensitivity analysis   Hall et al. (1981) made extensive analyses of how changes in HEPs might affect system unavailability, core melt probability, and radiation release probability. They started from nominal probabilities for salient events from the Nuclear Regulatory Commission Reactor Safety Study WASH-1400 (1975) for various accident scenarios. They considered all human error probabilities to be at least 10^{-5}, some of course much

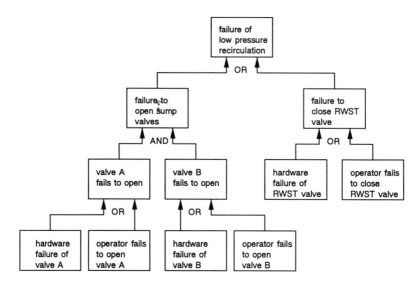

Figure 3.31
Fault tree (causality operates from bottom to top).

larger. Then, using a special computer program, they determined how making all HEPs 3, 10 ,or 30 times smaller or 3, 10, or 30 times larger would affect the "top events" within those accident scenarios (figure 3.32). Note that sensitivities to changes in HEPs are roughly comparable across various accident scenarios, and that these taper off quickly on the negative side as machine factors dominate. The apparent diminishing effect on the positive side is an artifact of the logarithmic scale.

Time-continuum failure models   Some risk investigators (Askren and Regulinski 1969) believe a more appropriate way to consider system reliability is in terms of *time until failure*, or, if one wishes to use empirical statistics, *mean time between failure* (MTBF). Confidence limits may be established for the MTBF based typically on a skewed distribution of times until failure such as the log-normal model. Assuming the human operator is good at recovery or repairing, one can incorporate data on mean time to repair (MTTR) and generate statistics for the fraction of time a given system is available.

Monte Carlo failure models   An approach to human reliability somewhat different from direct calibration of the above models by empirical data uses

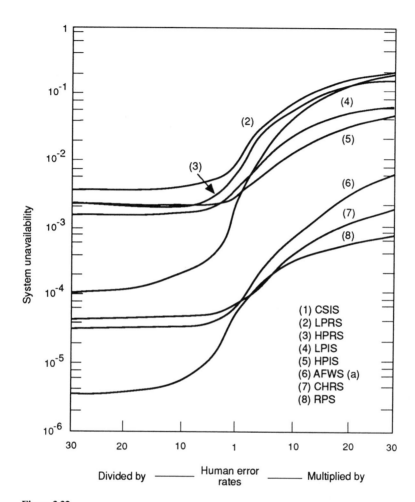

Figure 3.32
Sensitivity of nuclear plant unavailability (compulsory shutdown) to quantitative changes in human error probability. [From Hall et al. 1981.]

a computer-based Monte Carlo technique (Siegel et al. 1975; U.S. Navy 1977). Probabilities of error are assumed for human behavior elements such as finding the right display, reading and interpreting the display correctly, making the right decision, finding the right control, or operating it correctly. Each of these is conditioned on task or situational properties such as number of alternatives, size, distance, and familiarity. Then the appropriate combination of behavioral elements and task situation properties is assembled and "run" a large number of times in a computer, and distribution functions are generated for success (or failure) of the whole sequence of events. Such models, of course, can be made to fit empirical data by adjustment of their plentiful parameters. The latter characteristic also limits their usefulness for prediction.

Acquiring data

The usefulness of any of the above models depends on its correspondence with empirical events measured under circumstances that correspond to those for which predictions are to be made. From one viewpoint the models are nothing more than alternative ways of summarizing such empirical observations.In the nuclear power industry there are three available sources of such observations from which a "database" may be constructed: anecdotal accounts from the memory of operators or other participants, operating logs and formal accident or "event" reports, and runs on training simulators in which error-provoking conditions are present and errors are automatically measured and recorded. Of human errors in valve and switch operations noted in official licensee event reports from commercial nuclear power plants in the US, Luckas and Hall (1981) estimate human-error rates to approximate those used by Swain. The credibility of human-error data from simulators is most often questioned on the basis that realistic stress, boredom, and similar sources of behavior variability are lacking. Other neglected sources of variability are subjects' understanding of what they are supposed to do or what the criteria of success or failure are. Nevertheless, as is well proven by aircraft piloting simulators, the simulations approach may be the best way to estimate human reliability in complex operational situations.

Formal accident reporting schemes such as police reports or licensee event reports in nuclear plants are likely to be both simplistic and "sanitized"—data which are embarrassing to any of the parties involved are deleted, including most of what is useful for reliability research. The US

Department of Transportation (Federal Aviation Administration) has developed an excellent reporting scheme for aviation incidents (near-accidents) in which the anonymity of the person reporting is protected. Such a scheme could well be copied by the nuclear and other industries.

An important potential source of human-error data is the training simulator. Nuclear reactor operator training simulators have been programmed so as to monitor all control actions (or lack thereof) that are outside an acceptable range (in terms of what, when, in what order, and how). When errors are detected, segments from a continuously running videotape loop can be saved for later playback and analysis.

While simulators may be our best hope in understanding man-machine reliability in operations, they offer little hope for providing data on the types and stages of human "error" outside of operations. Finally, no matter how intelligent the human operator is, in many modern systems she is almost totally dependent upon displays and controls and mediation by computers. In view of computer-aided-design, computer-aided-manufacturing, computer-aided-test, and computer-aided-management systems, this computer dependence is gradually coming to be a condition of participation by humans all along the way. Identifying whether an "error" was due to a human or to a machine is coming to be more difficult, not less.

Recommended therapy: What can be done about human error

A first order of business is to make sure sufficient diagnosis has been performed. This means qualitatively reviewing the control boards or consoles and correcting obvious human-engineering deficiencies. It also means discovering, through quantitative reliability analysis, which sources of error are most critical. Finally it means acknowledging the social factors that cause neglect and sloppy work.

Given some understanding of the error situation, the usual wisdom proffered by the human-factors profession for keeping "bad errors" in check is (in order of efficacy) as follows.

Design to prevent error

Provide immediate and clear feedback from an inner loop (early in the consequence chain).

An outer loop (downstream consequences) should also be fed back to clarify and confirm earlier messages.

Provide special computer aids and integrative displays showing which parts of the system are in what state of health.

Give attention to cultural stereotypes of the target population—e.g., in Europe the expectation is that flipping a wall switch down turn a light on, so if designing for Europeans don't use the American stereotype.

Use redundancy in the information, and sometimes have two or more actors in parallel (though this does not always work).

Design the system to forgive, and to be "fail safe" or at least "fail soft" (i.e., with minor cost).

Train

Get operators to admit to and think about error possibilities and error-causative factors, since although people tend to catch errors of action, they tend not to catch errors of cognition.

Train operators to cope with emergencies they haven't seen before, using simulators where available.

Use skill maintenance for critical behaviors that need be exercised only rarely.

Restrict exposure   Be conscious that this limits actor opportunity.

Warn or alarm   Keep in mind that too many warnings or alarms overload or distract the observer, or condition her to ignore them.

Accept and try to repair any damage   It is best to strike a balance with tolerance of variability, and not expect people to be error-free zombie automatons. If automation is indicated, try to keep operator knowledgeable about what the automation is doing, provide opportunity for take-over from the automation if it fails, and engender some responsibility for doing this.

Further considerations about human error in relation to system context

Error vs. error consequences   It is undesirable consequences of error, not error itself, that we seek to reduce. Senders and Moray (1991) provide some relevant caveats:

"The less often errors occur, the less likely we are to expect them, and the more we come to believe that they cannot happen.... It is something of a paradox that the more errors we make the better we will be able to deal with them."

"Eliminating errors locally may not improve a system, and might cause worse errors elsewhere."

"Managerial styles and social dynamics of the work environment are potent factors for decreasing or increasing error."

Human error vs. machine error   It is commonly appreciated that humans and machines are rather different, and that thus a combination of both has greater potential for reliability than either alone. It is not commonly understood how best to make this synthesis. Humans are erratic. They err in surprising and unexpected ways. Yet they are also resourceful and inventive, and they can recover from both their own and the equipment's errors in creative ways. Machines are more dependable, which means they are dependably stupid when minor change of behavior would prevent a failure in a neighboring component from propagating. The intelligent machine can be made to adjust to an identified variable whose importance and relation to other variables are sufficiently well understood. The intelligent human operator still has usefulness, however, for she can respond to what at the design stage may be termed an "unknown–unknown" (a variable which was never anticipated, so that there was never any basis for equations to predict it or computers and software to control it).

Human errors beyond the operator   Reliability analysts of nuclear power plants, aircraft and air traffic control systems, and other large systems struggle to include not only human-operator errors but also human-operator-initiated recovery factors in their analyses. This is laudable but unfortunately still insufficient. This is because human error occurrence and recovery pervade the performance of these large systems in many locations and at many stages—not just in the control room. There are many other aspects of planning and design, plant construction and fabrication of equipment by vendors, installation, calibration, maintenance, administration, and management to which operator error and recovery can be traced.

A principal culprit is management of large system design. Subsystems are provided from many different sources. Typically each supplier provides alarms and special controls on its own component piece of equipment, independent of all other component subsystems. Often no objection is raised, on the ground that the designer of each component subsystem knows what is best for that subsystem. Then in an emergency there is an excessive number of alarm lights, and the operator finds herself overwhelmed and helpless. Clearly someone must be charged with the responsibility to see that the operator not be given more "help" than she can handle.

Another source of confusion and "error beyond the operator" is the tradeoff between design and cost. How much safety is acceptable (short of "100% safe," as demanded by a famous senator who should have known that such statements make no sense)? Naive demands that systems be "as safe as possible" often lead to political sham, which masks facing up to realistic safety needs and costs. We need to find better sources of data by which to calibrate our human-error models. Anecdotal error data are always available, but always suspect.

Supervisory errors: Different training needed?   As the supervisor's task becomes more cognitive, is the answer to provide training in theory and general principles? Curiously, the literature seems to provide a negative answer (Duncan 1981). Moray (1986) concludes: "There seems to be no case in the literature where training in the theory underlying a complex system has produced a dramatic change in fault detection or diagnosis." Evidence presented by Morris and Rouse (1985) suggests that diagnosis of the unfamiliar does not require theory and understanding of system principles. Apparently, frequent hands-on experience in a simulator (with simulated failures) is the best way to enable a supervisor to retain an accurate mental model of a process.

Human errors in distributed decision making and adversarial situations Whereas relatively tight control can be maintained over well-defined human activities of one or two persons, at higher organizational levels actual behavior and nominal previously-agreed-upon procedures can deviate dramatically and are more difficult to predict. The top level of the National Command Authority has been described by a White House aide as "mashed potatoes" (Bloomfield 1987). Bracken (1985) discusses how command can become "ambiguous" and how "the deeper into the unusual conditions of a high alert or a controlled nuclear exchange the more likely ambiguous command is to gain importance."

Some observers believe that often what is alleged to be operator error is in reality management's way of disguising its inability to administer effectively and to negotiate fairly with union workers, plus everyone's inability to cope with interpersonal problems—the real provocation for human error. This allegation was put succinctly: "To err is human factors" (Egan 1982).

Most reliability analysts shy away from considering acts of intentional malevolence as a source of system error. While overt attacks and sabotage are properly the domain of guards and professional security investigators and analysts, there probably exists a large "gray area" of carelessness and neglect by operators as well as by maintenance and administrative personnel provoked by malevolent feelings or apathy.

Error, experimentation, and requisite variety   Rasmussen has argued, and I concur, that the human operator is an inherent error maker, and it is questionable whether the goal should always be to keep her from making errors. Error making, along with active participation, is a proven ingredient of learning, and to isolate the human operator from error making is to make her into a zombie. Particularly as systems become controlled in supervisory fashion, it seems important to allow the human operator to be experimental when she deems it appropriate. Experimentation may be synonymous with "error" in terms of tried and proven procedures. The trouble is, proven procedures are not available for many situations, and even if they were the operator might not be sure which procedure to use.

However, experimentation must be done in a way that is fail-safe. That way is by intermixing simulation with actual system operation. That is, the operator is provided the means to try out various supervisory commands and study their relative effects on a simulator before the actual system is committed. By the time the actual system is committed, the operator has a pretty good idea what is error and what is not. However, there is a limit to how much experimentation can be done, particularly under time stress.

System designers, operators and managers are not quite at liberty to adopt a Darwinian resignation—to let the *requisite variety* in design, operator behavior, and management style play out in actual operation, so that in time some designs, operators, and managers survive and others do not, and *then* we will know which is best! There is some obligation to be more proactive and protective. At least we should pay attention to and learn whatever we can from experience.

Responsibility   Finally, there is the question of responsibility for error, and how much lies with the individual and how much with society. Should actors be responsible for own errors? One might like individuals to take a bit more responsibility than they now are inclined to do. In 1711 the poet Alexander Pope wrote "To err is human, to forgive divine." Today's litigious society seems not to be very forgiving, and forgiveness based on religion, culture, or political norms seems to be on the wane. Human-factors engineers should strive for error forgiveness through engineering design, but be careful not to remove motivation for individual responsibility.

4 Social Implications of Telerobotics, Automation, and Supervisory Control

It is probably a bit unusual to conclude a book about a new technology with a discussion of the social implications, many of them negative. However, given what in the author's opinion are compelling social implications of telerobot technology, there seemed an obligation.

4.1 Trends toward Super, Tele, and Meta

At an earlier time in the history of human-machine interaction there was an invasion of relatively large and crude machines to replace the muscles of workers. Mostly those workers welcomed the machines, though the early mechanical intruders were noisy, dirty, and often unsafe. With time they got quieter, cleaner, and safer.

And then, about the time of the Second World War, came the earliest wave of computer technology, namely that of continuous analog signal processing and control. "Servomechanisms" provided true and faithful slaves in military systems for accurate control of ship rudders, aircraft ailerons, and the aiming of guns and radar antennas, all under remote control by human operators. Now the finer motor skills were being taken over by machines.

The third stage is occurring now, as implied throughout the preceding chapters. The computer is taking over functions heretofore regarded as non-rote "pattern recognition" and "thinking": interacting with sensing devices, building up databases of "knowledge" or "world models," associating what is known from the past with what is currently happening, making decisions about what actions to take, and implementing those actions. The human operator, at the same time, is becoming more and more a supervisor. This may be characterized by the Latin prefix *super* and the Greek prefixes *tele* and *meta*:

super—The human operator is above the computer hierarchically.

tele—The supervising is from a distance, both literally and figuratively.

meta—The human operator may oversee many tasks, and may interact with many other supervisors by communication channels.

4.2 The Intended Positive Effects of Telerobotics and Automation

Telerobotics and automation pose a serious challenge for the years ahead. The robot or automaton itself, i.e., the hardware integration of sensors, actuators, and computers, means nothing without the human designer/ programmer to configure it and assign it task goals and procedures for particular applications. When the human-robot interaction is sufficiently intimate we essentially have a telerobot. Whether our advanced forms of automation are robots or telerobots (and clearly the trend is toward the latter), our lives are being changed by them. The optimistic scenario is that telerobots will grow in number and variety, becoming available to us to do our beck and call in our homes, schools, and government facilities, in our vehicles, our hospitals, and across the entire spectrum of our workplaces— factories, farms, offices, construction sites, mines, and so on. Some will be of human size, some the size of insects, and some much larger than human size. Some will work much faster than we can work, and some will work exceedingly slowly and patiently. These sensor-computer-actuators are already much more widespread than most of us are aware of.

Telerobots and automatic systems have come into being because we want them for their positive efforts:

Improved task performance and reliability

Telerobots can work longer hours, and perform many tasks faster, more accurately, and with less variability, than human workers. In many cases they are far more reliable than humans.

Improved human safety

Telerobots can work in hazardous environments—at extremes of heat or cold, high or low pressure, chemical or nuclear toxicity, or in tasks where there are other forces which injure or kill people.

Reduction of human labor

This is the economic advantage. Increasingly, machine labor costs less than human labor.

Participative technology advancement: Cathedral building

The modern-day building and programming of telerobots is not unlike the building of cathedrals and temples in the middle ages. Both posed techno- logical challenges, requiring careful planning, group cooperation, and the satisfaction of seeing results. Whereas cathedrals were supposedly built to glorify God (and perhaps a few lesser religious leaders of the day claimed some attention in the process), telerobots may be said to glorify the scientific theories (and the scientists and engineers).

Better appreciation of human intelligence in relation to artificial intelligence

The challenge of building and programming telerobots may also be said to be motivated by a latent desire of humankind to replicate itself and thereby to understand itself. Our human progeny supposedly embody whatever intelligence we can pass on to them; so too our telerobotic progeny embody whatever artificial intelligence we can pass on.

4.3 Negative Implications of Telerobotics and Automation for the Individual: Separation and Alienation

Developments in broadband communication technology have allowed the human supervisor to become physically separated from the locus of action, i.e., where the telerobotic system performs its functions. Gradually, in factories, power plants, and other large man-machine complexes, the human supervisors are drawn into centralized control rooms to perform their instructing and monitoring activities. Gradually they are being aided by flexible and sophisticated command languages and means to communicate either through keyboards or voice, by exotic multi-color computer-graphic displays to summarize what is happening and to predict what will happen, and by computer-based "expert systems" to answer questions and give advice. For robotic systems which perform inspection and manipulation tasks in the hazardous environments of space or the deep ocean, the human supervisor is likely to be provided a comfortable control room on the ground (or in a ship on the ocean surface).

The result is that the human supervisor removes herself not only spatially but also temporally, functionally, and cognitively from the ongoing physical process she is directing. This is because what she does and what she thinks are likely to have different timing, different explicit form, and different logical content from what the telerobot does and thinks.

In this sense the human supervisor becomes an alien to the physical process—in the literal sense of the word. It is natural for aliens to become alienated, in terms of what they know and how they feel. People who have been pushed sideways into jobs which do not make use of the skills on which they pride themselves and in which they have had their identity will feel frustrated and resentful. People who no longer understand the basis of what they are asked to do will become confused and distrustful. Especially if they perceive a powerful computer to be mediating between them and what is being produced at the other end, people become mystified about how things work, question their own influence and accountability, and ultimately abandon their sense of responsibility. All of this can be called alienation (Sheridan 1980). The components of potential alienation are detailed below.

Threatened or actual unemployment

This is the factor most often considered. To accomplish the same task, more supervisory control means more automation, more efficiency, less direct control, and fewer jobs for human workers.

Silent failures

Automatic systems can be designed to detect their own failures, but so far the human operator is far better at this. When failures do occur in automatic systems, they tend to be "silent" and may go undetected for long periods. The person "in charge" is likely to be blamed.

Erratic mental workload and work dissatisfaction

Automation greatly affects not only the nature but also the pace of work, and makes it vary between extremes. Airline pilots and nuclear plant operators refer to their work as "hours of boredom punctuated by moments of terror." Some workers may feel that although automation has eliminated many mundane tasks from their work, it has not relieved the stress induced by on-the-job decisions. For example, some pilots feel that in times of emergency or high stress the automation is not sufficient to ensure safety, and that more pilots are needed even than in earlier times of pure manual control. Additionally, while workers are often glad that automation has broken the dull monotony of repetitive manual work, they may not get as much satisfaction from their new supervisory monitoring role. The satisfaction derived from putting in a hard day's work and producing something with their own wits and efforts may be gone.

Already some airline pilots are complaining about automation, and power plant operators who have experienced older, simpler, and very reliable plants are wondering if things haven't gone too far.

Centralization of management control and loss of worker control

One result of automation and the introduction of electronic technology often feared by workers is the possibility of secret monitoring of their work through the equipment. Rarely does management engage in such activities, but the mere possibility is often sufficient to produce worker anxiety. This anxiety does not occur only in production employees; it can also occur in office workers who are fearful that private data stored electronically may be accessed by others. Centralization of control, so easy with advanced automation, is sometimes seen by management as synonymous with efficiency. While in some cases centralization may enhance productivity, in other it may prove detrimental (Rijnsdorp 1981).

Desocialization

Though cockpits and control rooms now require teams of two or three, the trend is toward fewer people per team, and eventually one person will be adequate in many installations. Thus cognitive interaction with computers will replace that with other people. As supervisory control systems are interconnected, the computer will mediate more and more of what interpersonal contact remains.

Deskilling

Skilled workers "promoted" to supervisory controller may resent the transition because of fear that when called upon to take over and do the job manually they may not be able to. A skill such as machining or inspecting products, developed over a long time period, provides the worker a sense of dignity and self-respect. If the worker becomes a button-pushing supervisor and monitor, that skill may atrophy.

Intimidation of greater power and responsibility

Supervisory control will encourage larger aggregations of equipment, higher speeds, greater complexity, higher cost of capital, and probably greater economic risk if something goes wrong and the supervisor doesn't take the appropriate corrective action. The human supervisor will be forced to assume more and more ultimate responsibility. Depending upon one's personality, this could lead to insensitivity to detail, anxiety about being up to the job's requirements, or arrogance.

Technological illiteracy

In older manual control systems, the operator could understand how things worked. In the role of supervisory controller, the operator may lack the technological understanding of how the computer and the rest of the complex technology do what they do. Operators may come to resent this and resent the elite class who do understand.

Mystification and misplaced trust

Human supervisors of computer-based systems sometimes become mystified by and superstitious about the power of the computer, even seeing it as a kind of magic or a "big brother" authority figure. This leads quite naturally to naive and misplaced trust. This was particularly well articulated by Norbert Wiener (1964), who used as a metaphor a classic in horror literature, W. W. Jacobs' *The Monkey's Paw*:

In this story, an English working family sits down to dinner in its kitchen. Afterwards the son leaves to work at a factory, and the old parents listen to the tales of their guest, a sergeant major in the Indian army. He tells of Indian magic and shows them a dried monkey's paw which, he says, is a talisman that has been endowed by an Indian holy man with the virtue of giving three wishes to each of three successive owners. This, he says, was to prove the folly of defying fate.

He claims he does not know the first two wishes of the first owner, but only that the last was for death. He himself was the second owner, but his experiences were too terrible to relate. He is about to cast the paw on the coal fire when his host retrieves it, and despite all the sergeant-major can do, wishes for £200.

Shortly thereafter there is a knock at the door. A very solemn gentleman is there from the company that has employed his son and, as gently as he can, breaks the news that the son has been killed in an accident at the factory. Without recognizing any responsibility in the matter, the company offers its sympathy and £200 as a solatium.

The theme here is the danger of trusting the magic of the computer when its operation is singularly literal. "If you ask for £200 and do not express the condition that you do not wish it at the cost of the life of your son, £200 you will get whether your son lives or dies."

To a naive user the computer can be simultaneously so wonderful and intimidating as to seem faultless, and if the computer produces other than what its user expects, that can be attributed to its superior wisdom. Such discrepancies are usually harmless, but if allowed to continue can, in some complex and highly interconnected systems, endanger lives. It is therefore crucial, as new computer and control technology is introduced, that it come to be accepted by users for what it is—a tool meant to serve and be controlled ultimately by human beings.

Sense of not contributing

Though the efficiency and mechanical productivity of a new supervisory control system may far exceed that of an earlier manually controlled system which a given person has experienced, that person may come to feel that with automation she is no longer the basis of value added, no longer a significant contributor.

Diffusion and abandonment of responsibility

As a result of the factors described above, supervisors may eventually feel they are no longer responsible for what happens—the computers are. A worker with her own set of hand tools or simple self-powered but manually controlled machine, though she may try to place the blame for difficulties elsewhere, has the primary responsibility for use and maintenance of her tools or machine. She is accountable for what is produced. When a worker's actions in using a machine are mediated by a powerful control system (e.g. a computer), however, the lines of responsibility are not so clear, and the worker may not be sure which should get the credit or the blame for a situation—the computer or herself. As a result the worker may, in effect, abandon her responsibility for the task performed or the good produced, believing instead it is "in the hands" of the computer. Even when computers are installed to aid information flow from one worker to another, or to act as a processor or storer of data, individuals using the system may feel that the machine is in complete control, and disclaim personal accountability for any error or performance degradation.

Blissful enslavement

To many writers the worst form of alienation, the worst tragedy, occurs if the worker is happy to accept a role in which she is made to feel powerful while in actuality she is enslaved. Engelberger (1981) reminds us that "it will always be far easier to make a robot of a man rather than to make a robot like a man."

In regard to the impacts of the computer on a person's self-perception, I am fond of citing Bruce Mazlish (1967), who refers to the computer as the "fourth discontinuity" in this self-perception. At first, says Mazlish, humans saw themselves as the center of all things, but Copernicus jarred this perception by showing that man was an isolated dweller of a tiny planet of a minor star (which turned out to be at the edge of but one galaxy). Darwin came along and rudely asserted that we were descended from the apes and they from lower creatures still. Later Freud suggested that we humans are not even consciously in charge of our own faculties, that our egos and ids drive us. Now the computer may be dealing us the ultimate affront—surpassing us intellectually—beating us in our best suit, and seemingly inviting us to give in.

Surely there are promises of greater product quality, better energy and economic efficiency, and improved worker safety which motivate the new technology changes. Nevertheless, we must then look at the potential negative impacts, which need to be reduced to achieve a satisfactory adoption of automation by a society.

4.4 Negative Implications of Telerobotics for Society

Machine productivity instead of human productivity

Today nations are consumed with productivity. Balance of payments and national well-being are at stake. With the intent to increase productivity, computers integrated with sensors, actuators, and robots have been installed in factories, power and chemical plants, aircraft, ships, automobiles, banks, hospitals, schools, and homes. The computer has invaded the entire infrastructure of technology, and most people would not turn back the clock. But what kind of productivity is being increased? Is it the kind of productivity that, at the end of our careers and indeed of our lives, gives us the satisfaction of having best served other human beings? Is machine productivity synonymous with human productivity, or are the two different, even in conflict with one another?

Daily living by remote control: Reduction of social contact

With future constraints on energy potentially inhibiting free travel, and with microelectronic advances furthering communication technology in many ways, we have new capability to use local telephones, facsimile machines, and personal computer terminals to order fast food or supplies delivered to our homes, to shop from electronic catalogs, to buy and sell stocks, to pay bills or make bank transfers, and do business without leaving our homes. At the moment this is not regarded the same as remote control of a dynamic robot which moves and does useful mechanical work—only as an extension of the telephone for communication purposes. But consider that in using such "extended telephones" one really is commanding some person or machine to prepare and/or deliver food or other goods. In one sense it is truly telerobotic control.

Future scenarios may see people browsing up and down the aisles of the supermarket or discount store, or inspecting and handling merchandise, though remote communication links, and possibly doing the remote browsing and manipulating in virtual environments rather than real ones. It is too early to predict the benefits and hazards of such radical changes in living style. But no significant "breakthroughs" in technology are required for such a scenario to occur. The tendency to return home and perform many more of our daily functions by remote control requires fundamental rethinking of the meaning of home, commerce, transportation, education, and human fulfillment.

Electronic tele-governance by the powerful over the powerless

The use of modern communication technology can provide not only "feedforward" of information from those in power down to the masses of citizens, but also "feedback" from the masses to the powerful. Already there have been many experiments with people watching TV programs and talking back through the telephone to vote on questions posed. Optical fiber and synchronous satellite communication technology greatly expand the bandwidth currently available on telephone circuits. Conceivably, democratic governance could extend to all citizens and be essentially instantaneous, possibly even eliminating layers of elected representatives.

This vision may have advantages for some purposes, for example to educate and test public opinion on certain issues. But such possibilities of electronic governance also conjure up visions of a kind of "brave new world" which could rapidly leave too much power in the hands of whoever controlled the media. Indeed, such arguments have already been made against the national media networks of today, and similar arguments underlay the antitrust motivations for breaking up the Bell Telephone monopoly.

Automation of ecoexploitation

The great debate about "limits to growth" is not finished. Most planners of future automation systems believe that it is especially important that the "technological imperative"—that we build automatic systems because we can—be restrained, especially with respect to use of energy and other precious natural resources (Aida 1982). Many nations of the world are lucky enough to have many such resources. Others are not so lucky. Proper use of automation will produce the same or greater benefits for people while reducing demands on energy and other (especially non-renewable) resources. It would be criminal to employ automation which, for the sake of short-term productivity, gluttonously exhausts these resources and leaves none for less developed nations and for future generations. Certain wealthy nations now recovering cobalt and other mineral nodules from the ocean bottom using high-tech robotic suction devices is a salient example.

We may be said to be facing a new stage of Hardin's (1968) "tragedy of the commons." Much as the wealthy sheepherders purposively monopolized the benefits of the English common grazing lands until there was none left for anyone, so too the technologically advanced nations are automating and expanding the machines which foul the air and water and use up the oil and other natural resources. The story of the sorcerer's apprentice comes to mind.

Telerobotic soldiers, spies, and saboteurs

The current interest in telerobotics has encouraged us to think hard about the relation of humans to machines in doing useful work. When evaluating the industrial robot for its societal advantages and disadvantages, one normally thinks in term of the economic-productivity advantage and the unemployment-producing disadvantage. Advantages and disadvantages of the telerobot tend to be seen in a different realm: Certainly the outstanding advantage is seen as that of removing the human operator from hazards to her health and risks to her safety. The principal disadvantage, possibly also related to health and safety, is subtler and on a different scale.

Consider a future teleoperator which has good mobility on land, or in the sea, or in the air or space—all are possible, all are being developed. Assume good telecommunication, reasonable sensors, and manipulative dexterity (full "telepresence" is not necessary). Assume a good battery pack or electric generator, or the possibility that the teleoperator can be controlled from afar to "plug itself in" from time to time to reenergize itself. This teleoperator may be sent by its human operator to do mischief in anyone's back yard. Its human operator need have no empathy for its welfare, for it is only a mechanical slave. Further, at any time its human operator can cease to communicate with it, and with ease can abandon responsibility and accountability for its present or past behavior.

Now consider a future telerobot, with a computer to help it see, hear, and touch, some motor reflex skills to conserve energy and adapt to its environment, and enough knowledge and instruction to understand how to implement its programmed goals in spite of disturbances or obstacles it encounters. This telerobot may be sent to do even more mischief, since it can go surreptitiously for long periods without need for communication. It can (and has) been used to spy, sabotage, set explosives, and perform a host of other duties. And of course, because it is controlled in supervisory fashion, any one human supervisor can multiply her own bodily capability manyfold. In this case it is even easier for the human operator to abandon responsibility. She can find herself very busy with a brood of other tele-robots, and anyway every telerobot can be claimed to have a mind of its own.

In past arguments, fights, and wars, individuals who feel they must resort to violence toward other individuals put themselves at some bodily risk in doing so—at least more risk than those not so inclined. Tradition-ally such behavior has been lauded as courage or bravery, and at least posed a high cost on the initiator. However, technology has been changing all that, as "weapon teleoperators" have evolved from clubs to arrows to bullets to bombs dropped from airplanes. The human operators no longer put themselves at risk so much as they jeopardize the safety of others. Telerobot technology is merely the next step.

Some have heralded the dawn of "smart weapons," battlefield robotics, and "telegladiators" as a new day when international disputes will be fought on a large technological playing field (space, undersea, or surely somewhere well away from real people) where technological prowess will win the day and no real people will get hurt. Certain military planners seem to be moving toward that fantasy even now.

Already we have telerobotic sonar spying devices in the oceans and similar optical spying devices in orbit above us—all over the protests of the helpless poorer nations. Now we see space becoming militarized—possible eventually in the form of an ultimate man-machine system pro-grammed in top-down supervisory fashion with the purpose of defending us, but demanding ultimately that we abandon responsibility to its computer.

I cannot help but recall again the theme of Norbert Wiener's *God* and *Golem, Incorporated* (1964), in which the Golem—the half-man, half-monster of Hebraic tradition—is the computer. Wiener clearly made the point that the computer can be programmed with the full expectation that it will do what its programmer intended. The computer, however, is literally single-minded; it will do as programmed—which may not correspond to what was intended. This by now is not a novel theme; it has been put forward by science fiction writers and political realists alike. I hope that as technologists we take seriously our social responsibility for the control of our telerobots.

4.5 Trust in Technology

Trustworthiness, and more generally trust-causation, since not all of what is trusted is worthy of trust, seems at first to be a characteristic applicable only to humans. Is it appropriate or useful to talk of trustworthiness (or trust-causation) of machines or of human-machine interaction? In today's world there are increasingly many situations where our use and appreciation of technology is closely tied to our trust in it. This is particularly true of large-scale technological systems such as air traffic control, electric power generation, computerized banking and funds transfer, and military command and control systems.

Definitions of trust

Webster's Third International Dictionary (1965) defines trust in four categories:

- assured reliance on a person or thing
- dependence on something future or contingent
- an equitable right or interest in property
- a charge or a duty imposed in faith or confidence.

Muir and Moray (1987), who especially consider trust in relation to technology, consider trust to be a function of three attributes: persistence, technical competence, and responsibility.

Below are proposed seven attributes of trust. (Perhaps these are better stated as causes of trust, whether rational or irrational.) On the basis of these attributes, trust in command and control systems and other technology might be defined operationally, measured, and modeled.

• **Reliability** of the system, in the usual sense of repeated, consistent functioning. This is the same as the first attribute of Webster. A person who observes repeated, consistent events under a particular circumstances may be said to be *conditioned to trust* (in the sense of operant conditioning) that those events will occur in the future when the appropriate circumstances occur. If the circumstances occur but the expected events do not, the conditioned trust will be *extinguished*.

• **Robustness** of the system, meaning demonstrated or promised ability to perform under a variety of circumstances. This is essentially the same as the Muir-Moray *competence*. We trust systems that will perform "correctly" under a variety of circumstances. We normally call people who do this "competent."

• **Familiarity**, meaning that the system employs procedures, terms, and cultural norms which are familiar, friendly, and natural to the trusting person. We tend to inherit trust in our family and friends and those who culturally are like us and who "speak the same language," both literally and metaphorically. The motto "In God we trust" might be an example with respect to Americans, who grow up with pennies in their hands. In human-machine interaction this translates to familiarity and therefore naturalness of displays and controls and console arrangement and procedures and system dynamics. "Computer friendliness" is a common term that supposedly connotes naturalness. It is important to point out that friendliness and familiarity can and often do engender irrational and unwarranted trust. Many of us trust ourselves to drive when we have been drinking alcohol, and at the same time may not trust airplanes or nuclear power plants, when the available statistics militate strongly in the reverse direction.

• **Understandability**, in the sense that the human supervisor or observer can form a mental model and predict future system behavior. Understandability is not the same as familiarity, though familiarity may be said to aid in understandability. However, we all are familiar with people who are not understandable or predictable, and we're not sure whether to trust them or not. A complex technological system which is easy to operate and become familiar with superficially may not be understandable and predictable in terms of its inner workings. Such a system can instill fear and distrust. This phenomenon has been seen again and again when sophisticated computer-control technology, often "human factored" to be "friendly," has been imposed on workers in industry without sufficient explanation. (I have discussed this phenomenon elsewhere as *alienation*; see Sheridan 1980.) Lack of understanding may account for much distrust which is ultimately quite irrational, e.g., distrust of foreigners and physical processes like computers and nuclear power, which appear mysterious.

• ***Explication of intention***, meaning that the system explicitly displays or says that it will act in a particular way (as contrasted to its future actions having to be predicted from a model). *Explication of intention* must be distinguished from *understandability*. In the former, intentions of future actions are specified outright by built-in computer-based decision, control, and automation systems; in the latter, future actions must be inferred from deeper understanding of how the system works. Other things being equal, we trust people who tell us what they intend to do and then do it (e.g., those who have taken an oath or publicly announced a policy) over those who just do things. Having a written contract makes most Westerners more trusting than having none, though somehow in Japan and other Asian countries trust in business deals is engendered by long discussions. Well-structured control loops and explicit computer-programs provide the equivalent characteristics in command-and-control and other technological systems. If this attribute corresponds to any of those used by Webster, it is to *charge or duty imposed in faith or confidence.*

• ***Usefulness***, or utility of the system to the trusting person in the formal theoretical sense. *Usefulness* accords with *responsibility*, literally "able to respond" (respond in a useful way). It is essentially the same as the attribute of *right* or *interest in property* of Webster. This is also the classical notion of utility as developed by Bentham, Mill, and von Neumann.

• ***Dependence*** of the trusting person on the system. My *dependence* attribute is the same as Webster's *dependence*. It could be said that we come to trust what we depend upon because we have to, but rationally, of course, we should place our dependence upon what warrants trust; trust should precede dependence rather than follow it.

Trust and the Turing test: Is it human or machine? real or virtual?

In the foregoing discussion we looked at attributes commonly applied in deciding whether to trust another person, and considered their application to machines or to human-machine systems. The presumption was that it would be clear in each case when we were dealing with a person and when with a machine. When an observer cannot tell whether observed behavior is the result of a person or of a machine, trust may be eroded. This special trust problem can occur in three situations: when the machine is actually "intelligent," when the behavior of human or machine is sufficiently constrained, and when the simulation of the environment is sufficiently compelling.

The intelligent machine   The accepted test of whether a machine (computer) is intelligent is the Turing test: whether a judge, not able to see the machine (say it is in another room) but able to specify inputs (through a human assistant) and observe responses, cannot determine whether it is a human or a machine. If a machine proved "intelligent" by this test, would the observer's trust be indifferent relative to its being a person? This is doubtful, since the observer would likely make assumptions of it beyond what showed up in the "intelligence" test. Present telerobots are not so intelligent that the Turing test is credible.

Parsons (1990) notes that Turing (1950) actually used the terms *thinking* and *intellectual* rather than *intelligence* when he proposed his famous test, and that he particularly emphasized behavior. Parsons quotes the two eminent psychologists C. L. Hull and E. G. Boring as having suggested (before Turing) that comparing robot behavior to human behavior might help us understand ourselves.

Constrained human or machine   If a telerobot or other machine, whether driven by a human or by a computer, is sufficiently constrained in its behavior (say it is can only receive a limited number of input signals and only perform a limited repertoire of controlled movements), the observer cannot put to it proper tests of "intelligence." This is not unlike the problem of determining the intelligence of a person with severe physical handicaps. When the Turing criterion cannot be applied, are there other ways to discriminate human vs. computer? It is unlikely, assuming the observer has no way of knowing the degree of constraint. This situation is a reality today for the non-operator observer.

Compelling simulation   The uncertainty may exist because of simulation technology sufficiently sophisticated and compelling that it can easily fool the observer. In time we are likely to have virtual environments that are indistinguishable from reality—virtual people or virtual machines or both in combination. Aircraft simulators provide the most compelling example of virtual reality today. The robots at Disney parks probably fool many people, especially children. A Turing-like test is probably the appropriate measure of "virtual reality" or "virtual presence."

A trustworthiness comparison of military C³I and nuclear power plants

The public is ever more aware of technology-induced risks on all sides. Familiar risks, such as fast driving in combination with alcohol ingestion, are accepted all too readily. Certain other risks, presumably because they do not involve familiar experiences, seem to cause greater public anxiety and outcry. Telerobotic technology, it has been suggested, fits the latter category, and is likely to impose ever greater anxiety. Without belaboring the point, and without examining all forms of technological risk, it is instructive to compare the trustworthiness of two large telerobotic systems: military command, control, communication, and information systems (C³I) on the one hand, and nuclear power plants on the other. The purpose is to show how different two telerobot application areas can be, to the end of having engineers and planners and eventually politicians and the public understand the differences.

During the last decade especially, military command and control systems have been infused by many billions of dollars' worth of research and development. Certainly some fraction of this vast expenditure has been directed to human behavior and human-machine interactions, including quantitative models of information processing in command hierarchies (Boettcher and Tenney 1986), timeliness and effectiveness (Cothier and Levis 1987), Petri nets (Andreadakis 1988), time-pressured distributed decision making (Tuler 1987), and compilations of experiential wisdom (Wohl et al. 1984; Perrow 1984; Carter et al. 1987). Curiously, the word *trust* and its essential concepts are seldom touched upon, perhaps because of the fuzziness of the word's meaning.

Complex military command and control systems are known to be particularly vulnerable to "bugs" in their electronic and human organizations' "nervous systems" and in their programs and procedures. Much information, certainly including performance data, is classified and not exposed to public scrutiny and critique. Vulnerability is aggravated in crises, when physical systems are likely to operate outside their normal ranges of variables and when humans are likely to be rushed, tired, frightened, and confused (and often not very experienced). To make matters worse, the whole C³I system is subject to malevolent interference by a powerful opponent. And this is further aggravated by the impossibility of fully testing such a system until it is used in war. (The author has observed some very limited military "war games" and has noted an interesting tendency to avoid the unexpected and to have the "bad guys" behave in rather stereotypical ways, the rationale being that the commanders cannot learn proper procedure and doctrine if events are too chaotic.) Such a system's trustworthiness may be in some question (Sheridan 1986).

A statement issued by the 1986 Pugwash Workshop on Accidental Nuclear War notes: "The most probable initiators of nuclear war are irrational acts, mistakes and malfunctions. Irrational leaders and groups may come into control of nuclear weapons. Leaders who are ordinarily rational may act irrationally under the intense pressure of a crisis or simply may fail to correctly perceive the consequences of their actions. And mechanical or electronic malfunctions may precipitate chains of events leading to nuclear war in spite of corrective action—or in concert with irrational or mistaken actions—by the human participants in the process." Since (we all pray that) there is no real opportunity to observe actual full-scale nuclear war, whatever determines our sense of trust in these systems determines our feelings of security.

Nuclear power plants, though they have their problems (many discussed in earlier sections), are designed to operate in normal and known conditions, and are shut down otherwise, while military systems are just the opposite. There is extensive operating experience with nuclear power technology, while with military systems there is relatively little experience in the current technology in the mode for which the systems are designed. In nuclear plants operators tend to be more experienced at their jobs and do not move so rapidly from billet to billet as in the military. In the nuclear industry serious errors and problems are reported publicly and technical information is shared much more openly, while errors and problems and much of the technology are kept secret by the military. In the nuclear industry accidents are simulated as a normal part of training, while in military war games the evidence suggests that commanders are loath to admit to and simulate accidents. In the past they have preferred "design-basis wars"; however, this may be changing. In any case real war is much more difficult to imagine and to simulate than various kinds of nuclear power accidents. Finally, nuclear plant operators are working only against nature, not against an intelligent malevolent opponent.

Table 4.1
Trustworthiness comparisons of nuclear power plant to military command and control system.

Factor	Nuclear power plant	Military command and control system
engineering design	plant startup <u>only if</u> everything is normal	initiation <u>because of</u> stress and abnormality
	automatic plant shutdown on significant abnormality	hard to stop once initiated
actual experience	hundreds of plant years	essentially none in mode anticipated
personnel	semipermanent	rapid turnover of many key personnel
error records	required public reporting	secret
simulation	"accidents" routinely simulated	difficult to simulate in realistic mode
type of formal game	game against nature	game against intelligent opponent
scientific analysis	open international forum	secret

The comparisons between C^{3}I and nuclear plants are summarized in table 4.1. The main point is that risk is a function of a variety of factors, and varies widely for different telerobotic applications.

Are we overtrusting technology?

We seem not to trust one another as much as would be desirable. In lieu of trusting each other are we putting too much trust in our technology? Should we continue expecting our manufactured products to be be flawless, so that mindless abuse and misuse resulting in accident makes the manufacturer liable for whatever happens and reinforces an ever-increasing promotion of ambulance-chasing litigation? Should we expect technology to provide happy and healthy lives in addition to extending them well beyond what they would be without certain technological props? Is it fair to trust our natural environment to go on supporting wanton waste of energy and natural resources to feed our technological addiction to production and consumption? Is it appropriate to trust military command and control systems to protect us from each other while we continue to feed our insatiable desire to be more powerful than our neighbor? I think not.

Perhaps we should blame the media, which condition us unrelentingly to want and expect more of technology. Perhaps we are not educating our children sufficiently well to understand the reasonable uses and limits of technology. Perhaps we are not governing ourselves to consider our children's children, our Third World neighbors, and the vulnerability of our fragile biosphere. Perhaps human-machine system scientists are giving insufficient attention to difficult but somehow important concepts such as trust and trustworthiness, and to the interdependence of trust with the ultimate performance of technological systems.

4.6 Is Using Technology to Love Harder than Using It to Hate?

In this section I bring up a problem which is by no means unique to automation and telerobotics but which certainly applies to them.

Is technology more easily applied to destruction than to construction?

It is obviously quicker and easier for a child to knock down a tower of blocks than to build it up. Building it takes discipline, care, and patience, but the result is usually one of satisfaction of having created something. Knocking it down takes none of these, and the lasting satisfactions are questionable. The same is true for an adult with a bomb. Building the tower or other structure is an example of increasing order, or negentropy. Knocking it down, whether suddenly and intentionally, or slowly and erratically, is an example of increasing disorder, or entropy. Physics, if "left to itself," seems to be on the side of increasing disorder—the second law of thermodynamics. Yet it is asserted that the creative aspects of life, of both individual life (conception, gestation, birth, growth) and the evolution of species, defy the second law.

Just as it is easier for the child, so too it is easier for a machine to knock the tower down, particularly if the machine is automated. So too for child and toy machine working together. So too for human adult and telerobot!

Destruction of life is quick and easy, as with non-living structures. Gestation and child rearing and human relationships are slow and labor intensive. By and large they do not seem particularly amenable to being improved by technology. True, medical and educational technology have much to offer, but neither is as straightforward as the capability of current technology to destroy human life.

Technology has many of its historical roots in making war. The profession of engineering grew out of the military—the design and construction of weapons and fortifications and armor and warships. Civil engineering was the first domesticated variety of engineering, and it was so named to distinguish the engineering of civilian roads and bridges and dams and buildings from military projects. Mechanical and electrical and chemical and metallurgical and ocean and aerospace engineering all came later, and now the distinction from military engineering no longer seems relevant (especially since all these engineering disciplines today derive much of their funding from the military).

Today commerce in the technology of hate thrives. International trade in addictive and debilitating drugs and in military weapons are major components of the economy. The US continues to sustain a great arms industry, spurred on by the largest fraction of academic technological research being directed from the Pentagon. The military pervades the national scientific establishment. The most exciting new technological research (e.g., in computers, artificial intelligence, lasers and optics, and superconductivity) is largely controlled by the military. Strategic defense and battlefield telerobots are the latest technological fashions. Things have not been so different in the Soviet Union and many other developed nations. Is this the ultimate Rasmussen "capture error"—getting caught in a militarization of technology that was never intended but which matched our habituated behavior?

Most tragic of all, poor Third World nations, which should be putting all their technological effort into providing water and sanitation and roads and buildings and domestic industrial infrastructure, are squandering their meager capital by purchasing arms from the superpowers.

Is it easier to produce and employ new technology than to understand and predict its social and cultural impacts?

The answer appears to be yes. There are several reasons for this. The production of new technology is driven mostly by extrapolation from existing technology plus new scientific discovery, not by societal need. Both existing technology and new scientific discovery tend to be well documented in objective terms. There is seldom controversy about what the new technology is and what its direct intended physical impacts are.

On the other hand there is usually little or no public understanding about the indirect physical impacts (e.g., the drift of air pollutants geographically or of water pollutants through aquifers, the drift of DDT through the food chain). This often is in spite of good and available scientific evidence (e.g. the effects of acid rain on putrifaction of lakes and deforestation). Technologies, at least in a democracy, are brought forth mostly by the initiative of an individual or a small group. After the promise (usually of the positive aspects only) has been evidenced, a much larger number of people will participate in the development, manufacture, and marketing of the product.

The social and cultural impacts appear long after the technology is in place, and only after exposure of the technology to the whole community and after the multiple cause-effect chains have had time to work. Not until this later stage does society encounter the inherent threats to the "commons" resources—e.g., depletion of arable land, deforestation, air and water pollution, and exhaustion of mineral resources. Only then does the "tragedy of the commons" become apparent. Thus the opponents of a technology are likely to mount their efforts much later than the proponents, that is, only after the protagonists have had a good start, and the deleterious impacts are finally in evidence. The protagonists are likely to be working together on a cooperative basis, usually a relatively wealthy and powerful group. The antagonists, once they appear, are likely to be diffuse and without much of a power base.

Anyway, who enjoys being against something new and creative and exciting? Thus, the initial production and deployment of the new technology is relatively unfettered by its negative impacts. Typically, the engineers of a new technology will seek to quantify as much as possible the "trade-offs" among the various objective attributes of the product, for example size, material, strength, speed, and cost. They will assert that safety has not been compromised, though necessarily it always must be, since maximum safety requires infinite monetary cost, which most of us cannot afford. These engineers may even claim to be providing an "optimum" design (military suppliers are fond of making such claims) when all engineers should know that optimality exists only when all considerations are expressed precisely in mathematical form. It is rare, for any actual physical product, that more than a few of its attributes can be expressed mathematically in relation to the others, this limitation being especially true of economic and human behavioral attributes. Seldom do the initial tradeoffs include the long-term social costs, since they are neither clear nor manifest at the time.

4.7   How Far to Go with Automation

The all-or-none fallacy

At the present time the layman tends to see automation as "all-or-none"—
a system is controlled either manually or automatically, with nothing in
between. In the case of robotized factories the media tend to focus on the
robots, with little mention of various design, installation, programming,
monitoring, fault detection and diagnosis, maintenance, and learning functions which are performed by humans. In the space program the same is
true—options are seen to be either "automated" or "astronaut in EVA,"
without much appreciation for the potential of supervisory control. The
truth, as has been discussed extensively in the preceding sections, is that
humans and automatic machinery are, and will continue to be, working
together.

Supervisory control relative to degree of automation and task predictability

Figure 4.1 helps in considering the future of supervisory control relative to
various degrees of automation, and to the complexity or unpredictability

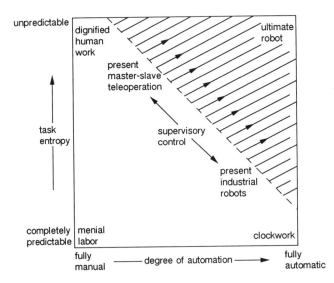

Figure 4.1
Supervisory control relative to degree of automation and task predictability.

of task situations to be dealt with. The meanings of the four extremes of this rectangle are worth considering. The lower left is labeled "menial labor" because to employ a human being to perform completely predictable tasks is demeaning (though the truth is that many of us operate voluntarily pretty close to this in doing many small tasks each day). The upper right, "use of machines for totally unpredictable tasks," is mostly not attainable, and might be considered an ideal for technology. However, in special and narrowly defined cases, such as the use of computers to generate random numbers or to experiment with "chaos" (Prigogine and Stengers 1984) for art or mathematics, we might have to admit that machines are already working. The upper left is where most of us feel humans belong: working on problems undefined and unpredictable. Indeed, this seems to be where creativity and dignity, at least of the intellectual sort, are to be found. The lower right, in contrast, seems an entirely appropriate locus for full automation; however, none but the simplest fully automatic machines already exist. Few real situations occur at these extremes. Supervisory control may be considered to be a frontier (diagonal line in figure 4.1) advancing gradually toward the upper right corner with improved technology.

A scale of degrees of automation, and where to stop

How far, in any particular application, should the system designer go with automation? Should the technological imperative to automate whatever can be automated serve as the prevailing principle? Should automation, at some level, be curtailed? In particular applications the answer is probably yes to both.

Table 4.2 suggests a scale of "degrees of automation," a refinement of a similar scale proposed by Sheridan and Verplank (1978). Each succeeding level of the scale below assumes some previous ones (when ANDed) or imposes more restrictive constraints (when ORed).

Each new level carries with it additional opportunities for machine error. Each precludes human intervention to a greater extent.

Clearly, for some tasks we are happy to let the computer go to the last level, while for others we would prefer to limit automation at a level well up in the list. We may give as a reason to stop that systems are more safely operated with people in charge (at whatever level). What we may mean is that we trust people more out of lack of understanding or inability to

Table 4.2
Scale of degrees of automation.

1.	The computer offers no assistance, human must do it all.
2.	The computer offers a complete set of action alternatives, and
3.	narrows the selection down to a few, or
4.	suggests one, and
5.	executes that suggestion if the human approves, or
6.	allows the human a restricted time to veto before automatic execution, or
7.	executes automatically, then necessarily informs the human, or
8.	informs him after execution only if he asks, or
9.	informs him after execution if it, the computer, decides to.
10.	The computer decides everything and acts autonomously, ignoring the human.

predict what the machine will do. Alternatively, the real motivation for deferring to human operators may be political—other people will be more accepting of that decision. We see evidence of these motivations in both the nuclear power and the commercial aviation industry today, where acceptance of computers has been limited even though the technology might be capable of far more. Meanwhile there are serious efforts to determine numerical reliability for various alternatives from fully manual to fully automatic.

The tendency, for obvious reasons, has been to automate what is easiest and to leave the rest to the human. From one perspective this dignifies the human contribution; from another it may lead to a hodgepodge of partial automation, making the remaining human tasks less coherent and more complex than they need be and resulting in overall degradation of system performance (Bainbridge 1981).

4.8   Roseborough's Dilemma, and a Possible Resolution

There is a profound problem in the engineering of supervisory control systems in general and decision aids in particular that has been put off until this point in the book, though the discussion has danced around it. This problem has consistently frustrated those who seek an objective basis for designing the human operator into complex technological systems. This includes the author and his graduate students—among them James Roseborough, who provoked considerable discussion about the problem among his colleagues and as a result motivated them to name the problem *Roseborough's dilemma*.

One comes upon the dilemma as follows:

(1)   In a complex control system the controlled process cannot be fully and explicitly modeled, nor can the objective function.

(2)   Therefore, as has been asserted in previous chapters of this book, one appropriately falls back on the supervisory human operator to complement the mechanized embodiment of these functions.

(3)   Since the human makes mistakes, it is evident that he can be helped by a computer-based decision aid, so one tries to provide such an aid.

(4)   To design the decision aid and evaluate the human operator's use of it, a relatively complete process model and objective function must be used as a norm. But step 4 is in conflict with step 1.

(5)   Further, if such a relatively complete process model and objective function were available, then why not use these in place of the human operator to provide an automatic decision maker, thus leaving the human out?

Roseborough (1988) concluded that "in any system requiring a human operator, the objective validity of a specific decision aid can never be established." On the basis of the above line of reasoning, this is self-evident IF the decision aid is intended to be used for decisions requiring information that is not explicitly modelable. However, a way out of the dilemma is to assume the following:

(1)   The human decision maker is necessary for the information that is not explicitly modelable. No valid decision aid can be built to provide such information when it is needed.

(2)   Some, perhaps most, decision situations the human operator will encounter require only information that is modelable. She will make mistakes in such decisions, and can benefit from a decision aid for these cases, and in such cases the decision aid can be validated. (So it makes sense to provide such a decision aid for those situations.)

(3)   Assume the human can properly decide when the situation includes elements the decision aid can properly assess, and for which elements the decision aid should be ignored.

Assumption 3 is a big one. One could argue that operators, when provided with decision aids, tend to accept and follow the advice given, so that having no decision aid is better than having one that is wrong some fraction of the time. However, in normal multi-person teams and organizations it is common to have one person designated for routine matters and another for non-routine or unusual situations, and somehow between the two (or more) of them they sort out which situations are appropriate for which decision maker. If, for example, the decision maker for non-routine situations is the other's supervisor, she may monitor the subordinate using some low information rate or sampling basis. Then, whenever there are indications that the situation may be non-routine, she could ask the subordinate to explain or defend that subordinate's decision making, or else she could simply impose her own will. The supervisor of the automatic machine is in a similar role. The computer could be asked to explain, or could simply be overridden for any input deemed unusual.

Could the computer be made wise enough to know when it needed the human operator's help? Surely the answer must be yes or no, depending upon the context. If the computer needs a well-defined set of information elements, and some elements are clearly missing or exceed some predefined bounds, then the human is called in. This is essentially what happens now in automatic systems with alarms, as already discussed. Our concern here is with the subtler situations where the computer does not know its own limits.

4.9 Other Dilemmas in Systems Design: Tilting in the Human Direction

In addition to deciding how much to automate (and how far to trust automation) and how much to "help" the human operator with decision aiding, the designer of a telerobot system must consider several additional aspects of treating the human element(s) in the system. This section summarizes six such issues which have already been alluded to in earlier discussion. It puts them in the form of design dilemmas. Easy resolutions are not available, but some directions are suggested.

New technology vs. prevention of user alienation: How to retain human responsibility and accountability?

The system designer is naturally motivated to employ new telerobot or automation technology where it has the prospect of increased efficiency and decreased cost. However, as has been pointed out, the human operator can be alienated by new technology in many ways. The designer, therefore, at the same time she designs the system hardware and software, must design an organization and a social system that keep the operator alert and motivated and allow her to retain her sense of responsibility and accountability (*teleresponsibility* and *superaccountability*?!).

Operator free will in systems vs. designer-fixed goals and criteria: Who decides what is good?

Most of us believe that human operators of machines have always had free will, and that includes supervisory operators of telerobots. The tendency toward greater complexity and robustness in telerobot technology as compared to older classes of human-machine systems and the changed role of the human in becoming a supervisor call particular attention to this free will, seeming almost to defy closed-form modeling. At the same time the designer feels obliged to assist or even constrain the human, to explicate goals, constraints, and tradeoffs between relative worths of decision alternatives, and to embody these in computer models. Where the designer does feel confident to advise or constrain the human, reasons should be presented in an understandable and convincing way. Otherwise the operator will assume that design decisions are arbitrary and may try to overcome or "second guess" the design.

Reliability vs. creativity: How to consider human variability?

From one perspective the most reliable system is one that works the same way every time and is quite predictable, never deviating from an established norm. However, more and more with advanced telerobotic control and computer technology, it becomes clear that anything for which a procedure can be established can be automated. The human, in contrast, is most useful to provide creativity in unusual circumstances. Telerobot systems should be designed to encourage creativity under such circumstances, particularly when off-line simulation experiments can help evaluate the implications of novel solutions in time that control actions are recoverable, and in any case should not regard the exercise of creativity as "error" until unrecoverable abnormalities threaten.

Complexity to cope with complexity: An unstable process?

Generally, the greater the variety of states a controlled process can get itself into, the greater the variety of actions required to measure and control its performance and the more support required to monitor the measurement and control equipment. And, as though hardware and software complexity were not enough, the more paperwork to accompany it all, some say according to a power function with exponent much greater than 1. Some types of systems have tended toward complexity seemingly without bound. Allegedly this is what was happening to nuclear power plants in the US before the accident at Three Mile Island, where safety "add-ons" themselves invited more add-ons until the operating personnel complained that they could no longer cope. Furthermore, the lack of standardization in the industry meant every plant was a different design. The designer should always be conscious of the undesirability of added complexity and too much variety when there are common purposes to be served, and always seek a simple design solution in preference to a complex one.

Information acquisition vs. processing and control: How to balance?

An automated system can seek and acquire more seemingly relevant data than can be handled by available resources to process the data and produce refined control. Alternatively such a system can have capability for processing and control which far exceeds its capability to acquire information. Such limitations, if they exist, are likely not to be "hard limits," but rather to be constraints and inefficiencies that become manifest gradually. In consideration of realistic constraints on time, money, and tolerable complexity, the designer often faces a tradeoff between getting more information and doing a better job of control.

Such a tradeoff also exists within the human operator—a compromise between sensed and perceived data, on the one hand, and decision and control on the other. Experimental psychologists have used the notions of data limitations and process limitations to characterize human behavior in this respect (Norman and Bobrow 1975). Either can be the primary constraint on human behavior. In any given situation the operator or behavioral analyst can usually identify which constraint is most important.

It is not clear, when human and machine are put together, that what is most constraining for the machine will be most constraining for the human, or vice-versa. The problem of "joint constraint" needs additional analysis.

Objectivity vs. advocacy: By what method to consider human interests?

Scientists and engineers like to claim objectivity. Perhaps that is the reason why many interests of human users and human operators are neglected—

the designer simply hasn't found an objective way to accommodate such "soft" considerations. In contrast to technology, Western justice operates not on the basis of objectivity but on the basis of advocacy—advocates for various alternatives try to convince juries or judges. Of course we all know that real decision making in technological design and implementation involves advocacy at many levels. Unfortunately the human user or operator has often been left without an advocate. This is changing. The human-factors profession, while at the same time trying for objectivity, has taken on such advocacy. So have unions, government regulators, and consumer groups. However, these groups need to be educated about automation and telerobotics—the possibilities and the problems.

4.10 Public Appreciation and Signs of Hope

The general public is aware of both the positive and the negative aspects of technology as never before, and this is cause for hope. Ordinary people are now very concerned about the constructive and destructive aspects of technology. There is also a new appreciation for the difficulty of discovering or anticipating the social and cultural impacts of technology, and a tacit understanding that such impacts are usually more subtle than just the potential for catastrophe. Particular world events, such as the accidents at Three Mile Island, Bhopal, and Chernobyl, as well as airline, train, and automobile accidents, combined with the widespread availability of television, have brought people everywhere in contact with the limits of technology. The claims of the proponents of technology are certainly being eyed with more suspicion than they were earlier. The public realizes that current benefits tend to bring future costs which are not very predictable as to when and where they will appear—only that they will.

Developing countries such as China want very much to have the modern technology of the West, but they are anxious not to bring along other aspects of Western technological culture which are threatening to their traditions.There are many new academic programs in universities which seek to integrate the "two cultures." They aim not simply to make engineers more culturally refined (who disputes that we need it?!), or to ensure that all humanists know about the Second Law of Thermodynamics. The new programs are more directed to teaching people how to do technology forecasting and assessment, how to involve various kinds of expertise in the forecasting, and how to incorporate the public into the assessment.

Science and engineering journals now include many more articles on the social impacts of technology than appeared two decades ago. Technology is now more acceptable as a subject of historical analysis, art, and literature. Both the general public and the political establishment have also come to appreciate that such analysis can be judgmental (often negative relative to the establishment), far from an exact science, and expensive.

Insofar as telerobotics and supervisory control are concerned, it should now be evident that we have not been so successful at developing good predictive models which put everything neatly in place and clearly light the way for us to go. The technology continues to outpace the researchers, especially the researchers in social sciences. It seems that for the immediate future we are destined to run breathless behind the lead of technology, trying our best to catch up. This means we may never fully exploit what we might possibly do with technology. At the same time it makes us humble—which can't be all bad.

Homo faber (man the maker) produces technology which may be said to ennoble the human spirit but at the same time to corrupt it. The computer, as it elevates the worker to a new and more powerful supervisory role, at the same time alienates him in many ways. It is crucial that engineers and scholars encourage this more enlightened and mature perception of our machines. Along with the development of the new technology, we must make every effort to improve our capabilities for timely and comprehensive assessment of the best role for humans.

References

Adams, J. A. 1982. Issues in human reliability. *Human Factors* 24, no. 1: 1–10.

Aida, S., ed. 1982. *Humane Use of Human Ideas—Introduction To Eco-Technology*. Pergamon.

Akin, D. 1986. EASE, an overview of selected results. In Proceedings of NASA Space Construction Workshop. NASA Langley Research Center.

Albus, J. S. 1981. *Brains, Behavior, and Robotics*. McGraw-Hill.

Albus, J. S., McCain, H. G. and Lumia, R. 1987. NASA/NBS Standard Reference Model for Telerobot Control System Archetecture (NASREM). NBS Tech. Note 1235.

Ammons, J. C., Govindaraj, T. and Mitchell, C. M. 1988. Decision models for aiding FMS scheduling and control. *IEEE Trans. Systems, Man and Cybernetics* 18, no. 5.

Anderson, R. J. and Spong, M. W. 1987. Hybrid impedance control of remote manipulators. *IEEE Trans. on Robotics and Automation* 4.

Andreadakis, S. K. 1988. Analysis and Synthesis of Decision-making Organizations. Ph.D. thesis, MIT.

Asada, H. and Liu, S. 1990. Acquisition of task performance skills from a human expert for teaching a machining robot. In Proceedings of 1990 American Control Conference: 2827–2832.

Asada, H. and Slotine, J-J. E. 1986. *Robot Analysis and Control*. Wiley.

Asada, H. and Yang, B-H. 1989. Skill acquisistion from human experts through pattern processing of teaching data. In Proceedings of 1989 IEEE International Conference on Robotics and Automation, Scottsdale, AZ, May 14–19: 1302–1307.

Askren, W. B. and Regulinski, T. L. 1969. Quantifying human performance for reliability analysis of systems. *Human Factors* 11, no. 4: 393–396.

Bainbridge, L. 1981. Mathematical equations or processing routines? In Rasmussen, J. and Rouse, W. B. (eds.), *Human Detection and Diagnosis of System Failures*, Plenum.

Bainbridge, L. 1991. Mental models in cognitive skill: the example of industrial process operation. In Rutherford, A. and Rogers, Y. (eds.), *Models in the Mind*, Academic Press.

Ballard, R. D. 1986. A last long look at Titanic. *National Geographic* 170, no. 6, December.

Barber, D. 1967. MANTRAN, a symbolic language for supervisory control of an intelligent manipulatror. SM thesis, MIT.

Baron, S. 1984. A control theoretic approach to modelling human supervisory control of dynamic systems. In Rouse, W. B. (ed.), *Advances in Man-Machine Systems Research*, Vol. 1. JAI Press.

Baron, S., Feehrer, C., Muralhidaran, R., Pew, R., and Horowitz, P. 1982. An approach to modelling supervisory control of a nuclear power plant. NUREG-2988. ORNL/SUB/81-70523/1, Oak Ridge National Laboratory.

Baron, S., Zacharias, G., Muralhidaran, R., and Lancraft, R. 1980. PROCRU: a model for analyzing flight crew procedures in approach to landing. In Proceedings of 8th IFAC Congress, Tokyo, 15: 71–76. See also NASA Report CR-152397.

Barrett, D. S. 1981. A computer-graphic method for visual search through multi-attribute data. SM Thesis, MIT, June.

Bejczy, A. K. 1980. Sensors, controls, and man-machine interface for advanced teleoperation. *Science* 208, no. 4450: 1327–1335.

Bejczy, A. K. 1983. Smart Hand, Manipulator Control through Sensory Feedback. University of Arizona, Report JPL D-107.

Bejczy, A. K. and Handylykken, M. 1981. Experimental results with six-degree-of-freedom force-reflecting hand controller. In Proceedings of 7th Annual NASA-Univ. Conference on Manual Control, Los Angeles, CA, Oct. 15: 465–477.

Bejczy, A. K., Brown, J. W. and Lewis, J. L. 1980. Evaluation of "smart" sensor displays for multidimensional precision control of space shuttle remote manipulator. In Proceedings of 16th Conference on Manual Control, MIT, Cambridge, MA, May 5–7.

Bejczy, A. K., Dotson, R. S. and Mathur, F. P. 1980. Man-machine speech interaction in a teleoperator environment. In Proceedings of Symp. on Voice Interactive Systems, DOD Human Factors Group, Dallas, TX, May: 11–13.

Bell, B. J. and Swain, A. D. 1983. A Procedure for Conducting a Human Reliability Analysis for Nuclear Power Plants. Sandia Natl. Labs. NUREG CR-2254, Washington, DC, US Nuclear Regulatory Commission.

Bellingham, J. G. and Humphrey, D. 1990. Using layered control for supervisory control of underwater vehicles. Conference Proceerings ROV 90, IEEE Marine Technology Society, Vancouver, BC, June 25–27: 175–182.

Berg, S. L. and Sheridan, T. B. 1985. Effect of Time Span and Task Load on Pilot Mental Workload. Man-Machine Systems Lab. Report, Cambridge, MA: MIT.

Bergeron, H. P. and Hinton, B. S. 1985. Aircraft automation: the problem of the pilot interface. *Aviation, Space and Environmental Medicine*, February.

Bernotat, R. K. 1970. Rotation of visual reference system and its influence on control quality. *IEEE Trans. on Man-Machine Systems* MMS-11: 129–131.

Billings, C. E. 1991. *Human-Centered Aircraft Automation: A Concept and Guidelines*. Book manuscript in preparation. Moffet Field, CA: NASA Ames Research Center.

Birkhoff, G. 1948. Lattice theory. *Amer. Math. Soc. Collected Publications* 25.

Black, J. H. 1971. Factorial Study of Remote Manipulation with Transmission Time Delay. SM Thesis, MIT.

Bliss, J. C. 1967. Optical to tactile image conversion aids for the blind. *Archives of Physical Medicine Rehabilitation* 48.

Bloomfield, L. 1987. Personal communication.

Boettcher, K. L. and Levis, A. 1982. Modeling the interactive decision-maker with bounded rationality. *IEEE Transactions on Systems, Man and Cybernetics* SMC-12, no. 2.

Boettcher, K. L. and Tenney, R. R. 1986. Distributed decision-making with constrained decision-makers: a case study. *IEEE Trans. Systems, Man and Cybernetics* SMC-16, no. 6: 813–823.

Bolt, R. 1980. "Put that there": voice and gesture at the graphics interface. In Proceedings of SIGGRAPH 80. Also in *Computer Graphics* 14, no. 3, July: 262–270.

Bolt, R. A. 1984. *The Human Interface*. Lifetime Learning Div. of Wadsworth.

Bracken, P. 1985. Accidental nuclear war. In Allison, G., Carnisale, A. and Nye, J. (eds.), *Hawks, Doves and Owls*, Norton.

Brehmer, B. 1981. Models of diagnostic judgments. In Rassmussen, J. and Rouse, W. B. (eds.), *Human Detection and Diagnosis of System Failures*, Plenum.

Brooks, F. 1988. Grasping reality through illusion: interactive graphics serving science. In Proceedings of SIGCHI-88, May: 1–11.

Brooks, M. 1989. Proposal for a pattern matching task controller for sensor-based coordination of robot motions. In Proceedings of NATO Advanced Research Workshop: Robots and Biological Systems, Il Ciocco, Tuscany, Italy, 26–30 June.

Brooks, R. 1986. A robust layered control system for a mobile robot. *IEEE J. Robotics and Automation* 2: 75.

Brooks, T. L. 1979. SUPERMAN: a System for Supervisory Manipulation and the Study of Human-Computer Interactions. SM thesis, Cambridge, MA: MIT.

Brooks, T. L. 1988. Supervisory control of multiple vehicles. In Proceedings of 15th Annual Symposium Association for Unmanned Vehicles, San Diego, CA, June 6–8.

Buckner, D. N. and McGrath, J.J. 1963. *Vigilance: a Symposium*. McGraw-Hill.

Buharali, A. and Sheridan, T. B. 1982. Fuzzy set aids for telling a computer how to decide. In Proceedings of 1982 IEEE International Conference on Cybernetics and Society, 82-CH-1840-8, Seattle, WA.

Busby, F. 1979. Remotely Operated Vehicles. U.S. Dept. Commerce Rep. 03-78-603-0136.

Buzan, F. 1989. Control of Telemanipulators with Time Delay. ScD Thesis, Cambridge, MA: MIT.

Buzan, F. and Sheridan. T. B. 1989. A model-based predictive operator aid for telemanipulators with time delay. In Proceedings of 1989 IEEE International Conference on Systems, Man and Cybernetics, 14–17 Nov. 1989, Cambridge, MA.

Cannon, D. 1992. Point-and-Direct Telerobotics: Interactive Supervisory Control at the Object Level in Unstructured Human-Machine System Environments. PhD Thesis, Stanford, CA: Stanford University.

Card, S. K., Moran, T. P. and Newell, A. 1986. The model human processer. In Boff, K., Kaufman, L. and Thomas, J. (eds.), *Handbook of Perception and Human Performance*, Wiley.

Carroll, J. D. and Wish, M. 1975. Multidimensional scaling: methods, models, and relations to Delphi. Chapter 6C in Linstone, H. A. and Turoff, M. (eds.), *The Delphi Method*, Addison Wesley.

Carter, A. B., Steinbruner, J. D. and Zraket, C.A. (eds.) 1987. Managing Nuclear Operations. Washington, D.C.: Brookings Institute.

Chambers, A..B. and Nagel, D. C. 1985. Pilots of the future: human or computer? *Computer*, ACM/IEEE, Nov.

Chao, A. I. 1989. A Feedback Monitoring Control scheme for the Cable-Controlled Parallel-Link Manipulator. SM Thesis, MIT.

Chapanis, A. 1975. Prelude to 2001: exploration in human communications. *Amer. Psychologist*: 949–961.

Charny, L. and Sheridan, T. B. 1989. Adaptive goal setting in tasks with multiple criteria. In Proceedings of 1989 IEEE International Conference on Cybernetics and Society, Cambridge, MA.

Chatten, J. B. 1972. Foveal hat: a head-aimed television system with foveal-peripheral image format. In Proceedings of Symposium on Visually Coupled Systems; Developments and Applications. Aerospace Medical Division, Brooks AFB, Texas.

Cheng, C-C. 1991. Predictor Displays: Theory, Development and Application to Towed Submersibles. ScD Thesis, MIT, June.

Cherry, C. 1953. Some experiments on the recognition of speech with one and two ears. *J. Acoustical Society of America* 22, 61–62.

Chin, K. P. 1991. Stable Teleoperation with Optimal Performance. PhD thesis, MIT.

Chiruvolu, R. K. 1991. Virtual Display Aids for Teleoperation. SM Thesis, MIT.

Chu, Y. Y. and Rouse, W. B. 1979. Adaptive allocation of decision making responsibility between human and computer in multi-task situations. *IEEE Trans. on Systems, Man and Cybernetics* SMC-9, no. 12: 769–788.

Chu, Y. Y., Steeb, R. and Freedy, A. 1980. Analysis and Modeling of Information Handling Tasks in Supervisory Control of Advanced Aircraft. Tech. Rep. PATR-1080-80-6, Woodland Hills, CA: Perceptronics.

Chubb, G. P., 1964. A Comparison of Performance in Operating the CRL-8 Master-Slave Manipulator under Monocular and Binocular Viewing Conditions. Wright Patterson AFB, OH: Report AMRL-AD-608791.

Cicciarelli, A. 1981. Fiber Optic Tactile Sensing Devices for Telemanipulators. SB thesis, MIT, June.

Cohen, H. and Ferrell, W. R. 1969. Human operator decision-making in manual control. *IEEE Trans. on Man-Machine Systems* MMS-10, no. 2: 41–53.

Conant, R. C. 1976. Laws of information which govern systems. *IEEE Trans. Systems, Man and Cybernetics* 6: 240–255.

Conway, L., Volz, R. and Walker, M. 1987. Teleautonomous systems: methods and architectuires for intermingling autonomous and telerobotic technology. In Proceedings 1987 IEEE International Conference on Robotics and Automation, March 31–April 3, Raleigh, NC: 1121–1130.

Cooper, G. E and Harper, R. P., Jr. 1969. The use of pilot rating in the evaluation of aircraft handling qualities. Report No. NASA TN-D-5153, NASA Ames Research Center, Moffett Field, CA.

Corker, K and Bejczy, A. K. 1985. Recent advances in telepresence technology development. In Proceedings of 22nd Space Congress, Kennedy Space Center, FL, April 22–25.

Corker, K, Bejczy, A. K., Stark, L., Lyman, J., and Lehman, S., 1987. Space Teleoperation, Human Factors and Technology. Unpublished report, Jet Propulsion Laboratory.

Corliss, W. R. and Johnsen, E. G. 1968. Teleoperator Controls. NASA SP-5070, Washington, DC: NASA Office of Technology Utilization.

Cothier, P. H and Levis, A. H. 1986. Timeliness measures of effectiveness in command and control. *IEEE Trans. Systems, Man and Cybernetics* SMC-16, no. 6: 844–853.

Crane, H. D. and Clark, M. R. 1978. Three dimensional visual stimulus deflector. *Applied Optics* 17, no. 5, March: 705–714.

Crossman, E. R. F. W., Cooke, J. E. and Beishon, R. J. 1974. Visual attention and the sampling of displayed information in process control. Reprinted in Edwards, E. and Lees, F.P. (eds.), *The Human Operator in Process Control*, Taylor and Francis.

Cunningham, H. A. and Pavel, M. 1990. "Rotational wind" indicator enhances control of rotated displays. In Proceedings of Engineering Foundation Conference on Teleoperators and Virtual Environments, Santa Barbara, CA, March.

Curry, R. E. 1981. A model of human fault detection for complex human processes. In Rassmussen, J. and Rouse, W.B. (eds.), *Human Detection and Diagnosis of System Failures*, Plenum.

Curry, R. E. and Ephrath, A. R. 1976. Monitoring and control of unreliable systems. In Sheridan,T.B., and Johannsen, G. (eds.), *Monitoring Behavior and Supervisory Control*, Plenum.

Curry, R. E. and Gai, E. G. 1976. Detection of random process failures by human monitors. In Sheridan, T. B. and Johannsen, G. (eds.), *Monitoring Behavior and Supervisory Control*, Plenum.

Dalkey, N. 1975. An elementary cross-impact model. In Linstone, H. A. and Turoff, M. (eds.). *The Delphi Method*, Addison Wesley.

Das, H. 1989. Kinematic Control and Visual Display of Redundant Teleoperators. PhD Thesis, MIT.

Deghuee, B. J. 1980. Operator-Adjustable Frame-Rate, Resolution and Gray-Scale Tradeoffs in Fixed Bandwidth Remote Manipulator Control. SM thesis, MIT.

deKleer, J. and Brown, R. 1983. The origin, form and logic of qualitative physical laws. In Proceedings of 8th International Joint Conference on Artificial Intelligence IJCAI 8.

deKleer, J. 1979. Causal and Teleological Reasoning in Circuit Recognition. PhD Thesis, MIT, AI-TR-529.

DiCesare, F. and Desrochers, A. A. 1991. Modeling, control and performance analysis of automated manufacturing systems using Petri nets. In Leondes, C. T. (ed.), *Advances in Control and Dynamic Systems*, Vol. 45, Academic Press.

Dumbreck., A. A., Abel. E. and Murphy, S. 1990. 3-D TV system for remote handling: development and evaluation. In Proceedings of SPIE Symposium on Electronic Imaging, Santa Clara, CA , Feb.

Duncan, K. D. 1981. Training for fault diagnosis in industrial process plant. In Rassmussen, J. and Rouse, W. B. (eds.), *Human Detection and Diagnosis of System Failures*, Plenum.

Edwards, E. and Lees, F. P. (eds.) 1974. *The Human Operator in Process Control*. Taylor and Francis.

Egan, J. 1982. To err is human factors. *Technology Review 85*.

Ellis, S. R. and Gruenwald, A. J. 1989. The dynamics of orbital maneuvering: design and evaluation of a visual display for human controllers. In Proceedings of NATO AGARD Symposium on Space Vehicle Flight Mechanics, 13–16 Nov., Laxenburg, Austria, Ch. 29.

Ellis, S. R. (ed.) 1991. *Pictorial Communication in Virtual and Real Environments*. Taylor and Francis.

Embry, D. E. 1976. Human Reliability in Complex Systems: an Overview. Report NCSR-R10. Warrington, England: Natlional Center of Systems Reliability, UK Atomic Energy Authority.

Engelberger, J. l98l. A remark originally attributed by the *IFAC Newsletter*. no. 2, March: 4.

Ephrath, A. R. and Young, L. R. 1981. Monitoring vs. man-in-the-loop detection of aircraft failures. In Rassmussen, J. and Rouse, W.B. (eds.), *Human Detection and Diagnosis of System Failures*, Plenum: 143–154.

Ernst, H. 1961. MH-1, a Computer-Operated Mechanical Hand. ScD Thesis, MIT.

Featherstone, R. 1983. Position and velocity transformations between robot end-effector coordinates and joint angles. *International J. Robotics Research 2*, no. 2.

Ferrell, W. R. 1965. Remote manipulation with transmission delay. *IEEE Trans. Human Factors in Electronics* HFE-6, no. 1.

Ferrell, W. R. 1966. Delayed force feedback. *Human Factors*, October: 449–455.

Ferrell, W. R. and Sheridan, T. B. 1967. Supervisory control of remote manipulation. *IEEE Spectrum 4*, no. 10, October: 81–88.

Fisher, S. S, McGreevy, M., Humphries, J., Robinett, W. 1987. Virtual interface environment for telepresence applications. In Berger, J. D. (ed.), Proceedings of ANS International Topical Meeting on Remote Systems and Robotics in Hostile Environments.

Fitts, P.M. 1954. The information capacity of the human motor system in controlling the amplitude of movement. *J. Experimental Psychology 47*: 381–391.

Freedy, A., Madni, A. and Samet, M. 1985. Adaptive user models: methodology and applications in man-computer systems. In Rouse, W.B. (ed.), *Advances in Man-Machine Systems Research 2*, JAI Press.

Furness, T. 1986. The super cockpit and its human factors challenges. Proc 1986 Annual Meeting of the Human Factors Society, Vol. 1: 48–52.

Fyler, D. 1981. Computer graphic representation of remote environments using position tactile sensors. SM thesis, MIT, August.

Gadamer, H. G. 1976. *Philosophical Hermeneutics*. Linge, D. (translator), Univ. of California Press.

Gadamer, H. G. 1975. *Truth and Method*. Barden, G. and Cummings, J. (translators and editors), Seabury Press.

Gai, E. G. and Curry, R. E. 1976. A model of the human observer in failure detection tasks. *IEEE Trans. on Systems, Man and Cybernetics* SMC-6, Feb.

Gai, E. G. and Curry, R. E. 1978. Perseveration effects in detection tasks with correlated decision intervals. *IEEE Trans. Systems, Man and Cybernetics* SMC-8: 93–101

Gentner, D. and Stevens, A. L., (eds.), 1983. *Mental Models*. Erlbaum.

Gibson, J. J. 1962. Observations on active touch. *Psychological Review* 69: 477–490.

Goertz, R. C. and Thompson, R. C. 1954. Electronically controlled manipulator. *Nucleonics*, 46–47.

Goertz, R. C. 1965. An experimental head-controlled television system to provide viewing for a manipulator operator. In Proceedings of 13th RSTD Conference: 57. See also Corliss and Johnsen 1967: 66.

Goodstein, L. P., Andersen, H. B. and Olsen, S. E. 1988. *Tasks, Errors and Mental Models*. Taylor and Francis.

Green, D. M. and Swets, J. A. 1960. *Signal Detection Theory and Psychophysics*. Wiley.

Grether, W. F. and Baker, C. A. 1972. Visual presentation of information. In VanCott, H. A. *Human Engineering Guide to Equipment Design*. US Government Printing Office.

Hall, R. E., Samanta, P. K., Swoboda, A. L. 1981. Sensitivity of Risk Parameters to Human Errors in Reactor Safety Study for a PWR. Brookhaven National Lab. Rep. 51322 NUREG/CR-1879, Jan.

Handlykken, M. and Turner, T. 1980. Control systems analysis and synthesis for a six degree-of-freedom universal force-reflecting hand controller. In Proceedings of 19th IEEE Conference on Decision and Control, Albuquerque, NM, Dec. 10–12: 1197–1205.

Hannaford, B., Wood, L., Guggisberg, B., McAffee, D. and Zak, H. 1989. Performance Evaluation of a Six-Axis Generalized Force-Reflecting Teleoperator. JPL Publication 89-18, Pasadena, CA: California Inst. of Technology JPL, June 15.

Hardin, G. 1968. The tragedy of the commons. *Science* 162, 13 December: 1243–1248.

Hardin, P. A. 1970. "AND-Tree" Computer Data Structures for Supervisory Control of Manipulation. PhD thesis, MIT.

Harmon, L. D. 1980. Touch sensing technology, a review. Technical Report MSRO 80-03, Society of Manufacturing Engineers.

Harmon, L.D. 1982. Automated tactile sensing. *International J. Robotics Research* 1, 2: 3–32.

Harmon, P. and King, D, 1985. *Expert Systems*. Wiley.

Hart, S. G. and Sheridan, T. B. 1984. Pilot workload, performance and aircraft control automation. In Proceedings of NATO/AGARD Conference 371, Human Factors Considerations in High Performance Aircraft, Nuilly sur Seine, France.

Hashimoto, T., Sheridan. T. B. and Noyes, M. V. 1986. Effects of predicted information in teleoperation through a time delay. *Japanese J. Ergonomics* 22, no. 2.

Hayati, S. and Venkataraman, S. 1989. Design and implementation of a robot control system with traded and shared control capability. In Proceedings of 1989 IEEE International Conference on Robotics and Automation, Scottsdale, AZ, May 14–19: 1310–1315.

Heer, E. (ed.) 1973. Remotely Manned Systems. California Institute of Technology.

Heidigger, M. 1962. *Being and Time*. Macquarrie, J. and Robinson, E. (translators), Harper and Row.

Heidigger, M. 1968. *What is Called Thinking?* Wieck, F. D. and Gray, J. G. (translators), Harper and Row.

Helander, M. (ed.) 1988. *Handbook of Human-Computer Interaction*. Elsevier North-Holland.

Held, R. 1990. Visual interfaces: the human perceiver. In Proceedings of Engineering Foundation Conference on Human-Machine Interfaces for Teleoperators and Virtual Environments (NASA SP), Santa Barbara, CA. Mar. 4–9.

Held, R. and Durlach, N. 1987. Telepresence, time delay and adaptation. In NASA Conference Publ. 10032. Also in Ellis, S.R. 1991.

Helmholz, H. V. 1925. *Treatises on Psychological Optics* 3. Southall, J. (translator and editor), Optical Society of America.

Hess, R. and McNally, B. D. 1986. Automation effects in a multi-loop control system. *IEEE Trans. Systems, Man and Cybernetics* SMC-16, no.1: 111–121.

Hick, W. E. 1952. On the rate of gain of information. *Quart. J. Experimental Psychology* 4: 11–26.

Hill, J. 1977. Two measures of performance in a peg-in-hole manipulation task with force feedback. In Proceedings of 13th Annual Conference on Manual Control, Cambridge, MA: MIT, 1977.

Hill, J. and Bliss, J. C. 1971. Tactile perception studies related to teleoperator systems. NASA Rep. CR-114346, FR-2, Proj. 7948, Menlo Park, CA: Stanford Research Institute.

Hillis, W. D. 1981. Active touch sensing. Memo. 629, MIT Artificial Intelligence Laboratory, April.

Hirabayashi, H. 1981. Supervisory Manipulation for Assemblying Mechanical Parts while Compensating for Relative Motion. SM Thesis, MIT.

Hirzinger, G. and Heindl, J. 1983. Sensor programming: a new way for teaching a robot paths and force-torques simulaneously. In Proceedings of 3rd International Conference on Robot Vision and Sensory Controls, Cambridge, MA, Nov. 7–10.

Hirzinger, G. and Lanzettel, K. 1985. Sensory feedback structures for robots with supervised training. *IEEE International Conference on Robotics and Automation*, Saint Louis, MO, March.

Hirzinger, G., Heindl, J., and Landzettel, K. 1989. Predictor and knowledge-based telerobotic control concepts. IEEE International Conference on Robotics and Automation, May 14–19, Scottsdale, AZ: 1768–1777.

Hogan, N. 1985. Impedance control: an approach to manipulation, Part 1: theory, Part 2, implementation, Part 3: applications. *ASME J. Dynamic Syst. Meas. and Control.*

Hollnagel, E. and Woods, D. D. 1983. Cognitive systems engineering: new wine in new bottles. *International J. Man-Machine Studies* 18: 583–600.

Hollnagel, E. 1989. *AI + HCI: Much ado about nothing?* Copenhagen: Computer Resources International, July.

Hong, J. and Tan, X. 1989. Calibrating a DataGlove for teleoperating the Utah-MIT hand. In Proceedings of IEEE 1989 International Conference on Robotics and Automation: 1752–1757.

Hutchinson, A. 1961. *Labanotation, the System for Recording Movement.* New Direction Books.

Jacobson, S. C., Iversen, E. K., Davis, C. C., Potter, D. M. and McLain, T. W. 1989. Design of a multiple degree-of-freedom, force-reflective hand master/slave with a high mobility wrist. In Proceedings of ANS/IEEE/SMC 3rd Topical Meeting on Robotics and Remote Systems, March 13–16, Charleston, SC.

Jacobson, S. C., Iversen, E. K., Knutti, D. F., Johnson, R. T., and Biggers, K. B. 1986. Design of the Utah/MIT dexterous hand. In Proceedings of 1986 IEEE International Conference on Robotics and Automation, April 7–10, San Francisco.

Jagacincki, R. J., Miller, D. P. and Gilson, R. D. 1983. A comparison of kinesthetic, tactual and visual displays in a critical tracking task. *Human Factors* 21: 79–86.

Jex, H. 1988. Four critical tests for control feel simulators. In Proceedings of 1988 Annual Conference on Manual Control, Cambridge, MA: MIT.

Johannsen, G. 1990. Towards a new quality of automation in complex man-machine systems. In Proceedings of 11th International Federation of Automatic Control World Congress, Tallinn, August.

Johannsen, G. 1991. Design issues of graphics and knowledge support in supervisory control systems. In Moray, N., Ferrell, W. R. and Rouse, W. B., *Robotics, Control, and Society,* Taylor and Francis.

Johannsen, G. and Rouse, W. B. 1979. Mathematical concepts for modeling human behavior in complex man-machine systems. *Human Factors* 21, no. 6: 733–747.

Johnsen, E. G. and Corliss, W. R. 1967. Teleoperators and Human Augmentation. NASA SP-5047, Washington, DC: NASA Office of Technology Utilization.

Johnsen, E. G. and Magee, C. B. 1970. Advancements in Teleoperator Systems. NASA SP-5081, Washington, DC: NASA Office of Technology Utilization.

Kalman, R. E. 1960. A new approach to linear filtering and prediction problems. *J. Basic Engineering, Trans. ASME* 82D: 33–45.

Kama, W. N. and DuMars, R. C. 1964. Remote Viewing: a Comparison of Direct Viewing, 2-D and 3-D Television. Wright Patterson AFB, OH: Report AMRL-TDR-64-15.

Kane, J. 1975. A primer for a new cross-impact language—KSIM. Chapter 5D in Linstone, H. A and Turoff, M. (eds.). *The Delphi Method,* Addison-Wesley.

Kazerooni, H., Sheridan, T. B. and Houpt, P. K. 1986. Robust compliant motion for manipulators. Part 1: fundamental concepts, Part 2: design method. *IEEE J. Robotics and Automation* RA-2, no. 2.

Keeney, R. L., and Raiffa, H. 1976. *Decisions with Multiple Objectives: Preferences and Value Tradeoffs.* Wiley.

Kelley, C. R. 1968. *Manual and Automatic Control.* Wiley.

Kim, W., Ellis, S. R., Tyler, M. and Stark. L. 1985. Visual enhancements for telerobotics. In Proceedings of 1985 IEEE International Conference on Systems, Man and Cybernetics, Tuscon, AZ.

Kleinman, D. L., Baron, S. and Levison, W. H. 1970. An optimal control model of human response, Part I. *Automatica* 6, no. 3: 357–369.

Knepp, L. 1981. Computer Graphics In Multi-Attribute Data Bases. SM Thesis, MIT.

Knepp, L., Barrett, D. and Sheridan, T. B. 1982. Searching for an object in four or higher dimensional space. In Proceedings 1982 IEEE International Conference on Cybernetics and Society, 82-CH-1840-8, Seattle, WA: 636–640.

Kobrinskii, A. 1960. The thought controls the machine: development of a bioelectric prosthesis. In Proceedings of First IFAC World Congress on Automatic Control, Moscow.

Kok, J. J. and Stassen, H. G. 1980. Human operator control of slowly responding systems: supervisory control. *Journal of Cybernetics and Information Science* 3: 123–174.

Kok, J. J., and VanWijk, R. A. 1978. Evaluation of Models Describing Human Operator Control of Slowly Responding Complex Systems. Delft, DUT, Lab. of Measurement and Control.

Kozinsky, E., Pack, R., Sheridan, T., Vruels, D., and Seminara, J. 1982. Performance measurement system for training simulators. Electric Power Research Institute, Report NP-2719, November.

Kramer, J. 1991. PhD thesis in progress, Stanford University.

Landsberger, S. and Sheridan, T. B. 1985. A new design for parallel link manipulators. In Proceedings of IEEE International Conference on Cybernetics and Society, Tucson, AZ, Nov. 12–13.

Laritz, J. and Sheridan, T. B. 1984. Experiments in the use of fuzzy sets in failure detection. In Proceedings 1984 IEEE International Conference on Cybernetics and Society.

Levis, A. and Boettcher, K. 1983. Decision makoing organizations with acyclical information structures. *IEEE Trans. Systems, Man and Cybernetics* SMC-13, no. 3.

Levis, A. H. 1990. Organizational information structures: quantitative models. In Sage, A. P. (ed.), *Concise Encyclopedia of Information Processing in Systems and Organizations*, Pergamon Press.

Linstone, H. A. and Turoff, M. (eds.) 1975. *The Delphi Method.* Addison-Wesley.

Loomis, J. M., and Lederman, S. J. 1986. Tactual perception. In Boff, K, Kaufman, L., and Thomas, J.P. (eds.), *Handbook of Perception and Human Performance*, Vol. 2, Wiley.

Luckas, W. J. and Hall, R. E. 1981. Initial Quantification of Human Errors Associated with Reactor Safety System Components in Licensed Nuclear Power Plants. Brookhaven Natl. Lab. Rep. 51323 NUREG/CR-1880, Jan.

Lynch, P. M. 1972. Rate Control of Remote Manipulators with Force Feedback. SM Thesis, MIT.

Machida, K., Toda, Y., Iwata, T., Kawachi, M. , and Nakamura, T. 1988. Development of a graphic simulator augmented teleoperator system for space applications. In Proceedings of 1988 AIAA Conference on Guidance, Navigation, and Control, Part I: 358–364.

Mar, L. E. 1985. Human Control Performance in Operation of a Time-Delayed Master-slave Manipulator. SB Thesis, MIT.

March, J. G., and Simon, H. A. 1958. *Organizations.* Wiley.

Massimino, M. and Sheridan, T. B. 1989. Variable force and visual feedback effects on teleoperator man-machine performance. In Proceedings of of the NASA Conference on Space Telerobotics, Pasadena, CA, January 31–February 2.

Massimino, M., Sheridan, T. B. and Roseborough, J. B. 1989. One handed tracking in six degrees of freedom. In Proceedings of 1989 IEEE International Conference on Systems, Man and Cybernetics, 14–17 Nov. 1989, Cambridge, MA.

Mazlish, B. 1967. The fourth discontinuity. *Technology and Culture* 8, no. 1.

McRuer, D. T. and Jex, H. R. 1967. A review of quasi-linear pilot models. *IEEE Trans. Human Factors in Electronics* HFE-4, no. 3: 231–249.

McRuer, D. T., Graham, D., Krendel, E. and Reisener, W., Jr. 1965. Human pilot dynamics in compensatory systems. Air Force Flight Dynamics Laboratory, Wright Patterson AFB, OH, Report AFFDL-TR-65-15.

Meek, S. G., Jacobson, S. C., and Goulding, P. P. 1989. Extended physiologic taction, design and evaluation of a proportional force feedback system. In *J. Rehabilitation Research and Development* 26, no. 3: 53–62.

Meister, D., 1964. Methods of predicting human reliability in man-machine systems. *Human Factors* 6, no. 6: 621–646.

Mendel, M. and Sheridan,T. B. 1989. Filtering information from human experts. *IEEE Trans. on Systems, Man and Cybernetics* 36, no. 1: 6–16.

Merritt, J. O. 1987. Visual-motor realism in 3-D teleoperator display systems. In Proceedingsof SPIE, Vol.761, True Imaging Techniques and Display Technologies.

Minsky, M. 1975. A framework for representing knowledge. In Winston, P. (ed.), *The Psychololgy of Computer Vision.* McGraw-Hill.

Mitchell, C. M. 1987. GT-MSOCC, a domain for research on human-computer interaction and decision-aiding in supervisory control systems. *IEEE Trans. on Systems, Man and Cybernetics* SMC-17, no. 4: 553–572.

Mitchell, C. M. and Forren, M. G. 1987. Effectiveness of multi-modal operator interfaces in supervisory control systems. *IEEE Trans. Systems, Man and Cybernetics* SMC-17. no. 4: 594–607.

Mitchell, C. M. and Saisi, D. S. 1987. Use of model-based qualitative icons and adaptive windows in workstations for supervisory control systems. *IEEE Trans. Systems, Man and Cybernetics* SMC-17, no. 4: 573–593.

Moray, N. 1981. The role of attention in the detection of errors and the diagnosis of failures in man-machine systems. In Rasmussen, J. and Rouse, W. B. (eds.), *Human Detection and Diagnosis of System Failures*, Plenum Press.

Moray, N. 1986. Monitoring behavior and supervisory control. In Boff, K., Kaufman, L. and Thomas, J. P. (eds.), *Handbook of Perception and Human Performance*, vol. 2, Wiley.

Moray, N. 1990. Mental models of complex systems. In Moray, N., Ferrell, W. R. and Rouse, W. B., (eds.), *Robotics, Control and Society*, Taylor and Francis.

Moray, N. Ed. 1979. *Mental Workload: Its Theory and Measurement*. Plenum.

Moray, N., Sanderson, P., Shiff, B., Jackson, R., Kennedy, S. and Ting, L. 1982. A model and experiment for the allocation of man and computer in supervisory control. In Proceedings of IEEE International Conference on Cybernetics and Society: 354–358.

Morris, N. M. and Rouse, W. B. 1985. The effects of type of knowledge upon human problem solving in a process control task. *IEEE Trans. Systems, Man and Cybernetics* SMC-15: 698–707.

Moses, J. 1984. Development of a Fiber-Optic Tactile Sensor, SB thesis, MIT.

Mosher, R. S. 1964. Industrial manipulators. *Scientific American* 211, no. 4: 88–96.

Mosher, R. S. and Wendel, B. 1960. Force reflecting electro-hydraulic servo-manipulator. *Electro-Technology* 66: 138.

Muir, B. M. and Moray, N. P. 1987. Operators' trust in relation to system faults. In Proceedings of 1987 IEEE Conference on Systems, Man and Cybernetics, Atlanta, GA.

Murphy, R. L. H., Fitzpatrick, T. B., Haynes, H. A., Bird, K. T. and Sheridan, T. B. Accurcy of dermatalogical diagnosis by television. *Archives of Dermatology* 105, June: 833–835.

Naish, J. M. and Von Wieser, M. F. 1969. Human factors in the all-weather approach. *Shell Aviation News* 374: 2–11.

Nilsson, N. J. 1965. *Learning machines*. McGraw-Hill.

Nof, S. Y. (ed.) 1985. *Handbook of Industrial Robotics*. Wiley.

Norman, D. A. 1981. Categorization of action slips. *Psychological Review* 88: 1–15.

Norman, D. A. 1986. Cognitive engineering. In Norman, D. A. and Draper, S. W. (eds.), *User Centered System Design: New Perspectives on Human Computer Interaction*. Erlbaum.

Norman, D. A. 1988. *The Design of Everyday Things*. Basic Books.

Norman, D. A. and Bobrow, D. 1975. On data-limited and resource-limited processing. *Journal of Cognitive Psychology* 7: 44–60.

Noyes, M. V. and Sheridan, T. B. 1984. A novel predictor for telemanipulation through a time delay. In Proceedings of Annual Conference on Manual Control, Moffett Field, CA, NASA Ames Research Center.

Noyes, M. V. 1984. Superposition of Graphics on Low Bit-rate Video as an Aid to Teleoperation. SM Thesis, MIT.

O'Donnell, R. D. and Eggemeier, F. T. 1986. Workload assessment methodology. In Boff, K., Kaufman, L., and Thomas, J. P. (eds.), *Handbook of Perception and Human Performance, vol.1, Sensory Processes and Perception*, Wiley.

Pao, L. and Speeter, T. 1989. Transformation of human hand positions for robotic hand control. In Proceedings of IEEE International Conference on Robotics and Automation: 1758–1763.

Papenhuijzen, R. and Stassen, H. G. 1987. On the modeling of a navigator. In Proceedings of 8th Ship Control Systems Symposium, The Hague, Vol. 2: 238–255.

Park, J. H. 1991. Supervisory Control of Robot Manipulators for Gross Motions. PhD Thesis, MIT, August.

Parsons, H. M. 1990. Turing on the Turing test. Chapter in Karwowski, W. and Rahimi, M. (eds.), *Ergonomics of Advanced Manufacturing and Hybrid Automated Systems II*, Elsevier.

Patrick, N. 1990. Design, Construction and Testing of a Fingertip Tactile Display for Interaction with Virtual and Remote Environments. SM Thesis, MIT.

Pattipati, K. R., Ephrath, A. E., and Kleinman, D. L. 1979. Analysis of human decision-making in multitask environments. Tech. Report EECS TR 79-15, Storrs. CT: Univ. of Connecticut.

Paul, R. P. 1981. *Robot Manipulators: Programming and Control*. MIT Press.

Perrow, C. 1984. *Normal Accidents*. Basic Books.

Peterson, J.L. 1977. Petri nets. *ACM Computing Surveys* 9, no. 3: 223–252.

Prigogine, I. and Stengers, I. 1984. *Order out of Chaos*. Bantam Books.

Raju, G. J. 1986. An Experimental Master-Slave Manipulator System to Study the Feasibility of Operator-Adjustable Impedance in Remote Manipulation, Man-Machine Systems Lab. Memo 86-1, Cambridge, MA: MIT.

Raju, G. J., Verghese, G. and Sheridan, T.B. 1989. Design issues in 2-port network models of bilateral remote manipulation. In Proceedings of IEEE International Conference on Robotics and Automation, Scottsdale, AZ, May 14–19: 1316–1321.

Ranadive, V. 1979. Video Resolution, Frame-Rate, and Grayscale Tradeoffs Under Limited Bandwidth for Undersea Teleoperation, SM Thesis, MIT, September.

Rasmussen , J. 1978. Notes on Diagnostic Strategies in the Process Plant Environment, Riso Natl. Lab. Report M-1983, Riso, Denmark.

Rasmussen, J. 1981. Models of mental strategies in process plant diagnosis. In Rasmussen, J. and Rouse, W. B. (eds.), *Human Detection and Diagnosis of System Failures*, Plenum.

Rasmussen, J. 1982. Human errors: a taxonomy for describing human malfunction in industrial installations. *J. Occupational Accidents* 4: 311–335.

Rasmussen, J. 1983. Skills, rules and knowledge: signals, signs and symbols, and other distinctions in human performance models. *IEEE Trans. Systems, Man and Cybernetics* SMC-133: 257–267.

Rasmussen, J. 1986. *Information Processing and Human-Machine Interaction*, Elsevier North-Holland.

Rasmussen, J. 1976. Outlines of a hybrid model of the process plant operator. In Sheridan, T. B., and Johannsen, G. (eds.), *Monitoring Behavior and Supervisory Control*, Plenum.

Rasmussen, J. and Rouse, W. B. (eds.) 1981. *Human Detection and Diagnosis of System Failures*. Plenum.

Reason, J. T. 1990. *Human Error*. Cambridge University Press.

Reason, J. T. and Mycielska, K. 1982. *Absent Minded? The Psychology of Mental Lapses and Everyday Errors*. Prentice-Hall.

Reid, G. B., Shingledecker, C. A. and Eggemeier, F. T. 1981. Application of conjoint measurement to workload scale development. In Proceedings of Human Factors Society 25th Annual Meeting: 522–526.

Ren, J. 1990. PhD thesis, in progress, MIT.

Rijnsdorp, J. E. 1981. Some cases of human factors in process automation. In Proceedings International Federation of Automatic Control 1981 World Congress, Kyoto, Japan, August.

Roseborough, J. 1988. Aiding Human Operators with State Estimates. PhD thesis, MIT, May.

Rouse, W. B. and Rouse, S. H. 1983. Analysis and classification of human error. *IEEE Trans. System, Man and Cybernetics* SMC-13, no. 4: 539–599.

Rouse, W. B. 1977. Human-computer interaction in multi-task situations. *IEEE Trans. System, Man and Cybernetics* SMC-7, no. 5: 384–392.

Rouse, W. B. and Hunt, R. M. 1984. Human problem solving in fault detection tasks. In Rouse, W. B. (ed.), *Advances in Man-Machine Systems Research*, vol. 1, JAI Press.

Ruffell-Smith, H. P. A. 1979. A Simulator Study of the Interaction of Pilot Workload with Error, Vigilance and Decisions. NASA TM-78482, Moffett Field, CA, NASA Ames Research Center.

Salisbury, J. K. 1981. Articulated hands: force control and kinematic issues. In Proceedings of 1981 JointAutomatic Control Conference. See also Mason, M. T. and Salisbury, J. K. 1985. *Robot Hands and the Mechanics of Manipulation.* MIT Press.

Salvendy, G. 1987. *Handbook of Human Factors.* Wiley.

Sanderson, P. M. 1988. The Human Planning and Scheduling Role in Advanced Manufacturing Systems: a Critical Review of Field and Laboratory Research. Engineering Psychology Research Labratory, Urbana: Univ. of Illinois.

Sanderson, P. M. 1991. Towards the model human scheduler. *Human Factors in Manufacturing* 1, no. 3: 195–220.

Schank, R. C. and Abelson, R. P. 1977. *Scripts, Plans, Goals and Understanding.* Erlbaum

Schneider, S. A. and Cannon, R. H. 1989. Experimental object-level strategic control with cooperating manipulators. In Proceedings of 1989 ASME Winter Annual Meeting.

Schneiter, J. 1982. An optical tactile sensor for robots. SM Thesis, MIT.

Schneiter, J. and Sheridan, T. B. 1984. An optical tactile sensor for manipulators. *Robotics and Computer-Integrated Manufacturing* 1, no. 1: 65–74.

Schneiter, J. L. 1986. Automated Tactile Sensing for Object Recognition and Localization. PhD thesis MIT, June.

Schwartz, A. 1986. Head tracking stereoscopic display. *In Proceedings of Society for Information Display* 27, no. 2: 133–137.

Senders, J. W. and Moray, N. P. 1991. *Human Error Cause, Prediction and Reduction.* Erlbaum.

Senders, J. W., Elkind, J. I, Grignetti, M. C. and Smallwood, R. P. 1964. An investigation of the visual sampling behavior of human observers. NASA-CR-434. Cambridge, MA: Bolt, Beranek and Newman, Inc.

Shannon, C. E. 1949. Communication in the presence of noise. *Proceedings of IRE* 37: 10–22.

Sharit, J., Cheng, T. C. and Salvendy, G. 1987. Technical and human aspects of computer-aided manufacturing. In Salvendy, G. (ed.), *Handbook of Human Factors*, Wiley.

Sheridan, T. B. 1960. Human metacontrol. In Proceedings of Annual Conference on Manual Control, Wright Patterson AFB, OH.

Sheridan, T. B. 1966. Three models of preview control. *IEEE Trans. Human Factors in Electronics* HFE-6, June.

Sheridan, T. B. 1970a. On how often the supervisor should sample. *IEEE Trans. Systems Science and Cybernetics* SSC-6: 140–145.

Sheridan, T. B. 1970b. Optimum allocation of personal presence. *IEEE Trans. Human Factors in Electronics* HFE-10: 242–249.

Sheridan, T. B. 1976a. Toward a general model of supervisory control. In Sheridan,T. B., and Johannsen, G. (eds.), *Monitoring Behavior and Supervisory Control*, Plenum.

Sheridan, T. B. (ed.) 1976b. Performance Evaluation of Programmable Robots and Manipulators. US Dept. of Commerce, National Bureau of Standards Special Publ. 459.

Sheridan, T. B. 1980. Computer control and human alienation. *Technology Review* 83, Oct.: 60–73.

Sheridan, T. B. 1981. Understanding human error and aiding human diagnostic behavior in nuclear power plants. In Rassmussen, J. and Rouse, W. B. (eds.), *Human Detection and Diagnosis of System Failures*, Plenum.

Sheridan, T. B. 1983. Measuring, modeling and augmenting reliability of man-machine systems. *Automatica* 19.

Sheridan, T. B. 1984. Supervisory control of remote manipulators, vehicles and dynamic processes. In Rouse, W. B. (ed.), *Advances in Man-Machine Systems Research*, vol. 1, JAI Press.

Sheridan, T. B. 1986. On trusting C^3I, particularly in SDI: when the pie meets the sky. In Proceedings of IFAC Conference on Contributions of Technology to International Conflict Resolution, Cleveland, OH, June 3–5.

Sheridan, T. B. 1987. Supervisory control. In Salvendy, G. (ed.), *Handbook of Human Factors*, Wiley.

Sheridan, T. B. 1989. Telerobotics. *Automatica* 25, no. 4: 487–507.

Sheridan, T. B. and Ferrell, W. R. 1974. *Man-Machine Systems*. MIT Press.

Sheridan, T. B. and Hennessy, R. T. (eds.) 1984. Research and Modeling of Supervisory Control Behavior. National Research Council, Committee on Human Factors, Washington, DC, Natl. Acad. Press.

Sheridan, T. B. and Rouse, W. B. 1971. Supervisory sampling and control: sources of suboptimization in a prediction task. Proceedings 7th Annual Conference on Manual Control, Univ. Southern California.

Sheridan, T. B. and Schneiter, J. 1986. *Opto-Mechanical Touch Sensor*. US Patent 4,599,908.

Sheridan, T. B. and Simpson, R. W. 1979. Toward the definition and measurement of the mental workload of transport pilots. MIT Flight Technology Laboratory Report R79-4, January.

Sheridan, T. B. and Verplank, W. L. 1978. Human and Computer Control of Undersea Teleoperators, MIT Man-Machine Systems Lab. Report.

Sheridan, T. B. and Johannsen, G. (eds.) 1976. *Monitoring Behavior and Supervisory Control*. Plenum.

Sheridan, T. B., Kruser, D. S. and Deutsch, S. (eds.) 1987. Human Factors in Automated and Robotic Space Systems: Proceedings of a Symposium, Washington, DC: National Research Council.

Sherrick, C. E. and Cholewiak, R. W. 1986. Cutaneous sensing. In Boff, K., Kaufman, L. and Thomas, J. P. (eds.), *Handbook of Perception and Human Performance*, vol. 1, Wiley.

Shladover, S. 1990. Advanced vehicle control systems, AVCS. SAE Paper No. 901129. In Proceedings International Congress of Transportation Electronics, SAE Conference P-233, October: 103–122.

Siegel, A. I., Wolf, J. J. and Lautman, M. R. A. 1975. A family of models for measuring human reliability. In Proceedings of IEEE Annual Reliability amd Maintainability Symposium.

Simon, H. A. 1969. *Sciences of the Artificial.* MIT Press.

Skinner, B. F. 1938. *The Behavior of Organisms: An Experimental Analysis.* Appleton-Century-Crofts.

Smith, D. C., Cole, R. E., Merritt, J. O. and Pepper, R. L. 1979. Remote Operator Performance Comparing Mono and Stereo TV Displays: the Effects of Visibility, Learning and Task Factors. Naval Ocean Systems Center, San Diego: TR-380.

Snyder, W. E. 1985. *Industrial Robots: Computer Interfacing and Control.* Prentice-Hall.

Stassen, H. G. 1991. Supervisory control behavior modeling: the challenge and necessity. In Moray, N., Ferrell, W. R. and Rouse, W. B., *Robotics, Control and Society,* Taylor and Francis.

Stein. A. C., Parseghian, Z. and Allen, W. 1987. A simulator study of the safety implications of cellular mobile telephone use. 31st Annual In Proceedings of Amer. Assoc. Automotive Medicine, Sept. 28–30, New Orleans, LA.

Stevens, S. S., (ed.) 1951. *Handbook of Experimental Psychology.* Wiley.

Strickler, T. G., 1966. Design of an Optical Touch Sensing System for a Remote Manipulator. SM thesis, MIT.

Sturgis, R. and Wright. P. 1989. A quantification of dexterity. *Journal of Robotics and Computer Integrated Manufacturing* 6, no. 1: 3–14.

Swain, A. D. and Guttman, H. E. 1983. Handbook of Human Reliability Analysis with Emphasis on Nuclear Power Plant Applications, Sandia Natl. Labs., NUREG CR-1278, Washington, DC, US Nuclear Regulatory Commission.

Tachi, S., Arai, H., and Maeda, T. 1988a. Tele-existence simulator with artificial reality I: design and evaluation of a binocular visual display using solid models. In Proceedings of IEEE International Workshop on Intelligent Robots and Systems, Tokyo, Japan, Oct. 31– Nov. 2: 719–724.

Tachi, S., Arai, H. and Maeda, T.1989. Development of anthropomorphic tele-existence slave robot. In Proceedings of International Conference on Advance Mechatronics, May 21–24, Tokyo: 385–390.

Tachi, S., Arai, H., Morimoto, I., and Seet, G. 1988b. Feasibility experiments on a mobile tele-existence system. In Proceedings of International Symposium and Exposition on Robots, 19th ISIR, Sydney, Australia, 6–10 Nov.: 625–636.

Tachi, S. and Arai, H. 1985. Study on tele-existence II: three-dimensional color display with sensation of presence. In Proceedings of 1985 International Conference on Advanced Robotics, Tokyo, Japan, Sept. 9–10.

Tani, K. 1980. Supervisory control of remote manipulation with compensation for moving target. MIT Man-Machine System Laboratory Report, July.

Taylor, F.W. 1947. *Scientific Management.* Harper Brothers.

Terano, T. and Sugeno, M. 1974. Conditional fuzzy measures and their applications. In Terano, T. and Sugeno, M. (eds.), *Fuzzy Sets and Their Applications to Cognitive and Decision Processes.* Academic Press: 151–170.

Thompson, D. A. 1977. The development of a six degree-of-freedom robot evaluation test, In Proceedings of 13th Annual Conference on Manual Control, Cambridge, MA, MIT.

Tomizuka, M. 1975. Optimal continuous finite preview problems. *IEEE Trans. on Automatic Control* AC-20, no. 3: 362–365.

Tomovic, R. 1969. On man-machine control. *Automatica* 5: 401–404.

Tsach, U., Sheridan,T. B., and Buharali, A. 1983. Failure detection and location in process control: integrating a new model-based technique with other methods. In Proceedings of American Control Conference, San Francisco, June 22–24.

Tsach, U., Sheridan, T. B., and Tzelgov, J. 1982. A new method for failure detection and location in complex dynamic systems. In Proceedings of 1982 American Control Conference, Arlington, VA, June.

Tuler, P. S. 1987. Human Behavior in Time-Pressured Distributed Decision Systems. SM thesis, MIT.

Tulga, M. K. and Sheridan, T. B. 1980. Dynamic decisions and workload in multi-task supervisory control. *IEEE Trans. on Systems, Man and Cybernetics* SMC-10, no. 5: 217–231.

Turing, A. M. 1950. Computing machinery and intelligence. *Mind* 59: 433–460.

Turoff, M. 1975a. The policy Delphi. In Linstone, H. A. and Turoff, M. (eds.), *The Delphi Method*, Addison-Wesley.

Turoff, M. 1975b. An alternative approach to cross-impact analysis. In Linstone, H. A. and Turoff, M. (eds.), *The Delphi Method*, Addison-Wesley.

Tversky, A. and Kahneman, D. 1981. The framing of decisions and the psychology of choice. *Science* 211: 453–458.

Tyler, C. W. 1982. Figure 7.28, page 265 in Schnor, C. M. and Ciuffreda, K. J. (eds.), *Vergence Eye Movements: Basis and Clinical Aspects*, Butterworths.

Tzelgov, J., Tsach, U., and Sheridan, T. B. 1985. Effects of indicating failure odds and smoothed outputs on human failure detection in dynamic systems. *Ergonomics* 28, no. 2: 449–462.

U.S. Congress Oversight Hearing 1979. *Testimony of the Three Mile Island Operators.* Serial 96-8, vol. 1, p. 138.

U.S. Navy Sea Systems Command 1977. *Human Reliability Prediction User's Manual.* December.

Uicker, J. J., Denavit, J., and Hartenberg, R. S. 1964. An iterative method for the displacement analysis of spatial mechanisms. *J. Applied Mechanics*: 309–314, June.

Vadus, J. R. 1976. International status and utilization of undersea vehicles 1976. In Proceedings of Inter-Ocean 76 Conference, June.

Van de Vegte, J. M. E., Milgram, P. and Kwong, R. H. 1990. Teleoperator control models: effect of time delay and imperfect system knowledge. *IEEE Trans. Systems, Man and Cybernetics* SMC-20, no. 6: 1258–1272.

Verplank, W.L. 1977. Is There an Optimal Workload in Manual Control? PhD Thesis, MIT.

Vertut, J. and Coiffet, P. 1986a. *Robot Technology, Volume 3A: Teleoperation and Robotics: Evolution and Development.* Prentice-Hall.

Vertut, J. and Coiffet, P. 1986b. *Robot Technology, Volume 3B: Teleoperation and Robotics: Applications and Technology,* Prentice-Hall.

Von Neumann, J. and Morganstern, O. 1944. *Theory of Games and Economic Behavior,* Princeton Univ. Press.

Warfield, J. N. 1974a. Toward interpretation of complex structural models. *IEEE Trans. on Systems, Man and Cybernetics* 4, no. 5.

Warfield, J. N. 1974b. Structuring Compex Systems. Monograph 4, Columbus, OH: Battelle Memorial Inst.

Webster's Third New International Dictionary, Unabridged 1965. P. Gove (ed.), Merriam.

Weissenberger, S. and Sheridan, T. B. 1962. Dynamics of human operator control systems using tactile feedback, *J. Basic Engineering*, June.

Wenzel, E. M., Wightman, F. I. and Foster, S. H. 1988. A virtual display system for conveying three-dimensional acoustic information. *Human Factors* 32: 86–90.

Wewerincke, P., 1981. A Model of the Human Decision Maker Observing a Dynamic System. Technical Report NLR-TL-81062-L, National Aerospace Laboratories, Netherlands.

Whitney, D. E. 1968. State Space Models of Remote Manipulation Tasks. PhD Thesis, MIT.

Whitney, D. E. 1969a. State space models of remote manipulation tasks. *IEEE Trans. on Automatic Control* AC-146.

Whitney, D. E. 1969b. Resolved-motion rate control of manipulators and human prostheses. *IEEE Trans. on Man-Machine Systems* MMS-10, no. 2.

Whitney, D. 1969c. Optimum step size control for Newton-Raphson solution of nonlinear vector equations. *IEEE Trans. on Automatic Control* AC-146, Oct.

Wickens, C. D., Tsang, P. and Pierce, B. 1985. The dynamics of resource allocation. In Rouse, W. B. (ed.), *Advances in Man-Machine Systems Research*, vol. 2, JAI Press.

Wiener, E. L and Curry, R. E. 1980. Flight-Deck Automation: Promises and Problems, NASA TM-81206, June. See also Wiener, E. L. 1989. Human Factors of Advanced Technology "Glass Cockpit" Transport Aircraft. NASA Ames Research Center Contract Report NCC2-337.

Wiener, N. 1964. *God and Golem, Inc.* MIT Press.

Wierwille, W. W. and Casali, J. G. 1983. A validated rating scale for global mental workload measurement applications. In Proceedings of Human Factors Society 27th Annual Meeting: 129–133.

Wierwille, W. W., Casali, J. G., Connor, S. A. and Rahimi, M. 1985. Evaluation of the sensitivity and intrusion of mental workload estimation techniques. In Rouse, W. B. (ed.), *Advances in Man-Machine Systems Research*, vol. 2, JAI Press: 51–127.

Wierzbicki, A. P. 1982. A mathematical basis for satisficing decision-making. *Math. Modeling* 3: 391–405.

Williges, R. C. and Weirwille, W. W. 1979. Behavioral measures of aircrew mental workload. *Human Factors* 21: 549–574.

Winey, C. M. 1981. Computer Simulated Visual and Tactile Feedback as an Aid to Manipulator and Vehicle Control. SM thesis, MIT, June.

Winograd, T. and Flores, F. 1986. *Understanding Computers and Cognition*. Addison-Wesley.

Wohl, J. G., Entin, E. E., Kleinman, D. L. and Pattipatti, K. 1984. Human decision processes in military command and control. In Rouse, W.B. (ed.), *Advances in Man-Machine Systems*, vol. 1, JAI Press.

Wood, W. T. and Sheridan, T. B. 1982. The use of machine aids in dynamic multi-task environments: a comparison of an optimal model to human behavior. In Proceedings of 1982 International Conference on Cybernetics and Society, 82-CH-1840, Seattle, WA: 668–672.

Yared, W. and Sheridan, T. B. 1991. Plan recognition and generalization in command languages with application to telerobotics. *IEEE Trans. Systems, Man and Cybernetics* 21, no. 2: 327–338. See also Yared, W. 1989. Plan Recognition and Generalization in Command Languages. PhD Thesis, MIT.

Yastrebov, V. S. and Stepanov, G. A. 1978. Underwater robot/manipulator development. *Marine Technology Society Journal* 12, no.1.

Yntema, D. B. and Klem, L. 1965. Telling a computer how to evaluate multi-dimensional situations. *IEEE Trans. Human Factors in Electronics* HFE-6: 3–13.

Yoerger, D. R. 1982. Supervisory Control of Underwater Telemanipulators: Design and Experiment. PhD thesis, MIT.

Yoerger, D. R. and Slotine, J.-J. E. 1987. Task-resolved motion control in vehicle manipulator systems. *International Jounal of Robotics and Automation* 2, no. 3.

Yoshikawa, T. and Nagai, K. 1991. Manipulating and grasping forces in manipulation by multi-fingered robot hands. *IEEE Trans. Robotics and Automation* 7, no. 1: 67–77.

Zadeh, L. 1965. Fuzzy sets. *Information and Control* 8: 338–353.

Zeltzer, F. D. 1990. Presentation at MIT Media Laboratory/Industrial Liaison Symposium, Cambridge, MA.

Author Index

Subject Index